New York, August 1991

second edition

SOCIAL WELFARE
politics and public policy

DIANA M. DINITTO
University of Texas at Austin

THOMAS R. DYE
Florida State University

PRENTICE-HALL, INC. ENGLEWOOD CLIFFS, NEW JERSEY 07632

Library of Congress Cataloging-in-Publication Data

DiNitto, Diana M.
Social welfare.

Bibliography: p.
Includes index.
1. Public welfare—United States. 2. United States—
Social policy. I. Dye, Thomas R. II. Title.
HV95.D56 1987 361.6'13'0973 86-16865
ISBN 0-13-819483-1

Editorial/production supervision and interior design: Marina Harrison
Cover design: Ben Santora
Manufacturing buyer: John Hall

FOR VINCENT, MARY, AND DANIEL DINITTO
FROM DIANA

Printed in the United States of America

10 9 8 7 6 5 4 3 2 1

ISBN 0-13-819483-1 01

Prentice-Hall International (UK) Limited, *London*
Prentice-Hall of Australia Pty. Limited, *Sydney*
Prentice-Hall Canada Inc., *Toronto*
Prentice-Hall Hispanoamericana, S.A., *Mexico*
Prentice-Hall of India Private Limited, *New Delhi*
Prentice-Hall of Japan, Inc., *Tokyo*
Prentice-Hall of Southeast Asia Pte. Ltd., *Singapore*
Editora Prentice-Hall do Brasil, Ltda., *Rio de Janeiro*

Contents

8

FIGHTING HUNGER: FEDERAL NUTRITION PROGRAMS 167

9

WARRING ON POVERTY: VICTORIES, DEFEATS, AND STALEMATES 188

10

IMPROVING HEALTH CARE: TREATING THE NATION'S ILLS 206

11

CHALLENGING SOCIAL WELFARE: RACISM AND SEXISM 233

Preface

Social Welfare: Politics and Public Policy, 2nd ed., is intended to introduce students to the major social welfare programs in the United States and to stimulate them to think about major conflicts in social welfare policy today. By focusing on "issues," we hope to emphasize that social welfare in America involves a series of *political* questions about what should be done about the poor, the near-poor, and the nonpoor—or whether anything should be done at all.

Social Welfare: Politics and Public Policy describes major social welfare programs—their histories, trends, and current problems and prospects. But more important, it tackles the difficult conflicts and controversies which surround these programs. Social welfare policy is *not* presented as a series of solutions to social problems. Instead, social policy is portrayed as public conflict over the nature and causes of poverty; over what, if anything, should be done about poverty; over who should do it; and over who should decide about it.

Major public programs—

Social Security
Unemployment Compensation
Supplemental Security Income
Aid to Families with Dependent Children
General Assistance
Food Stamps
School Lunches

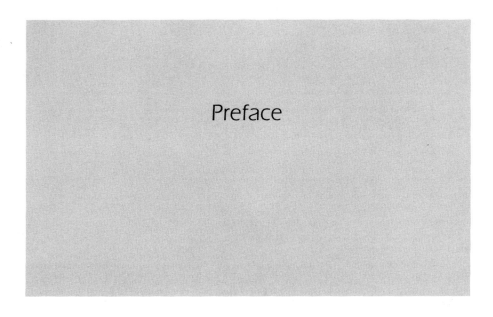

Community Action
Job Training Partnership Act
Mental Health
Care of the Elderly
Child Welfare Services
Legal Services
Vocational Rehabilitation
Medicare
Medicaid

are described and analyzed, and alternative proposals and "reforms" are considered.

This book is designed for undergraduate and beginning graduate courses in social welfare policy. It does not require prior knowledge of social work, nor does it attempt to introduce students to all aspects of the social work profession.

Many books on social policy treat social insurance, public assistance, and social service programs *descriptively;* by so doing they tend to obscure important conflicts and issues. Other books on social policy treat these programs *prescriptively;* by so doing they imply that there is only one "right" way to resolve social issues. *Social Welfare: Politics and Public Policy* views social policy as a *continuing political struggle* over the issues posed by poverty and inequality in society—conflicting goals and objectives, competing definitions of problems, alternative approaches and strategies, multiple programs and policies, competing proposals for "reform," and even different ideas about how decisions should be made in social welfare policy. A distinguishing feature of the book is that it provides an up-to-date discussion of Reagan's welfare reforms for each of the major social welfare programs.

We would like to acknowledge the reviewers who commented on the second edition of this book: David A. Hardcastle, University of Maryland at Baltimore and Sheldon R. Gelman, Pennsylvania State University. We would like to thank Allene Novy, Virginia Hula, and Joyce Pryor for their assistance with the second edition.

chapter 1

Politics, rationalism, and social welfare

POLITICS AND SOCIAL WELFARE POLICY

No one is really happy with the nation's welfare system—not the working taxpayers who must support it, not the social work professionals who must administer it, and certainly not the poor who must live under it. Since the Social Security Act of 1935, the federal government has tried to develop a rational social welfare system for the entire nation. Today a wide variety of federal programs serve the aged, the poor, the disabled, and the sick. "Income maintenance" (social insurance and public assistance) is the largest single item in the federal budget, easily surpassing national defense. The Department of Health and Human Services is the largest department of the federal government, and many additional welfare programs are administered by other departments. Yet even after fifty years of large-scale, direct federal involvement, social welfare policy remains a central issue in American politics.

Social welfare policy involves a series of *political* issues about what should be done about the poor, the near-poor, and the nonpoor—or whether anything should be done at all. The real problems in social welfare are not problems of organization, administration, or service delivery. Rather, they are political conflicts over the nature and causes of poverty and inequality, the role of government in society, the burdens to be carried by taxpayers, the appropriate strategies for coping with poverty, the issues posed by specific social insurance and public assistance programs, the relative reliance to be placed on cash versus services for the poor, the need for reform, and the nature of the decision-making process itself. In short, social welfare policy is a continuing political struggle over the issues posed by poverty and inequality in society.

Policy making is frequently portrayed as a *rational* process in which policy makers identify social problems, explore all of the alternative solutions, forecast all of the benefits and costs of each alternative solution, compare benefits to costs for each solution, and select the best ratio of benefits to costs. In examining social welfare policy, we shall explore the strengths and weaknesses of this rational model.

More important, we shall portray social welfare policy as a "political" process—as conflict over the nature and causes of poverty and over what, if anything, should be done about it. Social welfare policy is "political" because of disagreements about the nature of the problems confronting society; about what should be considered "benefits" and "costs"; about how to estimate and compare benefits and costs; about the likely consequences of alternative policies; about the importance of one's own needs and aspirations in relation to those of others; and about the ability of government to do anything "rationally." We shall see that the *political* barriers to *rational* policy making are indeed very great.

SCOPE OF SOCIAL WELFARE POLICY

Social welfare policy is anything government chooses to do, or not to do, that affects the quality of life of its people. Broadly conceived, social welfare policy includes nearly everything government does—from taxation, national defense, and energy conservation, to health, housing, and public assistance. More elaborate definitions of social welfare policy are available;[1] most of these definitions refer to actions of government which have an "impact on the welfare of citizens by providing them with services or income."[2] Some scholars[3] have insisted that government activities must have "a goal, objective, or purpose," in order to be labeled a "policy."* For practical purposes, we will limit our concerns to the policies of government which *directly* affect the income and services available to the aged, sick, and poor. We would discourage lengthy discussions of the definition of social welfare pol-

*This definition implies a difference between governmental actions and an overall plan of action toward a specific goal. The problem, however, in insisting that government actions must have *goals* in order to be labeled as "policy" is that we can never be sure what the goal of a particular government action is. We generally assume that if a government chooses to do something there must be a goal, objective, or purpose, but often we find that bureaucrats who helped write the law, lobbyists who pushed for its enactment, and members of Congress who voted for it all had different goals, objectives, and purposes in mind! The stated intentions of a law may also be quite different from what government agencies actually do. All we can really observe is what governments choose to do or not to do.

Political scientists Heinz Eulau and Kenneth Prewitt supply still another definition of public policy: "Policy is defined as 'standing decision' characterized by behavioral consistency and repetitiveness on the part of those who make it and those who abide by it" [*Labyrinths of Democracy* (Indianapolis: Bobbs Merrill, 1973), p. 465)]. Now certainly it would be a wonderful thing if government activities were characterized by "consistency and repetitiveness"; but it is doubtful that we would ever find a public policy in government if we insisted on these criteria. As we shall see, much of what government does is *in*consistent and *non*repetitive.

icy. These discussions are often futile, even exasperating, since few people can agree on a single definition of social policy. Moreover, these discussions divert attention away from the study of specific welfare policies.

Note that we are focusing not only on government action but also on government *in*action—that is, what government chooses *not* to do. We contend that government inaction can have just as important an impact on society as government action.

The boundaries of social welfare policy are fuzzy. But this should be viewed as a challenge, not an obstacle. Specifically, we will be concerned with major government programs in

- Income Maintenance
  - Aid to Families with Dependent Children (AFDC)
  - General Assistance
  - Social Security
  - Supplemental Security Income (SSI)
  - Unemployment Compensation
  - Workers' Compensation
- Nutrition
  - Food Stamps
  - School Breakfasts
  - School Lunches
  - Special Supplemental Nutrition Program for Women, Infants and Children (WIC)
  - Meals on Wheels
- Health
  - Medicaid
  - Medicare
  - public health
- Social Services
  - Community Action programs
  - community mental health
  - Job Training Partnership Act (JTPA)
  - legal services
  - social services for children and families
  - social services for the elderly
  - Vocational Rehabilitation

Some of these programs are labeled *public assistance* programs because people must be poor (according to legal standards) in order to receive benefits; benefits are paid out of general revenue funds. Public assistance programs include AFDC, Food Stamps, Medicaid, SSI, School Lunches, and General Assistance. Other programs are labeled as *social insurance* programs because they are designed to prevent poverty; people pay into these programs during their working years and are entitled to their benefits whether poor or not. Social insurance programs include Social Security, Medicare, Unemployment Compensation and Workers' Compensation.

Still other programs are labeled *social service* programs because they provide care, training, and assistance to children, the elderly, the poor, sick, or disabled. Social service programs are included in children's and family services, care for the elderly, community action, JTPA, legal services, mental health, public health, and vocational rehabilitation.

We shall endeavor, first of all, to *describe* these programs. But we shall also be concerned with the *causes* of social welfare policy—why policy is what it is. We want to learn about some of the social, economic, and political forces that shape social welfare policy in America. We shall be concerned with how social policies have developed and changed over time. We shall also be concerned with the *consequences* of welfare policies—their effects on target groups and on society in general. We shall consider some alternative policies—possible changes, "reforms," improvements, or phaseouts. Finally, we shall be concerned with *political conflict* over the nature and causes of poverty—and conflict over what, if anything, should be done about it.

SOCIAL WELFARE POLICY: A RATIONAL APPROACH

Ideally, social welfare policy ought to be rational. A policy is rational if the ratio between the values it achieves and the values it sacrifices is positive and higher than any other policy alternative. Of course, we should not measure benefits and costs in a narrow dollars-and-cents framework, while ignoring basic social values. The idea of rationalism involves the calculation of *all* social, political, and economic values sacrificed or achieved by a public policy, not just those that can be measured in dollars.

Rationalism has been proposed as an "ideal" approach to both studying and making public policy.* Indeed, it has been argued that rationalism provides a single "model of choice" that can be applied to all kinds of problems, large and small, public and private.[4] We do *not* contend that government policies are in fact rational, for they are not. Even so, the model remains important because it helps us to identify barriers to rationality. It assists us in posing the question: Why is policy making not a more rational process?

Let us examine the conditions for rational policy making more closely:

1. Society must be able to identify and define social problems and agree that there is a need to resolve these problems.
2. All of the values of society must be known and weighed.
3. All possible alternative policies must be known and considered.
4. The consequences of each policy alternative must be fully understood in

*Other major theoretical approaches to the study of public policy include institutionalism, elite theory, group theory, systems theory, and incrementalism. For an introduction to these approaches, see Thomas R. Dye, *Understanding Public Policy*, 5th ed. (Englewood Cliffs, N.J.: Prentice-Hall, 1984), especially chapter 2.

terms of both costs and benefits, for the present and for the future, and for target groups and the rest of society.

5. Policy makers must calculate the ratio of benefits to costs for each policy alternative.
6. Policy makers must choose the policy alternative that maximizes *net* values—that is, the policy alternative that achieves the greatest benefit at the least cost.

Because this notion of rationality assumes that the values of *society as a whole* can be known and weighed, it is not enough to know the values of some groups and not others. There must be a common understanding of societal values. Rational policy making also requires *information* about alternative policies and the *predictive capacity* to foresee accurately the consequences of each alternative. Rationality requires the *intelligence* to calculate correctly the ratio of costs to benefits for each policy alternative. This means calculation of all present and future benefits and costs to both the target groups and nontarget groups in society. Finally, rationalism requires a *policy-making system* that facilitates rationality in policy formation. The Israeli political scientist Yehezkel Dror provides a diagram of such a system in figure 1–1.

Identifying *target groups* means defining the segment of the population for whom the policy is intended—the poor, the sick, the disabled, dependent children, or others in need. Then the desired effect of the program on the target groups must be determined. Is it to change their physical or economic conditions—for example, to increase the cash income of the poor, to improve the housing conditions of ghetto residents, to improve the nutrition of children, or to improve the health of the elderly? Or is the program designed to change their knowledge, attitudes, or behavior—for example, to provide job skills, to improve literacy, or to increase awareness of legal rights? If several different effects are desired, what are the priorities among them? What are the possible *unintended consequences* on target groups—for example, does public housing improve the physical environment for many poor blacks at the cost of increasing housing segregation between blacks and whites? What is the impact of a policy on the target group in proportion to that group's total need? A program that promises to meet a recognized national need—for example, to end poverty altogether—but actually meets only a small percentage of that need may generate great praise at first but bitterness and frustration later when it becomes known how insufficient the impact really is, relative to the need.

Policies have different effects on various segments of the population. Identifying important *nontarget groups* for a policy is an important but difficult process. For example, what is the impact of welfare reform proposals—such as a guaranteed annual income—on groups other than the poor (government bureaucrats, social workers, working-class families, taxpayers)? Rational policy making requires consideration of "spill-over effects." These nontarget effects may be benefits as well as costs—for example, the benefits to the construction industry from public-housing projects or the benefits to farmers, food manufacturers, and grocers from the Food Stamp program.

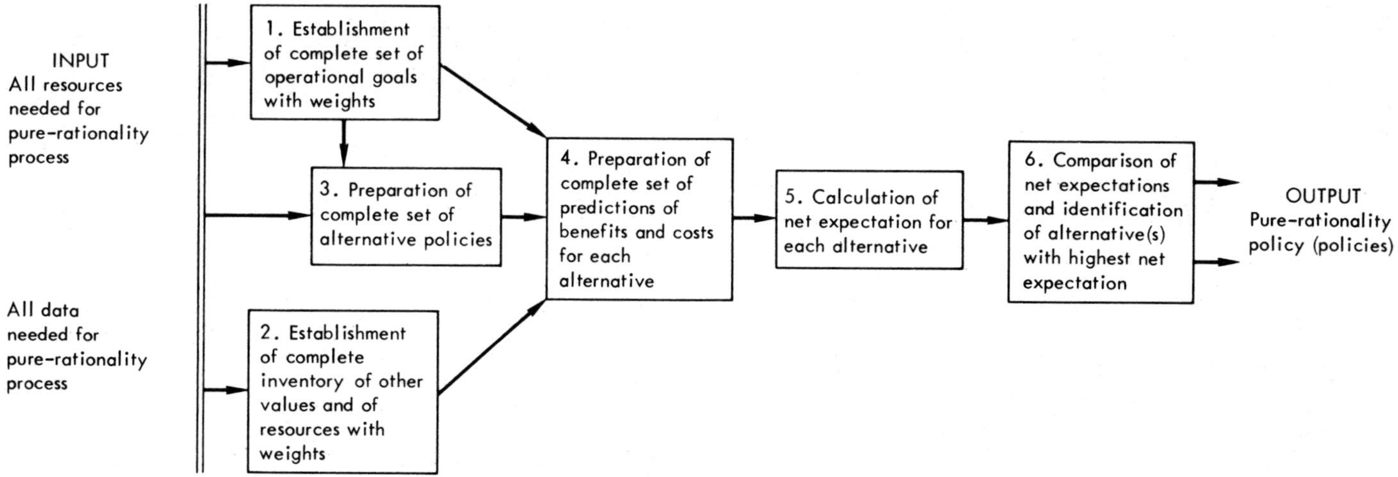

FIGURE 1-1 A rational model of a decision system. (Reprinted from Thomas R. Dye, *Understanding Public Policy*, 4th ed., Englewood Cliffs, N.J.: Prentice-Hall, 1981, p. 33.)

When will the benefits or costs be felt? Is the policy designed for short-term emergency situations or is it a long-term, developmental effort? If it is short-term, what will prevent bureaucrats from turning it into a long-term program, even after immediate needs are met? Many studies have shown that new or innovative programs have short-term positive effects—for example, Head Start and other education and job-training programs. However, the positive effects sometimes disappear as the novelty and enthusiasm of new programs wear off. Other programs experience difficulties at first—for example, in getting physicians and hospitals to accept Medicare and Medicaid patients—but turn out to have "sleeper" effects—as in the widespread acceptance of Medicare and Medicaid today.

Rational policy makers must measure benefits and costs in terms of general social well-being. Government agencies have developed various forms of cost-benefit analysis to identify the direct costs (usually, but not always, in dollars) of providing aid and assistance to the *average* family, worker, or job trainee. It is more difficult to identify and measure general units of social well-being. We need to know, for example, how to measure improved health, improved job skills, better nutrition, and greater employment opportunities. We are still struggling with better ways to measure these social values.

Actually *comprehensive* rationality in public policy making may not really be rational. This apparent contradiction was noted many years ago by Herbert A. Simon, a Nobel Prize winner for his studies of the decision-making process in large organizations. It is so costly and time consuming to learn about all of the policy alternatives available to decision makers, to investigate all of the possible consequences of each alternative, and to calculate the cost-benefit ratio of each alternative that the improvement in the policy selected is not worth the extra effort required to make a comprehensive rational selection. Simon developed a theory of *bounded rationality,* which recognizes the practical limits to complete rationality: "It is impossible for the behavior of a single isolated individual to reach *any high degree of rationality.* The number of alternatives to be explored is so great and the information to evaluate them so vast, that even an approximation of objective rationality is hard to conceive."[5]

In contrast to completely rational decision making, the notion of "bounded rationality" means that policy makers consider a limited number of alternatives, estimate the consequences of these alternatives using the best available means, and select the alternative that appears to achieve the most important values without incurring unacceptable costs. Instead of maximizing the ratio of benefits to costs, policy makers search for a "satisfying" choice—a policy alternative that is good enough to produce the desired benefits at a reasonable cost. This means that policy makers do not try to create the best of all possible worlds but rather seek to get by, to come out all right, to avoid trouble, to compromise.

Rationalism, then, presents an ideal model of policy making—in social welfare and in other policy fields. But policy making in "the real world" is not usually a rational process. Policy making occurs in a political context which places severe limits on rationality.

SOCIAL WELFARE POLICY: A POLITICAL APPROACH

Social welfare policy is "political." By *political* we mean that social welfare policy arises out of conflict over the nature of the problems confronting society and what, if anything, should be done about them.

Politics has been described as "who gets what, when, and how";[6] it is an activity through which people try to get more of whatever there is to get—money, jobs, prestige, prosperity, respect, and power itself. Politics, then, is conflict over the allocation of values in society, and the conflict is central to politics and policy making. "Politics arises out of conflicts, and it consists of the activities—for example, reasonable discussion, impassioned oratory, balloting, and street fighting—by which conflict is carried on."[7]

Why do we expect conflict in society over who gets what? Why can't we agree on "a theory of justice" according to which everyone would agree on what is fair for all members of society, particularly the poor, the aged, and the sick.?[8] Why can't we have a harmonious, loving, caring, sharing society of equals? Philosophers have pondered these questions for centuries. James Madison, perhaps the first American to write seriously about politics, believed that the causes of "faction" (conflict) are found in human diversity—"a zeal for different opinions concerning religion, concerning government, and many other points . . . [and] . . . an attachment to different leaders ambitiously contending for preeminence and power." More important, according to Madison, "the most common and durable source of faction has been the various and unequal distribution of property. Those who hold and those who are without property have ever formed distinct interests in society" *(The Federalist,* no.10). In short, differences among people, particularly in the sources and amount of their wealth, are the root cause of social conflict.

It is the task of government to regulate conflict. It does so by (1) establishing and enforcing general rules by which conflict is carried on, (2) arranging compromises and balancing interests in public policy, and (3) imposing settlements which the parties to a dispute must accept. Governments must insure that conflicts are channeled into elections, legislatures, bureaucracies, or courts, rather than into street fighting, terrorism, or civil war. Governments must arrange settlements in the form of public policy—settlements that allocate values in such a way that they will be accepted by both "winners" and "losers" at least temporarily. Finally, governments must impose these settlements by enforcing public policy and by promising rewards or threatening punishments.

From a "political" perspective, public policy is the outcome of conflicts in government over who gets what, and when and how they get it. A policy may be considered *politically* rational when it succeeds in winning enough support to be enacted into law, implemented by executive agencies, and enforced by the courts. Or it may be considered *politically* rational if it is supported by influential groups and believed to be popular among the voters. But this is not the same type of rationality that we described earlier in the rational model.

Indeed, the political approach raises serious questions about rationality in policy making. It suggests that:

1. There are no *social* values that are generally agreed upon, but only the values of specific groups and individuals, many of which are conflicting.
2. Problems cannot be defined because people do not agree on what the problems are. What is a problem to one group may be a benefit to another group.
3. Many conflicting costs and values cannot be compared or weighed; for example, how can we compare the value of individual dignity with the cost of a general tax increase.
4. Policy makers, even with most advanced computerized analytic techniques, cannot predict the consequences of various policy alternatives or calculate their cost-benefit ratios when many diverse social, economic, and political values are involved.
5. The environment of policy makers, particularly the political system of power and influence, makes it virtually impossible to forecast the consequences of public policy or accurately weigh many social values, particularly those that do not have active or powerful proponents in or near government. The poor and the sick may have little access to governmental representation.
6. Policy makers are not necessarily motivated to make decisions on the basis of social values. Instead they often seek to maximize their own rewards—power, status, reelection, money, and so on. Policy makers have their own needs, ambitions, and inadequacies, all of which can prevent them from performing in a highly rational manner.
7. Large, segmented government bureaucracies create barriers to coordinated policy making. It is difficult to bring all of the interested individuals, groups, and experts together at the point of decision. Governmental decision making is "disjointed."

How can we bridge the differences between an ideal model of *rational* policy making and the realization that policy making is a *political* activity? Political scientist Charles E. Lindblom first presented an "incremental" model of policy making as a critique of the rational model. Lindblom observed that government policy makers do *not* annually review the entire range of existing and proposed policies, or identify all of society's goals, or research the benefits and costs of all alternative policies to achieve these goals. They, therefore, do not make their selections on the basis of all relevant information. Limits of time, knowledge, and costs pose innumerable obstacles in identifying the full range of policy alternatives and predicting their consequences. Political limitations prevent the establishment of clear-cut societal goals and the accurate calculation of cost-benefit ratios. The incremental model recognizes the impracticality of comprehensive rational policy making and describes a more "conservative" process of public decision making.

Incremental policy making considers existing policies, programs, and expenditures as a base. It concentrates attention on newly proposed policies and programs and on increases, decreases, or other modifications of existing programs. Incrementalism is conservative in that policy makers generally accept the legitimacy of established policies and programs. The focus of attention is on proposed *changes* in these policies and programs. This narrows the attention of policy makers to a limited number of new initiatives and increases or decreases in the budget.

There are important *political* advantages to incrementalism in policy making. Conflict is reduced if the items in dispute are only increases or decreases in existing budgets or modifications of existing programs. Conflict would be greater if policy making focused on major policy shifts involving great gains or losses for various groups in society or "all-or-nothing," "yes-or-no" policy decisions. To have existing policies reconsidered every year would generate a great deal of conflict; it is easier politically to continue previously accepted policies.

Policy makers may also continue existing policies because of uncertainty about the consequences of completely new or different policies. Forecasting is never perfect. It is safer to stick with known programs when the consequences of new programs cannot be accurately predicted. Under conditions of uncertainty, policy makers continue past policies or programs whether they have proven effective or not. Only in a "crisis" do political decision makers begin to consider new and untried policies as preferable to existing ones. Thus, groups and individuals who seek more than incremental change in public policy usually try to generate a "crisis" atmosphere.

Policy makers also realize that individuals and organizations—executive agencies, congressional committees, interest groups—accumulate commitments to existing policies and programs. For example, it is accepted wisdom in Washington that bureaucracies persist over time regardless of their utility, that they develop routines that are difficult to alter, and that individuals develop a personal stake in the continuation of organizations and programs. These commitments are serious obstacles to major change. It is easier politically for policy makers to search for alternatives which involve only a minimum of budgetary, organizational, or administrative change.

Finally, in the absence of generally agreed-upon social goals or values, it is politically expedient for governments to pursue a variety of different programs and policies simultaneously, even if some of them are overlapping or even conflicting. In this way, a wider variety of individuals and groups in society are "satisfied." Comprehensive policy planning for specific social goals may maximize some people's values, but it may also generate extreme opposition from others. A government that pursues multiple policies may be politically more suitable to a pluralistic society comprising persons with varying values.

THE POLICY-MAKING PROCESS

Policy making involves a combination of processes in society. These processes are not always clear-cut and distinguishable in the complex world of policy making. But we can identify them for purposes of analysis.

Identifying Policy Problems: the identification of policy problems through publicized demands for government action.
Formulating Policy Alternatives: the formulation of policy proposals through political channels by policy-planning organizations, interest groups, government bureaucracies, and the president and Congress.

Legitimizing Public Policy: public statements or actions by the president, Congress, or courts, including executive orders and budgets, laws and appropriations, rules and regulations, and decisions and interpretations, which have the effect of setting policy directions.
Implementing Public Policy: the implementation of public policy through the activities of public bureaucracies and expenditure of public funds.
Evaluating Policy: the evaluation of policies by government agencies, by outside consultants, by interest groups, by the mass media, and by the public.

The foregoing is a formal breakdown of the policy-making process used by many students of public policy.[9] What it says is that some groups succeed, usually through the help of the mass media, in capturing public attention for their own definition of a problem. Various government bureaucracies, private organizations, and influential individuals, then, propose solutions in terms of new laws or programs, new government agencies, or new public expenditures. These proposals twist their way through the labyrinths of government and eventually emerge (generally after many alterations and amendments) as laws and appropriations. Government bureaucracies are created to carry out these laws and spend these funds. Eventually, either through formal evaluation studies or informal feedback, the successes and failures of these laws, bureaucracies, and expenditures are examined.

All of this activity involves both rational problem solving and political conflict. That is true whether we are describing Social Security or the Food Stamp program, employment training or free school lunches, Medicaid or legal services. Both rational and political considerations enter into each stage of the policy-making process.

Agenda Setting

Deciding what is to be decided is the most important stage of the policy-making process. We might refer to this stage as "agenda setting." Societal conditions not defined as problems never become policy issues. These conditions never get on the "agenda" of policy makers. Government does nothing, and conditions improve, remain the same, or worsen. On the other hand, if conditions in society are defined as problems, then they become policy issues, and government is forced to decide what to do.

Policy issues do not just happen. Creating an issue, dramatizing it, calling attention to it, and pressuring government to do something about it are important political tactics. These tactics are employed by influential individuals, organized interest groups, policy-planning organizations, political candidates and office holders, and perhaps most important, the mass media. These are the tactics of agenda setting.

Nondecisions

Preventing certain conditions in society from becoming policy issues is also an important political tactic. "Non-decision making" occurs when influential individuals or groups act to prevent the emergence of challenges to their own interests in society. According to political scientists Peter Bachrach and Morton Baratz:

> Non-decision making is a means by which demands for change in the existing allocation of benefits and privileges in the community can be suffocated before they are even voiced; or kept covert; or killed before they gain access to the relevant decision-making arena; or failing all these things, maimed or destroyed in the decision-implementing stage of the policy process.[10]

Non-decision making occurs when powerful individuals, groups, or organizations act to suppress an issue because they fear that if public attention is focused on it, something which may not be in their best interest will be done. Non-decision making also occurs when political candidates, office holders, or administrative officials anticipate that powerful individuals or groups will not favor a particular idea and therefore do not pursue the idea. They do not want to rock the boat.

The Mass Media

The power of the mass media is its ability to set the agenda for decision making—to decide what problems will be given attention and what problems will be ignored. Deciding what is "news" and who is "newsworthy" is a powerful political weapon. Television executives and producers, and newspaper and magazine editors, must decide what people, organizations, and events will be given public attention. Without media coverage, the general public would not know about many of the conditions or government programs affecting the poor or about alternative policies or programs. Without media coverage, these topics would not likely become objects of political discussion, nor would they likely be considered important by government officials even if they knew about them. Media attention can create issues and personalities. Media inattention can doom issues and personalities to obscurity.

The Budget

The budget is the single most important policy statement of any government. The expenditure side of the budget tells us who gets what in public money, and the revenue side of the budget tells us who pays the cost. There are few government activities or programs that do not require an expenditure of funds, and no public funds may be spent without legislative authority. The budgetary process provides a mechanism for reviewing government programs, assessing their costs, relating them to financial resources, and making choices among alternative expenditures. Budgets determine what programs and policies are to be increased, decreased, allowed to lapse, initiated, or renewed. The budget lies at the heart of all public policies.

In the federal government, the Office of Management and Budget (OMB), located in the Executive Office of the President, has the key responsibility for the preparation of the budget. OMB begins preparation of a federal budget more than a year before the beginning of the fiscal year for which it is intended. (For example, work began in January 1985 on the budget for the fiscal year beginning October 1, 1986, and ending September 30, 1987.) Budget materials and general instructions go out from OMB to departments and agencies, which are required to submit their budget requests for increases or decreases in existing programs and for new programs to OMB. With requests for spending from departments and agencies in hand, OMB begins its own budget review. Hearings are held for each agency. Top agency officials support their requests as convincingly as possible. On rare occasions a dissatisfied department head may ask the OMB director to present the department's case directly to the president. As each January approaches, the president and the OMB director devote a great deal of time to the budget document, which is by then approaching its final stages of assembly. Finally, in January the president sends "The Budget of the United States Government" to the Congress. This will be the budget for the fiscal year beginning October 1 and ending on September 30 of the following year. After the budget is in legislative hands, the president may recommend further amendments as needs dictate.

ILLUSTRATION: PUBLIC OPINION AND GOVERNMENT SPENDING

There is a great deal of concern in this country about government expenditures in general, and social welfare expenditures in particular, because of the nation's large budget deficit. The budget deficit has been running at about $200 billion annually (see figure 1–2). This means that the federal government is currently spending far more than the revenues it collects each year. The problem is analogous to what happens when you continually spend more than your income each month. The amount you owe accumulates, and your debt grows larger and larger. The federal government's deficit has grown faster under the Reagan administration than under any previous administration. Deficits have accumulated into a national debt that now stands at $1.5 trillion!

Congress recently took drastic steps to prevent the federal government from continuing to operate in the red by passing the Balanced Budget and Emergency Deficit Reduction Act of 1985, known as Gramm-Rudman after its sponsors, Senators Phil Gramm (R-Texas) and Warren Rudman (R-New Hampshire). It requires deficit reductions each year until 1991 when the goal of a balanced budget must be met. Failure to reduce the deficit could have resulted in automatic across-the-board cuts for most domestic and defense programs, although a number of the major social welfare programs are exempt from automatic reductions. Some see Gramm-Rudman as a meat-axe approach to solving budget problems while others see it as an act of desperation to bring government spending in line. The Supreme Court has upheld the goal of a balanced budget by 1991 but ruled unconstitutional the automatic budget cutting procedure, leaving Congress to once again decide where to cut the budget.

Since social welfare expenditures account for the largest portion of federal expenditures, the presidential administration is concerned that the government should do more to curb social welfare spending; but how does the American public feel about this issue? Recent Gallup Polls provide some interesting information about America's attitudes toward government spending. Periodically, Gallup interviewers ask a scientific sample of Americans questions like the following:

At present the Federal budget deficit is running at the rate of over $200 billion per year. Basically, there are only a few ways this deficit can be reduced. Please tell me whether you approve or disapprove of each of the following ways to reduce the deficit:

	APPROVE		DISAPPROVE		NO OPINION	
	JAN. 1983	APRIL 1985	1983	1985	1983	1985
Raise income taxes	18%	18%	77%	76%	5%	6%
Make further cuts in government spending for social programs	41	39	52	55	7	6
Make cuts in defense spending	57	66	35	28	8	6
Make cuts in "entitlement" programs such as Social Security, Medicare, and the like?	12	9	83	87	5	4

Responses have been relatively consistent in recent years. A review of the results indicates that the alternative favored most frequently to reduce the deficit is to cut defense spending, but a number of the individuals surveyed are also willing to cut social programs. Although social programs were not specifically identified, the public probably thinks of these as "welfare" programs for the poor such as Aid to Families with Dependent Children and Food Stamps. On the other hand, very few respondents wish to cut social insurance programs such as Social Security in order to achieve a balanced budget. There is also little public support for raising taxes.

Looking at the 1985 results more closely, men (22 percent) are somewhat more willing to raise taxes than women (14 percent), and blacks (20 percent) are slightly more willing than whites (17 percent) to consider raising taxes to solve the budget crisis. Hispanics (7 percent) are least likely to favor this alternative. Those with college educations are also somewhat more willing to consider this alternative than respondents with less schooling. Democrats and Republicans feel similarly on the issue of raising taxes. Only about 20 percent of each group favors raising income taxes.

Men (47 percent) are more willing than women (31 percent) to cut social programs, and whites (42 percent) and Hispanics (33 percent) are more likely to favor social program cuts than blacks (16 percent). Republicans (54 percent) are twice as likely as Democrats (26 percent) to favor cuts in social programs.

Men and women responded similarly to cuts in defense spending. Blacks (74 percent) were more likely than whites (65 percent) and Hispanics (55 percent) to favor defense cuts. Democrats (76 percent) were more likely than Republicans (56 percent) to approve this approach, and college graduates were somewhat more likely to approve defense cuts than those with less education.

Cuts in entitlement programs were unpopular among all groups with men (10 percent) approving this alternative slightly more than women (7 percent), and whites (9 percent) approving it slightly more than Hispanics (7 percent) and blacks (6 percent). Those with college educations also were somewhat more likely to approve cuts in entitlement programs than those with less formal education. Republicans (14 percent) favored this alternative three times as frequently as Democrats.

Public opinion does not necessarily decide public policy, even in a Democracy. While Americans are in general agreement on some issues such as reluctance to cut Social Security or raise taxes to reduce the budget deficit, there is a good deal less agreement on other issues. Although cuts in defense spending is the most popular alternative for reducing the deficit, 28 percent of Americans do not approve of this approach. Americans are even more divided on whether to cut social programs to achieve a balanced budget. Each of these disagreements generates an abundance of conflict over public policy which is not easily resolved. As a result, public policy making in the United States has been a political and incremental process.

Sources: The Gallup Poll, 1983, survey #207-G and the Gallup Report, June 1985, report no. 237.

Congress has established separate House and Senate budget committees and a joint Congressional Budget Office to review the president's budget after its submission to Congress. These committees initially draft a concurrent resolution setting target totals to guide congressional actions on appropriations and revenue bills considered throughout the year. Thus, congressional committees considering specific budget appropriations have not only the president's recommendations to guide them but also the guidelines established by the budget committees. If an appropriations bill exceeds the target set by the earlier resolution, it is sent back to the budget committees for reconciliation.

FIGURE 1–2 United States budget deficits, 1947–89 in billions of dollars by presidential administration. (Source: House Budget Committee, August 20, 1984.)

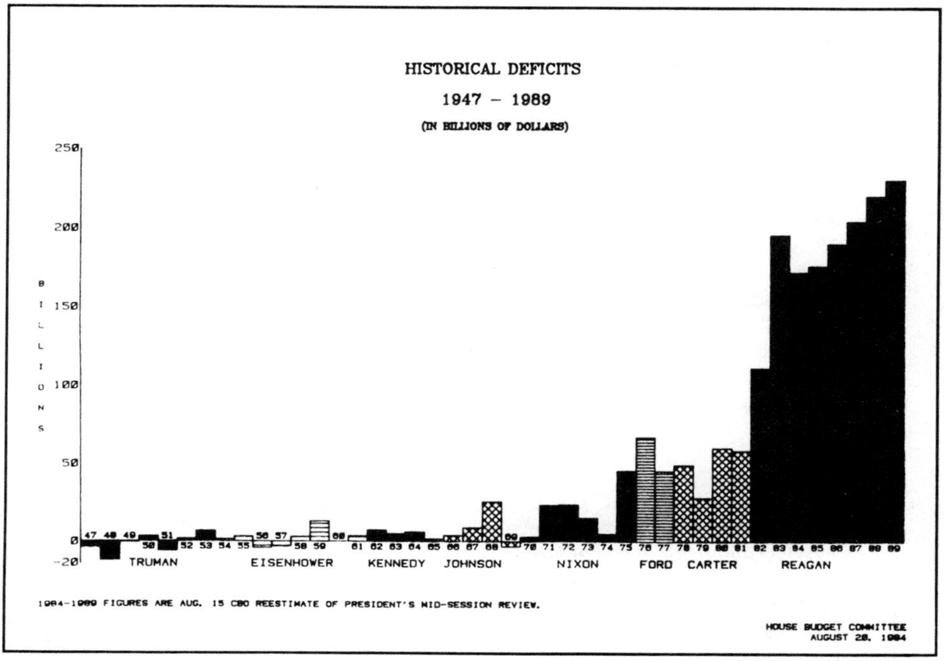

ILLUSTRATION: THE POOR AND THE NONPOOR: ATTITUDES TOWARD SOCIAL WELFARE

What do Americans think about the poor? Do the poor and the nonpoor feel differently about poverty? In a Los Angeles Times Poll, poor and nonpoor individuals were asked their opinions on a number of questions about poverty. Here are their perceptions of some of the issues:

	NOT IN POVERTY	IN POVERTY
Most poor people prefer to stay on welfare, or most would rather earn their own living.		
Prefer welfare	25%	20%
Earn their own living	62	68
Don't know	13	10
Most poor people are lazy, or most are hard working.		
Lazy	26	22
Hard working	48	58
Don't know	24	15
Poor people find it very hard to get work, or there are jobs available for anyone who is willing to work.		
Very hard to get work	39	59
Jobs are available	59	31
Don't know	2	9
Some people think welfare encourages husbands to avoid family responsibilities because it's easier for wives to get aid for children if the father has left. This happens almost always, often, seldom, or almost never.		
Often	61	60
Seldom	34	32
Don't know	5	8
Poor young women have babies so they can collect welfare: almost always, often, seldom, or almost never.		
Often	44	64
Seldom	51	23
Don't know	5	13
We are coddling the poor—poor people live well on welfare, or they can hardly get by on what the government gives them.		
Coddling	23	26
Hardly get by	68	64
Don't know	8	9

Antipoverty programs have almost always, often, seldom, or almost never worked.		
Often	33	31
Seldom	59	56
Don't know	8	13
Welfare benefits give poor people a chance to stand on their own two feet and get started again, or make poor people dependent and encourage them to stay poor.		
Get started again	16	31
Neither	11	9
Encourage people to stay poor	61	43
Don't know	11	16
Even if government were willing to spend whatever is necessary to eliminate poverty in the United States, does government know enough about how to do this?		
Yes, we know how	22	28
No, we don't know how	73	56
Don't know	4	15
Reagan's budget cuts left truly needy unprotected, or "safety net" still in place		
Unprotected	47	61
"Safety net" in place	43	22
Don't know	9	16
Greatest responsibility for helping the poor:		
Voluntary charities	8	4
Churches	16	24
Families and relatives	13	5
Government	33	34
Poor themselves	20	28
Other	0	0
Don't know/all about equally	9	4

From the results of this public opinion poll, we see that two-thirds of the poor and nonpoor interviewed believe that the poor would rather "earn their own living" than live on welfare, and half think the poor are "hard working." But in spite of these positive attitudes about the poor, the poor and the nonpoor disagree about the availability of work. Poor people feel it is more difficult to find work than the nonpoor do.

Nearly half of the nonpoor and nearly two-thirds of the poor believe that poor young women often have babies in order to receive welfare, and both the poor and the nonpoor have negative attitudes toward the current welfare system. Almost two-thirds of both groups believe that welfare benefits often contribute to family breakup. They also believe that the poor "can hardly get by" on the benefits they receive. Many respondents believe that welfare encourages people to stay poor, although the nonpoor believe this happens more than the poor do. There is also a great deal of pessimism about the government's ability to eliminate or reduce poverty. More than half of the nonpoor and the poor believe that antipoverty programs seldom work, and more than half of the poor and nearly three-fourths of the nonpoor do not believe that the government knows how to eliminate poverty even if unlimited funds were available to solve the problem.

These results reveal that there is considerable agreement between the poor and the nonpoor on many of the questions about welfare, but there is less agreement about the effectiveness of the Reagan "safety net" in helping the poor. The nonpoor are evenly divided in their opinions of the effectiveness of the Reagan approach to poverty. About half think the poor are not protected while an equal number believe that the safety net remains in place. But nearly two-thirds of the poor believe that they have been left unprotected while only one-fifth feel the social safety net remains in place.

Finally, there are many different responses to the question of who should have the *major* responsibility for the poor. The answer selected most frequently by both the poor and the nonpoor was the government. One-third of both groups chose this alternative. But it is also interesting to note that one-fifth of the nonpoor and one quarter of the poor believe that the poor should have major responsibility for helping themselves. Churches and relatives were the next most frequently chosen alternatives. Public opinion is, therefore, divided on the question of who should have primary responsibility for the welfare of the poor.

Source: Based on I. A. Lewis and William Schneider, "Hard Times: The Public on Poverty," *Public Opinion,* June/July 1985, pp. 1–7, 59–60.

Consideration of specific appropriations is a function of the appropriations committees in both houses. Each of these important committees has about ten fairly independent subcommittees to review the budget requests of particular agencies or groups of related functions. These subcommittees hold hearings in which department and agency officials, interest groups, and other witnesses testify about new and existing programs and proposed increases or decreases in spending. The appropriations subcommittees are very important because neither the full committees nor the Congress has the time or expertise to conduct in-depth reviews of programs and funding. Although the work of the subcommittees is reviewed by the full committee, and the appropriations acts must be passed by the full Congress, in practice most subcommittee decisions are routinely accepted.

In overall programs and expenditures, however, it is rare that Congress ever makes more than a 5 percent change in the budget originally recommended by the president. Most appropriations are determined by executive agencies interacting with the OMB. In spite of recent budget battles between Congress and the Reagan administration, Congress usually makes only minor adjustments in the president's budget.

Implementation

Policy implementation includes all of the activities which result from the official adoption of a policy. Policy implementation is what happens after a law is passed. We should never assume that the passage of a law is the end of the policy-making process. Sometimes laws are passed and nothing happens! Sometimes laws are passed and executive agencies, presuming to act under these laws, do a great deal more than Congress ever intended. Political scientist Robert Lineberry writes:

> The implementation process is not the end of policy-making, but a *continuation of policy-making by other means*. When policy is pronounced, the implementation process begins. What happens in it may, over the long run, have more impact on the ultimate distribution of policy than the intentions of the policy's framers.[11]

Specifically, policy implementation involves:

1. The creation, organization, and staffing of new agencies to carry out the new policy, or the assignment of new responsibilities to existing agencies and staff
2. The development of specific directives, rules, regulations, or guidelines to translate new policies into courses of action
3. The direction and coordination of personnel and expenditures toward the achievement of policy objectives.

The best laid plans of policy makers often do not work. Before a policy can have any impact, it must be implemented. And what governments *say* they are going to do is not always what they end up doing.

Traditionally, the implementation of public policy was the subject matter of public administration. And traditionally, administration was supposed to be free of politics. Indeed, the separation of "politics" from "administration" was once thought to be the cornerstone of a scientific approach to administration.

But today it is clear that "politics" and "administration" cannot be separated. Opponents of policies do not end their opposition after a law is passed. They continue their opposition in the implementation phase of the policy process by opposing attempts to organize, fund, staff, regulate, direct, and coordinate the program. If opponents are unsuccessful in delaying or halting programs in implementation, they may seek to delay or halt them in endless court battles. In short, conflict is a continuing activity in policy implementation.

The federal bureaucracy makes major decisions about the implementation of public policy. There are over two million civilian employees of the federal government. This huge bureaucracy has become a major base of power in America—independent of the Congress, the president, the courts, or the people. The bureaucracy does more than simply fill in the details of congressional policies, although this is one power of bureaucratic authority. Bureaucracies also make important policies on their own by (1) proposing legislation for Congress to pass; (2) writing rules, regulations, and guidelines to implement laws passed by Congress; and (3) deciding specific cases in the application of laws or rules.

In the course of implementing public policy, federal bureaucracies have decided such important questions as the safety of nuclear power plants; the extent to which blacks, women, and minorities will benefit from affirmative-action programs in education and employment; whether opposition political parties or candidates will be allowed on television to challenge a presidential speech or press conference; and whether welfare agencies will search Social Security Administration files to locate nonsupporting parents.

The decisions of bureaucracies can be overturned by Congress or the courts if sufficient opposition develops. But most bureaucratic decisions go unchallenged.

SUMMARY

Although there are elements of rationalism in policy making, the policy process is largely political. Our abilities to develop policies rationally are limited because we cannot agree on what constitutes social problems and on what, if anything, should be done to alleviate these problems. We also hesitate to make drastic changes in our current welfare system because we fear making large, costly errors that may be difficult to reverse.

The federal budget deficit, which now stands at about $200 billion annually, is a major concern of government. Americans are divided on their opinions about the best way to tackle the problem. Very few are willing to raise taxes to reduce the deficit, and there is also strong sentiment against cutting certain social welfare programs like Social Security. Stronger support exists for cutting some other types of social programs as well as cutting defense spending. These differences of opinion mean that public policy making generates conflict, and this conflict is generally resolved incrementally. The wheels of progress move slowly when it comes to social welfare policy making.

Social welfare policy development and implementation is much more a political "art and craft"[12] than a rational science. It is not enough for human-service professionals to know the needs of people and to want to provide services to help them. Policy advocates must both understand the political process and be adept at working within it if they are to have a voice in shaping social policy.

NOTES

1. See David G. Gil, "A Systematic Approach to Social Policy Analysis," *Social Service Review* 44 (December 1970) 411–26; also cited in Neil Gilbert and Harry Specht, *Dimensions of Social Welfare Policy,* 2nd ed. (Englewood Cliffs, N.J.: Prentice-Hall 1986), pp. 2 and 4.
2. T.H. Marshall, *Social Policy* (London: Hutchinson University Library, 1955), p.7. The distinction between *social policy* and *social welfare policy* is discussed in George Rohrlich, "Social Policy and Income Distribution," in Robert Morris, ed., *Encyclopedia of Social Work* (New York: National Association of Social Workers, 1971), pp. 1385–86.
3. See Carl T. Friedrich, *Man and His Government* (New York: McGraw-Hill, 1963), p. 70; Harold Lasswell and Abraham Kaplan, *Power and Society* (New Haven: Yale University Press, 1970), p. 71.
4. Edith Stokey and Richard Zeckhauser, *A Primer of Policy Analysis* (New York: W.W. Norton, 1978).
5. Herbert A. Simon, *Administrative Behavior* (New York: Macmillan, 1945), p.79. See also his *Models of Man* (New York: John Wiley, 1957); and *The Sciences of the Artificial* (New

York: John Wiley,1970). Simon was trained as a political scientist; he won the Nobel Prize in economics in 1978.

6. Harold Lasswell, *Politics: Who Gets What When and How* (New York: Free Press, 1936).
7. Edward C. Banfield and James Q. Wilson. *City Politics* (Cambridge: Harvard University Press, 1963), p. 7.
8. John Rawls. *A Theory of Justice* (Cambridge: Harvard University Press, 1972).
9. See Charles O. Jones. *An Introduction to the Study of Public Policy* (North Scituate, Mass: Duxbury Press, 1977); Thomas R. Dye, *Understanding Public Policy,* 5th ed. (Englewood Cliffs, N.J.: Prentice-Hall, 1984).
10. Peter Bachrach and Morton S. Baratz, *Power and Poverty* (New York: Oxford University Press, 1979), p. 7.
11. Robert L. Lineberry, *American Public Policy* (New York: Harper & Row, 1977), p.71.
12. Aaron Wildavsky, *The Art and Craft of Policy Analysis* (Boston: Little, Brown, 1979).

chapter 2

Government and social welfare

HISTORICAL PERSPECTIVES ON SOCIAL WELFARE

Social welfare policy as we know it today dates back to the beginning of the seventeenth century in Elizabethan England. Colonists who settled in the New World brought with them many of the English welfare traditions. In the colonies as in England, the earliest sources of welfare aid for the destitute were families, friends, and churches. Later, local and state governments intervened as a last resort. However, the twentieth century brought an increased number of social welfare problems for Americans. The magnitude of these problems caused the federal government to enact its own welfare legislation during the New Deal era of the 1930s. With the Great Society programs of the 1960s—another large-scale attempt on the part of the federal government to alleviate poverty and suffering—the federal government's role in social welfare continued to grow.

During the 1980s, however, a different response to hardship in America emerged. Concerned with growing costs and disillusioned with the perceived failure of many welfare programs, President Reagan's administration attempted to limit the federal government's role in social welfare and to increase reliance on state governments and the private sector in providing welfare services.

In the following pages, we briefly review the history of social welfare, discuss factors which have contributed to the growth of welfare programs in the United States, and consider recent initiatives to control the growth of welfare spending.

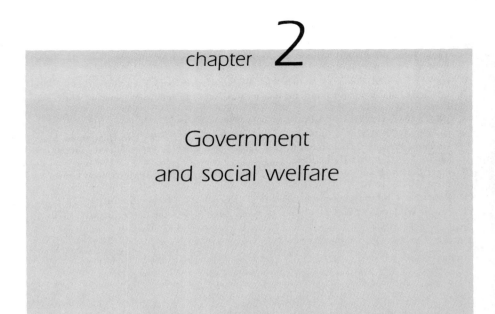

Elizabethan Poor Law

In the Old World, the first sources of welfare assistance—family, friends, the community—provided mutual aid. Aid was mutual because people relied on one another. If a family's food crop failed or the breadwinner became ill and unable to work, brothers, sisters, or neighbors pitched in, knowing that they would receive the same assistance if they should need it one day. Later, it became the duty of the church and of wealthy feudal lords to help the needy.[1] During much of the Middle Ages emphasis was placed on doing charitable works as a religious duty.[2] Attitudes toward the poor were benevolent. Those destitute through no fault of their own were treated with dignity and respect and were helped through the hard times.[3]

These early systems of aid were informal systems. There were no formal eligibility requirements, no application forms to complete, and no background investigations. But as the structure of society became more complex, so did the system of providing welfare assistance.

The first laws designed to curb poverty were passed in England during the fourteenth and fifteenth centuries. In 1349 the Black Death drastically reduced the population of the country. King Edward III responded with the Statute of Laborers to discourage vagrancy and begging; all able-bodied persons were ordered to work, and the giving of alms was forbidden.[4]

Changes in the structure of society eventually forced the Elizabethan government to intervene in providing welfare. The Industrial Revolution that occurred in England meant a shift from an agrarian-based economy to an economy based on the wool industry. People left their home communities to seek industrial employment in the cities. The feudal system of life fell apart as the shift away from agriculture and toward industry was completed. Government was becoming more centralized and played a stronger role in many aspects of society, including social welfare, while the role of the church in welfare was diminishing.[5]

The interplay of new social forces—the breakdown of the feudal system, the Industrial Revolution, and the reduction of the labor force—brought about the Elizabethan Poor Law of 1601,[6] the first major event in the Elizabethan government's role in providing social welfare benefits. The law was passed mostly as a means of "controlling" those poor who were unable to locate employment in the new industrial economy and who might cause disruption.[7] Taxes were levied to finance the new welfare system, but rules were harsh. Children whose parents were unable to support them faced apprenticeship. Able-bodied men dared not consider remaining idle.

Distinguishing the "deserving" from the "nondeserving" poor was an important part of Elizabethan Poor Law. Affluent members of society did not want to be burdened with assisting any but the most needy. The deserving poor were the lame, the blind, orphaned children, and those unemployed through no fault of their own. The nondeserving poor were vagrants or drunkards—those considered lazy, shiftless, and unwilling to work. "Outdoor" relief was help provided to some deserving poor in their own homes. "Indoor" relief was also provided to those unable to care for themselves, but such relief was generally provided in "almshouses," which were institutions that housed the poor. The nondeserving poor were sent to "workhouses," where they were forced to do menial work in return for only the barest of life's necessities.[8]

Stringent residency requirements had to be met by all recipients. Welfare aid was administered by local units of government called parishes. Parishes were specifically instructed to provide aid only to persons from their own jurisdictions. There was little sympathy for transients.

Early Relief in the United States

Many aspects of the Elizabethan welfare system were adopted by American colonists. For example, residency requirements were strictly enforced through the policies of "warning out" and "passing on."[9] Warning out meant that newcomers were urged to move on to other towns if it appeared that they were not financially responsible. More often, "passing on" was used to escort the transient poor back to their home communities. These practices continued well into the nineteenth century. In one year alone, eighteen hundred persons were transported from one New York community to another as a result of these policies.

Life was austere for the colonists. The business of making America livable was a tough job, and the colonists were by no means well-off. "Many of them were paupers, vagrants, or convicts shipped out by the English government as indentured servants." Life in the colonies, while better for many, still brought periods when sickness or other misfortune might place a person in need.

The colonists used four methods to "assist" the needy. "Auctioning" the poor to the family that was willing to care for them at the lowest cost was the least popular method. A second method was to put the poor and sick under the supervision of a couple who were willing to care for them at as little cost as possible. The third method, outdoor relief, was provided to most of the needy. And the fourth method was the use of almshouses. Many claimed almshouses were the best method of aid because of the quality of medical care they provided to the sick and elderly. Almshouses in the cities provided a much higher level of care than rural almshouses, which were often in deplorable condition and little more than rundown houses operated by a farm family. Politicians, almshouse administrators, and doctors seemed pleased with the progress they had made in assisting the needy during the eighteenth and nineteenth centuries.

The Great Depression and the New Deal

From 1870 to 1920 America experienced a period of rapid industrialization and heavy immigration.[10] Private charities, churches, and big city political "machines" and "bosses" assisted the needy during this period. The political machine operated by trading baskets of food, bushels of coal, and favors for the votes of the poor. To finance this primitive welfare system, the machine offered city contracts, protection, and privileges to business interests, which in return paid off in cash. Aid was provided in a personal fashion without red tape or delays. Recipients did not feel embarrassed or ashamed, for after all, "they were trading something valuable—their votes—for the assistance they received."

As social problems mounted—increased crowding, unemployment, and poverty in the cities—the states began to take a more active role in welfare. "Mothers' aid" and "mothers' pension" laws were passed by state governments to assist children in families where the father was deceased or absent. Other pension programs were established to assist the poor, aged, blind, and disabled. Federal government involvement in welfare was not far away.

The Great Depression, one of the bleakest periods in American history, followed the stock market crash in October 1929. Prices dropped dramatically, and unemployment was rampant. By 1932 one out of every four persons had no job, and one out of every six persons was on welfare. Americans who had always worked lost their jobs and depleted their savings or lost them when banks folded. Many were forced to give up their homes and farms because they could not continue to meet the mortgage payments. Economic catastrophe struck deep into the ranks of the middle classes. Many of the unemployed and homeless were found sleeping on steps and park benches because they had nowhere else to go.[11]

The events of the Great Depression dramatically changed American thought. The realization that poverty could strike so many forced Americans to consider large-scale economic reform. President Franklin Delano Roosevelt began to elaborate the philosophy of the "New Deal" that would permit government to devote more attention to the public welfare than did the philosophy of "rugged individualism" so popular in the earlier days of the country. The New Deal was not a consistent or unifying plan; instead it was a series of improvisations which were often adopted suddenly, and some of them were even contradictory. Roosevelt believed that the government should act humanely and compassionately toward those suffering from the depression. The objectives of the New Deal were "relief, recovery, and reform" and Roosevelt called for

> full persistent experimentation. If it fails, admit it frankly and try something else. But above all try something. The millions who are in want will not stand by silently forever while the things to satisfy their needs are in easy reach.[12]

Americans came to accept the principle that the entire community has a responsibility for welfare.

Included in the New Deal were a number of social welfare provisions. The Social Security Act of 1935, the cornerstone of social welfare legislation today, included Social Security retirement benefits administered by the federal government. Work programs established through projects such as the Works Progress Administration and the Civilian Conservation Corps provided jobs for many Americans. Federal grants-in-aid programs to states and communities were initiated to fund assistance programs for dependent children, the elderly, and the blind. Other programs included unemployment compensation, employment services, child welfare, public housing, urban renewal, and vocational education and rehabilitation.

Declaring War on Poverty

From 1935 through the 1950s, welfare programs did not change very much. Eligibility requirements were loosened, payments were increased, and a few new categories of recipients were added, but there were not many major changes in the system of providing welfare benefits. But the 1960s brought unusual times for Americans. The beginning of the sixties was a period of prosperity for most Americans, but civil rights issues and the depressed condition of minorities came to the foreground. Most Americans were relatively affluent, but there were twenty-five million people who remained poor. Influenced by the writings of economist John Kenneth Galbraith, who had directed attention to the existence of poverty in the midst of this affluent culture, President John F. Kennedy began to address the problem of poverty.

After Kennedy's assassination in 1963, President Lyndon Baines Johnson followed in the tradition of his predecessor by "declaring war on poverty" in March 1964. The war on poverty comprised many social programs designed to "cure" poverty in America. The goals of the "war" were to allow ghetto and poor communities to develop their own programs to arrest poverty and to root out inequality in the lives of Americans. Model cities programs, community-action agencies, and other devices were tried, but many of these strategies proved unsatisfactory. As the 1970s approached, the new presidential administration of Richard Nixon began dismantling the agencies of the War on Poverty. The "welfare rights movement" had come and gone.

President Nixon, determined to clean up the "welfare mess," attempted another type of reform in 1970—a guaranteed annual income for all poor persons. Parts of the plan were adopted, notably the Supplemental Security Income (SSI) program in 1972. But for the most part, the concept of a guaranteed annual income was rejected by Congress. Some members of Congress were concerned that Nixon's proposal was too much welfare, and others were concerned that it was too little welfare.

Meanwhile, another type of welfare movement had arisen as social services designed to address problems other than poverty grew increasingly popular in the 1960s and 1970s. Consequently, legislation was passed to assist abused children, to provide community mental health services, and to develop social services programs for the elderly.

"The Revolution No One Noticed"

While Americans were preoccupied with the turmoil of the 1960s—the civil rights movement and the war in Vietnam—a revolution no one noticed was taking place.[13] For many years, the argument on behalf of social welfare in America had followed clear lines: The United States was spending the largest portion of its budget for defense; programs for the poor, the sick, the aged, and minorities were underfinanced. It was argued in the 1960s that in order to be more responsive to the needs of its citizens, the nation should "change its priorities" and spend more for social programs to reduce poverty and less on wars like Vietnam. The argument ended with a call for a revolution in national priorities.

In a single decade America's national priorities were reversed. In 1965 national defense expenditures accounted for 42 percent of the federal government's budget, while social welfare expenditures (social insurance, health, and public assistance) accounted for less than 25 percent. While the mass media focused on the war in Vietnam and on Watergate, a revolution in national policy making was occurring. By 1975, defense accounted for only 25 percent of the federal budget and social welfare expenditures had grown to 43 percent of the budget (see figure 2–1).

Social welfare is now the major function and major expenditure of the federal government. This reversal of national priorities occurred during both Democratic and Republican administrations and during the nation's longer war.

> The mid to late 1960s were quite prosperous years. The unemployment rate fell under 4 percent, real income rose briskly. In the flush of affluence, new programs could be introduced with minimal fiscal strain, even as the Vietnam War expenditures were swelling.[14]

FIGURE 2–1 Welfare and defense priorities (percentage of total federal spending).

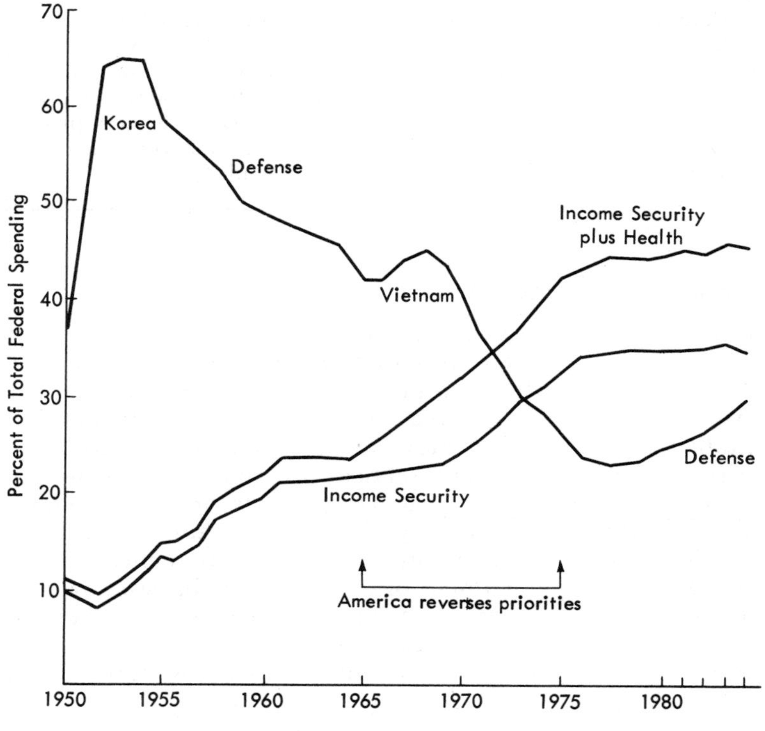

In short, ideas that welfare expenditures are not likely to increase during Republican administrations or during times of war turned out to be wrong. America's commitment to social welfare was growing.

But not everyone was comfortable with this revolution in public spending. There was fear that the nation was sacrificing national defense in order to spend money on social welfare programs which might not work. As the 1970s ended and the 1980s emerged, a more cautious attitude toward social welfare spending had developed.

ILLUSTRATION: WELFARE AND WARFARE

Today federal expenditures for social welfare (including social insurance and public assistance) far exceed federal expenditures for national defense. In the 1986 federal budget, direct benefit payments to individuals accounted for 41 percent of the federal budget. These direct benefit payments include social insurance payments (like Social Security and Medicare) and public assistance payments (like Food Stamps and Supplemental Security Income and the federal portion of AFDC and Medicaid). Health programs, primarily Medicaid and Medicare, alone comprise nearly 10 percent of the total budget. Only 29 percent of the 1986 budget is devoted to national defense.

Until a few years ago, the relationship between federal spending for "welfare" and "warfare" (or "guns and butter" as it was once called), was reversed: before 1973 the federal government spent more on national defense than it did on social welfare. Figure 2–1 shows the changing trends in spending for welfare and defense. Note that defense spending jumped up at the beginnings of the Korean War (1950–52) and the Vietnam War (1964–68) and recently in the military buildup begun under President Carter and continued under President Reagan. In contrast, social welfare spending rose slowly for many years and then "exploded" in the 1970s after the Great Society programs were in place. Social welfare and health spending have remained at high levels despite a significant increase in defense spending.

Social Welfare—Toward the 1990s

In some ways, social welfare has come a long way. The number of people served by the various welfare programs in the United States and the amount of money spent on these programs is impressive. But in other ways, the social welfare programs of today are not so different from social welfare in Elizabethan and colonial times. Payments to recipients are often low, and the conditions under which services are rendered can be demeaning. There are many other problematic aspects of social welfare. While helping many, the expansion of social welfare has also resulted in a mixture of public policies and programs which are often inconsistent, conflicting, and overlapping. A number of critics believe that welfare programs encourage dependency and have contributed to the numbers of people receiving welfare rather than reducing these numbers.

These problems have caused disillusionment with the welfare system.

This disillusionment has eroded many of the liberal ideas and hopes of the 1960s and 1970s. As a result, more conservative philosophies about welfare have gained popularity in the 1980s with the support of the Reagan administration. These philosophies suggest that (1) government spending for welfare should be kept to a minimum; (2) government, especially the federal government, should minimize its role in welfare policy and programs; (3) only those in extreme circumstances—the "truly needy"—should receive welfare assistance; and (4) welfare should be provided on a short-term rather than long-term basis whenever possible. Changes in many social welfare programs reflect these ideas. For instance, the rate of government spending in public assistance programs such as Aid to Families with Dependent Children has been slowed, eligibility requirements for many programs have been made more stringent, and there is a reluctance to establish new programs. There are many critics of the current conservative approach to social welfare. Among them are Michael Harrington, Frances Fox Piven and Richard Cloward, and Nancy Amidei, who have written on various aspects on the problems of the poor.[15] The conservative approach to welfare is frequently blamed for increases in the number of jobless, homeless, and medically needy individuals. As we approach the 1990s, social welfare policy remains a struggle between those who support a conservative and selective approach to assist those in need and those who believe in a more open, generous, universal system of aid. In the chapters that follow, we will continue to explore these struggles.

THE EXPANSION OF SOCIAL WELFARE

Since the early 1900s, several factors have contributed to the increase in the number of social welfare programs, the number of people receiving assistance, and the amount spent on welfare programs. Among these are (1) the rural-to-urban migration; (2) the elimination of residency requirements; (3) the welfare rights movement; (4) cost-of-living increases; (5) the aging of America, and (6) increases in single-parent families.

The Rural-to-Urban Migration

During the late 1800s and early 1900s, America experienced some of its sharpest growing pains as the Industrial Revolution reached its peak. America changed from a rural, agrarian society to an urban, industrial society. People migrated from poor rural farming communities hoping to find jobs and brighter futures in the cities. In addition, foreigners were also emigrating to American cities, seeking an improved standard of living. The dreams of many persons were shattered. Those who found jobs were often forced to work long hours for low pay under poor working conditions. Housing was often crowded; sanitation and health problems were common. Persons who had come to the cities to "make good" were often far from their families and could not receive financial and psychological support from them. Social problems became more and more a problem for governments. As the Great Depression unfolded, the cities and states were no longer able to cope with worsening social problems. The response to this major economic crisis was the Social Security Act of 1935, by which the federal government assumed its role as the major financier of social welfare programs.

Residency Requirements Eliminated

Residency requirements were traditional means for restricting the number of persons eligible for welfare assistance. During Elizabethan and colonial times, people believed that residency requirements were needed because the poor and needy should be provided for by their home communities. The financially dependent were not welcome in new communities. However, as society became more mobile and people moved more frequently to seek jobs and other opportunities, the argument for residency requirements no longer seemed to hold up. But states and communities continued to impose these restrictions to limit the number of persons dependent on welfare. Requiring that potential recipients had to reside in the city or state for six months or a year or even requiring that they intended to reside in the city or state were ways of keeping welfare caseloads small. Following a number of court challenges, the Supreme Court declared residency requirements unconstitutional in 1969.[16] It became easier to qualify for assistance, and as a result, welfare caseloads grew, especially during the 1970s.

Welfare Rights

In the 1960s blacks and other poor Americans showed their discontent with the welfare system through the "welfare rights movement." It arose in the wake of the civil rights movement, as the poor expressed their dissatisfaction with a political system that had denied them the standard of living that other Americans were enjoying. The welfare rights movement was a stormy time in American domestic history, especially from 1964 to 1968, when major cities experienced a series of riots. As the number of disturbances increased, so did the number of people applying for welfare. Also, a greater percentage of welfare applications were being approved than ever before. The welfare rights movement brought changes in the behavior and attitudes of welfare recipients. [17]

> The mood of applicants in welfare waiting rooms had changed. They were no longer as humble, as self-effacing, as pleading; they were more indignant, angrier, more demanding. [18]

The mood of welfare administrators and caseworkers had also changed. Many of the practices that had been part of lengthy background investigations ceased. The process of obtaining aid was speeded up; welfare agencies were not so quick to eliminate benefits when recipients did not comply with the rules.

> For all practical purposes, welfare operating procedures collapsed; regulations were simply ignored in order to process the hundreds of thousands of families who jammed the welfare waiting rooms. [19]

By 1968 the welfare rights movement was coming to a close. Riots were ceasing, but despite the demise of the movement and the National Welfare Rights Organization, which had been formed to improve the plight of the poor, a record number of people were being certified for welfare benefits. The rolls were continuing to grow.

Cost-of-Living Adjustments

Some of the welfare spending increases during the 1970s and 1980s have been due to congressional approval of cost-of-living adjustments, known as COLAs, designed to keep welfare benefits in line with inflation. Political scientist Aaron Wildavsky tells us that in the past, Congress had often increased Social Security payments by taking a special vote each time an increase was considered. But later, Congress decided to make automatic cost-of-living adjustments in the Social Security, Food Stamp, and SSI programs. [20] This practice is also called indexing. Each year these social welfare payments have been adjusted to account for the increased cost of living. Wildavsky comments on the purpose of automatic cost-of-living adjustments:

> Such action was not intended to provide greater benefits to recipients, but only to automatically assure them of constant purchasing power. The index makes changes non-discretionary. . . . Legislators may see such automatic increases as either favorable or unfavorable. Some may miss the almost yearly opportunity to show their constituents how much they have contributed to the nation's welfare. Others may be happy to continue constant benefits without being seen as wasteful spenders. [21]

By the early 1980s the rationale for COLAs had come under attack. While social welfare payments were being adjusted according to the increased cost of living, the wages of many workers in the sluggish economy had not kept pace with inflation. Some modifications have been made to control COLAs (see, for example, chapter 4 on the Social Security program), but COLAs continue to be an important concept in these federally controlled social welfare programs.

The Aging of America

The growing number of elderly persons in the United States has put an increasing strain on the social welfare system. Today, those over age sixty-five comprise 11 percent of the population, as compared to 4 percent at the turn of the century. By the year 2000 the figure will be near 12 percent. [22] The elderly have considerable health, financial, and other social welfare needs. Advances in nutrition and medicine including recent breakthroughs in the development of artificial organs and organ transplants have helped Americans look forward to longer lives than ever before.

But as people grow older they become increasingly vulnerable and are sometimes unable to meet their own needs. There is widespread agreement in the United States that the elderly deserve publicly supported care. The tripling of the size of the elderly population during this century has meant the need for greater planning and additional services to insure that older Americans receive proper treatment.

Increase in Single-Parent Families

The changing patterns of American family life are another factor that explains some of the increase in welfare expenditures. Divorce is rampant. The pregnancy rate among teenagers who are unmarried and ill-equipped to care for children has caused national alarm. As a result of these new patterns, the number of single-parent families, especially those headed by women, has grown considerably. From 1950 to 1975 the number of female-headed households doubled to over seven million, and 70 percent included children.[23] Many of these households are poor. According to Senator Daniel Patrick Moyniham, who has long been interested in family structure and its relationship to poverty, women and their children continued to stand out in the poverty picture of 1983.

> About 7.6 million families were below the poverty line [in 1983]; 3.8 million were married-couple families; 3.8 million were single-parent families, of which 3.6 million were families headed by a female householder. Between 1982–83, increases in the number of poor female-headed households accounted for 95 percent of the increased number of all poor families.[24]

We would like to think that the women's rights movement increased opportunities for education and job advancement that would have raised many female-headed households out of poverty during the last decade, but the bleak picture for women and their children remains. As a result, welfare programs such as Aid to Families with Children, Medicaid, and Food Stamps continue to be expensive but critical resources for the poor.

FINANCING WELFARE

Prior to the Great Depression, local and state governments shouldered the major responsibility for welfare programs; the federal government was virtually uninvolved. But today the picture is quite different. Since 1935 there have been important changes in the way social welfare programs are financed. While federal, state and local welfare expenditures have all increased, the federal government is clearly the largest welfare spender. In 1975 the federal government spent nearly $160 billion for welfare, three times as much as the combined state and local government expenditures of $50 billion. Today the federal government spends about three and a half times more than the states for health and welfare.[25]

But how does the federal government acquire the funds to pay for these programs? The answer, of course, is through the taxes that are paid by individual citizens and corporations. As shown in figure 2–2, individual income taxes are the largest source of federal government revenues (budget receipts). Income taxes account for 37 percent of budget receipts. These taxes are channeled to the federal government's general revenue fund, which is used for many purposes, among them the financing of public assistance programs. The second major source of budget revenue is the Social Security tax. This is a special tax levied against an individual's income which is used to finance the social insurance programs. Social insurance receipts account for 30 percent of the federal budget. The federal government also collects revenues through corporation income taxes, excise taxes (taxes on products) and other sources, but individual income taxes and Social Security taxes combined constitute a significant portion (67 percent) of the total budget. There is another source of government funding that does not appear in figure 2–2. Federal budget deficits are now so large that the government must resort to borrowing considerable sums of money in order to meet its budget commitments.

The states collect taxes in several ways. Like the federal government

FIGURE 2–2 Budget receipts of the United States government. (Office of Management and Budget. *Budget of the United States Government, Fiscal Year 1986,* p.4–19.)

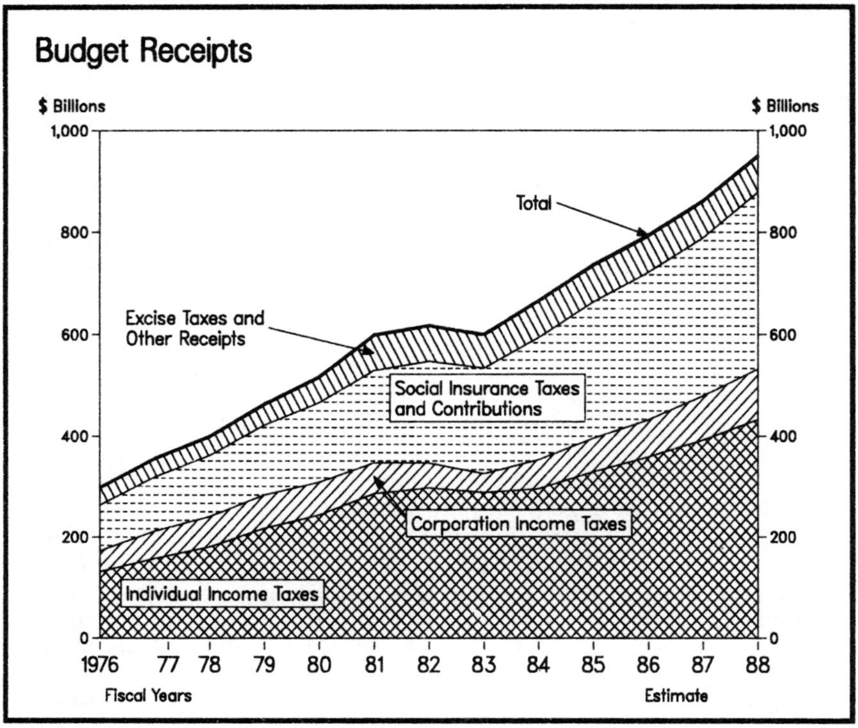

most states levy a personal income tax, although state income taxes are much less than federal income taxes. The sales tax is another mechanism used by states to generate revenue. A portion of these taxes is used to provide social welfare services. At the local level, the property tax, principally used to fund education, is the major source of revenue. Local governments (cities, counties, and municipalities) provide the smallest share of welfare services. These governments are mainly concerned with providing other types of services, such as police and fire protection to citizens.

Finances are an important aspect of providing welfare services, but setting welfare policy—determining the scope of welfare programs and rules governing eligibility and payment levels—is also important. Since 1935 the federal government's role in setting welfare policy has also grown. However, since President Reagan took office, he has made attempts to reduce the federal government's role in welfare and to return to the states greater responsibility for determining public assistance services, payment levels, and eligibility requirements. Although his successes in reducing federal government involvement to date may be considered modest, the issue of federalism—the appropriate roles of the federal, state, and local governments in determining policy—has received renewed attention from social welfare policy makers and analysts.

"REAGANOMICS" AND WELFARE

The economic ideas which have been labeled "Reaganomics," ideas which represent important political forces, have certainly affected social welfare policy. Whether or not one agrees with the ideas, it is essential to understand the Reagan administration's approach to welfare and the economy. Any brief description of Reaganomics risks oversimplification of many complex issues—inflation, economic growth, "supply-side" economics, capital investment, and money supply. However, we can briefly describe some of the central ideas guiding the Reagan administration through its first and second terms.

The "Misery Index"

An important component of Reaganomics is the belief that past Keynesian policies to reduce unemployment and hold down inflation have failed. (Keynesian economics is based on the notion that government can boost employment or cut inflation by manipulating the "demand side" of the economy—increasing government spending and expanding the money supply to boost employment, and doing just the opposite to hold down inflation.) According to Reagan, the most important cause of the nation's economic problems—unemployment, inflation, low productivity, and low investment—is the government itself. "The federal government through taxes, spending, regulatory, and monetary policies, has sacrificed long-term growth and price stability for ephemeral, short-term goals."[26]

According to Keynesian economic ideas, unemployment and inflation should not occur together. (Unemployment should reduce income, which in turn would force down prices.) But according to government figures, *both* unemployment and inflation remained high during the 1970s. Government efforts to reduce unemployment simply added to inflation; and government efforts to cut inflation simply added to unemployment. Reagan decided to combine the unemployment rate with the inflation rate and to call it the "misery index." In 1960 the misery index was 7.3, but by 1980 it had mushroomed to 17.2.[27] During the first term of the Reagan presidency, the misery index dropped owing to improvements in the economy, and this factor probably accounted for much of the president's popularity and his victory in the 1984 election.

Taxes and the Inflation Ratchet

Reducing taxes has been a central component of the President's economic policy. Because of the progressive rates of the federal personal income tax, the percentage of income claimed by the income tax increased with inflation. The current federal personal income tax begins at 12 percent of the *first* $1,000 of *taxable* income. (Generally, the first $6,000 of income for a family of four is *non-taxable*.) Tax rates increase to higher percentages for each $1,000 of additional income. A tax of 50 percent is levied on taxable income over $38,000. Prior to the Reagan-initiated tax cuts in 1981, the highest tax bracket of 70 percent was levied on taxable income over $200,000.

In the 1970s, inflation pushed Americans into higher tax brackets even though their buying power remained the same. Goods simply cost more. This meant that Americans were paying an increasing amount of their incomes to the federal government as inflation pushed up their salaries, even though their salary increases did not enable them to live a better life. These automatic tax increases caused by inflation were labeled "bracket creep."[28]

In 1981 the Reagan administration persuaded Congress to cut personal income taxes for all income groups by 25 percent over a three-year period. Moreover, Reagan persuaded Congress to "index" tax rates in the future to eliminate bracket creep. This means that if inflation carries taxpayers into higher tax brackets, their taxes will be adjusted, "indexed," so that the taxpayers will *not* carry a heavier tax burden.

"Supply-Side" Economics

President Reagan recommended a package of four sweeping policy directives designed to achieve "economic recovery."

1. Budget reform to cut the rate of growth in federal spending
2. Tax reductions of 25 percent over three years on personal income and additional tax reductions on business investment
3. Relief from federal regulations that cost industry large amounts of money for small increases in safety
4. Slower growth of the money supply, to be delivered with the cooperation of the Federal Reserve Board

All of these policies were designed to provide incentives for Americans to work, save, and invest. Theoretically, the economy will grow more rapidly because Americans can keep more of what they earn and purchase more goods with their earnings. Inflation will be brought under control by producing more goods rather than by limiting demand. Americans will also be encouraged to save a greater proportion of their incomes, and businesses will be encouraged to build new plants and provide more jobs.

Critics of the new "supply-side" economics argued that it is really a return to an old and discredited "trickle-down" approach to the economy. Taxes and regulations on businesses and affluent Americans are reduced in the hope that they will reinvest their profits and expand job opportunities for the poor and working classes. In other words, incentives are provided for the wealthy in the hope that benefits will "trickle down" to the poor.

Tax Cuts

According to the new Reaganomics, large tax cuts will not necessarily reduce government income or create large government deficits, at least in the long run. Taxes discourage work, productivity, investment, and economic growth. Reduce taxes, and the paradoxical result will be an *increase* in government revenue because more people will work harder and start businesses knowing they can keep a larger share of their earnings. Tax cuts will stimulate increased economic activity, and although tax rates are lower, this increased activity will eventually produce more government revenue.

Economist Arthur Laffer developed the diagram shown in figure 2–3.

FIGURE 2–3 The Laffer curve. (Reprinted from Thomas R. Dye. *Understanding Public Policy,* 4th ed. Englewood Cliffs, N.J.: Prentice-Hall, 1981, p. 272.)

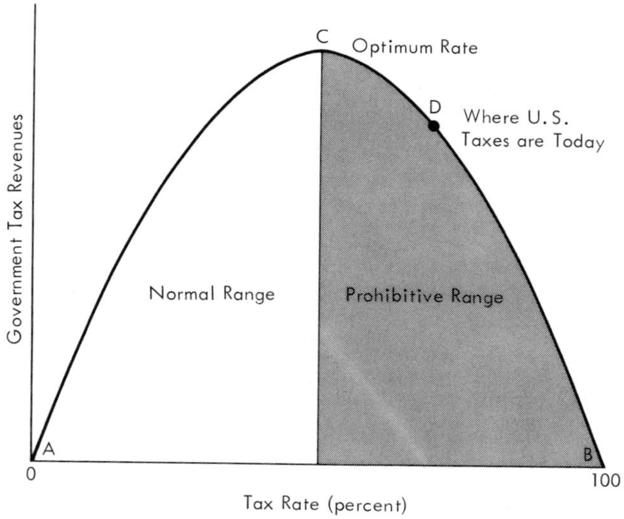

If the government imposed no taxes (a zero tax rate), the government would receive no revenue (point A). Initially, government revenues rise with increases in the tax rate. However, when tax rates become too high (beyond point C), they discourage workers and businesses from producing and investing. When this discouragement occurs, the economy declines and government revenues fall. Indeed, if the government imposed a 100 percent tax rate and confiscated everything that workers or business produced, then everyone would quit working. Then government would receive *no* revenues (point B).

According to the "Laffer curve," modest increases in tax rates will result in increased government revenues, up to an optimum point (point C), after which further increases will discourage work and investment. Laffer does not claim to know exactly what the optimum rate of taxation should be. But Laffer (and the Reagan administration) believed that the United States was in the "prohibitive range." Tax reductions, they concluded, would actually increase government revenues. Even before Reagan won his first term as president, Representative Jack Kemp (R-N.Y.) and Senator William Roth (R-Del.) proposed drastic cuts in personal income taxes over three years. President Reagan committed himself to support the Kemp-Roth bill during the campaign. Although these tax cuts were expected to create temporary increases in budget deficits, it was hoped that they would eventually stimulate enough new economic activity to raise additional revenues and balance the budget.

In his second term in office the president offered proposals for more sweeping changes in federal income taxes. He called for reducing the existing fourteen tax brackets to three at 35, 25, and 15 percent of income. This would mean that the top tax bracket would again be reduced, this time from 50 to 35 percent. According to estimates, the biggest winners would be those at the top and the bottom of the income scales. At the bottom, most people whose incomes fall just above the poverty line or below it would pay *no* income tax. That would be because of lowered tax rates and an increase in the personal income tax exemption, which would rise from $1,040 to $2,000. Three deductions popular with the middle class would be retained. First, interest on a home owner's primary residence would continue to be deductible; however, there would be severe restrictions on tax breaks for other property. Second, deductions for charitable contributions would be retained but only for those who itemize deductions. (The president's proposal calls for further simplifying the tax system by reducing the number of people who file itemized returns.) Third, medical expenses would also continue to be deductible, but only if they were more than 5 percent of gross income. Many deductions used by the upper classes, for example, business entertainment, would be restricted or eliminated, and many loopholes would be tightened. Currently, some people in very high income brackets pay very little tax or are able to avoid paying income taxes altogether. Other deductions which are popular with many taxpayers would also go by the wayside. State and local sales, income- and property-tax deductions might be scrapped. To make up for much of the income tax savings to individuals and families and the concomitant loss of federal revenues, there would be substantial increases on taxes that businesses and corporations pay.

The president is not the only one backing additional tax reform. Almost everyone is, but there are other proposals being offered. Republicans Jack Kemp and Senator Robert Kasten (Wis.) proposed a "flat tax"—a single tax rate for all taxpayers, and Democrats Senator Bill Bradley (N .J.) and Representative Richard Gephardt (Mo.) sponsored a plan which also lowers personal income taxes but utilizes three income brackets. The House Ways and Means Committee offered its version, with four tax brackets. Given the amount of effort being exerted by Congress and the Reagan administration, tax reform may not be far away.

Safety Nets and Tiers

Originally, the Reagan administration asserted that it would protect the "truly needy" by not making significant cuts in many of the income security programs. These programs included: Social Security, Medicare, Unemployment Compensation, veterans' benefits, Supplemental Security Income, Head Start, summer jobs for disadvantaged youths and free school lunches and breakfasts. The Reagan administration referred to these as the "social safety net programs." Note, however, that many of these programs belong to what is known as the "upper tier" of social welfare benefits. This upper tier consists largely of social insurance programs which are funded through payroll taxes and are given to beneficiaries regardless of their incomes. In addition, Social Security, Medicare, and veterans' benefits (which together account for most of the safety-net spending) really affect the *aged* more than the poor. SSI does affect the poor aged, blind, and disabled; and Head Start, summer jobs, and free school lunches and breakfasts do affect poor children, but they comprise a much smaller portion of the safety net.

Many programs which constitute the "lower tier" of social welfare programs are for the *poor*, and potential recipients must prove that they are poor in order to obtain these services.[29] Many of these programs were not included in the safety net and were targeted for substantial budget savings. They included: Aid to Families with Dependent Children, Food Stamps, Medicaid, housing assistance, CETA, social services, compensatory education, and legal services. The Reagan administration objects to overlapping programs—programs through which poor people receive more than one type of benefit. It also objects to programs which supplement the incomes of working families. The Reagan administration has been successful in tightening eligibility requirements in a number of the public assistance programs, such as AFDC and Food Stamps.

Block Grants, Revenue Sharing, and the New Federalism

A major goal of the president has been to restructure federal-state relations—specifically to turn over to the states many of the domestic programs of the national government. For example, during his first term, the president suggested a "swap" in which the federal government would assume full responsibility for the Medicaid program, and the states would in return take over the Food Stamp program and the federal portion of the AFDC program. (Chapter 10 describes Medicaid; chapter 8 describes Food Stamps and chapter 6 describes AFDC.) The swap was intended to "end cumbersome administration" and make the programs "more responsive to both the people they are meant to help and the people who pay for them."[30] Critics of the proposal contended that the swap would be a step backward in social welfare policy. Many social welfare programs were launched by the federal government *because* the states failed to respond to the needs of the poor. Even if state governments were well motivated to care for their poor, differences in the economic resources of the states would result in unequal treatment from state to state.

Although such a swap of programs is unlikely to occur, the Reagan administration has been successful in using block grants as a means of establishing a "new federalism." *Block grants* are federal payments to state or local governments for general functions, such as health, welfare, education, law enforcement, and community development. The money must be spent for the function specified in the block grant, but states and communities are free to decide specific uses for the funds. The purpose of block grants is to reduce the power of "the Washington bureaucrats," to return decision making to state and local governments, and to make federal money available for various purposes with "no strings attached." The Reagan administration considers block grants preferable to *categorical* grants, which are made by federal departments and agencies after reviewing specific applications of state or local governments on a project-by-project basis. The concept of block grants was developed as a reaction to centralization of power in the Washington bureaucracy. The first major block grants came in the field of law enforcement (the Crime Control and Safe Streets Act of 1968) and later in housing and urban affairs (the Housing and Community Development Act of 1974).

By consolidating many social welfare programs into state block grants, the president has been able to reduce social welfare spending because the amount of the block grants has been less than the sum of money previously spent on the individual social welfare programs. Block grants also shift decision making about specific uses of federal social welfare dollars to state political arenas where support for social welfare programs is not always as great as it is in Washington. As decision making is shifted to the states, much of the politicking and competition over funds is also shifted from Washington to state and local levels. For example, many health interests must now compete with each other to obtain scarce federal dollars, which are distributed through state welfare agencies.

Federal revenue sharing, another method of funding social welfare programs, was also attacked by the Reagan administration,[31] and Congress slated it for phaseout in 1987. Revenue sharing for specific purposes, such as health needs, housing, and nutrition, began in the 1960s and was targeted for poor communities. In 1972 President Nixon initiated general revenue sharing. However, most cities eventually became eligible for the funds, and many began using them for services originally paid for by local governments, such as police and fire protection. The arguments against federal revenue sharing were that the federal government has a huge budget deficit and can no longer afford revenue sharing and that some state governments are actually showing budget surpluses and are better able to afford to pay for these services themselves.

THE POLITICS OF BUDGET AND TAX CUTTING

Republican Ronald Reagan has secured two impressive presidential campaign victories. In 1980 he won the presidency with 51 percent of the popular vote; Democrat Jimmy Carter, the incumbent, received 41 percent of the vote, and Independent John Anderson received 7 percent of the vote. Reagan's victory was portrayed as a "landslide" by the media, and spokespersons for the Reagan administration talked about a popular "mandate" to cut government spending, reduce taxes, and strengthen the military. In 1984 Reagan won his second landslide victory, capturing 59 percent of the popular vote and more electoral-college votes than any other president in the history of the country. Many presidents have found it difficult to transform their electoral victory into a mandate for policy change. However, Reagan has been more successful than most modern presidents in convincing Congress that his "program for economic recovery" ought to be enacted.

Reagan's political popularity (as judged by national opinion polls) has remained high during both his terms in office. His popularity soared after an assassination attempt and his courageous recovery. Following an operation for cancer early in his second term, the president again seemed undaunted, and his popularity was stronger than ever. The president's age does not seem to concern voters. Regardless of the political problems that have occurred during his administration, they have not hurt or "stuck to" the president for long. As a result, Reagan's administration has been dubbed the "Teflon presidency."

Unlike many presidents, Reagan has used his personal popularity to advance his budget and tax-cutting programs. Before Jimmy Carter left office in January 1981, he submitted a $740 billion budget for fiscal year 1982. In March Reagan proposed a $695 billion budget for that same year. Reagan made $45 billion in cuts from the Carter budget, all of them from domestic programs. The image of heavy budget cuts in welfare programs by Reagan grew out of the reductions made by Reagan's Office of Management and Budget and its former director, David Stockman, in the requests made by the outgoing Carter administration. Carter, for example, requested a total of $255 billion for Social Security and public assistance in 1982; Regan reduced this request to $241 billion. But *both* the Reagan and Carter requests were well *above* the $232 billion spent in 1981. The press labeled Reagan's reductions in Carter's request as "cuts," but the Reagan figures were increases over the previous year's budget.

Nonetheless, the Reagan administration has enacted changes in welfare that have had serious consequences for many of the poor. Figure 2–4

Changes in Major Welfare Programs

The following table lists the major federal welfare programs and those changes made during the first three years of the Reagan administration that resulted in significant spending cuts. Hundreds of other program changes were made that also affected the poor and the near-poor.

Aid to Families with Dependent Children (AFDC)	**Purpose:** Federal-state program providing cash support to low-income families with children **Major Changes:** Reduced eligibility for families with earned income by limiting "work incentive" benefits; eliminated or reduced benefits for students beyond high school; limited benefits for pregnant women with no children to last trimester of their pregnancy.
Medicaid	**Purpose:** State-federal program to pay for medical care for the poor **Major Changes:** Reduced federal Medicaid grants to states 3 percent in 1982, 4 percent in 1983, and 4.5 percent in 1984 (states could avoid reduction by reducing error rates and benefit growth); states could require recipients to pay part of costs.
Food Stamps	**Purpose:** Coupons, good for food purchase, issued to low-income households **Major Changes:** Eliminated inflation adjustment in 1982 and postponed later adjustments; revoked eligibility of households with monthly incomes over 130 percent of the poverty line, unless they have elderly or disabled members; penalized states for excessive error rates in food stamp distribution.
Housing aid	**Purpose:** Rent subsidies for low-income families; aid to public-housing projects to help cover construction and operating expenses **Major Changes:** Gradually increased the tenant share of rent from 25 percent to 30 percent (the federal government pays the remainder); eliminated most federal housing construction subsidies.
Title XX Social Services	**Purpose:** Grants to states for providing services such as day care, foster care and family planning **Major Changes:** Congressional Budget Office (CBO) estimated funding cut of 22 percent.
Community Services block grant	**Purpose:** Grants to local community action agencies for social services to low-income persons **Major Changes:** Community Services Administration abolished and its programs made into a block grant. CBO estimated 39 percent funding cutback.

FIGURE 2-4 Major changes in social welfare programs under the Reagan administration. (*Editorial Research Reports* 1, no. 10, Congressional Quarterly, March 9, 1984.)

summarizes the major changes in the largest public assistance programs under the Reagan administration.

Reagan knew he could rely on the Republican-controlled Senate to support his budget. However, in the House of Representatives the Democrats were in the majority. The Speaker of the House, Democratic Congressmen Thomas P. "Tip" O'Neill, confidently predicted that the house would restore moneys cut from social programs. But Reagan outsmarted O'Neill by appealing to Southern, Democratic, conservative representatives—the so-called bollweevils—whom Reagan invited to the White House to appeal to their conservative instincts. Reagan went on national television to make a plea for his budget and ask viewers to write their representatives in support of the president. The response was overwhelming: thousands of calls, messages, and letters flooded into congressional offices. In the key vote on the budget, 62 House Democrats joined all 191 House Republicans to support the Reagan budget. Table 2–1 shows how Republicans and Democrats voted in response to President Reagan's budget and tax cuts.

Following his victory on the budget, Reagan introduced the largest tax cut in American history. This tax cut was the core of the new supply-side economics: the cut was supposed to improve investment, create employment, and expand output.

Again, Reagan was able to count on support from a Republican-dominated Senate, but House Democrats tried to reduce the size of the tax cut and change its upper-income tilt. Reagan, however, emerged as the master in political persuasion. He lobbied individual members of Congress and made many special taxing and spending concessions to win votes. In the end, he persuaded forty-eight House Democrats to join the Republicans in winning a clear victory for his tax-reduction program.

Later, David Stockman confided that he had serious doubts that the tax cut would expand the economy enough to cover the revenue loss to government. Stockman supported the budget cuts, but he believed the tax cuts would simply add to the government's deficits. Indeed Stockman even suspected that the real idea behind cutting taxes was to lower the top rate for those with highest incomes from 70 to 50 percent. According to Stockman, the tax cut was only a "Trojan horse" used to disguise a "trickle-down" economic program.[32]

It should be noted, however, that most major political figures in 1980 and 1981 (with the possible exception of Senator Edward M. Kennedy) supported budget and tax reductions. This is true of both Democrats and

TABLE 2-1 House Votes, Reagan Budget, and Tax Cuts, 1981

	BUDGET CUTS		TAX CUTS	
	Yes	No	Yes	No
Republicans	191	0	189	1
Democrats	62	182	48	196
Total	253	182	237	197

Republicans, liberals and conservatives. The only differences concerned how much to cut and how and where to cut. Most members of Congress felt a conservative "mood" in the nation favoring a reduction in government and taxation.

As the 1984 presidential campaign began, the federal budget deficit was larger than ever, but recovery in other aspects of the economy (inflation and employment) helped Reagan to win handily over Democratic challenger Walter Mondale, vice president during the Carter administration. The campaign got off to a rather lackluster start. Mondale's television personality and the image of Democrats as wasteful spenders proved to be hindrances. Although Mondale introduced cost-saving measures as part of his campaign, the president's image remained strong. Mondale did, however, make history when he chose Representative Geraldine Ferraro of New York—the first woman ever to run on a presidential ticket—as his running mate. Ferraro's candidacy added a new dimension to the campaign, and it was hoped that she would help widen the "gender gap." The gender gap refers to the differences in political preferences expressed by men and women. It appeared that women were less likely to favor Republican President Ronald Reagan and more likely to favor a Democratic candidate. Choosing a woman as the vice-presidential running mate might widen the gap considerably. After all, the president had not supported the equal rights amendment, and many welfare cuts made in his first term hit women hardest because poverty among women is higher than it is among men. But none of these strategies worked. Reagan vigorously launched a second term in office.

Mounting concern about the budget deficit by the president, the House, and the Senate did not have much effect on the 1986 budget. The budget allowed defense and Social Security spending to rise with inflation with no new tax increases. The budget total was $967.6 billion dollars. (The president had wanted more money for the military and more cuts in social welfare programs.) Much of the savings in the budget came from agricultural spending, Medicaid, Medicare, rural housing, small-business loans, and student loans. No one seemed happy with the budget compromise. According to the nonpartisan Congressional Budget Office, the deficit in 1988 will still be high—$160 billion.

POLITICS, THE WELFARE LOBBY, AND PACS

The poor are not represented in Washington in the same fashion as other groups in society.[33] The poor rarely write letters to members of Congress, and the poor are unlikely to make any significant campaign contributions. They are not usually found on a representative's home-state lecture circuit—service-club lunches, civic meetings, memorials, and dedications. The poor seldom come to Washington to visit their representative's office. Indeed, the poor do not turn out at the polls to vote as often as the nonpoor.

To the extent that the poor are represented at all in Washington, they are represented by "proxies"—groups that are not poor themselves but claim to represent the poor. Many of these groups have organized and reorganized themselves under various names over the years—the National Welfare Rights Organization (dissolved in the mid-1970s), the Children's Defense Fund, the National Anti-Hunger Coalition, the Low Income Housing Coalition, the Food Research and Action Center.

Lobbyists for the poor can be divided roughly into three categories: (1) churches, civil rights groups, and liberal organizations, (2) organized labor, and (3) welfare-program administrators and lawyers.

The churches (the National Conference of Catholic Bishops, the National Council of Churches, B'nai Brith, and others) often support programs for the poor out of a sense of moral obligation. Likewise, liberal activist groups (Common Cause, Americans for Democratic Action, and others) often support social programs out of an ideological commitment. Civil rights organizations (the National Urban League, the National Association for the Advancement of Colored People [NAACP], and others) support programs for the poor as a part of their general concern for the conditions affecting minorities.

Yet very often the success of lobbying efforts on behalf of the poor depends upon the addition of organized labor's considerable political power to the coalition of churches, civil rights groups, and liberal activists. Organized labor—for example, the AFL-CIO—does all of the things that the poor find difficult to do in politics—political organizing, campaign financing, letter writing, personal lobbying. Historically, organized labor has tended to support programs for the poor, even though union pay scales have moved a great distance from the poverty line. Labor *leaders* may be more likely to support social programs than the rank-and-file membership. Of course, the first concern of organized labor is labor legislation—labor relations, minimum wages, fair labor standards, and so on. But when labor leaders join others in support of social programs, the result is a strong political coalition.

Welfare-program administrators and lawyers have a direct financial interest in supporting social welfare spending. These groups may take the lead in trying to organize the others into coalitions that support particular programs. Supporters of proposals to reduce spending for social programs complain: "Virtually all of the lobbying has come from people who are involved directly or indirectly in administering these programs."[34] The welfare bureaucracy is said to create a powerful "poverty lobby," which consists of "people doing well by the government's doing good."

Prominent among the organizations representing social-program administrators and lawyers are the American Federation of State, County, and Municipal Employees (AFSCME), and the Legal Services Corporation. Affiliated with the AFL-CIO, AFSCME is a labor union that includes many public workers whose jobs are directly affected by cutbacks in social programs. As a labor union, it is funded primarily by the dues of its own members. But the Legal Service Corporation, whose five thousand attorneys across the nation provide legal assistance to the poor, is itself funded by the federal government. Because the Legal Service Corporation has lobbied on its own behalf, its critics have charged that it is misusing its funds. The same charge was leveled against the now defunct Community Services Administration, which was supposed to assist antipoverty programs throughout the country and was not supposed to lobby Congress. However, there are very few government bureaucracies—from the Defense Department, to the National Aeronautics and Space Administration, to the Department of Agriculture—which do not, directly or indirectly, lobby Congress for their own programs.

The "welfare lobby" is strongest when its separate groups—churches, civil rights organizations, liberal groups, organized labor, and social welfare administrators—are unified and coordinated in their efforts.

Lobbying on behalf of vulnerable groups and supporting legislation that is favorable to these groups is one form of political activity that goes on every day with members of Congress and state legislatures. Another important form of political activity is support of individual candidates. It is no surprise that those who are interested in seeing specific types of legislation passed or defeated support candidates who share their views. Support may come verbally through endorsements, or financially through campaign contributions at election time. Many special interests today are supported through the use of political action committees (PACs). PACs are used by all types of interest groups—the American Medical Association operates one of the wealthiest PACs. All forms of business and industry—real estate, building, agricultural, automobile, insurance, hospital—have PACs. The National Association of Social Workers, AFSCME, and other groups interested in social welfare issues also operate some form of PAC. The number of PACs has grown from 608 in 1974 to 3,400 in 1983.[35] In the 1984 elections PACs contributed about $75 million to the successful congressional candidates.[36] Many PACs have a vested interest in social welfare spending. The American Medical Association, once opposed to programs like Medicare and Medicaid, is now a strong supporter and defender of these programs. It is interested in the health of the nation and also wants to protect the interests of its own physician members. Other groups that provide social welfare services also do not wish to see their own colleagues adversely affected by budget cuts and government regulations, and they raise money to prevent this. Although *some* politicians refuse to accept PAC money, support of candidates through PACs rather than through individual contributions is becoming increasingly popular. The fear, however, is that as elected officials become even more beholden to special interests, it will be increasingly difficult to resolve public-policy issues.[37]

SUMMARY

The roots of the American welfare system can be traced back to Elizabethan times. English poor laws stressed local government responsibility for welfare and emphasized distinguishing the deserving poor from the nondeserving poor. Welfare in the United States today is similar in many respects.

In the early days of the country there were no large governmental welfare programs. Welfare was provided by families, friends, private charities, and churches. But by the late nineteenth and early twentieth centuries, social problems were mounting. The Industrial Revolution had taken its toll on the country. Overcrowding in the cities led to a variety of social problems, including poverty. State governments began to enact programs for dependent children, the elderly, and disabled persons. When the Great Depression hit, state and local aid was no longer enough. In 1935 the federal government passed the Social Security Act as part of America's New Deal. But none of these social welfare programs eliminated poverty and suffering. In the 1960s President Johnson declared war on poverty by pouring millions of dollars into grassroots social welfare programs. The Medicaid and Medicare programs and the Food Stamp program were also born in the sixties, but millions remained poor. The welfare rights movement sprang up and died, and Americans witnessed a change in national budget priorities with welfare spending overtaking defense spending.

The expansion of welfare has occurred for many reasons. Among these are the increased numbers of people who moved to urban cities around the turn of the century to find work and had no families on whom to rely when bad times struck. Residency requirements, used to restrict the number of people who received help, were eliminated in 1969, making it easier to receive aid. Potential welfare recipients saw many changes during the "welfare rights movement" of the 1960s, which made it easier to apply and qualify for benefits that might legally be theirs. Payments in some of the largest social insurance and public assistance programs now automatically increase as the cost of living rises, and this also increases the cost of welfare. As the aged population grows so does the demand for more health care and social services. Finally, the number of single-parent families has increased. They are generally headed by women whose risk of being in poverty and requiring welfare assistance is high.

Americans became disillusioned as they spent more on welfare without the results they had expected. In the 1980s America's welfare policies continued to be the focus of political conflict, and a more conservative mood had developed. President Reagan, who won two sound presidential victories, was successful in tightening eligibility requirements in many welfare programs, reducing spending, and consolidating many federal welfare programs. He also introduced a number of other economic reforms. These reforms are based on certain economic theories about how the rate at which people are taxed affects their incentive to work. The president's program for economic recovery was intended to increase the incentive to work and slow inflation by reducing taxes and slowing down the growth of the money supply. Another important aspect of Reagan's plan was to return to the states much of the decision-making power over how welfare dollars should be spent. While he pledged to continue aid to the "truly needy" and to maintain a "social safety net," many critics claimed that he was attempting to "balance the budget on the backs of the poor." Although it is difficult to pinpoint the exact causes, the economy improved after Reagan took office. Inflation decreased and more people went back to work, but this is only part of the picture. The number of poor had also risen, and the federal deficit grew tremendously. While the president has suggested more reductions in welfare spending, he continues to advocate increased defense spending. The activity of lobbying groups that represent the poor and political action committees with vested interests in social welfare has grown in the light of the activities of the Reagan administration.

NOTES

1. See Ronald C. Federico, *The Social Welfare Institution: An Introduction,* 3rd ed. (Lexington, Mass.: D.C. Heath, 1980), p. 42; and Blanche D. Coll, *Perspectives in Public Welfare: A History* (Washington: Department of Health, Education and Welfare, 1973), pp. 1–2 for an elaboration of the role of the church and feudal land holders in the provision of welfare benefits.
2. Coll, *Perspectives in Public Welfare,* p. 2.
3. Ibid., pp. 2–3.
4. Federico, *Social Welfare Institution,* p. 104; Coll, *Perspectives in Public Welfare,* p. 4.
5. See Federico, *Social Welfare Institution,* pp. 42–43 for further elaboration.
6. Ibid.
7. Philip Klein, *From Philanthropy to Social Welfare* (San Francisco: Jossey-Bass, 1968), p. 10, cited in Federico, *Social Welfare Institution,* p. 53.
8. See Federico, *Social Welfare Institution,* p. 53; and Coll, *Perspectives in Public Welfare,* pp. 5–6 for elaboration on Elizabethan welfare.
9. This section relies on Coll, *Perspectives in Public Welfare,* pp. 17, 20, 21–22, 27–28.
10. This paragraph relies on Thomas R. Dye, *Understanding Public Policy,* 4th ed. (Englewood Cliffs, N. J.: Prentice Hall, 1981), pp. 116–17.
11. Paragraphs describing the Great Depression rely on Thomas R. Dye and L. Harmon Zeigler, *The Irony of Democracy,* 5th ed. (Monterey, Calif.: Duxbury Press, 1981), pp. 100–101.
12. Cited in Richard Hofstadter, *The American Political Tradition* (New York: Knopf, 1948), p. 316.
13. See Aaron Wildavsky, *Speaking Truth to Power: The Art and Craft of Policy Analysis* (Boston: Little, Brown, 1979), especially pp. 86–89 for elaboration on this discussion of "the revolution no one noticed."
14. Robert D. Plotnick, "Social Welfare Expenditures: How Much Help for the Poor?" *Policy Analysis* 5, 2 (1979), 278.
15. Michael Harrington, *The New American Poverty* (New York: Holt, Rinehart & Winston, 1984); and Frances Fox Piven and Richard Cloward, *The New Class War* (New York: Pantheon Books, 1982). Nancy Amidei writes for the *Los Angeles Times* and *Commonweal* and is a commentator on National Public Radio's "All Things Considered." See for example, "Poor People and Health: Dollars and Sense," *Los Angeles Times,* September 19, 1985, part II, p. 5; "In Hunger, Charity Begins at Home," *Los Angeles Times,* October 2, 1985, part II, p. 5.
16. *Shapiro* v. *Thompson,* 394 U.S. 618; and see Frances Fox Piven and Richard A. Cloward, *Regulating the Poor: The Functions of Public Welfare* (New York: Random House, 1971) for an elaboration on residency requirements, especially pp. 306–8.
17. See Frances Fox Piven and Richard A. Cloward, *Poor People's Movements: Why They Succeed, How They Fail* (New York: Vintage Books, 1977).
18. Ibid., p. 275.
19. Ibid.
20. Wildavsky, *Speaking Truth to Power,* p. 98.

21. Ibid.
22. Robert M. Moroney, *Families, Social Services and Social Policy: The Issue of Shared Responsibility* (Washington: Department of Health and Human Services, 1980), p. 58. SHHS publication no. (ADM) 80-846.
23. Ibid., p. 43.
24. Daniel Patrick Moynihan, "Family and Nation," The Godkin Lectures, Harvard University, April 8, 1985, p. 15.
25. Bureau of the Census, *Statistical Abstract of the United States, 1984* (Washington, 1983), p. 367.
26. President of the United States, *A Program for Economic Recovery,* February 18, 1981 (Washington: Government Printing Office, 1981).
27. Ibid.
28. Ibid., p. 6.
29. For more on the safety net and upper- and lower-tier programs, see D. Lee Bawden and John L. Palmer, "Social Policy: Challenging the Welfare State," in John L. Palmer and Isabel V. Sawhill, eds., *Reagan Record,* Cambridge, Mass.: Ballinger, 1984, pp. 177–215.
30. President Ronald Reagan, State of the Union Address, January 26, 1982.
31. See "The Drive to Kill Revenue Sharing," *Time,* March 11, 1985, pp. 30–31.
32. William Greider, "The Education of David Stockman," *Atlantic Monthly,* December 1981, pp. 27–54.
33. This discussion relies on "Special Treatment No Longer Given Advocates for the Poor," *Congressional Quarterly Weekly Report,* April 18, 1981, pp. 659–64.
34. Rep. Phil Gramm (D-Texas) quoted in ibid., p. 662.
35. Sean S. Price, "PACs Purchasing Politicians," *Daily Texan,* September 13, 1984, p. 2.
36. Brooks Jackson, "PAC Money Talks Louder Now," *Wall Street Journal,* December 24, 1984, p. 26.
37. Ibid.

chapter 3

Defining poverty: where to begin?

DEFINING POVERTY

The very first obstacle to a rational approach to reducing poverty in America lies in conflict over the definition of the problem. Defining poverty is a *political* activity. Proponents of increased governmental support for social welfare programs frequently make high estimates of the number and percentage of the population that is poor. They view the problem of poverty as a persistent one, even in a generally affluent society. They argue that many millions of Americans suffer from hunger, malnutrition, remedial illness, hopelessness, and despair. Their definition of the problem practically mandates the continuation and expansion of a wide variety of public welfare programs.

In contrast, others minimize the number of poor in America. They see poverty as diminishing over time. They view the poor in America today as considerably better off than the middle class of fifty years ago and even wealthy by the standards of most societies in the world. They deny that anyone needs to suffer from hunger, malnutrition, or remedial illness, if they make use of the public services already available to them. They believe that there are many opportunities for upward mobility in America and that none should suffer from hopelessness or despair. This definition of the problem minimizes the need for public welfare programs and encourages policy makers to reduce the number and size of these programs.

Political conflict over poverty, then, begins with contending definitions of the problem of poverty. In an attempt to influence policy making, various political interests try to win acceptance for their own definitions of the problem. Political scientist E. E. Schattschneider explained:

> Political conflict is not like an intercollegiate debate in which the opponents agree in advance on a definition of the issues. As a matter of fact, *the definition of the alternatives is the supreme instrument of power;* the antagonists can rarely agree on what the issues are because power is involved in the definition.[1]

Poverty has always been a concern during economic depressions, but poverty has been a political issue only for the last twenty-five years. Prior to the 1960s, the problems of the poor were almost always segmented into areas such as old age, disability, widows and orphans, unemployment, medical indigency, delinquency, slum housing, and illiteracy. According to one observer, it was not until the Kennedy and Johnson administrations that the nation began to see that these problems were tied together in a single "bedrock" problem—poverty:

> The measures enacted, and those proposed, were dealing separately with such problems as slum housing, juvenile delinquency, dependency, unemployment, illiteracy, but they were separately inadequate because they were striking only at surface aspects of what seemed to be some kind of bedrock problem, and it was the bedrock problem that had to be identified so that it could be attacked in a concerted, unified, and innovative way . . . the bedrock problem, in a word was "poverty." Words and concepts determine programs; once a target was reduced to a single word, the timing became right for a unified program.[2]

But even political consensus that poverty is a problem does not necessarily mean that everyone defines poverty in the same fashion.

POVERTY AS DEPRIVATION

Poverty can be defined as *deprivation*—insufficiency in food, housing, clothing, medical care, and other items required to maintain a decent standard of living. This definition assumes that there is a standard of living below which individuals and families can be considered "deprived." This standard is admittedly arbitrary; no one knows for certain what level of material well-being is necessary to avoid deprivation.

Each year the U.S. Social Security Administration (SSA) estimates the cash income required for individuals and families to satisfy minimum food, housing, clothing, and medical-care needs. These figures are known as the *poverty index* and are sometimes called the poverty line, poverty level, or poverty threshold. The index was first used in 1964. Each year the SSA updates the poverty index according to the Consumer Price Index. Some revisions have been made in calculating the index. Sex of the head of the household is no longer considered, and distinctions between farm and nonfarm families are no longer made. The poverty index is a crude measure of poverty. It is calculated by making an estimate of the costs of food for a household (determined according to the Thrifty Food Plan of the U.S. Department of Agriculture) and multiplying this figure by three, since it is assumed that one-third of an average household budget is or should be spent on food. In 1985 the guideline for determining whether a family of four was in poverty was $10,650—up from poverty levels of $8,414 in 1980, $3,968 in 1970, and $2,973 in 1959 (see table 3-1). The poverty index is an *absolute* measure of poverty because it provides one figure for the number of poor in the country, and individuals and families fall either above or below the poverty line. According to this definition, there were approximately thirty-four million poor people in the United States in 1984. This is a poverty rate of 14 percent of the population.

Even if we were to agree that poverty should be defined as deprivation, there would still be many problems in establishing an official poverty line based on money income as described above. First of all, the Social Security Administration's definition of poverty includes only cash income and excludes free medical care, food stamps, free school lunches, and public housing. If these benefits were "costed out" (calculated as cash income), there would be *fewer* poor people in America than shown in official statistics. It is also thought that many persons (poor and nonpoor) report their incomes at lower figures than they really are. Taking this into account might further reduce the number of persons counted as poor.[3]

There are other problems in this definition of poverty. It does not take into account regional differences in the cost of living, climate, or styles of living. (It is unlikely that a family of four can live on $10,650 in New York City, even if it is possible to do so in Hattiesburg, Mississippi.) It does not account for family assets. (An older family that has paid off its mortgage does not usually devote as much to housing as a family that rents.) It does not recognize differences in the status of families—for example, whether family members are students or retirees. Some of these people may not consider themselves "poor," although they are counted as poor in official government statistics. This definition does not recognize the special needs of families that may have incomes above the poverty line but have special problems or hardships that drain away income—chronic illnesses,

TABLE 3-1 Poverty Levels Based on Money Income and Size of Family

FAMILY	INCOME IN DOLLARS			
SIZE	*1970*	*1975*	*1980*	*1985*
1 Person	1,954	2,724	4,190	5,250
2 Persons	2,525	3,506	5,363	7,050
3 Persons	3,099	4,293	6,565	8,850
4 Persons	3,968	5,500	8,414	10,650
5 Persons	4,680	6,499	9,966	12,450
6 Persons	5,260	7,316	11,269	14,250
7 Persons	6,468	9,022	13,955	16,050

Sources: Figures for 1970–80 from the *Statistical Abstract of the United States, 1984,* p. 447, and poverty guidelines for 1985 from the *Federal Register, 50,* no. 46, Friday, March 8, 1985, p. 9518.

large debts, alcohol- or drug-abuse problems, and others. Finally, the estimate that one-third of family income is spent on food is probably outdated. Today, one-fourth of the family budget is generally spent on food. If the family food budget were multiplied by four, this would yield a higher poverty level.[4]

Despite these problems, some official definition of poverty is needed to administer government programs. As one observer commented:

> Although the existing poverty lines are arbitrary both for statistical purposes and for operational purposes, some arbitrary lines are needed, and these serve well simply because they already exist as a convention. To reopen an argument as to whether they are "correct" seems a fruitless exercise.[5]

As often happens, administrative efficiency rather than the needs of the poor turns out to be the underlying basis for an important policy decision—in this case, defining poverty.

IN-KIND BENEFITS: HOW MUCH ARE THEY WORTH?

There has been a great deal of concern that in order to measure poverty accurately, in-kind benefits must be considered. Although the Social Security Administration is responsible for determining the poverty index and setting income guidelines for determining who qualifies for government welfare programs, it is the Bureau of the Census which estimates the portion of the population that lived in poverty each year. In 1980 the bureau began conducting research to determine the value of noncash benefits.[6] This is not an easy task because there is disagreement about the best way to determine the value of in-kind benefits.

Currently, three different approaches are being considered. One is the *market-value* approach. Using this approach, the value of welfare benefits is based on what it would cost a private consumer to purchase the good or service. In some cases, this is a very easy approach to use. For example, calculating the value of food stamps is easy because the face value of the coupons used to purchase food items is equal to the amount it would cost any shopper to purchase the same item. Calculating the value of other benefits such as public housing is not as easy because there are no surveys which equate the value of comparable public and private housing.

A second method is the *recipient* approach. This is the cash value that recipients place on the in-kind benefits they receive. This approach is difficult to use because individual preferences vary. What is very valuable to one person is not necessarily as valuable to another. The market value of welfare benefits is considered to be higher than the recipient value, because it is believed that recipients would prefer cash to in-kind benefits. For example, it is estimated that recipients would trade $1,500 worth of food stamps for $1,440 in cash.

The *poverty budget share* is the third approach. It is based on the minimum amount of money a family or individual needs to meet basic living requirements or the amount that would be spent by near-poor persons who are not receiving welfare benefits.

The three approaches can produce rather different estimates of the cash value of in-kind benefits. In 1984 the lowest estimate of in-kind benefits (including food, housing, and medical) per poor family came from the recipient-value method—a total of $1,843. The poverty-budget-share approach produced a similar figure—$1,988. A different result was obtained using the market-value approach—$3,637. That approach reduced official poverty figures for families by 4 percent while the other methods reduced poverty figures by about 2 percent. Owing to the difficulties in making estimates of the value of in-kind benefits and the lack of agreement among experts about the best method to use, the government is not yet including them in official estimates of poverty.

WHO ARE THE POOR?

Poverty occurs in many kinds of families and many environmental settings. However, the incidence of poverty varies among groups in America (see table 3-2).

More whites are poor than blacks. Of the thirty-four million poor people in the nation, by government definition, about twenty-three million are white and nine million are black. However, the likelihood that blacks will experience poverty is nearly three times greater than it is for whites: *The poverty rate for the nation's black population is 34 percent compared to 12 percent for the white population.* In other words, whites outnumber blacks among the poor, but a much larger percentage of the nation's black population is poor. (This is because the total black population in the nation is only about 26 million or 12 percent of the total 227 million people.) Five million poor Hispanics reside in the United States. The poverty rate for Hispanics is 28 percent.

The real source of poverty today is families headed by women. The poverty rate for families headed by couples is 7 percent, and the poverty rate for families headed by males is 13 percent, but poverty in female-headed households is 35 percent. *For families headed by white women, the rate is 27 percent; for families headed by black and Hispanic women, the rates are 52 and 53 percent respectively.*[7] Needless to say, it is sad to know that many children live in poverty. There are approximately 14 million poor children in America, or about 20 percent of the total population under age eighteen.[8] For black children, the situation is especially bad; nearly half of all black children live in poverty.

There is some better news in the official poverty figures: poverty rates for the elderly are lower than ever before. Poverty among the elderly has been reduced from 25 percent in 1970 to 12 percent today. This is two percentage points below the national average for all Americans.

Poverty occurs not only in large central cities but in rural America as well. About 20 percent of the residents of urban cities are poor, and about 18 percent of rural residents are poor. There is some poverty in the na-

TABLE 3-2 Who Are the Poor?
(population by categories, with income below poverty level)

CHARACTERISTIC	NUMBER (THOUSANDS)	POVERTY RATE
All persons	33,700	14.4
White	22,955	11.5
Black	9,490	33.8
Spanish origin[a]	4,806	28.4
Under 15 years	11,455	22.2
15 to 24 years	6,581	17.0
25 to 44 years	7,938	11.0
45 to 54 years	2,100	9.4
55 to 59 years	1,131	9.9
60 to 64 years	1,167	10.9
65 years and over	3,330	12.4
Northeast	6,531	13.2
Midwest	8,303	14.1
South	12,792	16.2
West	6,074	13.1
All families	7,277	11.6
Married-couple families	3,488	6.9
Male householder, no wife present	292	13.1
Female householder, no husband present	3,498	34.5
All unrelated individuals	6,609	21.8
Male	2,575	18.7
Female	4,035	24.4

[a]Persons of Spanish origin may be of any race.

Source: Bureau of the Census, *Money Income and Poverty Status of Families and Persons in the United States: 1984,* Current Population Reports, series P-60, no. 149, August 1985, p. 3.

tion's suburbs, but proportionately this figure is lower—10 percent. Suburban areas experience less poverty because the poor are unlikely to find low-income housing there!

How persistent is poverty? There are very few families who live all their lives in poverty. Researchers at the Survey Research Center, University of Michigan, tracked five thousand American families for over ten years and found that only *3 percent* were persistently poor—that is, they were poor throughout this entire period. This is a much smaller figure than the percent reported as poor at any one time. This means that people slip into and out of the poverty category over time. People can lose their jobs, retire, divorce or separate, or become ill. Then later they may find new jobs, remarry, or get well, thus changing their financial condition.

Has the percentage of poor in this country changed? Franklin D. Roosevelt said in this second inaugural address in 1937, "I see one-third of a nation ill-housed, ill-clad, ill-nourished." He was probably underesti-

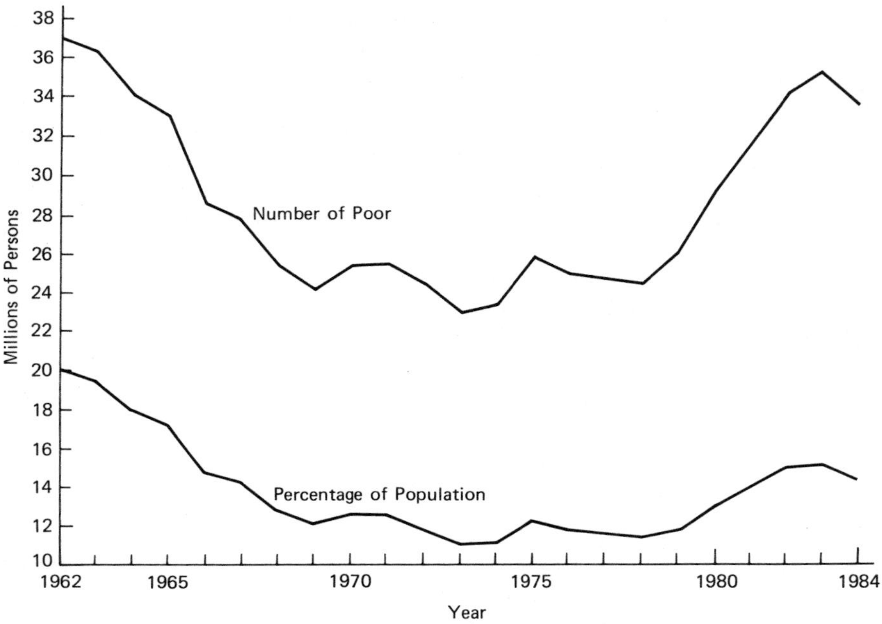

FIGURE 3-1 Poverty in the United States 1962–84

mating poverty; economic historians think that over 50 percent of the nation would have been classified as poor during the Great Depression. Since that time, the American political and economic system has succeeded in reducing the proportion of poor.

Figure 3-1 allows us to observe changes in the numbers and percentages of the poor since 1962. All of these figures account for the effects of inflation, so there is no question that poverty (as defined in official government statistics) declined considerably during the 1960s and reached lows of 11 to 12 percent during the 1970s. However, poverty increased in the early 1980s, rising to 15.3 percent by 1983, but dropped to 14.4 percent in 1984. A sluggish economy that resulted in increased unemployment along with some cuts in government social welfare programs explain much of the increase. The Reagan administration hailed the decrease in poverty as evidence that its economic policies do work, but others point to the fact that poverty remains higher than when the president took office.

POVERTY AS INEQUALITY

Poverty can also be defined as *inequality in the distribution of income*. This definition is not tied to any *absolute* level of deprivation. Instead, it focuses on *relative deprivation*—some people perceive that they have less income or material possessions than most Americans, and they believe they are entitled to more. Even with a fairly substantial income, one may feel a sense of "relative deprivation" in a very affluent society where commercial advertising portrays the "average American" as having a high level of consumption and material well-being.

Today the poor in America are wealthy by the standards that have prevailed over most of history and that still prevail in many areas of the world. Nonetheless, millions of American families are considered poor, by themselves and by others, because they have less income than most Americans. These people *feel* deprived—they perceive the gap between themselves and the average American family to be wide, and they do not accept the gap as legitimate. Eliminating poverty when it is defined as relative deprivation really means achieving greater *equality* of income and material possessions.

> By the standards that have prevailed over most of history, and still prevail over large areas of the world, there are very few poor in the United States today. Nevertheless there are millions of American families who, both in their own eyes and in those of others, are poor. As our nation prospers, our judgment as to what constitutes poverty will inevitably change. When we talk about poverty in America, we are talking about families and individuals who have much less income than most of us. When we talk about reducing or eliminating poverty, we are really talking about changing the distribution of income.[9]

How can we measure poverty as inequality? Economists frequently measure the distribution of total personal income across various classes of families. Since relative deprivation is a psychological as well as a social and economic concept, these classes or groups are difficult to establish, but a common method is to divide all American families into five groups—from the lowest one-fifth in personal income to the highest one-fifth. Table 3-3 shows the percentage of total personal income received by each of these groups since 1936. If perfect income equality existed, then each fifth of American families would receive 20 percent of all family personal income, and it would not even be possible to rank fifths from highest to lowest. But clearly, personal income in America is distributed unequally.

TABLE 3-3 The Distribution of Income in America (percent distribution of family personal income, by quintiles, and top 5 percent of consumer units, selected years)

QUINTILES	1936	1941	1950	1960	1970	1980	1983
Lowest	4.1%	4.1%	4.5%	4.8%	5.4%	5.2%	4.7%
Second	9.2	9.5	12.0	12.2	12.2	11.6	11.1
Third	14.1	15.3	17.4	17.8	17.6	17.5	17.1
Fourth	20.9	22.3	23.4	24.0	23.9	24.1	24.4
Highest	51.7	48.8	42.7	41.2	40.9	41.5	42.7
Total	100.0	100.0	100.0	100.0	100.0	100.0	100.0
Top 5 percent	26.5	24.0	17.3	15.9	15.6	15.6	15.8

Source: Bureau of the Census, *Statistical Abstract of the United States, 1980,* p. 454, and *1985,* p. 448.

The poorest one-fifth of American families receive only about 5 percent of all family personal income. This figure has remained relatively stable over the past fifty years. So even though poverty as defined by the government as a minimum subsistence level declined for many years, poverty defined as the proportion of total personal income received by the bottom one-fifth of the population has remained constant. Several definitions of poverty give us different perspectives on the success of the American political and economic system in dealing with poverty.

The wealthy, defined in table 3-3 as the highest one-fifth of Americans in personal income, received almost 49 percent of all family personal income in 1941; by 1983 this percentage had declined to 43. This group lost the most income in relation to other income groups, while the middle classes improved their relative income position. Another measure of the relative decline in the position of the wealthy was the decline in the percentage of income received by the top 5 percent in America. The top 5 percent received 24 percent of all family income in 1941 but less than 16 percent in 1983.

Not everyone in the lowest one-fifth suffers deprivation. Although the proportion of total personal income this group receives appears small (4.7 percent), some of the hardships of this lowest fifth are reduced by in-kind benefits (food stamps, public housing, Medicare and Medicaid, school lunches, and similar programs) which are not counted as income. Indeed, one economist estimates that if in-kind benefits were counted, the "adjusted income distribution" of the lowest fifth would be raised to 12 percent.[10]

WHY ARE THE POOR POOR?

Poverty is explained in many ways. We suspect that illness, old age, disability, lack of job skills, family instability, discrimination, unemployment, and general economic recessions all contribute to poverty. But how do these problems interact to create poverty?

Perhaps the most popular explanation among economists is the *human capital theory*. This theory explains income variations in a free market economy as a result of differences in productivity. The poor are poor because their economic productivity is low. They do not have the human capital—knowledge, skills, training, education—to sell to employers in a free market. As partial evidence for this theory, we can observe that poverty among families headed by a person with less than an eighth-grade education is 28 percent, while poverty among families headed by a person who completed high school is 10 percent.[11]

Economists recognize that poverty may also result from inadequate demand, either in the economy as a whole or in a particular segment of the economy. A serious recession and widespread unemployment raise the proportion of the population living below the poverty line. Full employment and a healthy economy do not directly reduce poverty among persons who have no marketable skills but nonetheless improve opportunities for marginal workers. Moreover, poverty can result from inadequate demand in a particular sector of the economy or in a particular region of the nation. For example, industrialization and technological development appear to have bypassed large segments of the Appalachian area. The closing of steel mills or auto plants in large eastern and midwestern cities can also force marginal workers into poverty.

Absence from the labor force is the largest single source of poverty. Over two-thirds of the poor are aged persons, children, or disabled people, who cannot reasonably be expected to find employment. No improvement in the federal economy is likely to affect these people directly. They are outside the labor market and are largely the responsibility of government rather than of the private economy.

Finally, we must consider poverty that is the direct effect of discrimination against blacks, other minorities, and women. It is true that *some* of the differences in black and white incomes are a product of educational differences between blacks and whites. However, *even if we control for education,* we can see that blacks with the same educational levels as whites earn less. As shown in table 3-4, white family income is substantially higher than black family income at every educational level. Blacks must finish high school to earn as much as whites with only an eighth-grade education. White families also earn more than Hispanic families at every educational level, although the income differences are not as large as those between whites and blacks.

If the human-capital theory operated freely—without interference in the form of discrimination—then we would expect very little difference between blacks and whites at the same educational levels. But, unfortunately, this is not the case.

When in 1776 Thomas Jefferson wrote on behalf of the Second Continental Congress that "all men are created equal . . . " he was expressing

TABLE 3-4 Black and White Family Income by Educational Level (1982)

	WHITE	BLACK	HISPANIC
Education			
Elementary School:			
Less than 8 years	12,708	9,796	11,479
8 years	15,783	11,390	15,014
High School:			
1–3 years	18,779	11,358	14,113
4 years	24,617	16,425	20,358
College:			
1–3 years	28,330	18,705	24,039
4 years	38,960	30,421	34,193

Source: Bureau of the Census, *Statistical Abstract of the United States, 1985,* p. 447.

the widespread dislike for hereditary aristocracy—lords and ladies, dukes and duchesses, and queens and kings. The Founding Fathers wrote their belief in equality of law into the U.S. Constitution. But their concern was *equality of opportunity,* not *absolute equality.* Indeed, the Founding Fathers referred to efforts to equalize income as "leveling," and they were strongly opposed to this notion. Jefferson wrote:

> To take from one, because it is thought his own industry and that of his fathers has acquired too much, in order to spare to others, who, or whose fathers have not, exercised equal industry and skill, is to violate arbitrarily the first principle of association, the guarantee to everyone the free exercise of his industry and the fruits acquired by it.[12]

Equality of opportunity requires that artificial obstacles to upward mobility be removed. Distinctions based on race, sex, ethnicity, birth, and religion have no place in a free society. But this is not to say that all persons' incomes should be equalized. Andrew Jackson, one of the nation's first democrats explained:

> Distinctions in every society will always exist under every just government. Equality of talents, education or wealth cannot be produced by human institutions. In the full enjoyment of the gifts of heaven and the fruits of superior industry, economy, and virtue, every man is entitled to protection by law; but when the laws undertake to add to these national distinctions, to grant titles, gratuities, and exclusive privileges, to make the rich richer . . . then the humble members of society have a right to complain of the injustice of their government.[13]

How much equality can we afford? Utopian socialists have argued for a rule of distribution: "From each according to his ability, to each according to his needs." In other words, everyone produces whatever he or she can, and wealth and income are distributed according to the needs of the people. There is no monetary reward for hard work, or skills and talent, or education and training. Since everyone's needs are roughly the same, everyone will receive roughly the same income. Collective ownership replaces private property. If such a Utopian society ever existed, then near-perfect income equality would be achieved, with each fifth of the population receiving roughly 20 percent of the income.

But all societies—capitalist and socialist, democratic and authoritarian, traditional and modern—distribute wealth unequally. It is not likely that income differences will ever disappear. Societies reward hard work, skill, talent, education, training, risk taking, and ingenuity. Distributing income equally throughout society threatens the work ethic. The real question we must confront is *how much* inequality is necessary and desirable for a society. We may or may not believe that the current distribution of income (as shown in table 3-3) is fair.

If the problem of poverty is defined as *inequality,* then it is not really capable of solution. Regardless of how well off the poor may be in absolute standards of living, there will always be a lowest one-fifth of the population receiving something less than 20 percent of all income. We might reduce income inequalities, but *some* differences will remain, and even these differences might be posed as a "problem."

POVERTY AS CULTURE

Some argue that poverty is a "way of life" passed on from generation to generation in a self-perpetuating cycle. This *culture of poverty* involves not just a low income but also attitudes of indifference, alienation, and apathy, along with lack of incentives and of self-respect. These attitudes make it difficult for the poor to utilize the opportunities for upward mobility that may be available to them. Increasing the income of the poor may not affect joblessness, lack of incentives, lack of educational opportunities, unstable family life, or the high incidence of crime, delinquency, and other social problems among the poor.

There are sharp differences between scholars and policy makers over the existence of a culture of poverty. The argument resembles the classic exchange between F. Scott Fitzgerald and Ernest Hemingway. When Fitzgerald observed, "The rich are different from you and me," Hemingway retorted, "Yes, they have more money." Observers who believe that they see a distinctive culture among the poor may say, "The poor are different from you and me." But opponents of the culture-of-poverty notion may reply, "Yes, they have less money." But are the poor undereducated, unskilled, poorly motivated, and "delinquent" because they are poor? Or are they poor because they are undereducated, unskilled, poorly motivated, and "delinquent"? The distinction is a serious one because it has important policy implications.

One especially controversial view of the culture of poverty is set forth by Harvard Professor Edward C. Banfield, who contends that poverty is really a product of "present-orientedness."[14] According to Banfield, individuals caught up in the culture of poverty are unable to plan for the future, to sacrifice immediate gratifications in favor of future ones, or to exercise the discipline that is required to get ahead. Banfield admits that some people experience poverty because of involuntary unemployment, prolonged illness, death of the breadwinner, or some other misfortune. But even with severe misfortune, he claims, this kind of poverty is not squalid, degrading, or self-perpetuating; it ends once the external cause of it no longer exists. According to Banfield, other people will be poor no matter what their "external" circumstances are. They live in a culture of poverty that continues for generations because they are psychologically unable to provide for the future. Improvements in their circumstances may affect their poverty only superficially. Even increased income is unlikely to change their way of life, for the additional money will be spent quickly on nonessential or frivolous items.

ILLUSTRATION: ESCAPING POVERTY—HOW ONE MAN DID IT

What is it like to live in poverty and then climb the ladder to success? What qualities are needed, what breaks along the way?

George E. Evans, a 36-year-old lawyer, has made such a journey. One of eight children raised by a widow in a public-housing project, he tells what it took to build a new life away from the old neighborhood.

Wilmington, Del. My mother only had an eighth-grade education and was working as a domestic when she died at age 59, but she was a motivator who believed the system could work, even for blacks, if you prepared yourself. "Play by the rules," she would say.

It was sound advice, though I had my doubts at times in the '60s when I was going through high school and college. We had no real role models for professional life. In grade school no one spoke about college. A classmate, when asked what she wanted to be when she grew up, said "a maid."

The most I hoped for then was to be an electrician, but I discovered in high school that unions offered few openings to blacks. So I dared to dream about college. My mother supported me, but she was realistic: "Where will the money come from?"

Money was always a problem in our house. We didn't live in misery, but there were some bad days, especially during my early childhood when we were on public assistance.

Toward the end of the month, money would run out. In winter, that might mean that my mother couldn't afford to buy the 5-pound bags of coal for the furnace of our row house. Then, we'd have to get our heat from the oven of the gas stove. I can remember an instance when three of us youngsters shared a single potato.

My mother wasn't to blame for this. She was a chin-up person, and we somehow understood that she was doing all she could. There was no shame to being poor because everyone we knew was in the same situation.

We always managed to have a good Christmas. An aunt in Philadelphia would send clothes, and I remember how good the fruit tasted from a food basket someone gave us one year.

Toys were often things we made ourselves, and we would spend hours playing in the woods near the project or at a nearby dump. That could be dangerous. One boy was murdered by a hobo in the woods.

Though I had my friends, maybe one reason I got out of the project was that I was always pretty much of a loner. By not getting caught up in a group or a gang, I had the time to think for myself and set goals. As for the "in crowd," few of them ever went to college. Some ended up hustling—or met an early death.

I got through college and law school by seeking loans, grants and scholarships. It was a better time for that because the civil-rights drive had pressured schools to open up more opportunities for blacks.

But I also worked—continuously—at many jobs. I started my freshman year at Delaware State working at the Chrysler plant in Newark, Del. When my shift was over at midnight or later, I'd drive—half asleep—to Dover for early-morning classes.

GRUELING DAYS

You could say I got through college partly on the shoulders of the auto industry. One summer, I worked at both a GM and a Chrysler plant—18 hours a day. When I awoke, my arms would automatically move to place a part on a car.

I had plenty of encouragement along the way. Besides my mother, there was a Delaware State professor, who happened to be white. He convinced me that a law career was possible and assisted me in applying to Rutgers University Law School.

After the King assassination in the spring of 1968, I thought about striking back by destroying property. I had done my share of protesting during college. But a chemist I worked with that summer at Du Pont cooled me down and introduced me to a company lawyer who reinforced my interest in law. I came to believe that law was the best way to change things I didn't like about society.

A DIFFERENT CLASS

Law school was harder than I ever thought, and the people I met there were different from those I grew up with. There were kids who had spent summers in Europe or hitchhiking around the country on a lark. I was a practicing lawyer before I even took my first plane trip.

But I survived. In 1973, another lawyer and I became the first blacks to be admitted to the Delaware bar since 1959. I started my law firm in 1981—one of only a half-dozen black attorneys in the entire state with their own practice.

Now, I have more than I ever dreamed of. I earn a very comfortable living, own a nine-room house in a nice neighborhood and three cars. My twin boys have a life that is Disneyland compared with my childhood. I force myself to say "No" at times so they can appreciate things.

Yet I still feel at home visiting the old neighborhood. I serve on the school board there, have represented the poor and hired them to work in my law office. One client charged with burglary lived in my old house.

Things have changed in the project, though. I see far more drugs, crime and vandalism—and less respect for adults and teachers. People watch their neighbors' habits and steal from them in broad daylight.

Poor kids now have a tougher time than I did. Those well-paying auto jobs are gone, and many youngsters won't work in fast-food places, though I don't know why. The money would give them some independence.

When I go to schools for talks on careers, I focus on turning students from the fast-money hustlers. I tell the kids those types are here today, gone tomorrow, but that those in legitimate professions have staying power. It's not always an easy selling job.

Source: *U.S. News & World Report*, March 26, 1984, p. 58. Copyright, 1984, *U.S. News & World Report*.

Opponents of the culture of poverty idea argue that this notion diverts attention from the conditions of poverty that *foster* family instability, present-orientedness, and other ways of life of the poor. The question is really whether the conditions of poverty create a culture of poverty or vice versa. Reformers are likely to focus on the conditions of poverty as the fundamental cause of the social pathologies that afflict the poor. They note that the idea of a culture of poverty can be applied only to groups who have lived in poverty for several generations. It is not relevant to those who have become poor during their lifetimes because of sickness, accident, or old age. The cultural explanation basically involves parental transmission of values and beliefs, which in turn determines behavior of future generations. In contrast, the situational explanation of poverty shows how social conditions and differences in financial resources operate directly to determine behavior. In this view, the conditions of poverty can be seen as affecting behavior not only directly but also indirectly through their impact upon succeeding generations. Perhaps the greatest danger in the idea of a culture of poverty is that poverty in this light can be seen as an unbreakable, puncture-proof cycle. This outlook may lead to a relaxation of efforts to ameliorate the conditions of poverty. In other words, a culture of poverty may become an excuse for inaction.

If one assumes that the poor are no different from other Americans, then one is led toward policies that emphasize opportunity for individuals as well as changes in their environment. If the poor are like other Americans, it is necessary only to provide them with the ordinary means to achieve—for example, job-training programs, good schools, and counseling to make them aware of opportunities that are available to them. The intervention that is required to change their lives, therefore, is one of supplying a means to achieve a level of income that most Americans enjoy.

On the other hand, if one believes in the notion of a culture of poverty, it is necessary to devise a strategy to interrupt the transmission of lower-class cultural values from generation to generation. The strategy must try to prevent the socialization of young children into an environment of family instability, lack of motivation, crime and delinquency, and so forth. One rather drastic means to accomplish this would be simply to remove the children from lower-class homes at a very early age and to raise them in a controlled environment that transmits the values of the conventional culture rather than of the culture of poverty. Such a solution is not realistic. More acceptable solutions use special day-care centers and preschool programs to remedy cultural deprivation and disadvantage. Theoretically, these programs would bring about change in young children through "cultural enrichment."

The culture of poverty idea leads to another policy implication. If one believes that such a culture exists, then one must also conclude that little can be done to help people escape from poverty until there has been sufficient change in their life condition to permit them to take advantage of opportunity programs. According to this line of reasoning, one cannot change people without changing their environment; the poor cannot advance through schooling or job training or programs to develop better attitudes while they are still poor. The emphasis on "self-help"—education, information, job training, participation—is incomplete and misleading unless it is accompanied by a program aimed at directly altering the conditions of poverty. Hence, it is argued that a *guaranteed minimum income* is required to bring the poor up to a level where they will be able to take advantage of educational and training information, along with other opportunity programs.

POVERTY AS EXPLOITATION

Both Marxist and non-Marxist writers have defined poverty as a form of *exploitation by the ruling class*. Sociologist Herbert Gans contends that poverty serves many functions for the middle and upper classes in America.[15] Specifically, Gans lists thirteen reasons why a poverty class is maintained in the nation:

1. The poor are available to do society's "dirty work" such as "physically dirty or dangerous, temporary, dead-end and underpaid, undignified, and menial jobs"—the jobs that others will not do.
2. The poor perform work that helps those who are financially better off. For example, they do domestic work that allows others to pursue more rewarding activities.
3. Poverty creates jobs in a number of fields such as welfare and law enforcement.
4. The poor buy old, used, and defective merchandise that others do not want.
5. The poor are often punished and accused of wrong-doing as a means of upholding societal norms. For example, the poor are called lazy because society values hard-working, industrious people.
6. The poor allow the rest of society to live vicariously in a world of uninhibited sexual, drug-taking, and alcoholic behavior, because society believes that this is how poor people live.
7. The poor provide a source of cultural works such as art, literature, and music that the affluent would not otherwise have.
8. Poverty allows those in the middle and upper classes to maintain their higher status in society.
9. The poor allow others to improve their position in society by providing a market for legal (and illegal) business activities in the slums.
10. The poor provide a source of activities for the affluent who pursue charitable causes on behalf of the poor.
11. The poor bear the burden of societal growth as they did when their homes were destroyed in the name of urban renewal.
12. The poor serve political functions. For example, the poor are identified with the Democratic Party, which can count on their votes regardless of whether or not Democratic legislators are responsive to the needs of the poor.
13. Since the poor are considered lazy and unwilling to work, they are the target of social criticisms which shift criticism for maintaining poverty away from the more affluent.

Gans's implication is that poverty is maintained by ruling classes in order to make their own lives more pleasant. Poverty does not have to exist; it could be eliminated with the cooperation of the middle and upper classes. But it is unlikely that these classes will ever give up anything they believe they have earned through their own hard work, useful skills, or business enterprise. Many Americans believe that they are immune from financial disaster and poverty.

THE INVISIBLE POOR

In an influential book of the 1960s, *The Other America,* Michael Harrington argued that most Americans were blind to the poverty of many millions of poor people.[16] Harrington spoke of two nations within America. One is the nation of comfortable and affluent Americans. The other is a nation of the poor—those forced to suffer deprivation and humiliation because they are without access to adequate education, housing, employment, and health care. Most Americans are blind to poverty because the poor are invisible—invisible because they do not live or socialize or receive their education with the more affluent. Rural poverty is masked by a beautiful American countryside. Mass production of decent clothing also hides poverty. A poor person may be relatively well dressed but unable to afford decent housing or health care. The elderly poor are invisible because they do not venture far from home owing to poor health, fear, and lack of somewhere to go. And finally, the poor are invisible because they have no political power; in fact, they are often the victims of political action.

Other authors have also written about the class-based nature of poverty. Influenced by the works of Harrington, two of these authors have called our society the "upside-down welfare state" because "the welfare state is a complicated system in which those who need help the most get the least, and those who need it least get the most."[17] They say that all Americans, rich or poor, benefit from government welfare programs. The poor receive government assistance through the Aid to Families with Dependent Children, Food Stamp, and Medicaid programs. The middle class receives government assistance in the form of home mortgage loans and educational grants. The rich receive government assistance in the form of income tax deductions, government contracts, and subsidies to business and industry. The difference is that government assistance to the poor is called "welfare," while government assistance to the rich is called "good business." In the final analysis, the poor receive only a pittance of all government assistance. Much government assistance goes to the middle and upper classes.

Social scientists Frances Fox Piven and Richard A. Cloward have also commented on the economic, political, and social utility that the upper classes see in maintaining poverty. In 1971 they published *Regulating the Poor: The Functions of Public Welfare* and claimed that "the key to an understanding of relief-giving is in the functions it serves for the larger economic and political order, for relief is a secondary and supportive institution."[18] Piven and Cloward argued, especially with regard to Aid to Families with Dependent Children, that welfare had been used as a device to control the poor in order to maintain social stability. Welfare programs were expanded in times of political unrest as a means of appeasing the poor, and welfare rules and regulations were used as a means of "forcing" the poor into the labor market during times of political stability, especially when there was a need to increase the number of people in the work force. Piven and Cloward have updated their original ideas. They now believe that this cyclical pattern of contraction and expansion of welfare has been replaced by a more permanent set of welfare programs.[19] These programs are a threat to "corporate America" because they provide basic subsistence, which makes people less dependent for their survival on business and industry and fluctuations in the labor market. Piven and Cloward believe in the right to welfare. They are hopeful that Americans will resist the philosophies of Reaganomics and preserve the welfare programs, thus ending the cyclical pattern of providing welfare benefits.

If poverty is defined as the exploitation of the poor by a ruling class, then it might be suggested that only a restructuring of society to eliminate class differences would solve the problem of poverty. Marxists call for the revolutionary overthrow of capitalist society by workers and farmers and the emergence of a new "classless" society. Presumably, in such a society there would be no ruling class with an interest in exploiting the poor. Of course, in practice, Communist societies have produced one-party governments that dominate and exploit nearly the entire population.

Nonetheless, these perspectives on poverty in America help us to understand that there are indeed class differences in views on poverty. If the upper classes do not deliberately exploit the poor, they sometimes express very paternalistic attitudes toward the poor. By paternalistic we mean that the upper classes have little understanding of the lives of poor people, yet they believe they "know what's best" for the poor in social welfare policy. Moreover, the upper classes frequently engage in charitable activities and support liberal welfare programs to demonstrate their idealism and "do-goodism," whether the poor are actually helped or not.

DOES WELFARE CAUSE POVERTY?

The belief that welfare programs can actually increase the number of poor persons is certainly not new. Since Elizabethan times, welfare payments have been kept minimal to discourage potential recipients from choosing welfare over work. Although the Great Depression of the late 1920s and early 1930s made the country realize that poverty could befall almost anyone, many have clung to the idea that welfare should be made an unattractive alternative to earnings. A good deal of attention has been given to the idea that much of today's poverty is a direct result of the social policies and programs of the 1960s and 1970s. The argument is presented this way: from 1947 to 1965 the poverty rate was reduced by more than half without massive government social welfare intervention, but by the mid-1960s it was thought that the poverty that remained was due to lack of opportunities and bad luck.[20] The solution was government intervention to reduce poverty and create more opportunities for the disadvantaged. Welfare spending and the numbers of welfare programs increased, but the number of poor did not decrease. During the 1970s the poverty rate remained at around 12 percent.

The first book to receive widespread attention that claimed welfare was to blame was George Gilder's *Wealth and Poverty,* published in 1981. Gilder discusses what he calls "the devastating impact of the programs of liberalism on the poor."[21]

> What actually happened since 1964 was a vast expansion of the welfare rolls that halted in its tracks an ongoing improvement in the lives of the poor, particularly blacks, and left behind—and here I chose my words as carefully as I can—a wreckage of broken lives and families worse than the aftermath of slavery.[22]

Gilder uses many Horatio Alger-type success stories, and he points to examples of how poor Americans and immigrants to the United States were able to achieve prosperity through their hard work and the advantages that a capitalistic economic system affords to those who are willing to "sacrifice" to "succeed." Gilder also contends that the expansion of the welfare system has led to an erosion of the work ethic and self-reliance. The book contains strong sexual biases because it focuses on the importance on jobs for men over those for women. Gilder contends that as welfare benefits (AFDC, Food Stamps, Medicaid, public housing) increase, the value of a *man's* labor to this family decreases, especially if that man earns low wages at his job. The welfare system saps his dignity and makes him less necessary to his family. This in turn leads to family breakup and to further reliance on welfare. Gilder also criticizes antidiscrimination policies, which he says favor credentials over the drive to succeed.

In 1984 Charles Murray made much the same argument in his book *Losing Ground: American Social Policy, 1950–1980.*[23] Relying on a number of statistical presentations, Murray concludes that there are more poor following the social programs of the Great Society; the underclass has fallen further behind and social welfare policy is responsible. Murray compares three measures of poverty—"official poverty," "net poverty," and "latent poverty"—to make his point. Official poverty, as discussed earlier, is the amount of poverty measured by the U.S. government's poverty index. Net poverty is official poverty minus the value of in-kind benefits. Latent poverty is the number of people who would be poor if they did not receive social insurance and public assistance payments. Murray claims that in-kind benefits have reduced the official poverty figures—but not as much as they should considering the large amounts of money spent on in-kind programs like Food Stamps and Medicaid. Much worse is the fact that latent poverty is much higher than official poverty. In 1980 official poverty stood at 13 percent. Latent poverty increased after 1968, reaching 22 percent of the population by 1980. The war on poverty was supposed to make people economically self-sufficient and get them off welfare. The unfortunate situation is that these programs failed to reduce the need for welfare.

Those critical of Murray's work contend that the statistics and the analyses can be misleading; that poverty is a complex issue and many factors must be presented in any discussion of the rising numbers of poor people.[24] For example, bad economic times result in higher unemployment (the lesson of the Great Depression). Lack of jobs and not just the desire to be on the dole adds to the ranks of the poor. In hard times it is not surprising that the underclass who are in marginal jobs are likely to be unemployed and will require welfare assistance.

But Murray's view leads him to suggest a drastic alternative to the current welfare system. He advocates ending all existing federal welfare programs for working-age people (AFDC, Food Stamps, Medicaid, and so on) except for Unemployment Insurance and leaving the rest of welfare to private charities and state and local governments. While Galbraith and Harrington were the topics of discussion in the 1960s, the talk is now of Gilder and Murray.

SUMMARY

Defining *poverty* is a *political* activity rather than a *rational* exercise. We have discussed four approaches to defining poverty—as deprivation, as inequality, as culture, and as exploitation. Society cannot agree on one "best" approach for defining poverty, and it cannot agree on solutions for alleviating poverty.

If we use the official government poverty line as our arbitrary yardstick, there were about thirty-four million poor people in the United States in 1984, or about 14 percent of the population. However, if we count in-kind welfare benefits as well as cash benefits, the number of poor persons is lower. Since the 1940s poverty has declined dramatically. Poverty levels reached lows of 11 to 12 percent in the 1970s; however, poverty began to rise again in the early 1980s, reaching a high of about 15 percent. Poverty is most frequently found in black households and households headed by women. Children make up a large number of the poor.

Poverty has many causes. Some people are poor because they lack the resources and opportunities of the nonpoor, and some, such as the elderly, children, and the disabled, are not able to work. Discrimination is another source of poverty. Even with the same number of school years completed, blacks and some other minorities earn less than whites; women earn less than men. Equality of opportunity remains an obstacle to the elimination of poverty in the United States.

The way in which poverty is defined has important implications for strategies to alleviate the problem. Human-service professionals have a commitment to increasing opportunities for poor persons as a means of reducing poverty. These professionals strive to maximize human potential whenever possible and believe the disadvantaged will make use of opportunities to overcome poverty. They reject the idea that many of the poor do not want to work and that they use their resources foolishly.

Some writers view poverty as a form of exploitation by the ruling classes. The dominant classes in society maintain poverty in order to produce a source of cheap labor and to "use" the poor economically, socially, and politically. This definition of the problem magnifies class conflict and implies that only a radical restructuring of the social system can reduce poverty.

Recent books have blamed the worsened condition of the poor and minorities on the social welfare policies of the Great Society. These authors believe that welfare became a more attractive alternative than low-paying jobs and has destroyed the incentives to self-sufficiency.

NOTES

1. E. E. Schattschneider, *The Semi-Sovereign People* (New York: Holt, Rinehart & Winston, 1961), p. 68.
2. James L. Sundquist, *Politics and Policy* (Washington, D.C.: Brookings Institution, 1968), pp. 111–12.
3. Sheldon Danzinger and Robert Haveman, "The Reagan Budget: A Sharp Break with the Past," *Challenge* 24 (May–June 1981), pp. 5–13.
4. Sar A. Levitan, *Programs in Aid of the Poor,* 5th ed. (Baltimore: Johns Hopkins University Press, 1985), pp. 3–4.
5. Robert A. Levine, *The Poor Ye Need Not Have with You* (Cambridge, Mass.: MIT Press, 1970), p. 19.
6. This section is based on Bureau of the Census, *Estimates of Poverty Including the Value of Noncash Benefits: 1984),* technical paper 55, August 1985.
7. Robert Pear, "U.S. Poverty Rate Dropped to 14.4% in '84, Bureau Says," *New York Times,* August 28, 1985, p. 12.
8. "Suffer the Children," *Time,* June 17, 1985, p. 37; "Study Says 1 of 5 Children in Poverty," *Florida Times Union,* March 11, 1984.
9. Victor R. Fuchs, "Redefining Poverty and Redistributing Income," *Public Interest,* no. 8 (Summer 1967), p. 91.
10. Edgar K. Browning, "How Much More Equality Can We Afford?" *Public Interest,* no. 43 (Spring 1976), pp. 90–110.
11. Bureau of the Census, *Statistical Abstract of the United States, 1984* (Washington, 1983), p. 476.
12. Cited in Richard Hofstadter, *The American Political Tradition* (New York: Knopf, 1948), p. 42.
13. Ibid., p. 45.
14. Edward C. Banfield, *The Unheavenly City* (Boston: Little, Brown, 1968).
15. Herbert J. Gans, "The Uses of Poverty: The Poor Pay All," *Social Policy,* 2, no. 2 (July–August 1971), 20–24.
16. Michael Harrington, *The Other America: Poverty in the United States* (New York: Macmillian, 1962).
17. Thomas H. Walz and Gary Askerooth, *The Upside Down Welfare State* (Minneapolis: Elwood Printing, 1973), p. 5.
18. Frances Fox Piven and Richard A. Cloward, *Regulating the Poor: The Functions of Public Welfare* (New York: Random House, 1971).
19. Frances Fox Piven and Richard A. Cloward, *The New Class War* (New York: Pantheon Books, 1982).
20. See James Gwartney and Thomas S. McCaleb, "Have Antipoverty Programs Increased Poverty?" Tallahassee: Florida State University, 1986.
21. George Gilder, *Wealth and Poverty* (New York: Bantam Books, 1981), p. ix.
22. Ibid., p. 13.
23. Charles Murray, *Losing Ground: American Social Policy, 1950–1980* (New York: Basic Books, 1984).
24. Robert Kuttner, "Declaring War on the War on Poverty," *Washington Post,* November 25, 1984, pp. 4 & 11. Also see Daniel Patrick Moynihan, "Family and Nation," the Godkin Lectures, Harvard University, April 8–9, 1985.

chapter 4

Preventing poverty: the social insurance programs

PREVENTING POVERTY THROUGH COMPULSORY SAVINGS

Why not require people to insure themselves against poverty, in much the same fashion as people insure themselves against other tragedies, such as deaths, accidents, and fires? The preventive strategy uses the *social insurance* concept. This involves compelling individuals to purchase insurance against the possibility of their own indigency, which might result from forces over which they had no control—loss of job, death of the family breadwinner, or physical disability. Social insurance is based on the same principles as private insurance—the sharing of risks and the setting aside of money for a "rainy day." Workers and employers pay "premiums" (Social Security taxes), which are held in trust by the government under each worker's name (and Social Security number). When age, death, disability, or unemployment prevents workers from continuing on the job, they or their dependents are paid out of the accumulated trust fund. Social insurance appears to offer a simple, rational approach for dealing with the causes of poverty.

It is important to distinguish between *social insurance* programs and *public assistance* programs. If (1) the beneficiaries of a government program are required to make contributions to it before claiming any of its benefits (or if employers must pay into the program on behalf of their workers) and if (2) the benefits are paid out as legal entitlements regardless of the beneficiaries' personal wealth, *then* the program is said to be financed on the social insurance principle. On the other hand, if (1) the program is financed out of general tax revenues and if (2) the recipients are required to show that they are poor in order to claim benefits, *then* the program is said to be financed on the *public assistance* principle.

Over the years, social insurance programs have been more politically viable than public assistance programs. Perhaps, people believe that social insurance is merely enforced savings and that eventually they will get back their own money (although we shall see that this not entirely true). In other words, people feel entitled to Social Security because they have paid specific Social Security taxes. But the public assistance recipients have never specifically "paid into" a public assistance fund. Their assistance checks come out of general tax funds. Moreover, while the vast majority of Americans expect to live to see some Social Security benefits returned to them, they do not expect to become public assistance recipients. Conservatives can support social insurance as a form of thrift; liberals can support it because it tends to redistribute income from workers to the aged, the sick, the disabled, the unemployed, and dependent children.

Government old-age insurance, the first social insurance program, was introduced in Germany in 1889 by the conservative regime of Chancellor Otto von Bismarck. The idea spread quickly and most European nations had old-age insurance pension programs before the beginning of World War I in 1914. Private old-age pension plans were begun in the United States by many railroads, utilities, and large manufacturers at the beginning of the twentieth century. The U.S. government began its own Federal Employees Retirement program in 1920. By 1931 seventeen states had adopted some form of compulsory old-age insurance for all workers. During the Great Depression, a California physician, Francis E. Townsend, began a national crusade for old-age pensions to be paid by the government out of taxes on banks. The "Townsend movement" was perceived by government and business leaders as radical and unworkable, but the combination of economic depression and larger numbers of aged in the population helped to develop pressure for some type of old-age insurance. Finally, in the presidential election of 1932, Franklin D. Roosevelt advocated a government insurance plan to protect both the unemployed and the aged. This campaign promise and party platform plank actually became law—the Social Security Act of 1935.

THE SOCIAL SECURITY ACT OF 1935

Through the Social Security Act of 1935, the federal government undertook to establish the basic framework for social welfare policies at the federal, state, and local levels. As amended, this act now provides for (1) federal Old Age, Survivors, Disability, and Health Insurance (OASDHI), (2) unemployment-compensation programs in the states, (3) federal public assistance to the aged, blind, and disabled under the Supplemental Security Income (SSI) program, (4) public assistance to families with dependent children under the Aid to Families with Dependent Children (AFDC) program, (5) federal health insurance for the aged (Medicare), and (6) federal-state assistance for the poor in paying medical costs (Medicaid). In this chapter we will examine OASDHI and unemployment compensation in detail. In chapter 5 we will examine SSI; in chapter 6 we will discuss AFDC; and in chapter 10 we will examine Medicare and Medicaid.

The original Social Security program, as enacted in 1935, covered only retirement and survivor benefits for workers in about half of the labor force; many farm and domestic workers and self-employed persons were exempted, as were state and local government employees. This old-age insurance was financed by employer-employee contributions of 1 percent each on a wage base of $3,000, or a maximum contribution by workers of $30 per year. It paid for retirement benefits at age 65 at a rate of about $22 per month for a single worker, or $36 per month for a married couple. Benefits were paid as a matter of right, regardless of income, as long as a worker was retired. Thus, retired workers were spared the humiliation often associated with public charity. Actually, no benefits were paid until 1940 in order to allow the trust fund to accumulate reserves. Economist Joseph A. Pechman writes of the original Social Security Act:

> The old age provisions in the Social Security Act were in part a first attempt to solve the long developing crisis of the aged and of economic security in general, in a reaction to the short-run crisis of the depression; and in part a compromise measure to blunt the political appeal of the enormously expensive and essentially unworkable Townsend Plan.[1]

One might attribute the Roosevelt administration's political success in gaining acceptance for the Social Security Act to several factors: (1) the decline of the extended family and the increasing inability of urban families to care for their aged members; (2) the economic insecurities generated by the Great Depression of the 1930s and the increasing fear of impoverishment even among the middle class; and (3) political movements on the left (the Townsend Plan, for example) and right which threatened the established order. One might add Roosevelt's skills as a national leader to these factors. Social Security was presented to the Congress as a *conservative* program which would eventually abolish the need for public assistance programs, in that individuals would be compelled to protect themselves against poverty.

The first major amendments to the original Social Security Act came in 1939 when Congress made survivors and dependents of insured workers eligible for benefits. In 1950 farmers and self-employed persons were added to the list of beneficiaries, bringing the total number of covered workers to over 90 percent of the work force. In 1956 disability insurance was approved for totally and permanently disabled workers. Later, workers were permitted to retire at age sixty-two rather than at sixty-five on the condition that they would accept 80 percent of the monthly benefit otherwise available at sixty-five. In 1965 prepaid medical insurance, Medicare, was added to the program. In 1977 an automatic cost-of-living index was added to Social Security benefit payments, and in 1981 some measures were taken to reduce program spending at President Reagan's request.

The minimum benefit of $122 per month was retained for current beneficiaries but was eliminated for new beneficiaries, and children ages eighteen to twenty-two of deceased, disabled and retired workers were no longer eligible for benefits.

OASDHI: THE NATION'S LARGEST SOCIAL PROGRAM

Today OASDHI is the nation's largest social program.[2] It covers approximately nine out of ten workers. Both employees and employers must pay equal amounts toward the employee's OASDHI insurance. Upon retirement, an insured worker is entitled to monthly benefit payments based upon age at retirement and the amount earned during working years. Average monthly payments, however, are modest—about $450 for each retired worker. In addition to retirement benefits, survivors' benefits are payable to the dependents of an insured worker. A lump-sum benefit is also payable upon the death of an insured worker. Disability benefits are payable to an insured worker with a total and permanent disability. And virtually *all* persons sixty-five years of age and over, whether or not they have ever paid into Social Security, are entitled to Medicare—hospital insurance which covers hospital and related services and voluntary supplemental medical insurance which covers a portion of physicians' services.

OASDHI is a completely federal program administered by the Social Security Administration in the Department of Health and Human Services. But it has an important indirect effect on federal, state, and local public assistance programs: By compelling people to insure themselves against the possibility of their own poverty, Social Security has reduced the welfare problems that governments might otherwise face.

The growth of OASDHI in numbers of recipients (beneficiaries), average monthly benefits, and as a percentage of the federal government's total budget is shown in table 4-1. Social Security taxes are the second largest source of income for the federal government; these tax revenues are exceeded only by the federal personal income tax. The Social Security

TABLE 4-1 Social Security Growth

	1940	1950	1960	1970	1975	1980	1984
Number of beneficiaries (in thousands)	222	3,477	14,845	25,312	31,598	35,900	36,300
Average monthly benefit for retired workers (in dollars)	23	44	74	100	183	360	450
Social insurance taxes as a percent of all federal revenue	—	—	15.9	22.5	29.0	32.0	29.0
Medicare expenditures (in millions of dollars)	0	0	0	6,800	11,181	31,376	57,540

tax is marked on the paycheck stubs of many workers with the abbreviation FICA, which stands for the Federal Insurance Contributions Act.

What began as a very modest "insurance premium"—a maximum annual tax contribution of $30—is now a major expense for both employers and employees. Currently, Social Security taxes are scheduled to grow to 15.3 percent combined contribution of employees and employers by 1990. The maximum annual employee contribution has grown from $30 to $3,000, a one-hundred-fold increase since the program was begun over fifty years ago (see table 4-2).

TABLE 4-2 Social Security Taxes

YEARS	TAX RATE	MAXIMUM WAGES TAXABLE	MAXIMUM ANNUAL TAX
1937–1949	1.00%	$ 3,000	$ 30
1950	1.50	3,000	45
1955	2.00	4,200	84
1960	3.00	4,800	144
1966	4.20	6,600	277
1969	4.80	7,800	374
1973	5.85	10,800	632
1978	6.06	17,700	1,071
1980	6.13	25,900	1,588
1981	6.65	29,700	1,957
1982	6.70	32,400	2,171
1984	7.00	37,800	2,646
1985	7.05	39,600	2,792
1986	7.15	42,000	3,003
1988	7.51	[a]	
1990	7.65		

[a]Maximum taxable wages are increased either by Congress or automatically in multiples of $300 if there is a cost-of-living increase in Social Security benefits.

THE BEST LAID PLANS: UNINTENDED CONSEQUENCES OF SOCIAL SECURITY

The original strategy of the Social Security Act of 1935 was to create a trust fund with a reserve that would be built from the insurance premiums (Social Security taxes) of working persons. This trust-fund reserve would earn interest, and both the interest and principal would be used in later years to pay benefits. Benefits for insured persons would be in proportion to their contributions. General tax revenues would not be used at all. The Social Security system was intended to resemble private, self-financing insurance. But it has not turned out that way at all.

By the early 1980s everyone knew that Social Security was in trouble. Rather than a reserve system, Social Security had become a "pay-as-we-go" program. Income from the program (about $200 billion per year) matched the outgo in Social Security benefits. The program was on the verge of bankruptcy. Today's generation of workers is paying for benefits of the last generation, and we can only hope that the next generation will be willing to make the same sacrifices. Over the years, political pressure to raise benefits while keeping taxes relatively low reduced the trust-fund reserve to a minor role in Social Security finance. Social Security taxes were lumped together with all other tax revenue in the federal government's budget. The insurance-fund idea had clearly been pushed aside in the first years of the program, when Roosevelt's planners quickly realized that building the reserve was taking money out of the depressed economy and slowing recovery. The plan to build a large self-financing reserve was soon abandoned in 1939 under political pressure to pump more money into the economy. Over the years, Congress has encountered pressure to increase benefit levels to retirees, even though these retirees never paid enough money into their accounts to actually justify higher benefits. In 1977 Congress voted to allow benefits to automatically increase with inflation (measured by rises in the official Consumer Price Index). This has been a very popular protection against inflation for older Americans, but Social Security ran into trouble. It could no longer cover these regular increases, especially in times of high inflation. Moreover, benefits under Social Security are no longer proportionate to contributions; benefits are figured more generously for those whose wages were low than for those whose wages were high. Today the only remaining aspects of an insurance program are that individuals must have paid into the system to receive benefits (although even this requirement has been dropped for Medicare), and beneficiaries are not required to prove that they are needy. Americans have come to view their Social Security benefits as a right.

To keep up with increased benefits, the Social Security tax has risen very dramatically in two ways: first, the tax rate assessed against both employer and employee has risen (see table 4-2); second, the wages subject to taxation have also risen. The Social Security tax is now the second largest source of federal revenue, and social insurance benefits are now the single largest expenditure of the federal government, even surpassing expenditures for national defense.

CAN THIS PROGRAM BE SAVED?: CRISIS INTERVENTION AND THE NATIONAL COMMISSION ON SOCIAL SECURITY REFORM

As the problems of Social Security intensified, it became clear that something would have to be done. A number of approaches to rescuing Social Security had been proposed. Some were proposed by Democrats and condemned by Republicans, and for other proposals it was just the other way around. Now partisan politics would have to be put aside in favor of solutions to the ailing retirement system. In 1981 President Reagan issued an executive order establishing the National Commission on Social Security Reform. The commission, also referred to as the Greenspan Commission after its chairperson, Republican economist Alan Greenspan, was comprised of fifteen individuals with backgrounds in business and industry, politics, labor organizations, and academia. Among the members were Senator Robert Dole (R-Kan.), Senator Claude Pepper (D-Fla.), Senator Daniel Patrick Moynihan (D-N.Y.), Martha E. Keys (former congresswomen from Kansas and former assistant secretary of Health and Human Services), Lane Kirkland (president of the AFL-CIO), and Robert Ball (former commissioner of Social Security and social insurance scholar).

Needless to say, there were many disagreements about the best way to tackle the problems of Social Security. Some wondered if there would be a compromise at all. Finally, the commission's report was issued with the joint support of President Reagan and Speaker of the House Thomas P. "Tip" O'Neill (D-Mass.). Numerous changes were then enacted by Congress. Among the most important were a delay of the popular cost-of-living adjustment (COLA) and a "stabilizer" that was placed on future COLAs. This stabilizer may reduce the increases that beneficiaries would have received in a given year under the old law. Today Social Security benefits are indexed according to the Consumer Price Index (CPI), but if Social Security trust funds fall below certain levels, future benefits will be indexed according to the CPI or the average increase in wages, whichever is lower.

Under former provisions, no Social Security benefits were counted as taxable income. Now, half of an individual's or couple's social security benefits are taxed if taxable income plus one half of Social Security benefits exceed $25,000 for single persons and $32,000 for couples. Young people can no longer look forward to retiring on their sixty-fifth birthdays. Higher retirement ages will be phased in beginning in the year 2003. (If you were born in 1938, you will be sixty-five in 2003). By 2027 the retirement age will reach sixty-seven for those planning to collect full benefits. (If you were born in 1960 you will be sixty-seven in 2027.) Beneficiaries will still be allowed to retire earlier, at age sixty-two, but the amount of benefits will fall from 80 percent to 70 percent of full retirement by 2027. The good news is that by 2008 those who choose to retire after age sixty-five will receive 5 percent more in benefits than they would today. Medicare benefits will still be available at age sixty-five. Other good news is that Social Security beneficiaries will be able to earn more and lose less. Today Social Security beneficiaries are able to earn about $7,000 from employment before they begin to lose Social Security benefits. Earnings over $7,000 are "taxed" at a rate of 50 percent. That is, beneficiaries lose $1 for every $2 they earn. This "tax" on benefits will be reduced to one-third, or $1 for every $3 earned. This new measure was designed to encourage older Americans to continue working. Since taxes are paid on their wages, more money is pumped back into the economy.

Beneficiaries who receive Social Security benefits as well as other government pensions (such as military retirement), but who paid into the Social Security system for only a short time may receive lower Social Security benefits under a new formula. This is called reducing "windfall" benefits.

The Social Security tax will rise once again. By 1990 it will reach 7.65 percent each for employers and employees. More workers are now included under the Social Security system. All new federal employees must participate as well as all members of Congress, the president and the vice president, federal judges, and all employees of nonprofit organizations, among others. Many of these persons were formerly included under separate systems. For example, federal employees were covered under a separate, more generous retirement system.

The commission made a few adjustments to eliminate sex discrimination in the program, but these changes did not address inequities which many of today's elderly women face. Some members of the commission wanted to do more to help women, but there was disagreement about whether the commission should tackle this problem; therefore, many issues related to women were not fully addressed. (See chapter 11 for a fuller discussion of sex inequalities under Social Security.)

Other changes suggested by the Social Security Commission and adopted by Congress included different accounting procedures to make the fund more efficient. Temporary interfund borrowing between the OASI, DI, and HI portions of the program was approved. Other changes are too numerous to mention, but reforms were intended to make the Social Security fund solvent without altering the basic structure of the program.[3] Predictions are that the system will be solvent for the next seventy-five years. As Wilbur Cohen, longtime champion of Social Security and former secretary of HEW under President Johnson, writes of the Social Security Commission:

> After more than a year of deliberation, this fifteen-member panel . . . came forward with the most unusual high-level policy agreement on controversial aspects in Social Security legislation since enactment of the original Social Security Act in 1935. . . . If the Commission's work represented a remarkable achievement in political statesmanship, so did the actions of the Congress in dealing with the legislative package. The bill moved through both houses of Congress in just over ten weeks.[4]

One thing that we know about public policy is that it generally takes a crisis before these types of concerted efforts to reduce governmental problems emerge.

INTERGENERATIONAL EQUITY

The current Social Security system might not be considered such a bad deal if (1) today's workers and employers did not view the Social Security tax as overly burdensome and (2) the number of aged persons supported by the working population was not increasing. However, Social Security taxes continue to increase, and the *dependency ratio*—the ratio of beneficiaries to workers—is also growing rapidly. In spite of assertions that the Social Security program is now on stronger footing, many young people doubt that Social Security will provide them an adequate living in their old age. Some argue that Social Security was never intended to support people fully during their retirement years. It was intended to help, but not fully subsidize, elderly citizens. Up to now, however, almost everyone who has retired has received Social Security benefits that have greatly exceeded what they contributed in Social Security taxes over the years. This helps to explain the political popularity of the Social Security program among its thirty-six million beneficiaries. But what about today's workers? They are not likely to get back as much as they will pay into the system during their working years. For example, if you are now twenty-seven, your contributions and those of your employer, from now until retirement at age sixty-five, will likely total over $225,000! But if these same monies were set aside in a private fund, such as an individual retirement account (IRA), in your own name and allowed to accumulate tax free at even a low interest rate of 7.5 percent, you would wind up with a nest egg at age sixty-five of over $1 million.[5] Needless to say, Social Security benefits, even including survivors, disability, and health provisions, will never amount to $1 million for an individual. So today's young workers are indeed paying a price far in excess of anything they might hope to regain. In addition to paying Social Security taxes, many young workers feel they must also invest in other retirement plans for fear that Social Security benefits will hardly be adequate in the twenty-first century. These payments take another chunk out of earnings.

An even greater problem for young workers is the increasing *dependency ratio.* This refers to the number of recipients as a percentage of the number of currently contributing workers. At present, each one hundred workers support about twenty-nine beneficiaries. But as the U.S. population grows older—because of lower birth rates and longer life spans (see figure 4-1)—we can expect forty-four beneficiaries per one hundred work-

FIGURE 4-1 The graying of America. (Bureau of the Census.)

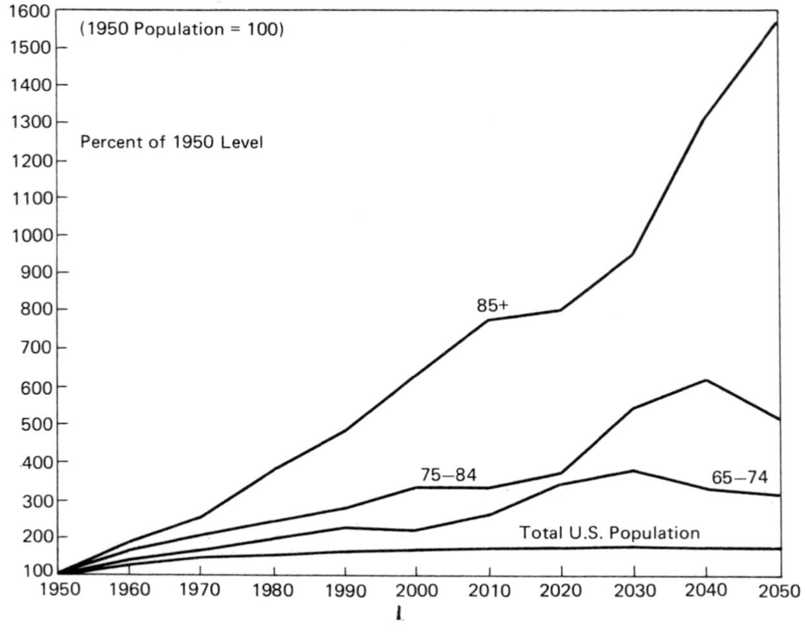

ers after the year 2000. This means that every two workers must support one Social Security recipient—a very heavy burden that will place additional pressures on current workers to keep the system financially solvent. If predictions are wrong, and the Social Security system cannot finance these promised benefits, political pressures will mount to force Congress to use general tax revenues to keep the system from bankruptcy. Many people already support the use of general revenues.[6] However, in light of the current budget deficit, the government would like to avoid this alternative.

Martha Ozawa believes that a key to the future of Social Security is to promote "intergenerational equity," that is, to be fair to both the old and the young.[7] Thus far, she says, politicians have focused on how to increase benefits to retired persons without consideration of how much current workers should be expected to pay into the system. Ozawa believes that in order to establish equity between the generations, future benefits should equal past contributions in addition to interest. This approach would work to prevent retirees from receiving benefits that are much higher than what they contributed and would eliminate undue tax burdens on younger workers. However, this approach could leave many older Americans with inadequate incomes in retirement if their contributions to the Social Security system during their working years were low. In order to rectify this problem of "intragenerational equity" (fairness among members of the same generation), Ozawa advocates paying the poor elderly at higher rates. Regardless of the approach to be used in the future, Social Security may not survive unless the ratio of contributions to benefits is brought into line for future workers. This may be a reasonable approach, especially because the financial status of older people has improved over the years.

OUT OF THE WOODS?

Are we out of the woods with Social Security?[8] Is the system really solvent for the next seventy-five years? Unfortunately, economic forecasts are not always correct. They assume that the economy will behave in certain ways. Factors that are not presently accounted for may result in unexpected deficits. For example, Medicare is part of the Social Security system, and many of its financial problems have not been addressed. (See chapter 10.)

Furthermore, Social Security has always been a regressive tax. It takes a larger share of the income of middle- and lower-income workers than the affluent. That is because (1) the Social Security tax is levied only against wages and not against dividends, interest, rents, and other nonwage income sources, which are more frequently sources of income for the wealthy; and (2) the wage base which is taxed stops at $42,000 and leaves all income in excess of this amount untaxed. This was not a problem when Social Security taxes amounted to very little, but today the size of Social Security revenues—30 percent of the federal government's income—has an important impact on the over-all equity of the revenue structure. Moreover, unlike the federal income tax, Social Security taxes make no allowance for family dependents or medical expenses. Finally, even though half of the full 14.3 percent Social Security tax is paid by the employee and half by the employer, most economists agree that the full burden of these taxes falls on the workers. The reason is that employers must consider the Social Security tax as a cost of hiring a worker, and the worker's take-home pay is reduced by the amount paid into the Social Security trust fund by both the employer and the employee. The 1983 amendments do not reduce the tax burden (the amount deducted from paychecks) for lower-income workers as compared to higher-income workers; however, they do tax part of the Social Security benefits of retirees in higher-income brackets.

Although it looks as though Social Security is on stable financial footing, the fact remains that it will continue to place a greater financial strain on workers in years to come. The thirty-six million beneficiaries of Social Security represent a large bloc of voters—older people vote more often than younger people—so it has been very difficult to modify Social Security. Any elected official who suggested reducing benefits or making other cuts in the program was said to be committing "political suicide." The Greenspan Commission did not recommend altering the basic structure of the program, and the president was forced to back off from any other thoughts he might have had for clamping down on benefits. However, future generations may view Social Security as too costly and too inefficient. It has been suggested that people be given an option to participate in Social Security. Many workers might prefer to put their funds in an IRA type of account with the hopes of doing better than what Social Security will afford them during retirement. The fear is that given the option, many people would fail to set aside anything at all, and this would place an even greater strain on the welfare system when these individuals retire. If wealthier workers chose to invest in IRAs rather than Social Security, and only lower-wage workers contributed to Social Security, there might be too little in the fund to pay adequate Social Security benefits to participants. It seems, therefore, that we are left with Social Security and that we must make the best of the situation, at least until another crisis occurs!

UNEMPLOYMENT COMPENSATION

A second major insurance program—unemployment compensation—was included in the original Social Security Act of 1935. Again, the underlying rationale was to compel employers to contribute to trust funds which would be held for the employees in the event of job loss. The federal government requires employers to pay into *state* unemployment insurance programs that meet federal standards. These programs are administered by the states. The federal standards are flexible, and the states have considerable freedom in shaping their own unemployment programs. In all cases, unemployed workers must report in person and show that they are willing and able to work in order to receive unemployment benefits. In practice, this means that unemployed workers must register with the U.S. Employment Service (usually located in the same building as the state unemployment compensation office) as a condition of receiving unemployment compensation. States cannot deny workers benefits for refusing to work as strikebreakers or refusing to work for less than "prevailing" rates. But basic decisions concerning the amount of benefits, eligibility, and length of time that benefits can be paid are largely left to the states. However, in all states, unemployment compensation is temporary (usually thirty-nine weeks maximum). Unemployment compensation is not a protection against long-term or "hard-core" unemployment.

ILLUSTRATION: 1983 SOCIAL SECURITY REFORMS UNFAIR TO MINORITIES AND THE YOUNG

The sweeping 1983 reforms of the Social Security system, when fully understood, may not endure. These so-called reforms ignore the interests and contributions of young workers and minorities.

By ignoring those who will be the mainstay of the system in the 21st century, Congress and the President may have set in motion an angry and powerful countervailing force that could radically restructure the Social Security system before the end of this decade.

The most unfair aspects of the Social Security reforms are the increase in the retirement age to 67, the increase in the tax rate to almost 8 percent by 1990, as well as the *reduction* in benefits to 21st century retirees. None of these changes would have been necessary if President Reagan had the courage and foresight to impose the Social Security tax on the income of the wealthy. . . .

An examination of the impact of the 1983 Social Security changes illustrates the potential for deep-seated dissatisfaction with the Social Security system, particularly among the young and minorities.

THE AVERAGE MALE HISPANIC WILL NEVER RECEIVE ANY SOCIAL SECURITY BENEFITS, EVEN IF HE WORKS FOR FORTY-FIVE YEARS

The average black and Hispanic, particularly the average male Hispanic, *never* retires. The median life expectancy of male Hispanics is 64, while the present full retirement age for Social Security is 65. As a result, approximately half of the Hispanic population in the United States never draws any retirement benefits from Social Security. In addition, the average Hispanic draws about nine years less in Social Security benefits than the typical Anglo whose life expectancy is 73 years of age.

As a result of this mortality disparity, the 1983 increase in the retirement age to 67 is a gross injustice to Hispanics who are presently disproportionately underserved by the current system. Equally important, the proposed increase in the retirement age unfairly harms those, such as Hispanics, whose primary occupations are in demanding physical labor (such as farmwork) that takes its toll long before the age of 67.

If all Americans drew from Social Security as little as the typical Hispanic retiree does, Social Security would have a substantial surplus rather than a deficit.

SOCIAL SECURITY WOULD BE INSOLVENT WITHOUT HISPANICS

The median age of the Hispanic population is eight years younger than the white population. (The median age is 23 versus 31 for the Anglo population; and only 4 percent of the Hispanic population, compared with 11 percent of the entire population, is over 65). This unique youth factor means that over the next two generations, the workforce supporting Social Security will be increasingly Hispanic and the retiree force increasingly and disproportionately Anglo.

ALL INCOME SHOULD BE TAXED FOR SOCIAL SECURITY

The Social Security tax is probably the world's most regressive tax. . . .

. . . A typical chief executive of a Fortune 500 corporation, earning $400,000 per year, pays only one-half of 1 percent of his/her earnings to Social Security. . . . *the typical American's contribution to Social Security is at a rate nine times higher than that paid by most chief executives.*

On the other hand, if Social Security taxes were imposed on *all* earnings, the Social Security system would be in the black every year and have an overall surplus of $1.1 *trillion* by the beginning of the next century. (The absence of an all-inclusive tax is of special significance to minorities since their median income is only two-thirds that of other Americans. . . .)

RECOMMENDATIONS TO PROTECT SOCIAL SECURITY AND ENSURE SUPPORT FROM MINORITIES AND YOUNG WORKERS

In recognition of these realities regarding the unfairly harsh impact of Social Security reforms on young workers and minorities, the League of United Latin American Citizens, the nation's largest Hispanic membership organization, offers four interrelated long-term recommendations to strengthen Social Security and ensure future worker support while fully protecting the rights of the elderly:

(1) The inclusion of "all earnings" for purposes of Social Security tax. This would produce an estimated $178 billion in additional revenue over the next six years and, based on similar projections, an additional $1.1 *trillion* over the next generation. This is more than *five times* the projected Social Security deficit over the next generation. It makes unnecessary all other so-called Social Security reforms.

(2) A return to age 65 for retirement.

(3) A moratorium on rate increases.

(4) No reduction in benefits for future retirees.

The continued ignoring of legitimate worker grievances could create an atmosphere in which a majority of the workers conclude that those who contribute the most will receive the least. It was just such unfair "taxation without representation" that inspired the American Revolution and President Reagan's 1980 election.

Source: Robert Gnaizda & Mario Obledo, *Gray Panther Network*, Spring 1985, p. 12.

Each state maintains an unemployment compensation trust fund of its own, financed from taxes on employers ranging from 1 percent to 4 percent of their total payroll. The federal government also maintains an unemployment compensation trust fund to bail out any state trust fund that becomes exhausted. Average state payments to the unemployed range from lows of $80 per week to highs of about $150.

WHAT IS UNEMPLOYMENT AND WHO IS UNEMPLOYED?

When unemployment compensation insurance was first adopted in 1935, the loss of one's job was an economic catastrophe. The alternative to work could be starvation. Most families depended on the support of one worker—usually the father. If he lost his job, the family's income was immediately reduced to zero. But today almost three-fifths of American families benefit from the earnings of more than one worker. Unemployment is still serious, but a second income provides a buffer against economic catastrophe. A combination of (1) short-term help from unemployment insurance, (2) food stamps, and (3) other forms of public assistance for the long-term unemployed reduce the real "cost" of becoming unemployed. The cost of unemployment can be viewed as the difference between income from unemployment insurance and other public assistance programs and the wages of a potential job. These changes have had an important effect on the motivations and expectations of the unemployed. The jobless need not jump at the first available job that comes along. They may now decide to pass up, at least for a while, low-paying or undesirable jobs in the hope of finding better-paying, more satisfying employment.

The unemployment rate is a monthly estimate by the U.S. Department of Labor of the percentage of the work force that is out of work and actively seeking jobs. Each year the total work force grows as the population increases. This means that the total number of jobs must grow each year to keep pace with population growth. An overall unemployment rate of 7 percent has become quite common. (See figure 4-2.) This is far below the 20 to 30 percent unemployment rate estimated during the depression of the 1930s but somewhat above the 3 to 4 percent lows achieved during the 1950s.

Clearly there is some unavoidable minimum unemployment. In a large, free economy, hundreds of thousands of people move and change jobs and temporarily find themselves unemployed. This "frictional" unemployment is estimated to be about half of the total unemployment during normal (nonrecession) periods. Others find themselves unemployed because of poor job skills, poor health, low mental capacities, or geographic locations far from work places. These "structurally" unemployed are estimated to be less than 20 percent of the total unemployed.

In order to determine the unemployment rate, a survey based on about sixty thousand household interviews is conducted each month. Those sixteen years of age and older are included in the survey. The Labor Department is frequently criticized because it counts part-time workers as employed; yet many part-time workers would prefer full-time work. It is also criticized because many of the poor in America are never counted as unemployed. That is because they have become discouraged and have

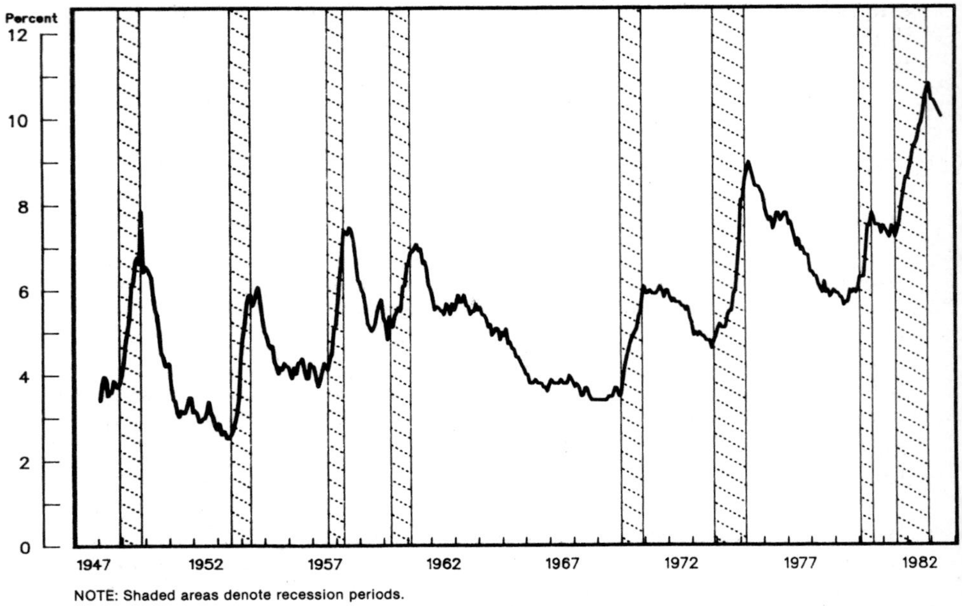

FIGURE 4-2 Unemployment Rate, 1948–1983 (Source: Department of Labor, *Workers without Jobs: A Chartbook on Unemployment* [Washington: Government Printing Office, July 1983], p. 39.) Note: Shaded areas denote recession periods.

given up even trying to find a job. These discouraged workers are excluded from unemployment statistics altogether.

On the other hand, in order to qualify for public assistance, such as food stamps, able-bodied individuals must sign up with the state employment office in their area. Some argue that this drives unemployment figures up, because some of these individuals may not really intend to seek employment.[9]

Women and blacks and teenagers suffer from higher unemployment rates than adult white males do. In good times or bad, the black unemployment rate is nearly double the white unemployment rate. Unemployment rates for women are slightly higher than unemployment rates for men. But the teenage (sixteen to nineteen years old) unemployment rate is usually three times higher than the adult male rate. The highest unemployment rate of all is for black teenagers; a 40 percent unemployment rate for this group is not uncommon.

How much unemployment is enough? There is an old saying: "When your neighbor is unemployed, it's a recession. When you are unemployed, it's a depression." It has been argued that unemployment among women and teenagers is not as urgent a problem as unemployment among male adults, who are generally the family breadwinners. Others reject this notion, contending that at least one-third of working women support their families alone and that many other women work because of low family income. It is also argued that jobs for teenagers produce long-term social benefits—teens learn work habits and the importance of holding a steady job in later life. The unemployment picture would improve considerably if jobs and unemployed workers were better matched. This could be done in two ways. First, those unable to locate employment near their homes could be encouraged or assisted to relocate to areas where jobs are available. Relocation assistance is often provided for higher-paid workers by their employers but not for low-wage earners, who may need this assistance the most. Second, more job training and retraining programs could be offered to help workers with outdated skills learn skills that employers are seeking. The Job Training Partnership Act (discussed in chapter 9) is intended to help with this problem.

REFORMING UNEMPLOYMENT INSURANCE

How can the unemployment insurance program be improved to better assist the unemployed? According to one task force studying unemployment, the program should be made ". . . more reliable for those who depend on it, more responsive to changes in the economy, and more effective in providing relief and helping put people back to work."[10] The task force cites four major problems with unemployment insurance. First, the program is too complex. Basic benefits are provided, and then there are "triggers" which allow additional benefits to be paid during periods when unemployment is especially high. These triggers and benefit periods change frequently, adding to confusion in the program. Second, the program is too rigid. It can fail to help states and areas with the highest unemployment. Many long-term unemployed persons are not counted when determining unemployment rates, so the severity of a state's unemployment is underestimated. Unless unemployment is high, the triggers are not set off, and extended benefits are not made available in that state. In addition, if unemployment in a particular area of a state is high, but the overall state unemployment rate is relatively low, the depressed area does not receive additional payments. Third, there are few inducements for workers to seek training that would qualify them for new jobs. The attitude is to take the first job available, whatever it is. Training opportunities are limited. Short-term solutions are used in favor of longer-term gains. Fourth, program financing should be altered so that the states with the highest unemployment receive more federal financial assistance rather than face the possibility of incurring additional financial burdens. When faced with heavy financial burdens, state economies become more depressed when growth is needed most. In order to improve the program, steps should be taken to simplify "triggers" and other regulations, provide more assistance to states and areas with high unemployment, more accurately count the number of unemployed, and provide more inducements for training and job searches that will better match jobs and workers.

ILLUSTRATION: HUNDREDS LINE UP FOR LOW-PAYING JOBS

Athol, Mass. (AP) Hundreds of unemployed residents of this depressed mill town began lining up at daybreak Monday, hoping for the chance to travel 70 miles each way to a $4-an-hour job in a city whose economy is so strong it can't find enough workers.

The round trip from Athol, tucked in the hills of central Massachusetts, to Framingham, a bustling metropolitan area west of Boston, could take three hours a day. But the jobseekers were not discouraged.

"I've been out of work for three years. I would take anything," said former machine operator Eugene Labor. "My benefits are completely exhausted now. If it wasn't for my parents, I'd be out in the streets."

Labor was among 400 people who filled out applications for five companies, including McDonald's and Burger King, which had come to town in search of employees for the Christmas rush. They offered $4-an-hour wages and free bus rides to and from work. The program was created and sponsored by the state Division of Employment Security.

Once a thriving factory town that churned out shoes, tables and tools, Athol, a town of 8,700 residents, now has an unemployment rate of 8.2 percent. Framingham, once a quiet Boston suburb, has become one of the state's fastest-growing urban areas with 70,000 residents. Its jobless rate is just 2.3 percent.

"I just need something to keep my head above water," said Herman Foster, a janitor who has been out of work since July. "You can survive on welfare, but you've got nothing. I have five kids. How can I buy them a pair of shoes?"

For the Framingham employers, the recruitment campaign was a success.

"They really want the jobs. Some of them are desperate. They all say they are hard workers, and that's what we need," said Doug Whyte, general manager of a Wendy's restaurant.

State officials said they expect 200 of those who turned out Monday to land jobs. The job applicants will hear within a few days whether they have been hired.

"I would love to get a job, even for two months. I don't care how far away it is," said 22-year-old Albert Bixby. "It's better than sitting around and doing nothing."

Source: *Austin American-Statesman,* January 8, 1985, p. A3.

Workers' Compensation

Workers' compensation (formerly called workmen's compensation) is another type of social insurance program. Each state operates a workers' compensation program but the programs vary by state. Workers' compensation provides cash payments and medical benefits to workers injured on the job. "All [workers' compensation] laws include some or all diseases attributable to the worker's occupation. Most exclude injuries due to the employee's intoxication, willful misconduct, or gross negligence."[11] Dependents of workers killed in job-related mishaps are generally entitled to benefits. Some states provide benefits to widowers as well as widows. Employers participate by insuring their workers. Some insure through a private insurance company, others self-insure, and in some cases, the state insures employers. The types of jobs covered by workers' compensation differ from state to state.

SUMMARY

One strategy for preventing poverty in the United States is through social insurance programs. The purpose of social insurance is to help workers insure themselves and their dependents against poverty, which may result from advanced age, death, disability, and unemployment. The major social insurance program is known as the Social Security program. It is financed through premiums paid by both workers and employers and is administered by the federal government.

Social insurance programs differ from public assistance programs. Social insurance programs require that beneficiaries make contributions to the program; contributors are entitled to benefits regardless of their wealth. Public assistance recipients must prove that they are poor before they receive benefits, and benefits are paid from general tax revenues rather than through recipients' contributions.

The Social Security Act of 1935 was the first major piece of federal welfare legislation. This act has been amended many times; today it includes a number of social welfare programs. The social insurance programs it includes are Old Age, Survivors, Disability and Health Insurance, Unemployment Compensation, and Medicare. The public assistance programs it includes are Aid to Families with Dependent Children, Supplemental Security Income, and Medicaid.

Social Security was originally intended to be a self-financing program, but it developed into a "pay-as-we-go" system because life expectancy increased, and payments were continually raised to keep up with the cost of living. In order to finance the growing program, the amount of taxable wages increased over the years and the rate at which these wages were taxed also increased. The thirty-six million recipients of Social Security are a strong voting bloc, and any changes that would reduce benefits have met with strong resistance. Eventually it looked as if the program would be bankrupt. In 1981 President Reagan appointed a bipartisan commission to come up with solutions to the ailing Social Security program. After many disagreements, the commission made a number of recommendations which were supported by both Democrats and Republicans and rapidly adopted by Congress. The changes included raising the retirement age, increasing the taxable wage base and the Social Security tax rate, taxing part of Social Security benefits of those in upper-income categories, increasing benefits to those who retire later and decreasing benefits to those who retire early, and allowing retirees to earn more while losing less in Social Security benefits. Accounting procedures were modified to make the program more efficient, cost-of-living adjustments were delayed, and methods of computing these adjustments were altered to provide cost savings if the trust fund runs low. Unfortunately, the Social Security program places a great strain on current workers, and future workers face an even greater responsibility to keep the system afloat. For the time being, it appears that the system is on steady footing, and no major alternatives to the program are likely to be instituted, barring another financial crisis.

Unemployment Compensation is another large social insurance program. While national unemployment rates have fluctuated at around 7 percent, unemployment among blacks, women, and teenagers is much higher. Minority youth have been hit hardest by unemployment. Unemployment insurance does not help with long-term unemployment. Unemployment would be reduced if unemployed workers were better matched with available jobs. Workers' compensation, another social insurance program, is designed to assist workers who have been injured or become ill in work-related situations.

NOTES

1. Joseph A. Pechman, Henry J. Aaron, and Michael K. Taussig, *Social Security: Perspectives for Reform* (Washington: Brookings Institution, 1968).
2. For further discussion of provisions under the Social Security Act, see Robert M. Ball, *Social Security Today and Tomorrow* (New York: Columbia University Press, 1978); Alice H. Munnell, *The Future of Social Security* (Washington: Brookings Institution, 1977); Bruno Stein, *Social Security and Provisions in Transition* (New York: Free Press, 1980); and Sar A. Levitan, *Programs in Aid of the Poor for the 1980s*, 4th ed. (Baltimore: John Hopkins University Press, 1980).
3. For a more detailed description of the work of the National Commission on Social Security Reform see "Report of the National Commission on Social Security Reform," *Social Security Bulletin* 46, no. 2 (February 1983), pp. 3–38. For a more thorough description of House and Senate action on Social Security reform see "Social Security Rescue Plan Swiftly Approved," *1983 Congressional Quarterly Almanac*, pp. 219–26. For a concise consideration of the changes adopted, see Wilbur J. Cohen, "The Future Impact of the Social Security Amendments of 1983," *The Journal/The Institute for Socioeconomic Studies* 8, no. 2 (Summer 1983), 1–16.
4. Wilbur J. Cohen, "Social Security: The Compromise and Beyond," Washington D.C.: Save Our Security Education Fund, 1983, pp. 4–5.
5. William G. Flanagan, "Social Security—Don't Count on It," *Forbes* 126, no. 12 (December 8, 1980), 161–162.
6. Cohen, "Social Security," pp. 33–34.
7. Martha N. Ozawa, "Benefits and Taxes Under Social Security: An Issue of Intergenerational Equity," *Social Work* 29, no. 2 (March 1984), 131–137.
8. For more on the future of Social Security see Cohen, "Social Security Amendments of 1983."
9. Kenneth W. Clarkson and Roger E. Meiners, "Government Statistics as a Guide to Economic Policy: Food Stamps and the Spurious Increase in the Unemployment Rates," *Policy Review* 1, no.1 (Summer 1977), 27–51.
10. Donald J. Pease and William F. Clinger, Jr., "Reform Unemployment Insurance," *Wall Street Journal*, January 29, 1985, p. 26.
11. Department of Health and Human Services, *Social Security Handbook 1984*, 8th ed., Social Security Administration, SSA publication no. 05-10135, July 1984, p. 387.

chapter 5

Helping the "deserving poor": aged, blind, and disabled

The aged, blind, and disabled are among the groups considered to be the "deserving poor"—those whom society has moral and ethical obligations to assist. Two major types of programs are available to these persons: (1) Public assistance programs serve the poor aged, blind, and disabled in cases where the individual's condition is not likely to improve and other means of support are not available; and (2) social service programs assist those who can benefit from a wide range of rehabilitation services.[1] In addition to these programs, recent legislation for the disabled is aimed at reducing discrimination in employment and education and at providing greater access to public facilities.

EARLY AID FOR THE DESERVING POOR

Most states had programs to assist the elderly poor before the Social Security Act of 1935 was passed. Massachusetts was among the first states to appoint a commission to study the problems of the elderly.[2] In 1914 Arizona passed a law establishing a pension program for the aged.[3] The territory of Alaska passed a law entitling elderly persons to pensions in 1915.[4] By the time the federal government adopted the Social Security Act, thirty states already had their own old-age assistance programs.[5] Eligibility requirements for state old-age programs were very stringent. In order to qualify, recipients generally had to be at least sixty-five years old, be citizens of the United States, and meet residency requirements in the location where they applied for benefits. In cases where relatives were capable of supporting an elderly family member, benefits were often denied. Often those elderly who did participate had to sign all of their assets over to the state in the event of their death.[6]

Old age was not the only disabling condition which concerned Americans. The blind were also considered "deserving." In fact, terms of residence and other entrance requirements were often more lenient in the state pension laws for the blind than they were for the elderly. By 1935, twenty-seven states had pension programs for the blind.[7] Other types of diseases, injuries, and handicaps were also considered disabling, but early in the 1900s policies to assist persons disabled because of conditions other than old age and blindness varied considerably from state to state,[8] and some states had no programs at all.

When the Social Security Act of 1935 was passed, its most far-reaching provision was the Social Security insurance program, which provided financial payments to retired workers. However, the Social Security Act also included public assistance programs for some special target groups. Following the precedent established by many states, the programs included were Aid to Dependent Children (ADC), Old Age Assistance (OAA), and Aid to the Blind (AB). In 1950 the Social Security Act was amended to include the Aid to the Permanently and Totally Disabled (APTD) program. OAA, AB, and APTD were called the adult categorical assistance programs. Although the programs were authorized by the federal government, each state could decide whether it wanted to participate in any or all of the programs. All states eventually adopted the OAA and AB programs, but several states chose not to participate in the APTD program. The federal government shared costs with the states and set minimum requirements for participation in the programs. Elderly persons had to be at least sixty-five years old to receive federal aid. Blind and disabled persons had to be at least eighteen years old. The states were primarily responsible for administering the programs and retained a great deal of discretion in determining eligibility requirements. Residency requirements and income limitations were determined by the states as were the amount of payments. The states also determined the definitions of disability and blindness.

State administration of the OAA, AB, and APTD programs had serious ramifications for some beneficiaries. An individual who moved to another state was often denied benefits until residency was reestablished. Benefits also varied drastically and were often meager. In the OAA program in 1964, the state of West Virginia paid an average monthly benefit of $50, while Wisconsin paid an average benefit of $111.[9] Beneficiaries from poorer states often received less because their states had less money to operate the program.

SSI: "FEDERALIZING" THE AGED, BLIND, AND DISABLED PROGRAMS

When President Nixon took office in 1972 he wanted to clean up the "welfare mess." Nixon's welfare reform was to provide a minimum income to poor Americans that would replace the AFDC, OAA, AB, and APTD programs and bring an end to the uneven treatment of welfare recipients from state to state. His *guaranteed annual income* proposal, known as the Family Assistance Plan (FAP), was the target of controversy in Congress. Liberals believed that the reforms were too stingy. Conservatives believed that the reforms provided too much in welfare benefits and would reduce the incentive to work. Daniel P. Moynihan, advisor to President Nixon, supporter of the FAP, and author of *The Politics of a Guaranteed Annual Income,* tells us that most of the controversy focused on the reform of the AFDC program.[10] AFDC was never reformed, but in the midst of the AFDC controversy, the OAA, AB, and APTD programs underwent substantial revisions that went almost unnoticed.[11]

In 1972 Congress made major changes in OAA, AB, and APTD by federalizing these programs under a new program called Supplemental Security Income (SSI). "Federalizing" meant that Congress largely took the programs out of the hands of state governments. The state governments would no longer determine basic eligibility requirements or minimum payment levels, nor would they directly administer the programs. These changes represented the most sweeping reform of the adult categorical assistance programs since APTD had been added in 1950. SSI replaced the OAA, AB, and APTD programs by establishing a minimum income for recipients and by standardizing eligibility requirements in all states; however, most states supplement the minimum payment to recipients.[12] State supplements may be administered by the federal government or the state. When administered by the federal government, it pays the administrative costs, but the state must agree to cover all SSI recipients. States which choose to set their own requirements by including only certain beneficiaries or by disregarding additional income administer their own supplementation programs at their own expense. Under the change to SSI no state could pay beneficiaries less than they had previously received.

How SSI Works

Because SSI is administered by the Social Security Administration, and because its name resembles that of the Social Security retirement program, some people think that these programs are the same, but they are quite different. SSI is a means-tested public assistance program while Social Security is a social insurance program. SSI is funded through general revenues while Social Security is funded through a special payroll tax. However, older persons may receive SSI benefits in addition to Social Security if their income from Social Security and other sources is lower than the income standard set under the SSI program.[13]

Sometimes a person qualifies for benefits under two of the SSI components. For example, a poor aged person may also be disabled. Due to the fact that there are more income exclusions under the portion of the program for the disabled, it may be more advantageous for the client to qualify under the disabled rather than the aged portions of the program.

Children as well as adults may qualify for benefits under the disabled and blind portions, since age is not a factor in determining eligibility. In determining benefits for children, their parents' income is considered.

Beneficiaries cannot receive SSI and AFDC benefits simultaneously. When a parent or child meets the qualifications for both programs, a determination must be made as to which program provides the most advantageous situation. Of all children receiving SSI, 54 percent are mentally retarded.

In most cases, residents of rest homes or halfway houses operated by a city or county cannot qualify for SSI payments, but there are some exceptions. For example, individuals living in public institutions may be eligible if their primary reason for residence is to acquire vocational or educational training. Others may qualify if they are living in public facilities with no more than sixteen residents.

The aged portion of the program is for those who are at least sixty-five years old and who have little or no income. Under the portion of the program for the blind, "a person whose vision is no better than 20/200 or who has a limited visual field of 20 degrees or less with the best corrective eyeglasses is considered blind."[14] Adults (those at least eighteen years of age) qualify as disabled if they cannot work because of a physical or mental impairment that "is expected to last for at least twelve months or to result in death."[15] Although children under eighteen are not expected to work, they qualify for SSI if their disability or impairment is similar in severity to that of an adult with the same condition. Persons who do not meet the definition of blindness but who are visually impaired may qualify as disabled. Drug addicts and alcoholics who are disabled may qualify for payments but must comply with a treatment program. In these cases, their payments are made to a responsible third party. A trial work period is offered to help disabled recipients determine if they are capable of gainful employment. Disabled recipients may work for nine months and still receive SSI payments if their income is within prescribed limits and/or recovery does not occur.

Those who qualify for benefits have limited resources. In 1984 an individual could have resources of up to $1,500 and a couple up to $2,250. These limitations are increasing gradually. By 1989 they will reach $2,000 and $3,000 respectively. Resources include items like real estate, savings accounts, and household goods. However, several types of resources are not included in determining eligibility. For example, the individual's home is not counted. Personal property which does not exceed a value of $2,000 is excluded and the value of a car up to $4,500 is not counted.

To qualify for SSI an adult's countable income must be less than $314 monthly. For a couple, the figure is $472. In the case of child beneficiaries, allowances are made which take into consideration parents' work expenses and living expenses of the family. Income is defined as "anything received that can be used to meet the needs for food, clothing, or shelter."[16] Income may be "earned" or "unearned." Examples of earned income are wages and income from sheltered workshops. Examples of unearned income are Social Security benefits, veteran's compensation, pensions, in-kind support, rent, and interest on savings. Certain items are not considered income, including medical and social services and bills that are paid by another party if they are not for food, shelter, or clothing. Some income is disregarded in calculating benefits. Generally, the first $20 a month of earned or unearned income is disregarded as well as an additional $65 of earned income, plus half of all remaining earned income. The idea of allowing beneficiaries to keep half of all earned income (up to prescribed limits) is to encourage employment.

The federal government pays a *maximum* of $314 to an individual living alone and $472 to a couple. One-third of the payment is deducted if the beneficiary resides in the home of someone who is contributing to his or her support. Payments are adjusted each year to keep pace with the cost of living. "The SSI program provides an annual income that in 1982 was approximately 71 percent of the poverty line for an aged individual and 85 percent of the poverty line for an aged couple."[17] The illustration that follows provides examples of how SSI payments are calculated.

Recipients' cases are generally reviewed at least every three years in order to determine if they are still eligible. For disabled beneficiaries, "continuing disability reviews" may also be required in which new medical information is submitted in order to determine if the person is still disabled. Most states automatically provide Medicaid benefits to SSI recipients.

Costs and Recipients of SSI

Since 1972, when the OAA, AB, and APTD programs were federalized, costs have generally continued to rise, even after accounting for inflation (see table 5-1). In 1940 the costs of OAA were $473 million. In 1983, under SSI, costs amounted to more than $2.8 billion. The AB program has not been as expensive a program because there are not as many blind recipients as there are aged and disabled. In 1940 the program cost $22 million to operate; today it costs $229 million. The most dramatic growth in expenditures has been for disabled recipients. Costs rose from $259 million in 1960 to more than $6 billion in 1983.

Payments to recipients have also increased, although they remain modest. And once we consider the high rate of inflation, especially in re-

TABLE 5-1 The Costs of the Adult Public Assistance and SSI Programs for Selected Years (in millions of dollars)

YEAR	AGED	BLIND	DISABLED
1940	473	22	—[a]
1950	1,485	53	8
1960	1,922	83	259
1970	1,862	98	1,000
1980	2,734	190	5,014
1983	2,814	229	6,357

[a]Program did not begin until 1950.

Sources: Bureau of the Census, *Historical Statistics of the United States, Colonial Times to 1970* (Washington, 1975), p. 356; and *Statistical Abstract of the United States, 1985,* p. 378.

TABLE 5-2 Average Monthly Payments for the Adult Public Assistance Programs for Selected Years (in dollars)

YEAR	AGED	BLIND	DISABLED
1940	19.30	26.10	—[a]
1950	43.05	25.35	44.10
1960	58.90	46.00	56.15
1970	77.65	104.00	97.65
1980	128.00	213.00	198.00
1983	158.00	256.00	245.00

[a]Program did not begin until 1950.

Sources: Bureau of the Census, *Historical Statistics of the United States, Colonial Times to 1970* (Washington, 1975), p. 356; and *Statistical Abstract of the United States, 1985,* p. 379.

cent years, payments may leave recipients with little more purchasing power than they had before the enactment of SSI. An elderly recipient now receives an *average* of $158 per month. This is lower than average payments to the blind and disabled. The blind receive the highest payments, averaging $256 monthly, and disabled recipients receive an average of $245 monthly (see table 5-2).

Over the years the number of elderly and blind SSI recipients has continued to decrease, especially when compared with the rate of growth in the general population. However, the number of disabled beneficiaries has increased rapidly (see table 5-3). In 1950 about 2.8 million people received old-age assistance. Today there are about 1.5 million recipients. The declining number of recipients can be attributed primarily to the increasing number of persons who have become eligible for Social Security insurance benefits. When SSI was enacted, however, it was anticipated that many more elderly would become eligible for some assistance. Low participation may be due to the stigma associated with being a welfare recipient.

TABLE 5-3 Number of Recipients of the Adult Public Assistance and SSI Programs for Selected Years (in thousands)

YEAR	AGED	BLIND	DISABLED
1940	2,070	73	—[a]
1950	2,786	97	69
1960	2,305	107	369
1970	2,082	81	935
1980	1,808	78	2,256
1983	1,515	79	2,307

[a]Program did not begin until 1950.

Sources: Bureau of the Census, *Historical Statistics of the United States, Colonial Times to 1970* (Washington, 1975), p. 356; and *Statistical Abstract of the United States, 1985,* p. 379.

Others do not apply, believing they do not qualify.[18] The Social Security Administration is currently studying why participation has been so low.[19]

Since 1960 the number of blind recipients has dropped from a high of more than 100,000 to about 79,000. The decrease can be attributed to advances in the prevention and treatment of blindness and to the growing numbers of blind persons who are self-supporting.

Most of the growth in SSI has been due to increases in the number of permanently and totally disabled recipients. Many states had strict definitions of disability. When the program was federalized, a standard definition of disability was adopted that helped many new recipients join the rolls. The number of recipients has grown from nearly 370,000 in 1960 to over two million today.

The Future of SSI

SSI has not fared badly under the Reagan administration because Congress has resisted attempts to cut benefits and to reduce the number of disabled recipients. In 1983 a measure was enacted which delayed the cost-of-living increase for beneficiaries for six months, but Congress counteracted the delay by increasing benefits by $20 per month for individuals and $30 for couples.[20] In order to reduce fraud and error, information is ob-

ILLUSTRATION: DETERMINING SSI PAYMENTS

Methods of calculating public assistance payments often seem complex and are not well known to those outside the welfare system. The following examples provided by the Social Security Administration illustrate how benefits are calculated for aged recipients of SSI.[1]

1

Sam Johnson is 66, lives alone in a small house he owns, and his only income is his Social Security benefit of $182.00 a month. He gets $167.40 of this in his check, after his $14.60 Medicare medical insurance premium is deducted.

Income not from current earnings:		
Monthly Social Security benefit	$182.00	
Less $20	−20.00	
Remainder: Countable income not from current earnings.	$162.00	$162.00
Income from current earnings:	None	+None
Total countable income for the month		$162.00
Basic SSI amount for the month	$314.00	
Less total countable income	−162.00	
Monthly SSI payment	$152.00	$152.00
His Social Security benefit is		+182.00
So his total monthly income will be		$334.00

2

Now let's say Mr. Johnson is married and lives with his wife who is 65. She gets $91.00 a month from Social Security—from which a Medicare medical insurance premium is deducted. The couple's total Social Security income is $273.00 a month.

Income not from current earnings:		
Couple's monthly Social Security benefits	$273.00	
Less $20	−20.00	
Remainder: Countable income not from current earnings..................................	$253.00	$253.00
Income from current earnings:...............	None	+None
Total countable income for the month		$235.00
Basic SSI amount for the month	$472.00	
Less total countable income	−253.00	
Monthly SSI payment	$219.00	$219.00
Their Social Security benefits are		+273.00
Their total monthly income will be		$492.00

3

Mr. Johnson takes a weekend job which pays $100 a month gross wa ges. Here's how these earnings affect Mr. and Mrs. Johnson's total income.

Income not from current earnings:		
Couple's monthly Social Security benefits	$273.00	
Less $20	−20.00	
Remainder: Countable income not from current earnings	$253.00	$253.00
Income from current earnings:		
Wages for the month	$100.00	
Less $65	−65.00	
Divide remainder by 2	2/35.00	
Countable income from current earnings	$17.50	+17.50
Total countable income for the month		$270.50
Basic SSI amount for the month	$472.00	
Less total countable income	−270.00	
Monthly SSI payment	$201.50	$201.50
Their Social Security benefit is		+273.00
And Mr. Johnson's monthly earnings are		+100.00
So their total monthly income will be		$574.50

4

Joe Jones, 68, lives with his daughter and son-in-law. Joe receives $182.00 in Social Security benefits. Since Joe lives with someone who provides food and shelter, he is receiving in-kind support and maintenance, which is valued at one-third of the basic SSI amount. This takes the place of setting the exact dollar value of the support and maintenance.

Income not from current earnings:		
Monthly Social Security benefit	$182.00	
Less $20	−20.00	
	$162.00	
Plus one-third of basic SSI amount	+104.66	
Countable income not from current earnings . . .	$266.66	$266.66
Income from current earnings	None	+None
Total countable income for the month		$266.66
Basic SSI amount for the month	$314.00	
Less total countable income	−266.66	
Monthly SSI payment	$ 47.34	$ 47.34
And his Social Security Check is		+182.00
Joe Jones' total monthly cash income will be		$229.34
And the value of his food and shelter is		+104.66
So his total monthly income will be		$334.00

[1]Benefits for blind and disabled recipients are calculated in a similar manner, however, other factors are considered in these portions of the SSI program. Additional income exclusions apply as well as provisions like trial work opportunities for disabled recipients.

Source: Department of Health and Human Services, Social Security Administration, "A Guide to Supplemental Security Income," January 1984 ed., SSA publication no. 05-11015, pp. 16–19.

tained from the IRS and the Social Security Administration (SSA) in determining eligibility for benefits in federally funded welfare programs like SSI.[21]

In a ten-year review of the SSI program, the SSA concludes that the program has done well in meeting most of its objectives.[22] With respect to age, race, and sex of recipients, the program appears to be reaching those most likely to be poor. In terms of future planning, the growth in the number of disabled recipients cannot be overlooked, since few disabled recipients work and most continue to remain on the rolls. Since the advent of SSI, more children have entered the program with disabilities such as mental retardation. This may mean that they will be eligible for benefits throughout their lifetimes.

DEFINING DISABILITY

Since considerable attention is devoted to the elderly in chapters 4 (Social Security) and 7 (social services), most of this chapter is devoted to an analysis of social policies and services for the disabled. Most Americans agree that the "disabled" are among the "deserving" poor. However, defining *disability* is not an easy task. There are many types of disabilities and handicaps. Amputations, arthritis, blindness, bone problems, brain injuries, burns, cancer, cerebral palsy, cleft lip and palate, deafness, diabetes, disfigurement, emotional disturbances, epilepsy, heart disease, mental retardation, mongolism, multiple sclerosis, muscular atrophy, muteness, paralysis, respiratory disorders, stroke, and stuttering are just some.[23] In addition to classifying these problems as disabilities or handicaps, one might classify them in terms of degree of impairment.[24] For instance, a person may be legally blind but still have some sight. Some persons are so severely handicapped that they can perform few of life's day-to-day functions, yet other disabled persons are able to function quite well in society. *Disabilities* have traditionally been defined as *health-related problems that prevent the individual from working*.[25] A broader definition might include not only employment limitations, but also limitations on all roles and tasks a person usually performs in society, especially if these limitations exist for long periods of time.[26]

The U.S. government, which supports a large number of programs for the handicapped and disabled, has developed a definition of disability. This definition is used to determine which individuals are eligible to participate in federally funded programs for the disabled.

> A handicapped person is anyone with any type of physical or mental disability that substantially impairs or restricts one or more such major life activities as walking, seeing, hearing, speaking, working, or learning. Handicapping conditions include but are not limited to:
>
> Cancer
> Cerebral palsy
> Deafness or hearing impairment
> Diabetes
> Emotional illness
> Epilepsy
> Heart Disease
> Mental Retardation
> Multiple Sclerosis
> Muscular dystrophy
> Orthopedic, speech, or visual impairment
> Such perceptual handicaps as
> Dyslexia
> Minimal brain dysfunction
> Developmental aphasia
>
> The U.S. Attorney General has ruled that alcoholism and drug addiction are physical or mental impairments that are handicapping conditions if they limit one or more of life's major activities.[27]

REHABILITATIVE SERVICES FOR THE DISABLED

Financial assistance through SSI is an important resource for elderly, handicapped, and disabled persons who are unable to work or who earn so little that they cannot maintain an adequate standard of living. However, handicapped and disabled persons often need more than financial assistance. Even the most severely and profoundly retarded person can benefit from programs of physical stimulation. For those with less severe disabilities, physical therapy or artificial limbs may be important in order to interact in society. Others need special educational programs and learning devices. Still others require vocational education and reeducation.

The Vocational Rehabilitation Program

One of the first training programs to assist the disabled was developed in Massachusetts in 1916.[28] Then in 1920 Congress passed the Vocational Rehabilitation Act to assist vocationally disabled civilians and disabled veterans returning from World War I by providing funds through a federal-state matching formula. The federal and state governments shared program costs on a fifty-fifty basis. The appeal of vocational rehabilitation is that it is less costly to rehabilitate people to work than to provide them with public assistance payments.

Today the federal government provides the majority of funding for the Vocational Rehabilitation (VR) program. Each state operates its own program according to federal guidelines and also supplements federal funding of the program. An individual who applies for VR services is evaluated by a doctor and/or other experts to determine whether a disability exists. Only those who have a reasonable chance of becoming employed or reemployed qualify for services. For women at home, the criterion is that they have the potential to perform independent living skills.[29] Each person who qualifies for assistance is assigned a VR counselor, who develops an individualized plan for the disabled client; the plan may include medical services, training, education, guidance, financial assistance, and job-placement services.

The concept of the individualized rehabilitation plan sounds like a rational way to optimize services to the disabled. However, in actuality, some clients may not receive all the services they need. For example, the emphasis of the vocational rehabilitation program changes from time to time. Some of the target populations have been the mentally ill, the mentally retarded, the culturally disadvantaged, and the severely handicapped.[30] When available funds cannot be stretched to meet the needs of all eligible participants, clients' needs must be prioritized. In addition, because each state administers its own program, persons with the same or similar disabilities may receive different types and amounts of services depending on the state in which they live.

The number of individuals referred for vocational rehabilitation services has declined. In 1975 more than one million new cases were processed. By 1977 the number had dropped to just below one million. Current figures indicate the processing of about 870,000 new cases annually. However, the percentages of individuals accepted into the program have remained relatively stable, with 46 percent accepted in 1975 and 43 percent accepted in 1981. Rehabilitation rates have declined somewhat from 70 percent in 1975 to 62 percent today. Federal and state spending increased from about $867 million in 1975 to $1.1 billion in 1981. Disabling conditions of clients, in order of the frequency of their occurrences from highest to lowest, are orthopedic impairment, mental illness, mental retardation, visual impairments, hearing impairments, substance abuse, digestive disorders, genito-urinary disorders, and missing limbs. The largest group of clients are placed in industrial jobs, followed by service, clerical and sales, homemaking, professional, technical and managerial, and agricultural and fishing.[31]

There are other provisions for employment of the handicapped in addition to the VR program. The state employment offices (see chapter 4) have a legal responsibility to assist the handicapped, and some handicapped individuals may qualify under the Job Training Partnership Act (see chapter 9).

Creaming

In its early days critics charged the Vocational Rehabilitation program with a practice called *creaming*. Creaming means accepting into the program those candidates who are most likely to become rehabilitated. While the goal of the program is rehabilitation, it is easier for some disabled persons to be rehabilitated than others. Most of the program's early clients were young, white males whose disabilities were neither chronic nor severe.[32]

> In 1938 the federal [vocational rehabilitation] office captured the policy that lay behind the selection of the vocational rehabilitation case load when it told the states that eligibility does not necessarily imply feasibility. Anyone over 18 was technically eligible for rehabilitation, but such factors as advanced age, extreme disability, bad attitude of mind, or low social status limited feasibility.[33]

Although this attitude has changed since the early days of the program, the fact remains that VR is not an entitlement program. Funds are limited. Not everyone who needs assistance can be served, and for those who are served, counselors may not be able to procure all the funds and services the client needs.

Normalization

One of the first responses of modern society to the severely physically and emotionally handicapped was "indoor" relief—the "warehousing" of these persons in large institutions. Over the years, conditions in institutions became more humane, but until recently these large facilities were the primary means of assisting those considered too severely handicapped to re-

ILLUSTRATION: UNDERSTANDING THE PROBLEMS OF PERSONS WITH HANDICAPS

Many capable, handicapped persons face a variety of barriers in everyday life. These barriers prevent us from developing a rational approach to assisting persons with handicaps. In the following examples, we see how prejudice, fear, ignorance, and administrative policies can limit full participation for the 36 million handicapped in the United States.

First grader Chris Powers was the only youngster left behind when his class went to the zoo. He was the only one asked to step aside when the class picture was taken. He was also the only pupil forbidden to eat with his classmates in the school cafeteria. In each instance, the principal felt that the emotional outbursts Chris is subject to would upset other children. Chris is an autistic child.

When George C. Jackson, a psychologist and professor at Howard University in Washington, D.C., was recuperating from surgery, the hospital staff insisted that he stay in his room rather than walk down the hall to visit with other patients in the solarium. The operation had nothing to do with the restriction. Dr. Jackson is blind. "They thought I might fall over something in the hallway," he recalls, "but they never offered to guide me through that hallway obstacle course a time or two."

Thomas Maske, disabled as a teenager by polio, knows most of the world's airline routes by heart, as his job with an agricultural supply firm in Wheeling, Illinois, requires almost constant foreign travel. Nonetheless, some airlines, citing safety factors, have refused to accept Mr. Maske as a passenger unless he flies with a companion. Other airlines have stored—and sometimes damaged—his wheelchair in aircraft luggage compartments after refusing to store it in the passenger cabin. Mr. Maske has threatened to go to court on both counts. He now flies alone and carries a special Federal Aviation Administration permit for passenger cabin storage of his wheelchair.

Barbara A. Hoffman, a clinical psychologist with a successful private practice in Houston, Texas, works primarily with brain-damaged children but is seldom invited to share her expertise with other psychologists at professional meetings. She has cerebral palsy. Conference planners assume, falsely, that she also has a speech impairment, a condition often associated with the disease. "I have learned not to waste my time showing my genuine interest in community projects," Dr. Hoffman says, "because the doors are closed to handicapped persons."

John Lancaster, a 1967 Notre Dame graduate, went to Viet Nam as a Marine Corps second lieutenant. Wounded in action, he came home paralyzed from the waist down. Despite his disability, he returned to college and earned a law degree. Looking back, he says that was the easy part. Finding a job was harder.

"I looked pretty good on paper," Mr. Lancaster says, "but when I showed up for an interview in a wheelchair, that was usually the end of it. I applied to more than 40 companies and government agencies before I finally landed a job."

Today Mr. Lancaster is director of Barrier-Free Design for Paralyzed Veterans of America.

Source: "It's a New Day for Disabled People," HEW Task Force on Public Awareness and the Disabled, *American Education,* December 1977, unpaginated.

main at home and in the community. Today there is greater concern for *normalization* of disabled persons. Normalization means that regardless of the severity of their disabilities, handicapped individuals should have the opportunity to live as much like other citizens as possible. For example, their homes should be located in regular residential communities and should resemble other homes in the community.[34] The advancement of educational techniques, physical therapies, and medical technologies has also made it possible for more persons to live independently. But while it seems logical from both humanistic and cost-savings perspectives, the normalization of the handicapped has met with serious problems. Although the trend has been toward normalization, consider these ten barriers which handicapped people continue to face:

> The existence of large residential facilities which provide minimal care at low cost without emphasis on rehabilitation.
>
> Lack of access to buildings; other architectural barriers.
>
> Lack of public transportation facilities.
>
> Negative attitudes among professional persons who do not believe that handicapped persons can function at a normal level.
>
> Negative attitudes of the general public.
>
> Community rejection of people with problems.
>
> Negative attitudes of professional people toward an establishment they believe is unconcerned.
>
> Negative attitudes by employers.
>
> The professionals and the public do not always understand each other's language making it difficult to arrive at solutions.
>
> Lack of manpower and resources to change the community.[35]

Mainstreaming

One issue faced by handicapped children, their families and their communities is *mainstreaming*. Mainstreaming requires that handicapped children be placed and taught in regular public school programs whenever possible rather than in separate schools or in separate classrooms. The Education for All Handicapped Children Act of 1975 states that every disabled child is entitled to an "appropriate elementary and secondary education." If a child must be placed in a private school by the local education authority in order to obtain an appropriate education, this service must be provided at no cost. Other services, including transportation and special devices, must also be provided. About $1 billion is appropriated annually for the program in the form of a block grant, with additional funds provided for supportive activities.

Some people hail mainstreaming as a sensible and effective way to insure that physically and mentally handicapped children are afforded the opportunity to learn and to interact with other children. In this way they are not made to feel more different than need be, and "normal" children learn how much they have in common with these "special" children. Children who are mainstreamed may attend some special classes, and their teachers in regular classrooms are assisted in developing educational programs to meet the needs of their handicapped pupils.

However, like other social policies and programs, mainstreaming is not without conflicts. An individual education program must be developed for each child, and parents have the right to participate in the development of these programs. Unfortunately, there is the possibility that these educational programs will not be carried out for students and that they will be left in regular classrooms without special assistance because of lack of time and resources. Others believe that the regular classroom teacher is already overburdened. Teachers who want to be helpful may have large classes and heavy workloads which prevent individualized instruction. Although Congress has appropriated only 30 percent of the funds that could be expended under the act, the House Education and Labor Committee reported in 1985 that 633,000 more handicapped children were receiving a public-school education.[36]

Developmental Disabilities Program

The Developmentally Disabled and Bill of Rights Act of 1975 (PL 94-103) is one piece of federal legislation authorizing a broad range of services for the disabled. Each state operates a developmental disabilities (DD) program and receives federal funds to insure that developmentally disabled individuals receive habilitation and other necessary services.[37] "The goal of the program is to improve the quality of services through comprehensive planning, coordination of resources, and developing programs to fill gaps in services."[38] Developmental disabilities are defined as "severe, chronic disabilities attributable to mental and physical impairment, which are manifested before age 22, result in substantial functional limitations in several areas of life, and require services over an extended period."[39] Like many other programs for the disabled, the DD program varies among states and communities.

Other services are targeted at specific disability groups. For example, every state has either a commission to serve the blind or a special unit in its vocational rehabilitation offices to assist blind persons. Throughout the country there are about fifty-five schools providing education and training specifically to blind children at the kindergarten through twelfth-grade levels. At the federal level the Deafness and Communicative Disorders Branch of the Rehabilitation Services Administration provides consultation to the states in developing services for those who are deaf or have other communication disorders. It also works on developing technological devices to assist handicapped persons. Sixty-two schools in the U.S. provide residential programs for deaf children from infancy through high school. In 1972 the Economic Opportunity Act was amended to include a goal that 10 percent of Head Start enrollees be handicapped children.

A Bill of Rights for the Handicapped

Strides have been made in integrating handicapped and disabled persons into society. In many cases, these strides have been made through the persistent political efforts of the handicapped and their families. Title V of the Rehabilitation Act of 1973 is an example of these accomplishments. All programs and facilities, such as schools and hospitals, receiving federal funds must comply with these rules:

1. Federal agencies must have affirmative-action programs to hire and promote qualified handicapped persons.
2. The Architectural and Transportation Barriers Compliance Board is charged with enforcing a 1968 law requiring that all buildings constructed in whole or in part with federal funds—as well as buildings owned or leased by federal agencies—have ramps, elevators, or other barrier-free access for persons who are blind, deaf, in wheelchairs, or otherwise disabled. More recently the board's activities have been expanded to include communication barriers.
3. All businesses, universities, foundations, and other institutions holding contracts with the U.S. government must have affirmative-action programs to hire and promote qualified handicapped persons.
4. Discrimination against qualified disabled persons—employees, students, and receivers of health care and other services—in all public and private institutions receiving federal assistance is prohibited.[40]

There are offices of civil rights in the Department of Education and the Department of Health and Human Services which have responsibility for enforcing federal laws that prohibit discrimination against handicapped persons.

But although restaurants, stores, and other establishments may choose to provide easy access for the handicapped, this so-called bill of rights for the handicapped does little to encourage private-sector participation. Suitable living environments are also difficult to find. For the wheelchair-bound, many apartment complexes and housing developments are not equipped with extrawide doorways or appliances that can be easily reached. Even if the individual can afford to make such changes in an apartment, permission must be granted by the owner. Many of the points contained in this bill of rights are still goals to be achieved. Negative attitudes and prejudices, while sometimes blatant, are often subtle and difficult to overcome.[41] The rewards of providing for the integration of handicapped persons may not be apparent; and so, people do not bother.

Access for the Handicapped

In recent years almost everyone in the United States has become familiar with the blue-and-white symbol of a person in a wheelchair shown in figure 5-1. In a parking lot it means that certain parking spots are reserved for handicapped drivers. On a building door it means that handicapped persons can move about in the building independently. On a restroom door it means that stalls are equipped with hand rails and raised toilets so that handicapped persons can use the facilities more easily.

Several steps have been taken to promote access for handicapped persons. In 1968 the Architectural Barriers Act adopted specifications aimed at making buildings accessible and safe for the blind, the deaf, and the

FIGURE 5-1
International symbol of access for the handicapped.

wheelchair bound as well as those with other handicaps. Making buildings accessible for the handicapped sounds like an expensive proposition, but one writer argues that the cost to the builder is only "one-tenth of one percent of the total cost of a new building."[42] The results of the legislation are far from adequate. Most buildings fall short of meeting the standards for restrooms, parking lots, doors, and warning signals.

The Federal Aviation Administration had mandated that all U.S. airlines develop policies access and services for the handicapped, but the Supreme Court recently said that ". . . airlines may discriminate against the disabled because a federal law protecting the rights of the handicapped does not apply to air travelers."[43] Most commercial airlines do not receive direct federal aid. However, Amtrak, the federally subsidized rail system, is taking steps so that all new cars will have facilities for the handicapped. There are many more public-policy issues that involve handicapped persons. The rights to refuse treatment and to informed consent, guardianship, treatment when accused of crimes, voting rights, and zoning restrictions on community residences are some that remain on the public agenda.[44]

GENERAL ASSISTANCE: THE STATE AND COMMUNITY RESPONSE TO WELFARE

Most major social policies and programs today are totally or partially the responsibility of the federal government. But there are some social welfare programs which are developed, administered, and financed by state and local governments, independent of the federal government. The term used to describe state and local financial aid to the poor is *General Assistance.*

General Assistance programs are administered differently from state to state and even from one locality to another. The types and amounts of services vary as well as the types of recipients served. In some states, the state government is entirely responsible for administering General Assistance. The state determines the policies and procedures for General Assistance, and state workers accept applications and provide assistance to recipients. However, in other states, the state sets policy and determines eligibility requirements, but General Assistance is administered through local governments—usually cities or counties. In still other states, the state government has no involvement in General Assistance. Local governments are free to establish General Assistance programs if they desire. If not, there may be no General Assistance available in a community. In other words, General Assistance programs are highly discretionary.[45]

Why is General Assistance needed when there are a number of federally mandated and funded programs designed to assist persons who are aged, blind, disabled, and dependent? General Assistance exists because the United States uses a fragmented approach to social welfare needs. *Some poor people do not meet the criteria for any of the major federal or federal-state welfare programs.* They may not be aged or blind or disabled, and they may have no dependent children. They may need immediate assistance, unable to wait for federal benefits which may take thirty days or more to begin. In other words, to qualify for most welfare programs, simply being "needy" is not always enough.

While most Americans have heard of the AFDC, Food Stamp, and Medicaid programs, General Assistance is not as well known. In some places it is referred to as "county aid" or "county welfare." Some programs provide cash assistance. Others rely on in-kind assistance. Some programs use a combination of the two. In some areas the bulk of aid is for medical costs.

General Assistance may provide help to persons who receive public assistance payments from federal or federal-state welfare programs because their payments are low and may be inadequate to cover an emergency. But in half of the states, SSI and AFDC recipients are not eligible for General Assistance. Others have received General Assistance because of advanced age, disability, unemployment, or as a supplement to very low wages.[46] Those who receive General Assistance are usually in dire circumstances. In communities which provide General Assistance, aid is often available on a short-term basis only. However, one study of twenty General Assistance programs indicated greater emphasis on meeting "continuing basic needs,"[47] and another study indicates that it is "unlikely that General Assistance plays a large role in covering emergency assistance and special needs at the local level."[48] Information on General Assistance should be interpreted cautiously because there are no federal regulations requiring reporting and because "record keeping is notoriously lax."[49]

When Congress passed the Social Security Act in 1935, General Assistance expenditures decreased sharply from almost $1.5 million in 1935 to about $450,000 in 1936.[50] Since then the amount states and communities have spent for General Assistance has fluctuated, but today expenditures are approximately $1.5 billion.[51] In 1950 the average monthly benefit per household was $47. In 1970 it was $108. Today about one million households receive an average of $160 a month.

ILLUSTRATION: GENERAL ASSISTANCE IN IOWA

ITEM	CHARACTERISTIC
	A. General Description
1. Type of program	General Assistance (General Relief) is administered by the 99 counties. Criteria of eligibility, amount of aid given, and dura-

	tion of aid vary among the counties and may not be consistent within a county. In about one-fourth of the counties the responsibility is given to an "Overseer of the Poor."
2. Most common uses	Generally provided on a short-term basis. Need pending categorical public assistance,* emergency needs for food, shelter, utility payments, medical and transportation, and, in many counties, to meet need for prescription drugs.
	B. Conditions of Eligibility
3. Definition	Applicants are considered on an individual basis. Aid is not limited to unemployables; however, employable persons are urged or required to register for employment.
4. Residence	Must reside in county for one year to gain legal settlement. General Assistance usually provided without regard to settlement; however, the county may bill the county in which applicant has legal settlement. Migrants and transients are given emergency assistance or referred to other available resources.
5. Citizenship	No requirement.
6. Employment and employability	Most counties will assist a family with an employed or employable person when the employed person is temporarily disabled or there is some other emergency basis.
7. Property limitations	Some counties follow AFDC-SSI guidelines. Some are less restrictive where the need is a medical one.
8. Lien and limitations	County may recover amount expended (1) from legally responsible relatives, (2) from the person himself within two years after he becomes able to repay such amounts, or (3) from estate of the person by filing claim as provided in statute.
9. Other	About half the counties have no other conditions. Others will not assist an SSI or AFDC recipient, but most will assist a person eligible for, but not receiving, AFDC or SSI. Some will provide assistance in an emergency to AFDC or SSI recipients.
	C. Standards of Assistance and Payment
10. Standards of assistance	Varies a great deal. Some counties use the AFDC-SSI standards as guidelines, but each county is free to vary the assistance given.

11. Limitations on payment	Usually given on a temporary basis; limitations on amount and duration vary among the counties.
12. Method of providing assistance	*Maintenance Items:* Usually a vendor payment. Some counties give cash assistance. *Medical care:* Vendor payments. Often hospital care at University of Iowa hospitals. General Assistance medical care is not covered under the State Medicaid program.
	D. Administration
13. State agency	No state agency responsibility for general assistance.
14. Local agency	County Boards of Supervisors in one-fourth of the counties place the responsibility with an "Overseer of the Poor." In three-fourths of the counties, the responsibility is delegated to the local office of the Department of Social Services.
15. Financing	General Assistance is paid out of county funds in the same manner as other county disbursements.

*The General Assistance program may make emergency or short-term payments to an individual or family that is applying for AFDC or SSI but whose application is pending approval.

ILLUSTRATION: GENERAL ASSISTANCE IN ARIZONA

ITEM	**CHARACTERISTIC**
	A. General Description
1. Type of program	General Assistance is administered by the Arizona Department of Economic Security throughout the six districts; in effect uniformly in all districts but not on Indian reservations. Two programs (1) General Assistance and (2) "Emergency Relief." (Characteristics of these two programs in subsequent entries are identified by these numbers.) The same agencies administer the federal-state public assistance programs.
2. Most common uses	(1) Response to any kind of need of an eligible individual. (2) Emergency situations pending receipt of categorical assistance,* short-term assistance to meet temporary need, transportation of nonresidents to place of legal residence, purchase of food stamps on emergency basis.
	B. Conditions of Eligibility
3. Definition	(1) General Assistance covers "either permanently or temporarily disabled, totally

	or partially"; couples, and nonfamily individuals. (2) "Emergency Relief" covers dire emergency needs for employable persons or families.
4. Residence	(1) If a person is present in the state and intends to remain, he or she is a resident. (2) *Nonresidents:* may be aided in emergency situations only, pending return to place of legal residence. *Transients or migratory labor:* aided only in emergency situations.
5. Citizenship	(1) must be a citizen of United States, a resident in United States for 15 years, or a legally admitted alien. (2) Not applicable to emergency situations.
6. Employment and employability	No requirements.
7. Property limitations	(1) Limitations on property holdings generally the same as for AFDC.
8. Lien and recovery	No lien provision. Recovery made only when there is fraud or ineligibility.
9. Other	None.
	C. Standards of Assistance and Payments
10. Standards of assistance	Same as for AFDC
11. Limitations on payment	(1) The assistance grant will be equal to the standard budgetary need amount multiplied by the percentage of need factor for which funds are available (80%), less income. (2) The payment is limited to $100 for one adult plus $25 for each additional individual. No emergency assistance for more than three months in any twelve-month period may be issued.
12. Method of providing assistance	*Maintenance items:* (1) Monetary payment to recipient, by warrant each month. (2) Monetary payment to meet "emergency needs . . . within the limits specified above." *Medical care:* None
	D. Administration
13. State agency	Arizona Department of Economic Security through its local county offices has administrative responsibility.
14. Local agency	District offices of the Department of Economic Security (6). Does not cover persons living on Indian reservations.

*General Assistance is provided to persons who have applied for AFDC or SSI and are waiting for payments to begin.

Source: *Characteristics of General Assistance in the United States,* 1978 edition, Department of Health, Education and Welfare, Social Security Administration, Office of Family Assistance, HEW publication no. (SSA) 78-21239.

Welfare and the New Federalism

American federalism—the constitutional division of power between the national government and the states—affects the administration and financing of social welfare programs. The major public assistance programs in the United States (AFDC, SSI, Medicaid, Food Stamps, and General Assistance) are administered and funded in different ways. AFDC and Medicaid are joint ventures of the federal and state governments, which share in funding the programs, but the states play a major role in determining eligibility requirements and payment levels. The Food Stamp and SSI programs are to a great extent controlled by the federal government, which finances minimum benefits and establishes basic eligibility requirements. The states may supplement basic SSI benefits, and many do. SSI checks are mailed directly to recipients by the Social Security Administration. Food stamps are generally distributed through state and local welfare offices. General Assistance is a highly discretionary type of program and is the only major public assistance program funded and administered by state and/or local governments with no federal participation. Most social service programs, like mental health and child welfare, are jointly funded by the federal and state governments. The federal government sets broad guidelines, and the states have responsibility for administering the programs.

Since President Reagan took office, debate over the appropriate approach to federalism in social welfare programs has taken on new vigor. Prior to the Reagan presidency, the trend in welfare programs was toward greater centralization or federalization of welfare programs, but President Reagan has been successful in returning more power to the states. He has consolidated hundreds of smaller categorical grants into nine large block grants covering health, mental health, and other social services.

Block-grant proponents claim that most welfare concerns are issues that belong to the states rather than the federal government, and they look at the cost savings of block grants as evidence that these measures work. Critics agree that block grants have indeed resulted in cost savings, but they contend that the savings have hurt those who need services. Others believe that there is not even much evidence of savings.[52] States have responded in different ways to the reduced funding. Some states have used more of their own monies to fund needed social services, but others have responded by replacing more expensive services with less expensive ones.[53] A case in point is Texas, which ". . . lowered its average daily cost for day care from $10.87 to $8.15 under the new Social Services Block Grant, when it was able to drop from its requirements proposed federal standards on staff-pupil ratios and staff training requirements."[54] In this case, the ironic result was that Texas was able to decrease total day-care spending while simultaneously increasing the number of children reached![55]

SUMMARY

Two major types of assistance are available to the aged, blind, and disabled: public assistance and rehabilitative services. The major cash assistance program for these groups is the Supplemental Security Income (SSI) program.

In 1972 Congress passed legislation that federalized the adult categorical assistance programs—Old Age Assistance, Aid to the Blind, and Aid to the Permanently and Totally Disabled under the SSI program. SSI has been one of the major innovations in providing welfare benefits to Americans since the original Social Security Act became law in 1935. Under SSI states no longer directly administer the adult categorical programs. The federal government now sets minimum payment levels and eligibility requirements for beneficiaries. The states may supplement payments. These changes helped to reduce inequitable treatment of recipients from state to state. SSI was the only portion of President Nixon's welfare-reform package that Congress passed.

One of the largest social service programs for the disabled is the Vocational Rehabilitation (VR) program, but it is a limited program because not everyone who is disabled is entitled to assistance. The primary criterion for participation is the individual's potential for returning to work. In the case of a homemaker, there must be potential to return to caring for the home. The VR program has been accused of creaming—taking on the clients who are most easy to rehabilitate while the more severely disabled may have to do without services.

Individuals with physical and mental handicaps face a number of obstacles in achieving independence. Some of the more severely handicapped are housed in large institutions with little chance of realizing their maximum potential. In other cases, community rejection, lack of transportation, and lack of access to buildings and other facilities prevent the disabled from interacting in society. Laws designed to eliminate structural and architectural barriers from buildings have not been very successful in removing many obstacles faced by the handicapped.

Handicapped children face as many problems as handicapped adults. Mainstreaming, an attempt to include handicapped children in as many regular school activities as possible, has met with resistance. Mainstreaming sounds like a good idea, but in practice handicapped children may not receive the attention they deserve. Proponents of mainstreaming believe that children are more likely to achieve their maximum potential if they are not made to feel different from other children by being isolated all day in special classrooms.

Title V of the Rehabilitation Act of 1973 prevents programs and agencies that receive federal funds from discriminating against the handicapped in terms of access, employment, and education. It is referred to as a "bill of rights for the handicapped." Many services to the handicapped are provided under the Developmentally Disabled and Bill of Rights Act of 1975.

Another program which helps the poor, aged, disabled, dependent children, and the unemployed is called General Assistance. General Assistance programs are solely funded and administered by state and local governments. There is no federal involvement in these programs. Administration of General Assistance varies from state to state and from community to community. Eligibility criteria and payment levels also differ considerably. In some cases, General Assistance is used as unemployment relief and as a means for assisting those who do not qualify for other welfare programs.

In many cases, it is used to help the indigent with medical expenses. Aid may be limited to emergency situations and is often short-term. Some communities have no General Assistance program at all.

There is a lack of consensus about the best methods for funding and administering welfare programs. While some believe that the federal government is best suited to perform these functions because of its large revenue base and its ability to treat recipients equally regardless of the state in which they live, others feel that welfare is a concern of the states. The president has been successful in consolidating many categorical grants into block grants, giving the states greater control over social welfare decisions. However, the amount of funds available under block grants has been reduced from previous spending levels, and critics contend that block grants have been used by the administration more as a means of cutting government spending than as a method of providing better welfare services. Americans cannot agree on the best arrangements for delivering social welfare services.

NOTES

1. For a discussion of available resources see Garry D. Brewer and James S. Kakalik, *Handicapped Children: Strategies for Improving Services* (New York: McGraw-Hill, 1979).
2. John G. Turnbull, C. Arthur Williams, Jr., and Earl F. Cheit, *Economic and Social Security* (New York: Ronald Press, 1967), p. 83.
3. Ibid.
4. Robert J. Myers, *Social Security* (Bryn Mawr, Pa: McCahan Foundation, 1975), p. 400.
5. Ibid.
6. Ibid., pp. 400–401.
7. Ibid., p. 401.
8. Ibid.
9. Bureau of the Census, *Statistical Abstract of the United States, 1965* (Washington, 1965), p. 309.
10. Daniel P. Moynihan, *The Politics of a Guaranteed Income* (New York: Random House, 1973).
11. *Future of Social Programs* (Washington: Congressional Quarterly, 1973), p. 15.
12. For a description of state supplementation programs see Donald E. Rigby and Elsa Ponce, *The Supplemental Security Income Program for the Aged, Blind, and Disabled, Selected Characteristics of State Supplementation Programs as of January 1982*, Department of Health and Human Services, Social Security Administration, SSA publication no. 13-11975, rev. March 1983.
13. The following paragraphs in this section are based on Department of Health and Human Services, Social Security Administration, "A Guide to Supplemental Security Income," January 1984 Edition, SSA publication no. 05-11015.
14. Ibid., p. 6.
15. Ibid.
16. Ibid., p. 12
17. Department of Health and Human Services, Social Security Administration, *Social Security Bulletin* 47, no. 1 (January 1984), p. 18.
18. John A. Menefee, Bea Edwards, and Sylvester A. Schieber, "Analysis of Nonparticipation in the SSI Program," *Social Security Bulletin* 44, no. 6 (June 1981), pp. 3–21.

19. John Trout and David R. Mattson, "A 10-Year Review of the Supplemental Security Income Program," *Social Security Bulletin* 47, no. 1 (January 1984), pp. 3–24.
20. John L. Palmer and Isabel V. Sawhill, eds., The Reagan Record (Cambridge, Mass.: Ballinger, 1984), p. 378.
21. Department of Health and Human Services, Social Security Administration, "Deficit Reduction Act of 1984: Provisions Related to the OASDI and SSI Programs," *Social Security Bulletin* 47, no. 11 (November 1984), p. 7.
22. Trout and Mattson, "A 10-Year Review."
23. This list was taken from Jane Mullins and Suzanne Wolfe, *Special People Behind the Eight-Ball: An Annotated Bibliography of Literature Classified by Handicapping Conditions* (Johnstown, Pa.: Mafex Associates, 1975).
24. Saad Z. Nagi, "The Concept and Measurement of Disability" in Edward D. Berkowitz, ed., *Disability Policies and Government Programs* (New York: Holt, Rinehart & Winston, 1979), p. 2; and Shirley Cohen, *Special People: A Brighter Future for Everyone with Physical, Mental, and Emotional Disabilities* (Englewood Cliffs, N.J.: Prentice-Hall, 1977), p. 8.
25. Monroe Berkowitz, William G. Johnson, and Edward H. Murphy, *Public Policy toward Disability* (New York: Holt, Rinehart & Winston, 1976), p. 7.
26. Nagi, *Concept and Measurement of Disability,* p. 3.
27. "It's a New Day for Disabled People," HEW Task Force on Public Awareness and the Disabled, *American Education* (December 1977).
28. Edward D. Berkowitz, "The American Disability System in Historical Perspective," in Berkowitz, *Disability Policies,* p. 43.
29. Berkowitz et al., *Public Policy toward Disability,* p. 34.
30. Ibid.
31. Information in this paragraph comes from *Statistical Abstract of the Unites States, 1984,* p. 392.
32. Berkowitz, *Disability Policies,* p. 45.
33. Ibid. Cites FBVE, "Administration of the Vocational Rehabilitation Program," bulletin 113, rev. under imprint of the Department of Interior, Office of Education (Washington, Government Printing Office, 1938).
34. B. Nirje, "The Normalization Principle," in R. Kugel and A. Shearer, eds., *Changing Patterns in Residential Services for the Mentally Retarded 231,* 1976, cited in Bruce Dennis Sales, D. Matthew Powell, and Richard Van Duizend and Associates, *Disabled Persons and the Law, State and Legislative Issues* (New York: Plenum Press, 1982), p. 310.
35. Roberta Nelson, *Creating Community Acceptance for Handicapped People* (Springfield, Ill.: Charles C. Thomas, 1978), pp. 12–22.
36. Barbara Coleman, "Education for Handicapped Seen as Policy Success Story," *Congressional Quarterly,* November 16, 1985, pp. 2375–78.
37. Information in this section is based on Office of Information and Resources for the Handicapped, Department of Education, "A Pocket Guide to Federal Help for the Disabled Person," September 1983, publication no. E-83-22002.
38. "Pocket Guide," p. 1.
39. Ibid.
40. "New Day for Disabled People."
41. Ibid.
42. Cohen, *Special People,* p. 132.
43. "Court Allows Discrimination Against Disabled Air Travelers," *Austin American-Statesman* (June 27, 1986), p. A6.
44. For an extensive consideration of these issues and others, see Sales et. al., *Disabled Persons and the Law.*
45. Joel F. Handler and Michael Sosin, *Last Resorts, Emergency Assistance and Special Needs Programs in Public Welfare* (New York: Academic Press, 1983).
46. For a discussion of how General Assistance has been used, see Duncan M. MacIntyre,

Public Assistance: Too Much or Too Little? (Ithaca, N.Y.: New York State School of Industrial and Labor Relations, Cornell University, 1964), p. 51.

47. Urban Systems Research and Engineering, *Characteristics of General Assistance in Twenty States* (Cambridge, Mass.: Urban Systems Research and Engineering, 1978); cited in Handler and Sosin, *Last Resorts.*
48. Handler and Sosin, *Last Resorts,* p. 94.
49. Ibid., p. 81.
50. *Statistical Abstract, 1943,* p. 193.
51. *Social Security Bulletin, Annual Statistical Supplement, 1983,* p. 255.
52. Palmer and Sawhill, *Reagan Record,* p. 17.
53. Ibid.
54. George E. Peterson, "Federalism and the States," in Palmer and Sawhill, *Reagan Record,* p. 245.
55. Ibid.

chapter 6

Assisting poor families: aid to families with dependent children

Aid to Families with Dependent Children (AFDC) is one of the most controversial of the public assistance programs. The purpose of AFDC is to provide cash assistance to poor families so that children can continue to be cared for in their own homes. If there is any segment of society for whom people have compassion, it is for children, who are completely dependent on others to meet their needs. Why, then, has the AFDC program been a political tug of war? The political controversy has focused less on the millions of dependent children served by the program and more on the *adult* beneficiaries.

THE DEVELOPMENT OF AFDC

Mothers' Aid

A dependent child, in terms of public assistance programs, is one whose parents or guardians lack the financial assistance to provide for the child's care. The states began formalizing laws to assist such children in the early twentieth century, with local governments often providing the financing. These laws were established to assist children whose fathers were deceased; sometimes assistance was also provided to children whose fathers were disabled or absent through divorce or desertion. These early programs were called *mothers' aid* or *mothers' pensions.*

ADC

The federal government stepped in to share responsibility for dependent children in 1935, when the Aid to Dependent Children (ADC) program was included as part of the original Social Security Act. At first the

ADC program was conceived of as a short-term device to assist financially needy children. It was intended that the program would diminish and eventually become *outmoded* as more and more families came to qualify for assistance under insurance programs of the Social Security Act.[1] "The program began," as Daniel P. Moynihan puts it, "as one whose typical beneficiary was a West Virginia mother whose husband had been killed in a mine accident."[2] But the emphasis of the early ADC program was not on providing aid for the wives of deceased workers; it was on providing assistance to mothers on behalf of their *children*.

Keeping the Family Together

From 1935 until 1950 the ADC program grew slowly. There were some changes made in the program, but they did not arouse much public notice. The needs of the adults in ADC families were eventually considered when in 1950 adult heads of families were also made eligible for ADC assistance. Other improvements were made in the program. Medical services, paid in part by the federal government, were made available to recipients. In 1958 a formula was developed so that states with lower per capita incomes received more federal financial assistance for their ADC programs than wealthier states.

But other parts of the program were becoming sore spots. One of the most stinging accusations leveled against the ADC program was that it contributed to the desertion of fathers from families. While the argument has been difficult to prove empirically,[3] we can see how the concern arose. Under the ADC program, families that had an able-bodied father residing at home were not eligible for benefits. In many cases, unemployed fathers qualified for other types of assistance—unemployment compensation, disability insurance, or Aid to the Permanently and Totally Disabled. But it was also possible that the father did *not* qualify for any of these programs or had exhausted his benefits. In other words, some fathers fell through the cracks. The unemployed, able-bodied father who could not find work did not qualify for ADC and could not support his family. However, if the father deserted the home, the family became eligible for ADC assistance. It is not known how many fathers did this. Fathers (or mothers) may be absent for many reasons. They may be in institutions or separated from their spouses because of incompatibility or other reasons. But regardless of the reason for absenteeism, when a father was at home and unemployed, the family could not receive ADC.

As a result, two changes were made in the ADC program. In 1961 a new component called the ADC-Unemployed Parent (UP) program was enacted. This made it possible for children to receive aid because of their parent's unemployment. In 1962 the name of the program was changed to Aid to Families with Dependent Children (AFDC) to emphasize the *family* unit. A second adult was considered eligible for aid in states with AFDC-UP programs and also in cases where one of the child's parents was incapacitated.

In 1967 the AFDC-UP program was changed to the AFDC-Unemployed Father (UF) program, but in 1979 the Supreme Court ruled that it was unconstitutional to provide benefits to unemployed fathers but not to unemployed mothers. The name of the program was changed back to the AFDC-UP program.

Since the AFDC-UP and UF programs were never made mandatory, states have been free to accept or reject them. Even today only half of the states have an AFDC-UP program. Eligibility requirements are strict, and the number of fathers who receive aid remains very small.

A review of studies of state AFDC-UP programs does not show that these programs are associated with increased marital stability. In fact, evidence points in the opposite direction.[4] However, studies of AFDC payments show that "while there is some support for high AFDC payment levels being a marriage destabilizer, there is very little support for its being a powerful destabilizer."[5] The relationship of the AFDC program to family stability remains a troublesome issue.

Man-in-the-House Rules

The number of able-bodied fathers who might receive welfare assistance is one area of public concern over the morality of welfare recipients. The work ethic is firmly entrenched in American culture. According to this ethic, no one who is capable of self-support should be entitled to public benefits.

This concern about the morality of welfare recipients was reflected in "man-in-the-house rules." It was clear that only in extreme circumstances, and only in certain states could able-bodied fathers be present while the family collected AFDC benefits. And before 1962 no able-bodied father could be present. These rules about fathers also carried over into welfare mothers' relationships with other men. The thought of welfare mothers allowing able-bodied men to reside with them presented a threat to those who wanted to insure that payments went to the "right" people. The AFDC check was intended for the *children* and their *mother,* and in some cases, the children's *father*. It was considered immoral and *illegal* for the mother to allow anyone else to benefit from the welfare check. "Midnight raids"—home visits to welfare mothers late at night—were sometimes conducted to insure that no able-bodied males resided in AFDC households. An able-bodied adult male who resided with the family was considered responsible for its financial support. Today midnight raids are considered unethical by most professional standards.

Making Parents Pay

In 1968 the Supreme Court determined that man-in-the-house rules could not be used as a method for "flatly denying" children public assistance. The emphasis today has shifted to methods of making children's *legal* fathers and mothers support their dependents. In 1974 federal law was amended for the purpose of enforcing child-support obligations owed by absent parents to their children by locating absent parents, establishing paternity, and obtaining child support. Concerns regarding these measures arose because of the rising number of children dependent on AFDC who are born to parents who are not legally married. Few absent parents of children receiving AFDC contribute to their children's support. The Office of Child Support Enforcement in the Department of Health and Human Services is responsible for this program.[6] The states see that the enforcement program is carried out under federal guidelines.

The Child Support Enforcement Amendments of 1984 have made it tougher for parents to avoid making child-support payments. Sentiments regarding the new measures were so strong that the bill passed both houses of Congress unanimously. In addition to AFDC families, the amendments extend assistance to all families in which children need financial support from their noncustodial parents. Under the new provisions, states establish procedures to (1) garner (withhold) a parent's wages if support payments are at least thirty days overdue, (2) impose liens against the delinquent parent's income, real estate, and other property, and (3) intercept federal and state income tax refunds. Judges across the country have also taken issue with delinquent parents, and many are resorting to jailing parents who fail to comply. Some communities print the names of nonsupporting parents in local newspapers.

WHO RECEIVES AFDC?

There are many misconceptions about the beneficiaries of AFDC. Here are some facts about AFDC families.[7]

1. Almost 79 percent of all AFDC families are headed by one parent, usually the mother. Only about 7 percent are headed by two parents. The remaining 14 percent of child recipients do not live with either parent but live with guardians or foster parents.
2. Contrary to common belief, AFDC families are usually small, and the trend is toward even smaller families. The average AFDC family has two children. Almost 68 percent of all AFDC families have one or two children while only 8 percent have five or more children.
3. The children in most AFDC families have fathers who do not live with the family and provide limited financial support, if any. Almost 34 percent of AFDC children have parents who are not married to each other.
4. Most (93 percent) AFDC children live with their mothers. Only 13 percent live with their fathers. Few AFDC children live with both parents. In many cases (41 percent) the father cannot be located, but only 2 percent of the mothers cannot be located.
5. Fourteen percent of all AFDC mothers are working full or part time. The primary reason that AFDC mothers are not working is that they remain at home to care for their small children. Many fathers (39 percent) receiving AFDC are unable to work because of mental or physical disability.
6. Most AFDC parents who have worked or are working are employed in blue collar and service jobs, rather than in professional jobs.
7. Young families are more likely to receive AFDC than older families. Most mothers (51 percent) are under age thirty and 8 percent are teenagers. Fathers tend to be older.

8. Thirty-five percent of AFDC children are five years of age or younger. This fact accounts for the large number of AFDC mothers who remain at home in order to care for their children.
9. Most AFDC families live in rented housing. Fifteen percent of all families rent public housing and 64 percent rent private housing. Only 10 percent own or are buying their own homes.
10. AFDC families move often. Forty-five percent have lived at their current address one year or less and 2 percent for two to five years. Only 12 percent have been at the same address six years or more.
11. Not all AFDC families receive food stamps, even though they are automatically eligible to participate in the Food Stamp program. Seventy-four percent of the recipients receive food stamps.
12. AFDC families are more likely to live in urban rather than rural areas. Fifty-six percent of all families live in central cities.
13. Similar numbers of black and white families receive AFDC. Whites comprise 41 percent of all recipients; blacks comprise 43 percent. An additional 12 percent are Hispanic. One percent are Native Americans.

In addition, it is important to note that the majority of these families are not on AFDC caseloads year after year. Receiving AFDC tends to be a short-term phenomenon. The Department of Health and Human Services reports that 25 percent of cases are closed within a six-month period and almost one-third within the first year. Half are closed within two years and three-fifths within three years.[8]

AFDC AND WORK

Historically, Americans have been unwilling to provide money and services to those who are able to work. This feeling is evident in the AFDC program. There have been two major approaches to encouraging adult AFDC recipients to work: (1) rehabilitating the poor for work and (2) job training and assistance in securing jobs.

Rehabilitation for Work

In 1962 social service amendments were added to the AFDC and other public assistance programs as a means of "rehabilitating" the poor. The rehabilitation approach was designed to reduce poverty by treating personal and social problems which stood in the way of financial independence.[9] Services included counseling, vocational training, child-management training, family-planning services, and legal services. States found a bonus in providing social services to clients. Offering social services meant that states received additional federal funds. For every dollar spent by the states, the federal government matched it with three dollars. States were criticized for claiming federal funds for many of the services they were already providing to clients.[10] To insure the success of the social service amendments, worker caseloads were to be small—no more than sixty clients—but it was difficult to find enough qualified social workers to provide services.[11] What had sounded good in theory could often not be put into practice.

Job Training and WIN

By 1967 enthusiasm for the rehabilitation approach to helping welfare clients began to fade. The approach had not been a booming success; welfare rolls continued to climb. A new approach was needed, and the chosen approach was tougher; the theme of the 1967 amendments was *work*, and both "carrot" and "stick" measures were employed to achieve this purpose.[12] The "stick" included work requirements for unemployed fathers on AFDC, as well as for mothers and some teenagers. The "carrot" was the Work Incentive Now (WIN) program, established by Congress to train recipients for work and to help them locate employment. The federal government threatened to deny federal matching funds to states that paid benefits to able-bodied recipients who refused to work or receive job training.

Other measures were also taken to encourage recipients to work. According to the "thirty plus one-third rule," welfare payments were not reduced for the first $30 of earned income, and one-third of all additional income was disregarded in determining eligibility until the limit on earnings was reached. Day-care services were provided for WIN participants, but in some cases shortages of licensed day-care facilities prevented placements for children while their mothers worked or trained for jobs. And the cost of working—clothes, transportation, and child care—often outweighed what the mothers earned.

Nonetheless, the AFDC rolls continued to climb. In other words, strategies aimed at encouraging welfare recipients to work did not produce the results that rational planners had intended. Perhaps the failure of these approaches had much to do with the fact that AFDC recipients may not have earned enough in marginal, low-income, or minimum-wage jobs to make work a rational alternative for them after deducting child care, transportation, and other work-related expenses. Short-term training programs generally do not enable recipients to substantially increase their earning capacities. Moreover, some recipients have disabilities or handicaps—mental, physical, or both—that do not allow them to work or to earn enough to support themselves. Some welfare recipients are forced to survive on a combination of "a little work and a little welfare."

Workfare

The WIN program remains in operation today, although funds have been reduced. President Reagan has attempted to get rid of WIN and to replace it with "workfare" (mandatory employment in return for welfare payments), but Congress has not complied fully. Federal law now permits states to operate workfare programs, but few have done more than test workfare on a pilot basis.[13] Workfare is certainly not a new concept. In its most punitive forms, the workhouses of the Elizabethan period and similar institutions in the United States fit under the rubric of workfare.[14]

Workfare is a controversial issue. Some believe that after three hundred years of various forms of workfare programs, both experience and empirical evidence indicate they have failed to improve the job skills of participants; they have failed to reduce the costs of welfare; they do not discourage malingering because the number of malingerers receiving welfare is already negligible; and welfare recipients who can would gladly take jobs if decent ones were available.[15] However, some positive findings about workfare programs may begin to change the attitude that these programs are inherently punitive. Funded by the Ford Foundation, studies by the nonprofit Manpower Demonstration Research Corporation show positive preliminary findings from programs in five states. Results differ from state to state, but in general, work participation by welfare recipients has increased, and recipients and employers have voiced support for the programs. It is true that the skill level of recipients has not been upgraded, but there is optimism that the work experience may prove to be valuable in competing for jobs in the regular labor market.[16]

One new job program that has received good press is the Massachusetts Employment and Training Program, which is called ET. Welfare recipients register for work, but they have options. Those who choose to participate in ET may decide between career counseling, education and training, on-the-job training, and job placement. Although Massachusetts has one of the highest AFDC payment levels, participation in ET is high. Those who participate in training get day-care services for a year, and their Medicaid benefits are assured for fifteen months. Employers do not know that these participants are welfare recipients. Initial results have been promising, saving the state millions of dollars and placing many people in jobs. ET offers flexibility to welfare recipients. It is based on the idea that welfare recipients are responsible individuals. A mandatory, more punitive approach to work programs is unlikely to produce the same success.[17] Future results of workfare and other job programs are likely to get serious attention from both liberals and conservatives concerned about welfare reform.

Separating Payments and Services

When social services were first introduced as a means of helping welfare recipients overcome obstacles to financial independence, the AFDC caseworker was responsible for seeing that the family got its benefit check and its social services. In fact, AFDC mothers may have feared that if they did not accept social services offered or urged by the caseworker, benefits might be terminated.

In 1967 Congress chose to separate the provision of social services to AFDC recipients from the issuance of benefit checks. A payments worker was responsible for matters related to the distribution of the welfare check, while another worker was responsible for obtaining social services for the recipients. This approach was based on the recognition that not all poor families are necessarily in need of social services, since poverty may be attributable to a variety of causes. The 1967 amendment was also aimed at eliminating some AFDC families' feelings that they must accept social services from the AFDC caseworker in order to receive their financial benefits. Families who wished to receive social services were still entitled and encouraged to do so.

GROWTH OF THE AFDC PROGRAM

The growth of welfare programs is generally measured by three factors: the number of program recipients, the total costs of the program, and the benefits received by each recipient. During the 1960s and 1970s the number of AFDC families rose sharply. As the rolls swelled, so did the total costs of the program, but today the number of families has stabilized, and so have program costs. Average payments have not grown as rapidly. Once inflation is taken into account, it is easy to see that payments have not begun to keep up with the cost of living.

Number of Recipients

ADC was originally designed as a short-term program to help dependent children whose deceased or disabled fathers were ineligible for Social Security insurance benefits. As more fathers became eligible for Social Security benefits, the need for the AFDC program was supposed to diminish. However, it did not turn out that way. AFDC is now more than fifty years old, and the number of families receiving assistance has grown dramatically (see figure 6-1). For example, in the ten-year period between 1968 and 1978, the number of families doubled. Considering the number of individuals receiving AFDC as a percentage of the total U.S. population, we see that in 1950 the group amounted to 1.5 percent; by 1970 the proportion had reached 4.7 percent; and at its peak it was 5.3 percent. Today 3.6 million families (10.5 million individuals) are supported in whole or in part through AFDC payments. The large number of families dependent on AFDC is directly related to the increase in the number of children who do not receive financial support from their fathers.

Increasing Costs

AFDC costs grew incrementally during the first thirty years of the program, but during the 1960s and 1970s they escalated rapidly. In 1940 the total costs were $133 million; by 1960 they were $750 million; but by 1980 they had risen to $12.5 billion. Even after controlling for inflation, costs spiraled. Today they are about $13 billion. Rising expenditures were a consequence of the large numbers of new families who joined the rolls during the "welfare-rights movement," a period of increased awareness of the needs and demands of the poor. Program expenditures are likely to remain stable at this time unless eligibility requirements are tightened further or drastic alternatives are considered.

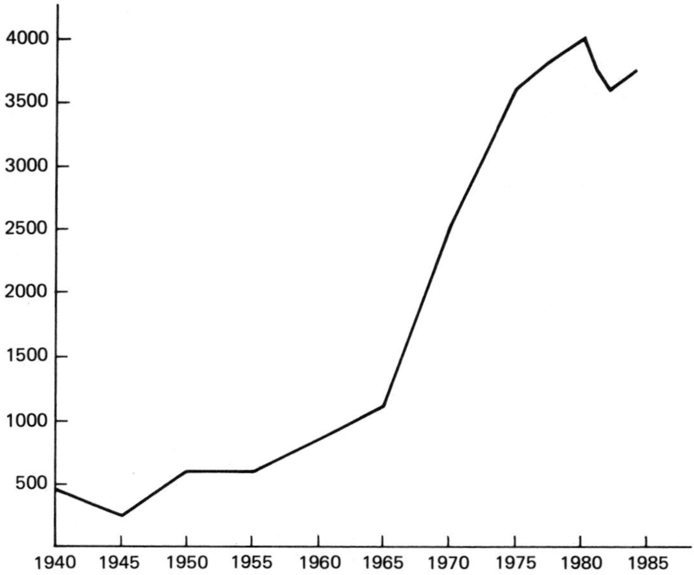

FIGURE 6-1 Aid to Families with Dependent Children Program, number of recipient families in thousands, 1940–84. (Sources: Bureau of the Census, *Historical Statistics of the United States, Colonial Times to 1970* [Washington: 1975], p. 356; *Statistical Abstract of the United States, 1977,* p. 345; *1981,* p. 343; *1984,* p. 393; *Social Security Bulletin* 48, no. 2 [February 1985], 56; and John L. Palmer and Isabel V. Sawhill, eds., *The Reagan Record,* Cambridge, Mass.: Ballinger Publishing Co., 1984, p. 363.)

Monthly Payments and the Cost of Living

Rising costs in the AFDC program might lead us to believe that payments to AFDC families have also increased, but this is not really the case. In 1963 the average AFDC family received $122 per month; by 1978 this payment had more than doubled to $250. But after controlling for inflation, AFDC recipients had no more purchasing power than they had in 1963. At the present time, AFDC payments average $310 monthly. More people have access to AFDC, but in the light of inflation, public assistance payments to AFDC families have not changed very much.

There is also a great deal of variation from state to state in AFDC payments (see figure 6-2). California has one of the highest payment levels—an average of $416 per month for a family. Texas is one of the lowest at $105. In other words, a recipient family in California is likely to receive four times more than a recipient family in Texas. Even taking into consideration differences in the cost of living between the two states, the difference in payments is great. Each state determines its payment levels in a seemingly rational manner. The costs of food, shelter, and other necessities are calcu-

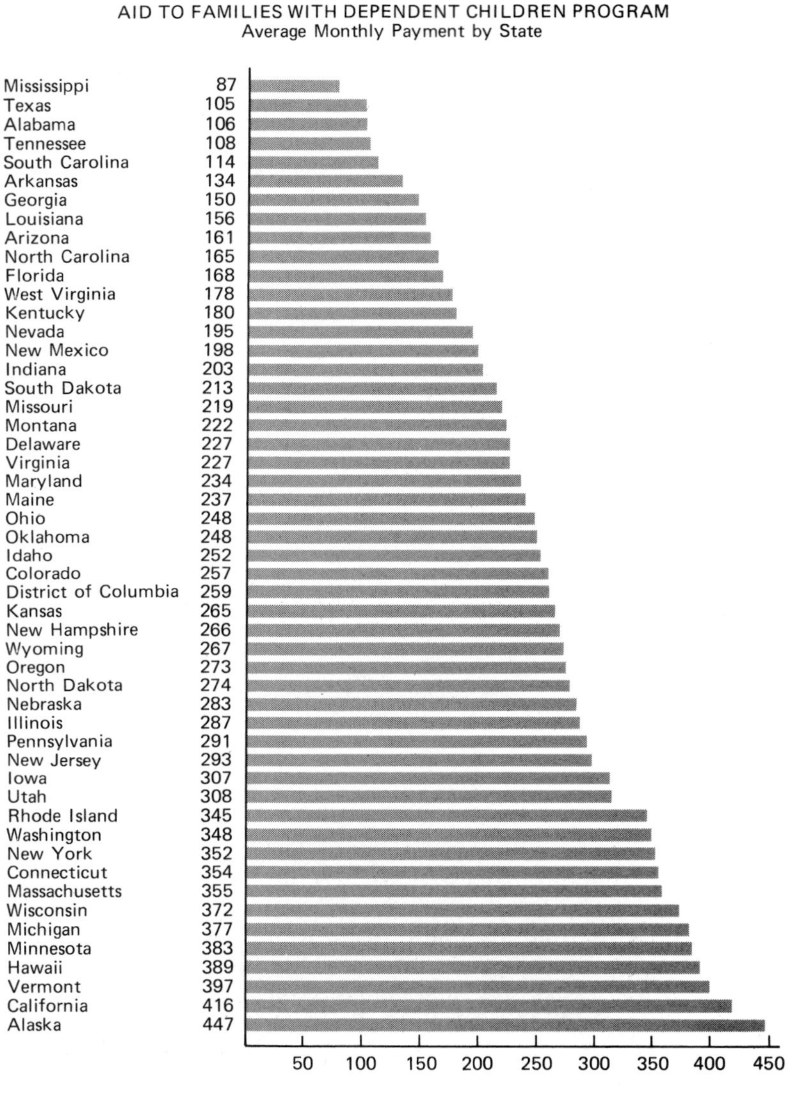

FIGURE 6-2 Aid to Families with Dependent Children Program, average monthly payment by state. (Source: Bureau of the Census, *Statistical Abstract of the United States, 1984* [Washington: 1983], p. 395.)

lated according to family size. The figure obtained is called the *standard of need,* but a number of states pay recipients less than the minimum standard of need, and the standard might stay the same for several years before adjustments are made, even though the cost of living has risen. Cost-of-living increases are not automatic in the AFDC program; state legislatures must vote to increase payments.

ILLUSTRATION: APPLYING FOR AFDC

Most Americans have never seen an AFDC application nor will they ever know what it is like to apply for public assistance. Application procedures and forms have been simplified over the years to make it easier to apply. In addition, because AFDC recipients are also eligible for Medicaid and food stamps, some states use a combined application form for the three programs. Florida's combined application form, a twelve-page application, is reproduced as an example of what it is like to apply for welfare. (See figure 6-3).

Applying for welfare is a cumbersome and sometimes uncomfortable process. After providing basic information—name, Social Security number, and address—the applicant is informed of the rights of AFDC recipients. Applicants are assured that they will not be discriminated against because of race, color, sex, age, handicaps, religion, national origin, or political belief. They are also told that they will be informed of whether or not they are eligible for assistance within thirty days and that they may request assistance in completing the application form.

There are also a number of responsibilities of AFDC recipients. Recipients must notify the public assistance office of any changes in income, employment, assets, family composition, and living arrangements. They must register for the Work Incentive Program unless exempt from work requirements. In addition, a controversial responsibility of applicants is that they cooperate in establishing paternity and obtaining child support unless there are reasons, such as a threat of physical harm to the child, the custodial parent, or the caretaker, which do not make this feasible. Providing incomplete or false information on the application may be punishable by fine, imprisonment, or both.

Information must be provided about each child for whom aid is requested, including the reason why the child is considered to be "deprived." Detailed information must also be provided about where the family resides and the amounts and types of living expenses. An individual's assets are also carefully considered since there are limitations, which vary from state to state, on the amount of assets an individual can possess while remaining eligible for AFDC. Sources of income must also be specified as must information about the work of those fourteen years of age or older for whom assistance is requested.

Applying for public assistance requires more than filling out an application form. It also requires evidence of expenses and income through rent and utility receipts, pay statements, and other documentation. The applicant must also agree to an investigation. The application states that the public assistance office has the right to "contact anyone necessary to determine the assistance group's eligibility for public assistance." A review of the application procedure makes it easier to see that applying for welfare can be a disconcerting process.

Applicants' expectations may also make a difference in the eligibility process. Qualified applicants may not be aware that it may be several weeks before payments begin. Applicants may be upset or angry when they are not able to receive on-the-spot payments or when they are deemed ineligible. Other factors also enter into the application process. The applicant may not come prepared with the proper documentation. The atmosphere of the waiting room and the treatment of applicants by the receptionist and the AFDC eligibility worker are also important considerations in the conduct of eligibility interviews. AFDC applicants are generally under stressful conditions when they come in to apply. Eligibility workers also find their jobs stressful as evidenced by their high turnover rates. Making the eligibility process better for both clients and workers is a challenge to those concerned about improving the welfare system.

REAGAN AND AFDC

Like other presidential administrations, the Reagan team is committed "to determine welfare needs more accurately, improve program administration, reduce fraud and abuse, and decrease federal and state costs."[18] In order to do this, the administration has implemented the following changes in the AFDC program: (1) counting the income of stepparents in determining a child's eligibility; (2) limiting deductible child-care costs and other work-related expenses; (3) limiting the thirty plus one-third rule to four months; (4) improving the states' efforts at child-support enforcement; (5) requiring states to determine eligibility based on previous actual income. Some changes reflect a desire to eliminate from the welfare rolls near poor recipients, especially those with some potential to work.

The Reagan policies have been especially harsh on AFDC recipients. As many as five hundred thousand families have been removed from the program.[19] Researchers at the University of Michigan's Institute for Social Research claim that changes in the AFDC program have plunged millions of children deeper into poverty.[20] According to their figures, in Michigan alone, seventeen thousand families were declared ineligible and another nineteen thousand families suffered sharp reductions in benefits following the Reagan initiatives. Interviews were conducted with three hundred mothers whose payments were terminated. Nearly half reported running out of all food; 42 percent were at least two months in arrears paying bills; 16 percent had had their utilities shut off; and 11 percent were without telephone service. They were using various methods to survive. Almost half got old produce from groceries, and one-fifth collected bottles and cans for refunds.

DO WELFARE RECIPIENTS REALLY WANT TO WORK?

Some people argue that many welfare recipients could work if they "really wanted to." However, many welfare recipients are not capable of regular, full-time employment. The largest group of AFDC recipients is children. The mothers of these children also comprise a considerable portion of those who receive benefits. Many of these women do not work because they must care for their young children; some are too ill, physically or mentally, to hold jobs; and many also lack the skills to earn a wage which is adequate to support their children. Recipients of other welfare programs, such as SSI, are too old or too disabled to hold jobs in today's labor market.

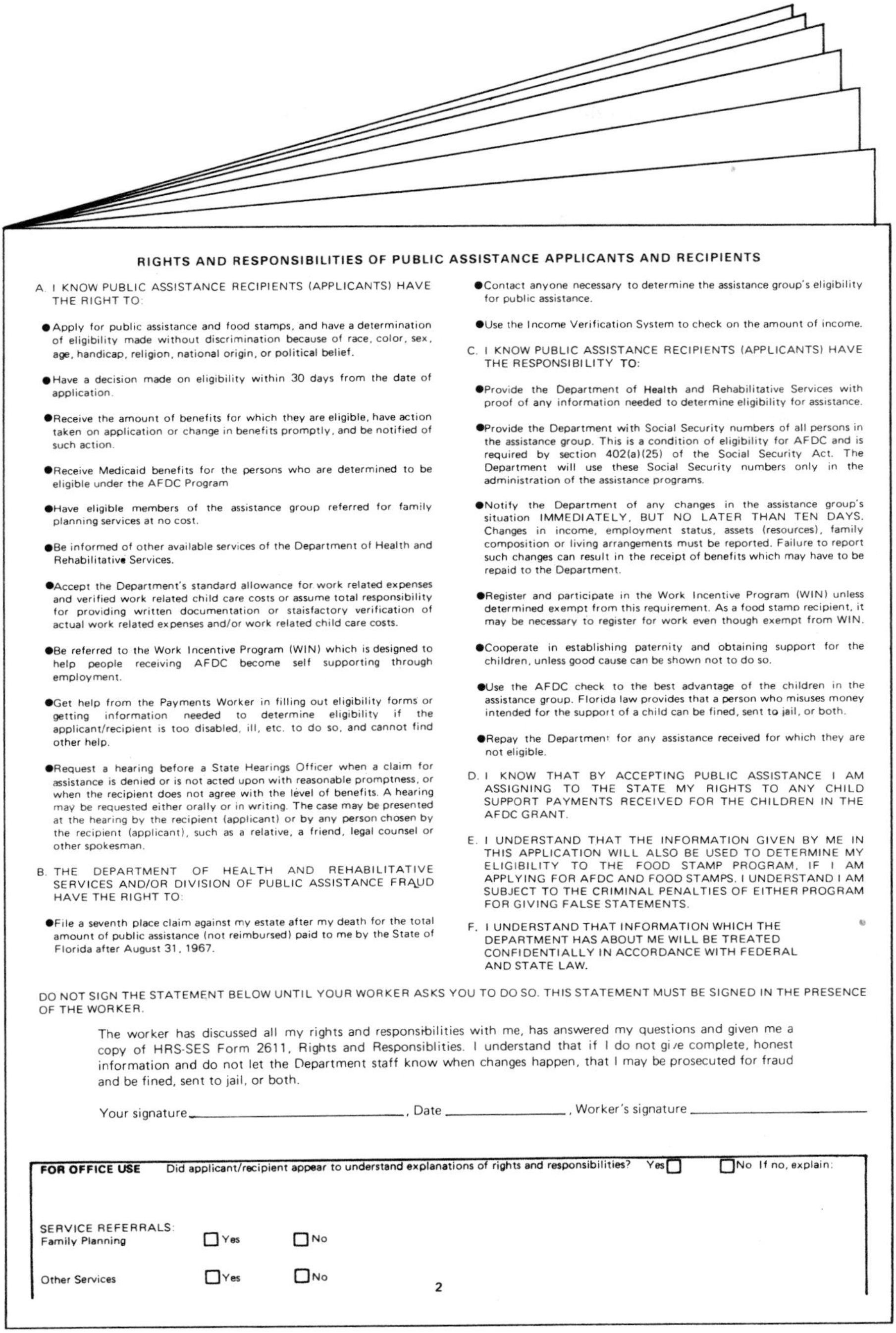

RIGHTS AND RESPONSIBILITIES OF PUBLIC ASSISTANCE APPLICANTS AND RECIPIENTS

A. I KNOW PUBLIC ASSISTANCE RECIPIENTS (APPLICANTS) HAVE THE RIGHT TO:

- Apply for public assistance and food stamps, and have a determination of eligibility made without discrimination because of race, color, sex, age, handicap, religion, national origin, or political belief.
- Have a decision made on eligibility within 30 days from the date of application.
- Receive the amount of benefits for which they are eligible, have action taken on application or change in benefits promptly, and be notified of such action.
- Receive Medicaid benefits for the persons who are determined to be eligible under the AFDC Program
- Have eligible members of the assistance group referred for family planning services at no cost.
- Be informed of other available services of the Department of Health and Rehabilitative Services.
- Accept the Department's standard allowance for work related expenses and verified work related child care costs or assume total responsibility for providing written documentation or staisfactory verification of actual work related expenses and/or work related child care costs.
- Be referred to the Work Incentive Program (WIN) which is designed to help people receiving AFDC become self supporting through employment.
- Get help from the Payments Worker in filling out eligibility forms or getting information needed to determine eligibility if the applicant/recipient is too disabled, ill, etc. to do so, and cannot find other help.
- Request a hearing before a State Hearings Officer when a claim for assistance is denied or is not acted upon with reasonable promptness, or when the recipient does not agree with the level of benefits. A hearing may be requested either orally or in writing. The case may be presented at the hearing by the recipient (applicant) or by any person chosen by the recipient (applicant), such as a relative, a friend, legal counsel or other spokesman.

B. THE DEPARTMENT OF HEALTH AND REHABILITATIVE SERVICES AND/OR DIVISION OF PUBLIC ASSISTANCE FRAUD HAVE THE RIGHT TO:

- File a seventh place claim against my estate after my death for the total amount of public assistance (not reimbursed) paid to me by the State of Florida after August 31, 1967.
- Contact anyone necessary to determine the assistance group's eligibility for public assistance.
- Use the Income Verification System to check on the amount of income.

C. I KNOW PUBLIC ASSISTANCE RECIPIENTS (APPLICANTS) HAVE THE RESPONSIBILITY TO:

- Provide the Department of Health and Rehabilitative Services with proof of any information needed to determine eligibility for assistance.
- Provide the Department with Social Security numbers of all persons in the assistance group. This is a condition of eligibility for AFDC and is required by section 402(a)(25) of the Social Security Act. The Department will use these Social Security numbers only in the administration of the assistance programs.
- Notify the Department of any changes in the assistance group's situation IMMEDIATELY, BUT NO LATER THAN TEN DAYS. Changes in income, employment status, assets (resources), family composition or living arrangements must be reported. Failure to report such changes can result in the receipt of benefits which may have to be repaid to the Department.
- Register and participate in the Work Incentive Program (WIN) unless determined exempt from this requirement. As a food stamp recipient, it may be necessary to register for work even though exempt from WIN.
- Cooperate in establishing paternity and obtaining support for the children, unless good cause can be shown not to do so.
- Use the AFDC check to the best advantage of the children in the assistance group. Florida law provides that a person who misuses money intended for the support of a child can be fined, sent to jail, or both.
- Repay the Department for any assistance received for which they are not eligible.

D. I KNOW THAT BY ACCEPTING PUBLIC ASSISTANCE I AM ASSIGNING TO THE STATE MY RIGHTS TO ANY CHILD SUPPORT PAYMENTS RECEIVED FOR THE CHILDREN IN THE AFDC GRANT.

E. I UNDERSTAND THAT THE INFORMATION GIVEN BY ME IN THIS APPLICATION WILL ALSO BE USED TO DETERMINE MY ELIGIBILITY TO THE FOOD STAMP PROGRAM, IF I AM APPLYING FOR AFDC AND FOOD STAMPS. I UNDERSTAND I AM SUBJECT TO THE CRIMINAL PENALTIES OF EITHER PROGRAM FOR GIVING FALSE STATEMENTS.

F. I UNDERSTAND THAT INFORMATION WHICH THE DEPARTMENT HAS ABOUT ME WILL BE TREATED CONFIDENTIALLY IN ACCORDANCE WITH FEDERAL AND STATE LAW.

DO NOT SIGN THE STATEMENT BELOW UNTIL YOUR WORKER ASKS YOU TO DO SO. THIS STATEMENT MUST BE SIGNED IN THE PRESENCE OF THE WORKER.

The worker has discussed all my rights and responsibilities with me, has answered my questions and given me a copy of HRS-SES Form 2611, Rights and Responsiblities. I understand that if I do not give complete, honest information and do not let the Department staff know when changes happen, that I may be prosecuted for fraud and be fined, sent to jail, or both.

Your signature ________________, Date ________, Worker's signature ________________

FOR OFFICE USE Did applicant/recipient appear to understand explanations of rights and responsibilities? Yes ☐ ☐ No If no, explain:

SERVICE REFERRALS:

Family Planning ☐ Yes ☐ No

Other Services ☐ Yes ☐ No

2

FIGURE 6-3 Part of AFDC application.

ILLUSTRATION: AID TO FAMILIES WITH DEPENDENT CHILDREN IN OHIO

The fifty state Aid to Families With Dependent Children (AFDC) programs vary in their administration, eligibility requirements, standards of need, assistance payments, and optional programs. In this illustration we take a look at how Ohio operates its AFDC program.

ADMINISTRATION

State Agency: The Ohio Department of Public Welfare is the state agency which supervises the administration of the AFDC program.

Local Agency: There are eighty-eight county Departments of Public Welfare that administer AFDC. Directors of the county departments are appointed by the county commissioners.

Financing: The state provides 40.6 percent of the assistance costs from general funds. Local funds cover 4 percent of the costs. The federal government pays the remaining 55.4 percent of the costs.

ELIGIBILITY

Eligible Persons: Children with insufficient income and resources to provide support and care requisite for health and decency are eligible. Other eligible persons may be the parent or caretaker relative with whom the child resides and the second parent in the home if one parent is incapacitated or is the unemployed principal wage earner.

Age: Dependent children must be under age nineteen. A child who is eighteen must be a full-time student in secondary school or receiving the equivalent level of vocational or technical training and expect to complete the program before reaching age nineteen.

Pregnancy: A pregnant woman with no other children may be eligible for an AFDC grant for one adult plus a $20 special-needs allowance if her pregnancy is verified. Coverage may not begin until the sixth month of pregnancy.

Employment: Participation in WIN is mandatory for adult recipients unless an individual is exempt. Exemptions are provided in several cases such as the need to care for a child under age six.

Community Work Experience Program*: The program is operating in five counties. All recipients nineteen to sixty-five years old must participate unless exempt because they are ill or incapacitated or meet certain other conditions such as care of a child under six or another member of the immediate family or attendance in an approved educational, vocational, or rehabilitation program. Exempt recipients may volunteer to participate.

Income and Resources: In determining eligibility, work expenses up to $75 may be disregarded from the monthly earned income of each person employed thirty-five or more hours per week, and up to $50 may be disregarded from the earned income of those who work fewer hours. Actual costs of care up to $160 for each child or incapacitated adult is disregarded from the income of persons working thirty-five or more hours, and $120 is disregarded for persons working fewer hours. Stepparent income is considered in determining payments. Property disregarded in determining eligibility is the homestead, the equity value of an automobile not exceeding $1,200, personal effects and household furnishings of limited value that are essential to basic day-to-day living, and other property, which may not exceed a total of $1,000 equity value.

ASSISTANCE PAYMENTS

Needs Standards: Basic needs include food, clothing, household supplies, shelter, utilities, personal-care items, laundry, school supplies, and recreational expenses. The state has determined that the full standard of need for a caretaker and one child is $430, and for a caretaker and two children, $537.

Methods of Limiting Payment: The state does not meet the full amount of the needs standard. The reduced standard is 49 percent of the full standard of need.

Payment: In cases where the family has no countable income, the basic-needs payment to AFDC families composed of a needy caretaker relative and one child is $216 and for two children is $263.

OPTIONAL PROGRAMS

Unemployed Parent: A parent is considered unemployed if the number of hours worked is less than one hundred per month. Unemployed parents register with WIN and the Bureau of Employment Security.

Emergency Assistance: Emergency assistance is available when children are without resources to meet immediate needs. Emergencies include the need for food, clothing, shelter, or medical care and needs arising from natural and civil disasters and unexpected, unavoidable financial crises. Payments can be made for delinquent rent in case of threatened eviction or utility bills in the case of shut-off. The maximum payment for necessary items is $300.

*This is a form of workfare.

Source: Adapted from *Characteristics of State Plans for Aid to Families With Dependent Children,* 1984 ed. Department of Health and Human Services, SSA Publication no. 80-21235, pp. 215–20.

Several researchers have concluded that welfare benefits, such as a guaranteed income, do *not* reduce the incentive to work,[21] but others, including some economists, do not view the problem in the same way. For example, earning even a small amount of money may result in the termination of Medicaid payments. Take the case of a near-poor working family with a chronically ill child that receives Medicaid benefits. Once the family reaches its limit of earnings, its Medicaid benefits are completely stopped. The family is forced to decide whether to continue working and face catastrophic medical bills *or* "go on welfare" so medical benefits will be provided to their child. There is little tapering off of benefits as earnings increase.

Economist Martin Anderson believes that these practices have created a "poverty wall" in America.[22] The poverty wall is the disincentive to work created by the structure of the welfare system in the United States.

Anderson believes the way to tear down the poverty wall is to adopt a welfare plan that would provide *only* for the needy and would include clearly defined *work requirements*.

But recent reforms of the Reagan administration may have increased disincentives to work. According to Rosemary Sarri of the Institute for Social Research, limitations on the thirty plus one-third rule punish women willing to take low-paying, undesirable jobs and give payments to those who do not work.[23] Consider the following illustration provided by researchers at the Urban Institute:

> [A] working AFDC mother with three children earning $450 a month (a below-poverty-level wage) in an average-benefit state would previously have received a monthly AFDC benefit (in 1984 dollars) of about $230; her benefits now have been reduced to about $50 per month after four months of employment.[24]

This means a reduction in total income of $180. Such policies do little to encourage employment. As Sarri says, this "defies rational public policy."[25] However, according to some researchers, "people removed from the welfare rolls appear to be continuing to work even when they might be better off quitting their jobs and reapplying for government assistance."[26]

TRYING TO REFORM WELFARE

There is widespread agreement that the welfare system in the United States is in urgent need of reform, but there is little agreement on how reform should take place.

One small step that has been taken through the Internal Revenue Service to provide relief to low-income families is the *earned-income credit*. Families with incomes below $11,000 may qualify. The maximum payment is $550, and the amount received is based on a percentage of the family's income. A family that paid no income taxes or paid taxes less than the amount of the credit may still qualify if other conditions are met. Families expecting to receive the earned-income credit in the next calendar year may get it in advance by requesting that it be included in the worker's regular paycheck.

Many proposals for major welfare reform center around the concept of a guaranteed annual income or a negative income tax. Examples of these proposals are Milton Friedman's negative income tax plan and President Nixon's Family Assistance Plan. Negative income tax and guaranteed annual income plans are based on the premise that welfare reform has not worked. The current welfare system could be replaced by a negative income tax which would guarantee everyone a minimum income and encourage recipients to work by allowing them to keep a portion of their earnings without severe reductions in benefits.

Each negative income tax or guaranteed annual income plan has its own set of procedures and requirements, but let us consider one example of how such a plan might work. Let us say that the guaranteed annual income for a family of four is set at $4,000 with an earnings deduction of 50 percent. A family with no income would receive $4,000. A family with $2,000 in earnings would receive a payment of $3,000 for a total income of $5,000. A family earning $6,000 would receive a payment of $1,000 for a total income of $7,000, while a family earning $8,000, the break-even point, would receive no payment. The program is a logical extension of the income tax system already in place in the United States. Everyone would file an income tax statement as they do today. Many citizens would pay taxes, but those at the lower end of the income scale would receive payments, or negative income taxes. Checks would be mailed through the U.S. Treasury Department as income tax refunds are mailed today. Since welfare applications, means tests, and other eligibility procedures would be eliminated, much of the welfare bureaucracy could be reduced.

But the United States has no practical experience with a guaranteed income or negative income tax. There is a possibility that near-poor persons would qualify for benefits and prefer accepting the guarantee. This threat to the work ethic is probably the greatest fear working against implementing such a proposal in the United States. Planners would need to estimate how many persons might qualify for payments at various levels. The plan would then be debated. A decision on payment levels, however, may be based not on what seems to be a fair standard of living but on how much decision makers believe the country can afford to make in guaranteed annual income payments.

In 1970 President Nixon proposed the Family Assistance Plan (FAP). The FAP, an example of a guaranteed income, was designed to address many of the problems of the welfare system: disincentives to work, discouragement of family life, inequities among the states, and discrimination against the working poor. "However, the FAP failed in Congress because of the combined opposition of those who felt it was too much welfare and those who felt it was not enough."[27] The problem of welfare reform is one example of how a rational approach to meeting the basic needs of Americans has failed. Americans have not been able to agree on who is poor, who should receive assistance, or what methods should be used to alleviate poverty. Until we agree on these questions, rational planning cannot take place. The policy process remains a series of political struggles over "who gets what, when, and how."

SUMMARY

Perhaps the most controversial of all the welfare programs is Aid to Families with Dependent Children. Most of the criticism is directed toward the adult beneficiaries of the program, who, some believe, are capable of "making it on their own." The first programs to assist dependent children were state mothers' aid programs. The federal government became involved as part of the 1935 Social Security Act. Midnight raids and man-in-the-house rules were used to insure that mothers were not "harboring" men who could support their children, but Supreme Court action has discouraged these practices.

Many Americans have an incorrect picture of the average AFDC family. AFDC families are usually small; most have only one or two children. There are about as many white AFDC recipients as black recipients, although blacks are overrepresented among the total. The majority of AFDC families stay on the program less than three years.

Various approaches have been used to get adult AFDC recipients to work. Rehabilitating AFDC recipients so that they could overcome personal problems which prevented them from being self-supporting was one method. Another method was job training and job development. But many adult AFDC recipients are the mothers of small children, day care is expensive, and these mothers may earn so little from what employment they can find that work programs may cost more than they are worth financially. Workfare programs offer another approach, but these programs are still in the experimental stage, so it is still too soon to know if they will make a difference.

AFDC caseloads and costs rose dramatically during the 1960s, the period called the "welfare-rights movement." Much of the growth was due to the increase in single-parent families, which are headed mostly by women. After controlling for inflation, it is not difficult to see that the purchasing power of AFDC recipients remains meager. AFDC caseloads have remained stable in the last few years and are not expected to grow much. Reforms of the Reagan administration have made it more difficult to qualify for payments, and payments vary considerably by state.

The question of whether welfare recipients "really want to work" has been the subject of much debate. Many people believe that the current system destroys the incentive to work, but others argue that if given the chance many welfare recipients would choose work over welfare. Disagreements over questions like the incentive to work have helped to bog down AFDC reform. Every president has taken his turn at welfare reform. In 1969 President Nixon proposed the Family Assistance Plan to guarantee all poor families a minimum income. The plan failed because liberals thought it was too little welfare and conservatives thought it was too much welfare. President Reagan has instituted cost-cutting measures in AFDC which have caused thousands of families to be removed from the rolls.

NOTES

1. Laurence E. Lynn, Jr., "A Decade of Policy Developments in the Income-Maintenance System," in Robert H. Haveman, ed., *A Decade of Federal Antipoverty Programs: Achievements, Failures, and Lessons* (New York: Academic Press, 1977), p. 60; and Martin Rein, *Social Policy: Issues of Choice and Change* (New York: Random House, 1970), p. 311.
2. Lynn, "Decade of Policy Developments," p. 73.
3. Gilbert Y. Steiner, *The State of Welfare* (Washington: Brookings Institution, 1971), p. 81.
4. John Bishop, *Jobs, Cash Transfers, and Marital Instability: A Review of the Evidence* (Madison, Wis.: Institute for Research on Poverty, University of Wisconsin, Madison). Written tes-

timony to the Welfare Reform Subcommittee of the Committees on Agriculture, Education and Labor, and Ways and Means of the U.S. House of Representatives, October 14, 1977, p. 9.

5. Ibid., p. 8.
6. *Paternity Determination: Techniques and Procedures to Establish the Paternity of Children Born Out of Wedlock,* Department of HEW, Office of Child Support Enforcement, April 30, 1977.
7. *Aid to Families with Dependent Children: A Chartbook.* Department of HEW, Social Security Administration, Office of Policy, Office of Research and Statistics, HEW publication no. (SSA) 79-11721, 1979.
8. *Welfare Myths vs. Facts,* Department of HEW, Social and Rehabilitation Service (SRS) 71–127.
9. Steiner, *State of Welfare,* p. 36; and Lynn, "Decade of Policy Developments," pp. 62–63.
10. Donald Brieland, Lela B. Costin, Charles R. Atherton, and contributors, *Contemporary Social Work: An Introduction to Social Work and Social Welfare* (New York: McGraw-Hill, 1975), p. 100; Steiner, *State of Welfare,* p. 37.
11. Steiner, *State of Welfare,* p. 37.
12. Lynn, "Decade of Policy Developments," p. 74.
13. John L. Palmer and Isabel V. Sawhill, *The Reagan Record* (Cambridge, Mass.: Ballinger, 1984), p. 366.
14. Leonard Goodwin, "Can Workfare Work?" *Public Welfare* 39 (Fall 1981): 19–25.
15. Ibid.
16. Alan Otten, "Study in 5 States Indicates Workfare Is Going Smoothly," *Wall Street Journal,* January 9, 1985, p. 16.
17. Ellen Goodman, "Volunteer Workfare Program Proves Worth," *Austin American Statesman,* March 5, 1985, p. A11.
18. Office of Management and Budget, *A Program for Economic Recovery,* February 18, 1981 (Washington: Government Printing Office, 1981), pp. 1–11.
19. Palmer and Sawhill, *Reagan Record,* p. 364.
20. "AFDC Cuts Hurt," *ISR Newsletter,* University of Michigan, Spring/Summer 1984, p. 3.
21. U.S. Office of Economic Opportunity, "Preliminary Results of the New Jersey Graduated Work Incentive Experiment," February 18, 1970; and David Kershaw and Jerelyn Fair, eds., *Final Report of the New Jersey Graduated Work Incentive Experiment* (Madison: University of Wisconsin, Institute for Research on Poverty, 1974).
22. The statement of Professor Martin Anderson of the Hoover Institution at Stanford University in *How to Think about Welfare Reform for the 1980s.* Hearings before the Committee on Public Assistance of the Committee on Finance, U.S. Senate, 96th Cong., 2nd sess., February 6 and 7, 1980.
23. "AFDC Cuts Hurt."
24. D. Lee Bawden and John L. Palmer, "Social Policy: Challenging the Welfare State," in Palmer and Sawhill, *Reagan Record,* p. 192.
25. "AFDC Cuts Hurt."
26. Palmer and Sawhill, *Reagan Record,* p. 25.
27. Thomas R. Dye, *Understanding Public Policy,* 3rd ed. (Englewood Cliffs, N.J.: Prentice-Hall, 1978), p. 131.

chapter 7

Providing social services: helping the mentally ill, children, and the elderly

DEFINING SOCIAL SERVICES

Social welfare programs are often equated with programs for the poor. But there are some social services that people may need regardless of their income and social status. Developing a list of all the social services provided in the United States is a major task, but such a list would include:

1. Day care and similar child-development and child programs (Head Start, family day care, group care for infants or for 3-to-5-year olds in centers, after school care, and so on)
2. Homemaker, home help, and chore services
3. Personal and family guidance and counseling, including marital counseling
4. Child welfare activities such as foster-home care, adoption, and protective services for neglected or abused children
5. Assessments for courts, schools, or camps of parental relationships (are parents neglectful? with which member of a separated couple should a child reside?) or of a child's personality and capacities (is he capable of adjusting to a normal group?)
6. Big Brother, Big Sister, and related volunteer helping and guidance efforts
7. Family planning services (advice, counseling, referral)
8. Community centers for the aged, for youth, for families
9. "Meals on wheels," nutrition, senior citizen programs, transportation, and special protective programs for the aged
10. A diversity of such group programs as therapeutic group work with adolescents, organization of tenants in a housing project, organization of the parents of retarded children

11. Home management counseling and educational activity, as well as home improvement services
12. Rural welfare programs and special programs for migrant laborers
13. Special programs to counsel potential migrants or immigrants and help them cope with new surroundings
14. Assistance to residents of poverty areas or members of underprivileged population groups, so that they may come together with mutual aid activity
15. Information, advice, referral, complaint, and advocacy services of many kinds
16. Institutional programs for the neglected, dependent, disturbed, or frail (state training schools, homes for the aged, adult homes, residential treatment for children, and so on)
17. Counseling, therapeutic, rehabilitation and education services for drug addicts and alcoholics
18. Social services in schools, hospitals, clinics, churches, industrial establishments, and other settings[1]

During their lifetimes, many Americans utilize the social services on this list.

WHO PROVIDES SOCIAL SERVICES?

Social services are provided by four types of organizations: (1) public agencies; (2) private not-for-profit corporations; (3) private profit-making corporations; and (4) self-help groups. Social services like day care are provided by several types of agencies. Other services, like child and adult protection, are provided by public agencies since these agencies have the legal right to intervene in cases where a child or adult might be the victim of neglect or abuse.

Public agencies are established by law and are operated by federal, state, or local governments. The Department of Health and Human Services is the major federal agency responsible for providing social services. Each state has a department which administers most of its social welfare programs, and some counties and cities also operate welfare agencies.

Private not-for-profit agencies, also called voluntary agencies, are governed by boards of directors or boards of trustees that are legally responsible for the agencies. These agencies may receive funds from donations, client fees, or government payments, such as grants or contracts. Private not-for-profit agencies provide a multitude of services, such as day care for children, mental-health services, and nursing-home care. Many of these agencies, such as community mental-health centers, charge fees to clients on a sliding scale, based on the clients' ability to pay for the services. Other not-for-profit agencies do not charge their clients. Socialization activities at senior citizen centers are often provided at no cost. Some not-for-profit corporations act as policy advocates for their clientele by lobbying policy makers and making them aware of their clients' needs. They may also educate the public about their clients' problems. The National Association of Retarded Citizens and its local affiliates, the Children's Home Society, and the National Council on Alcoholism are private not-for-profit agencies.

Private profit-making organizations are also called proprietary agencies. They too provide services like child care, nursing-home care, and mental health care, but private profit-making agencies charge their clients for services at the current market rate. Government agencies often purchase services from private agencies when they do not directly provide these services for their clients. For example, specialized medical services to disabled individuals are often purchased by the government from physicians engaged in private medical practices.

Self-help groups also provide social services but generally do not rely on governmental funding at all. The structure of self-help groups is less formal than other social service agencies. Alcoholics Anonymous is a self-help group which assists persons with drinking problems. The only requirement for membership is the desire to stop drinking. The group relies only on its members for support and does not accept outside contributions. Other self-help groups are Narcotics Anonymous, Gamblers Anonymous, and Parents Anonymous.

THE DEVELOPMENT OF SOCIAL SERVICES IN THE UNITED STATES

Before the 1900s, social services were historically provided by family members, neighbors, church groups, private charitable organizations, and local governments. State governments increased their involvement in social welfare services early in this century, when they began providing financial assistance and commodity foods to the destitute. The federal government did not become directly involved in financial and food programs until the 1930s. Other social welfare services remained largely outside the range of federal government activities until 1956 when the Social Security Administration encouraged Congress to amend the Social Security Act to provide social services to families on relief.[2]

The rationale for federal funding of social services was to rehabilitate the poor, help them overcome their personal problems, and thereby reduce their dependence on welfare. To carry out this plan, the federal government gave the states three dollars for every one dollar the states spent on social services. But this approach did not reduce poverty. Views on the causes of poverty have since changed. Today being poor does not necessarily imply a need for rehabilitation. In 1967 Congress officially recognized this position by separating welfare payments from social service provisions. Although welfare recipients are no longer expected to receive social services along with their checks, those services continue to be used by many clients.

Another development in the growth of social services has been the recognition that those who are not poor can also benefit from social services. The growth of public and private social service agencies which assist middle- and upper-class families, in addition to poor families, is an indication that mental health, family counseling, child guidance, and other types of social services can be useful to many Americans.

THE SOCIAL SERVICES BLOCK GRANT

The federal government's willingness to subsidize social services was a boon to the states that were willing to increase the amount of social services available to clients, but the costs of social services were rising so fast (from $282 million in 1967 to $1.7 billion in 1973)[3] that Congress decided to take action to curb spending. In 1976 Title XX was added to the Social Security Act to place a ceiling on expenditures and to insure that the majority of federally funded social services went to the poor. In 1981, the Reagan administration convinced Congress to replace Title XX with the Social Services Block Grant. Under this block grant, state matching requirements were eliminated, and the federal contribution to social services decreased. States can use these funds as they wish, and most of them go to assist the frail elderly residing at home and children of welfare mothers needing day care.[4] In fiscal year 1984 the federal government contributed $2.8 billion. According to some welfare experts, many states have reacted to federal spending reductions by appropriating more money for social services.[5]

Social services reach many types of people. The mentally ill, abused children, and the elderly are examples of social service beneficiaries who have gained increased attention since the 1960s. We have chosen to explore social welfare policy for these groups at greater length.

SOCIAL SERVICES FOR THE MENTALLY ILL

The first obstacle to rationalism in providing mental-health services is a lack of consensus about how to define mental-health problems. There is no single definition of mental illness.

Defining Mental Illness

Psychiatrists, mental-health workers, and the general public disagree about the definition of mental illness.[6] Mental health and mental illness may be thought of as two ends of a continuum. At one extreme are people who behave in an acceptable manner in the community. At the other extreme are psychotic persons who are unable to cope with reality and cannot function within the community. Depression is one common mental-health problem that can range from mild and temporary to depression so severe than an individual may become suicidal.

Everyone experiences emotional stress at some time in his or her life. For most, professional care is not needed, but today more emphasis is being placed on preventing mental-health problems. Mental-health professionals are as likely to see family members adjusting to a divorce or the loss of a loved one as they are to see the severely depressed, suicidal, or schizophrenic.

Most people needing assistance seek mental-health treatment voluntarily, but some persons with severe mental-health problems may not recognize their need for treatment. In these cases, state and local policies stipulate the conditions under which an individual may be judged mentally ill and in need of treatment. Involuntary admission to a mental-health hospital is generally reserved for persons who psychiatrists believe are dangerous to themselves or others and who may not perceive the need for treatment.

Estimating Mental-Health Problems

Although we cannot specifically define mental health or mental illness, estimates have been made of the numbers of persons who experience mental-health and related problems, such as alcohol and drug abuse. The federal government's Alcohol, Drug Abuse, and Mental Health Administration (ADAMHA) reports that:

> Recent surveys have shown that 15 and possibly 20 percent of American citizens need some form of mental health care in the course of a given year. There are today nearly 10 million adults with alcohol problems in the United States, plus an estimated 3.3 million youths having trouble related to alcohol abuse.[7]

Drug use among youths continues to be a serious concern. Although daily use of marijuana by high school seniors dropped from a high of 10.7 percent of students in 1978 to 7.0 percent in 1981, 17 percent of high school seniors have tried cocaine at least once.[8]

Only a small percentage of persons with mental-health, alcohol, and drug problems receive assistance. The ADAMHA reports that about one million people per year receive alcoholism treatment services in special programs for alcoholics. In addition, the general health-care sector assists another one-half million persons with alcohol-related problems. Approximately seven hundred thousand persons participate in Alcoholics Anonymous.[9] Yet these figures fall very short of the thirteen million adults and youths estimated to be directly harmed by alcohol problems. About one-half million persons receive drug-abuse services annually; mental-health services are provided each year to about seven million individuals.[10] While the number of persons who receive treatment for drug abuse and mental-health problems grows each year, many who are in need of treatment remain outside of the service-delivery system.

Discovering Mental Illness

The mentally ill were once thought to be possessed by the devil and were hidden away from public view, but by the nineteenth century treatment of the mentally ill began to take different forms. Phillipe Pinel, a French physician, introduced "moral treatment" for the mentally ill. Moral treatment consisted of treating the mentally ill with kindness and consideration, providing the opportunity for discussion of personal problems, and encouraging an active orientation to life.[11] Although this approach to treating mental illness sounded good, it was not the kind of treatment offered to most mentally ill persons.[12] For those who could not afford moral treatment, institutional treatment or incarceration was the general method of providing mental health care. Dorothea Dix, a social reformer during the mid-1800s, sought to improve the plight of severely mistreated mental patients. Dix succeeded in improving conditions within institutions for mental-health patients, but with the increasing numbers of persons being labeled mentally ill in the nineteenth century, institutions grew larger and larger and less capable of helping the mentally ill.

The Industrial Revolution intensified a number of social problems, including mental illness.[13] People came to the cities seeking jobs and wealth and instead found overcrowding, joblessness, and misery. Those migrating to the cities were often without support of family and friends, and coping with urban problems was difficult. Immigrants from other countries also flocked to the cities. Those who did not acculturate or assimilate quickly into American society were often labeled as deviant or mentally ill.[14] City dwellers, overwhelmed with problems, had little tolerance for what they considered deviation from normal behavior.[15] This increased the number of persons sent to mental-health institutions.

Apart from state institutions, there was little in the way of social policies and public programs for the mentally ill. Following Dix's efforts to reform mental institutions, Clifford Beers was responsible for introducing the "mental-hygiene movement" in the early twentieth century. Beers knew well the dehumanizing conditions of mental institutions; he himself had been a patient. Beers's efforts to expose the inhumane conditions of the institutions, like Dix's, resulted in better care, but the custodial and institutional philosophies of mental-health treatment continued.[16]

During World War II, a large number of young men were needed for military service. Part of the screening procedure for new recruits was a psychiatric examination. The number of young men rejected as unfit for military service or later discharged for psychiatric reasons was alarming. While the accuracy and methods of these psychiatric screening procedures have been criticized, the identification of so many young men with mental health problems brought about renewed concern for mental health.[17] This concern was reflected in the Mental Health Act of 1946. The act established the National Institute of Mental Health (NIMH), with its focus on training, education, and research.

In the 1950s another important development occurred in mental-health treatment—the discovery of improved psychotherapeutic drugs. These drugs reduced many of the *symptoms* of mental-health patients. This allowed hospital staffs to eliminate many restrictions placed on patients and made patients more acceptable to the community.[18]

But the use of drug therapy has been criticized, not only because of the potential side effects of drugs but also because drugs may be used to replace other forms of treatment. Consider, for example, the complaint of "radical therapists":

> Radical therapists—and others not so radical—ask a question we cannot ignore. Isn't the drug revolution an excuse for therapy on the cheap, for leaving therapy of the severely ill to social workers and paraprofessionals, for substituting a chemical reaction for the skilled deep human contact that alone can heal? Isn't it still another way of shortchanging the poor—since all studies show that the upper socio-economic groups are far more likely to get intensive psychotherapy, while the lower socio-economic groups get mostly somatic treatments?
>
> Fortunately, treatments are not necessarily second-rate because the poor get them—in spite of what radical therapists maintain. And unfortunately, deep human contact, though it may help a patient feel and act better, rarely heals severe mental illness—anymore than it heals severe physical illness. (On the rare occasions when it does, we have a word for it—a miracle.) Nor is it true that more drug treatment means less psychotherapy—rather, it's the reverse.[19]

The use of drug therapies has been widely debated. What *is* evident is that the advent of psychotherapeutic drugs has deemphasized the need for hospitalization for many patients.

Psychotherapeutic drugs laid some of the groundwork for the passage of the Community Mental Health Act in 1963. As part of an emerging community mental-health movement, the act emphasized more federal involvement in community-based care as well as coordination between community services and hospitals, improved services to the chronically mentally ill, a reduction in state hospital treatment, an increase in community treatment, education and prevention services, and greater utilization of paraprofessional staff.

The Community Mental-Health Center

The Community Mental Health Act of 1963 provided funds for the establishment and staffing of community mental-health centers (CMHCs) throughout the nation. Today there are over 781 CMHCs in the United States. Figure 7–1 shows the number of CMHCs in each state. Initially funding for CMHCs came from the federal government, with some state and local support, as well as from fees paid by clients. Persons with very low incomes may pay little or no fee for service.

The Community Mental Health Act originally mandated that federally funded CMHCs provide five "essential services." These services are (1) inpatient care, (2) outpatient care, (3) emergency care, (4) partial hospitalization, and (5) consultation and education. Inpatient care is usually provided within a psychiatric hospital or in a psychiatric unit of a general hospital within the community. Generally this care is short-term. If long-term care is needed, the patient may be transferred to a state mental health hospital or, if the patient can afford private care, to a private hospital outside the CMHC system.

Outpatient care covers a wide range of services. Among these services are individual therapy or counseling, group therapy, family therapy, and alcohol- and drug-abuse services. Among the personnel who provide care are psychiatrists, nurses, psychologists, social workers, counselors, rehabilitation specialists, and paraprofessionals.

FIGURE 7-1 Community mental-health centers, 1980: number by state. (Department of Health and Human Services, *Report of the Administrator, Alcohol, Drug Abuse, and Mental Health Administration, 1980* [Washington: Public Health Service, 1981], DHHS publication no. [ADM] 81-1165.)

Emergency services, also known as crisis services, are provided on a twenty-four-hour basis. They may include the use of telephone hot lines and outreach services to clients who cannot reach a mental-health facility in time of emergency. Crisis services are often used in responding to persons who are contemplating or who have attempted suicide, or who are experiencing other acute emotional problems.

Partial hospitalization is the name generally given to supervised activities and mental-health services that a client receives for several hours a day. One type of partial-hospitalization service provides a structured environment for mental-health clients during the day, with the clients' spending evenings at home. Partial-hospitalization services help clients who are attempting to reintegrate themselves back into the community, perhaps following a psychiatric hospitalization.

The fifth essential service is consultation and education (C&E), which also may be thought of as "prevention services." C&E services are provided to many groups throughout the community: medical professionals, courts, law-enforcement agencies, schools, civic groups, religious groups, social service agencies, the elderly and other citizens who want to learn about mental health and mental illness. C&E services are generally educational services that focus on the prevention of mental illness, on the identification of mental-health problems, and on what to do if mental-health problems occur.

In 1975 amendments to the Community Mental Health Act mandated more essential services, including special programs for children and the elderly, after-care and halfway-house services for patients discharged from mental-health hospitals, and services to courts and related agencies to screen persons who may be in need of treatment. CMHCs were mandated to spend 2 percent of their annual budgets on program evaluation, but this requirement has been eliminated. State governments may now use more discretion in determining CMHC evaluation requirements.

In 1980 Congress passed the Mental Health Systems Act, which continued many of the provisions of the Community Mental Health Act. The 1980 act also took to heart many of the recommendations of the President's Commission on Mental Health appointed by Jimmy Carter in 1977. It contained provisions for special groups, including the chronically mentally ill, severely disturbed children and adolescents, and those persons in communities who were unserved or underserved. However, CMHCs were no longer required to provide all the essential services in order to qualify for federal funding.

When Ronald Reagan took office, he collapsed funding for these services under the Alcohol, Drug Abuse and Mental Health Block Grant. The block grant has reduced the amount of funds available to states to provide these services. Critics contend that fiscal austerity has contributed to the number of homeless mentally ill persons and the inability of others to obtain services.

The Rights of Mental-Health Patients

Sometimes treatment cannot be provided to persons with mental-health problems on an outpatient basis or in community facilities. Community mental-health programs may not be equipped to assist persons whose mental-health problems are very severe, or specialized facilities may not exist in a community. Treatment in an inpatient mental-health facility may be necessary. This type of treatment restricts an individual from moving about in the community and conducting everyday affairs. In the nineteenth century and in the early twentieth century, mental-health patients had few rights. Today there is a greater concern for laws and policies which protect the rights of persons hospitalized in mental-health facilities. The federal and state governments are responsible for protecting the rights of mental-health patients. Patients must be informed of their rights to obtain and refuse treatment, and those who are not able to read must have this information explained to them.

Some obstacles prevent patients from receiving the best treatment in mental-health facilities. Patients should always be treated in a way that respects their individual dignity, but this manner of treatment is contingent on the quality of the treatment facility and of its staff. Facilities are often crowded and caseloads high. Some are located in remote areas where there may be an inadequate number of persons trained to provide mental-health services. Thus, qualified staff may be difficult to recruit and retain. Yet the decisions about a patient's day-to-day activities are largely staff decisions. The patient may have little influence in choosing these activities, short of refusing to participate. Moreover, when patients refuse to participate in activities, they are often considered to be uncooperative and resistant to treatment. This may serve to prolong their stay in the mental-health hospital.

Patients have the right to know the reason for their admission and what must happen before release can be granted. They should be provided access to mental health laws and legal assistance. Patients should be afforded privacy when they have visitors, and visits should not be denied unless there is reason to believe that they might be harmful to the patient or others. Unfortunately, when hospitals are located far from the patient's home, it is more difficult for family to visit or for the patient to visit family on short leaves of absence from the hospital. Well-intentioned policies relating to the care of the mentally ill persons may not always be implemented to serve the best needs of the client.

Deinstitutionalization

Persons with mental-health problems frequently face social rejection. While the public agrees that treatment should be provided to the physically and mentally handicapped and to the mentally ill, the public does not always believe that this treatment should be provided in their neighborhoods. This attitude persists for several reasons. Some people fear the mentally ill and believe they might endanger the safety of their families. Others believe that community-based facilities will cause their neighborhoods to become rundown if these facilities are not well maintained. There is also the fear that when community programs move in, neighborhood residents will decide to sell their homes, perhaps at a loss. An example of these concerns and a story about the problems faced in locating community treatment programs for the physically and mentally handicapped is reproduced below.

The phrase "treatment in the least restrictive manner" means that the freedoms of the individual receiving treatment should be preserved whenever possible. It is not appropriate to confine someone to treatment in a state hospital when a community facility can meet the individual's needs. Hospitals may compound patients' problems by making them "institutionalized." Patients may be forced to get up at certain times and to eat at certain times; their meals are prepared for them and their clothes washed for them; they may be told when to bathe and when to take their medication. As a result, patients become increasingly dependent on others for survival. When and if they return to their homes and communities, they may not have the skills to live independently.

But "deinstitutionalization"—reliance on community facilities—may also present problems. Some communities do not have enough local treatment and residential facilities. The discharge of large numbers of patients from state institutions to their home communities, in cases where the communities lack enough resources for newly released patients, may result in added stress for both patients and communities. Families are often not equipped to care for patients who may need supervision or special services within the home. Other families do not want to cope or do not know how to cope with the burdens placed on them by family members returning from institutional care.

ILLUSTRATION: MENTAL HEALTH AND LOCAL POLITICS

LaMar Silver is no rabble-rouser. . . .

His home in Orlando's Bel Aire Woods subdivision is a reward he worked hard to attain before retiring. . . .

When two group homes for the mentally retarded opened within a block of his home, LaMar Silver felt his neighborhood was changed, even ruined. He was determined to fight.

Bill Brandt, a data processing consultant in his early 30s, is a family man with a sense of civic duty. . . . When a detoxification program for alcoholics moved into his neighborhood, Brandt too came out fighting.

The same alcoholic treatment facility was bitterly fought again when mental health officials tried to move it into another location. This time, the main opponent was a self-styled conservative and opponent of big government. A 38-year-old businessman, he was—and still is—convinced the facility will ruin his business. He challenged the move legally and lost. Still angry about his new neighbor, he doesn't want his name published but he'll discuss his objections at length. . . .

Community acceptance—or lack of it—is a force to be reckoned with in the 1980s. As human service programs push to deinstitutionalize and open a gamut of community based programs, firefights are erupting in neighborhoods throughout the state and the nation.

At the very least, angry neighbors can cause costly delays and disrupt programs. Or, in the extreme, they can stop the opening of a facility and bring community programming to a grinding halt. . . .

Silver . . . said . . . "As far as I'm concerned and as far as the neighborhood's concerned, we have no objection to the clients. We don't object to the homes if they're not concentrated. . . ."

According to Silver, after the second home opened, "For Sale" signs began springing up in the neighborhood. He estimated that about a half-dozen homes were sold in the area adjacent to the group homes and said he was told the houses sold for $10,000 to $20,000 less than comparable homes in the other areas. Silver maintains that the reduced prices brought undesirable people into the neighborhood. Yet he said he has not actually surveyed prices of homes sold in the area. . . .

Two separate Tallahassee neighborhoods fought to stop the opening of an inpatient treatment program for alcoholics by the Apalachee Community Mental Health Center. One neighborhood won, the other lost. Yet the time-consuming and expensive battles caused the center to close the program for seven months. . . .

Bill Brandt, president of the Lafayette Park Neighborhood Association, said the detox center was the final straw for residents. He said many people were unhappy with the short-term psychiatric care program already located in the center. And with five other group homes and related facilities in the immediate area, they felt their social consciousness stretched thin. . . .

Apalachee officials said the move might have met less resistance had it not been for negative publicity about patients leaving the detox center and wandering through the neighborhood. No crimes were linked to detox clients and changes were made to prevent clients from wandering. But neighbors were unconvinced and feared clients might disturb them or their children.

Lafayette Park residents and Apalachee officials became adversaries, first before a zoning appeals board and then in court. Zoning officials said that the detox center—and the inpatient psychiatric unit—were prohibited in the area. The court agreed and gave Apalachee six months to move the programs.

As Apalachee looked at other sites, opposition spread to every area considered. When six months were up, a new site had not been firmed up and the agency had to close the two treatment programs. It would be seven months before they reopened in their new home.

Apalachee officials finally zeroed in on a building on commercially-zoned land east of Tallahassee. Across the street from a small cluster of businesses, it is about a half-mile from Eastgate, one of Tallahassee's newer single family subdivisions and home for many young families.

Although the zoning allowed for "clinics," Apalachee officials were geared for opposition. They went to work immediately to offset it by winning support from Eastgate residents and others. "We set up a Neighborhood Advisory Board of 14 people who live in Eastgate and nearby," said Apalachee's medical and educational consultant, Linda Cooper. "We educated them on the programs, who the supervisors were, who the clients were. We gave them honest, matter-of-fact answers to questions. We also stressed the fact we are a *resource* for their neighborhood—that one of them or a neighbor might need our services."

The advisory board formed a core of support for the treatment facility and members successfully overcame the objections of many of their neighbors.

But the welcome wasn't unanimous. A small group of businessmen fought the facility before the zoning appeals board and in court. At times their tactics were less restrained. "Do you want Mental patients and Drunks across from your children?" read the sign in front of a neighborhood skating rink.

Their efforts were unsuccessful. The center opened in December. . . .

But the conservative businessman who asked not to be named said he questioned the need for the programs as well as objecting to them being located across from his business. . . .

He said his concerns were twofold: the impact on his business and the safety of the children who often wait outside his skating rink for their parents.

So far, he said, there have been no incidents involving patients from the treatment facility. But he was skeptical about the future and vowed to take things in his own hands if an incident occurred. . . .

The man's anger is not atypical. And threats of violence can become very real. A recent CBS "Sixty Minutes" show featured a segment on efforts to locate a group home in a Michigan community. The same night the house was burned to the ground—the apparent victim of arsonists. . . .

Numerous studies have looked at the problem of community opposition to residential treatment facilities. Most conclude that neighbors oppose facilities because they believe:

—They will devalue property.

—Criminal activity and disturbances will increase.

—The character of the neighborhood will be negatively affected.

Yet, recent studies both in Florida and other states have concluded that these fears are generally unfounded.

A number of studies have examined the impact homes for the handicapped and other clients have on property values. They indicate there is no relationship between these facilities and property values—regardless of the age of the neighborhood, its relationship to downtown or the characteristics of its residents. In general, property values in communities with group homes had the same increase or decrease in market prices as comparable neighborhoods without such facilities.

One recent study, completed last summer by the Jacksonville Community Council, Inc., looked at the impact of residential treatment facilities on criminal activity. The study found that clients were more often the *victims* rather than suspects in criminal investigations. . . .

Most studies also advocate that social services agencies take a "high profile" approach and educate the community before moving into a neighborhood rather than the "low profile" approach, where the goal is to move in unnoticed. But those with first-hand experience say what works in theory may fail in practice. . . .

Richard Baron, project director for the Horizon House Institute of Research and Development in Philadelphia, said his organization favors the "community education" approach. Baron readily admits, however, that there's no conclusive data as to which approach is best and said there's much at stake in answering that question.

Baron said he believed the longterm solution lies in dispelling myths about handicapped and other clients and in educating the public as to their right to treatment in a community setting. Given an enlightened public, the task of overcoming pockets of opposition in specific neighborhoods would be easier, he said.

Client advocates believe that many confrontations can be avoided through implementation of the group home amendment to Florida's Local Government Comprehensive Planning Act. The amendment requires local governments to provide for group and foster homes in their local zoning plans.

Some client advocates, however, are fearful that special zoning may result in limiting residential facilities to "social services ghettos." And some advocates say special zoning shouldn't be necessary. "The purist position is that, constitutionally, these people have a right to live anywhere they want," said Linden Thorn of the Developmental Services Program office. "He [Mr. Silver] didn't have to have permission from his neighbors to buy his house."

Source: Pat Harbolt, "The Fight Against Community Programs" *Access: A Human Services Magazine* 4, no. 4, Feb. 81/Mar. 81/State of Florida, Department of Health & Rehabilitative Services, pp. 14–18.

CHILD WELFARE POLICY

The family has always been viewed as a sacred entity. Governmental interference in family life is generally viewed as an unnecessary intrusion. As a result, the United States has no official national family policy. Instead, there are many federal, state, and local laws that govern various aspects of family relations. There are also more than twenty separate federal government agencies that provide some type of services for children.[20] In this section we focus on one area of family relations—child welfare, especially child abuse and neglect.

According to Title IV–E of the Social Security Act, child welfare policy and services are aimed at accomplishing a number of purposes, including:

1. Protecting and promoting the welfare of all children, including handicapped, homeless, dependent, or neglected children;
2. Preventing or remedying, or assisting in the solution of problems that may result in the neglect, abuse, exploitation, or delinquency of children;
3. Preventing the unnecessary separation of children from their families by identifying family problems, assisting families in resolving their problems, and preventing breakups of the families where the prevention of child removal is desirable and possible;
4. Restoring to their families children who have been removed, by the provision of services to the child and the families;
5. Placing children in suitable adoptive homes in cases where restoration to the biological family is not appropriate; and
6. Assuring adequate care of children away from their homes in cases where the child cannot be returned home or cannot be placed for adoption.

Children Who Receive Social Services

Nearly two million children receive social services.[21] Slightly more boys (52 percent) than girls are served. The median age of these children is nine years. The majority are white, but almost 30 percent are black, and 9 percent are Hispanic, Asian-Pacific, and Indian-Alaskan. Over half of the children receiving services attend school, while the rest are not attending school or are too young to attend.

Only 15 percent of the children receiving services live with both parents. Forty percent of these children live only with their mothers, and 5 percent only with their fathers. Almost one-quarter live in foster homes, while the remainder live with adoptive parents, relatives or guardians, or in institutions or group homes.

Thirty percent of the children have parents who are married; 25 percent have divorced parents. The remainder either have a deceased parent, or parents who are legally separated or were never married. Thirty-eight percent of the children are recipients of AFDC.

The primary reasons children receive social services are neglect and abuse. Other reasons are financial need, emotional problems of the child or of a parent, conflict between child and parent, abandonment, and a parent's unwillingness to care for the child. In response to these problems, the services most often provided to children are protective services, health services, foster care, counseling, and day care. The services provided most frequently to the child's principal caretaker are counseling, financial aid, and health services.

Child Maltreatment

No one wants to think that there are adult members of society who would inflict harm on children, but the reality is that in 1982 over 900,000 cases of child maltreatment were reported, an increase of 123 percent since 1976 when nationwide reporting systems were improved (see table 7-1).[22]

TABLE 7-1 Reports of Child Maltreatment (abuse and neglect) in the United States

YEAR	TOTAL NUMBER OF REPORTS	ANNUAL INCREASE
1976[a]	416,033	—
1977	516,142	24%
1978	614,291	19%
1979	711,142	16%
1980	788,844	11%
1981	850,980	8%
1982	929,310	9%

[a]1976 is the first year for which these data were collected.

Source: *Highlights of Official Child Neglect and Abuse Reporting 1982* (Denver: American Humane Association, Child Protection Division, 1984), p. 2.

Maltreatment consists of both *child neglect and child abuse.* Neglect results when a parent or caretaker does not provide a child with the essentials needed to live adequately. Neglect may be due to the failure or inability of parents or caretakers to provide adequate food, shelter, or clothing for a child. It can also occur when parents or caretakers fail to see that a child receives an adequate education or adequate health care. Neglect may also result from psychological deprivation. Children who are isolated from others, locked in rooms, and denied normal stimulation may also be called neglected.

In contrast to child neglect, child abuse occurs when severe physical harm is inflicted on a child. Children who are beaten by parents or caretakers, and children who suffer broken bones, burns, lacerations, or other injuries as a result of such attacks, many be said to be abused.

A review of more than 250,000 reports of child maltreatment indicated th at abuse accounted for 26 percent of the cases, while neglect accounted for 43 percent and a combination of abuse and neglect comprised another 19 percent. The remaining cases were considered to be "at-risk' ' and other potentially problematic situations for children.[23] The Dep artment of Health and Human Services adds that while child abuse has received more media and government attention, "child neglect is the most pervasive, costly and intractable child maltreatment problem encountered by child protective service workers."[24]

What are the causes of child neglect and abuse? Many abusive parents were child-abuse victims themselves. This suggests that these parents may abuse their own children because this is the method of child rearing they experienced while growing up. There are other explanations for child maltreatment. Parents who are unable to cope with the stress of personal or economic problems or who suffer from mental illness may turn their frustrations toward their children. In other cases, parents may not be equipped to assume the responsibilities of child rearing. Young parents may underestimate the amount of time and attention a child requires. Like other social problems, child maltreatment is a problem for which researchers will be unlikely to isolate a single cause. In addition, there is no single profile of an abusive or neglectful parent. The vast majority of persons accused of perpetrating maltreatment are the child's natural parents (see table 7-2).

Table 7-3 gives the sources of reported cases of child maltreatment. According to these reports, child maltreatment is reported by a number of persons including friends, neighbors and relatives, law-enforcement agencies, medical professionals, and community and social service agencies. Some cases are reported by the victim or perpetrator.

The majority of cases (62 percent) are reported as the result of a child's being deprived of necessities (see table 7-4). This category includes neglecting to provide nourishment, shelter, clothing, and health care; failure of child to thrive; lack of supervision; and failure to see that a child receives education. The second largest category of maltreatment is considered minor physical injuries. This category accounts for 17 percent of cases and involves inflicting such injuries as minor cuts, bruises, and welts or

TABLE 7-2 Characteristics of Perpetrators of Child Maltreatment (number of reports: 255,472[a])

Average Age	31.2 years
Sex	
Males	38.6%
Females	61.4%
Race	
White	69.0%
Black	19.7%
Hispanic	9.2%
Other	2.1%
Relationship to Victim	
Natural Parent	85.1%
Step/Adoptive/Foster Parent	8.0%
Unspecified Parent Type	0.7%
Other Relative	4.1%
Other	2.1%

[a]Based on the reports of 36 U.S. jurisdictions.

Source: *Highlights of Official Child Neglect and Abuse Reporting 1982* (Denver: American Humane Association, Child Protection Division, 1984), pp. 8 and 9.

TABLE 7-3 Source of Reports of Child Maltreatment (number of reports: 252,506[a])

Professionals:		
Medical Personnel		11%
School Personnel		12
Law Enforcement		12
Social Services		11
Child Care Providers		2
	Total	48%
Nonprofessionals:		
Friends, Neighbors, Relatives, Self (victims and perpetrators)		41%
Anonymous		9
Other Sources		2
	Total	52%

[a]Data based on reports of 36 U.S. jurisdictions.

Source: *Highlights of Official Child Neglect and Abuse Reporting 1982* (Denver: American Humane Association, Child Protection Division, 1984), p. 6.

TABLE 7-4 Types of Child Maltreatment Reports[a] (total number of reports: 331,544[b])

TYPE OF MALTREATMENT	PERCENT OF CHILDREN
Major Physical Injury	2
Minor Physical Injury	17
Unspecified Physical Injury	5
Sexual Maltreatment	7
Deprivation of Necessities	62
Emotional Maltreatment	10
Other Maltreatment	9

[a]More than one category may be reported for each victim.
[b]Based on the reports of 36 U.S. jurisdictions.

Source: *Highlights of Official Child Neglect and Abuse Reporting 1982* (Denver: American Humane Association, Child Protection Division, 1984), p. 11.

twisting and shaking a child. The category of emotional maltreatment, which constitutes 10 percent of cases, includes both abuse and neglect. The 9 percent of cases included in the category of "other" represents abandonment, mixed forms of maltreatment, and problems not specified elsewhere. Sexual maltreatment—7 percent of reported cases—includes incest, exploitation, rape, intercourse, and molestation as well as other forms of this problem. Major physical injuries, accounting for 2 percent of cases, involve brain damage, skull fracture, subdural hemorrhage or hematoma, bone fracture, dislocation, sprains, internal injuries, poisoning, burns, scalds, and severe cuts, lacerations, and bruises. Victims are evenly divided between boys and girls. Children aged five and younger are the largest group of victims (43 percent) while those in the six-to-eleven-year-old age group constitute the next largest group (33 percent), and those ages twelve to seventeen represent the remaining 24 percent of cases. White children are 65 percent of victims; black children, 22 percent; and Hispanic children, 11 percent.[25]

Discovering Child Abuse

Historically, children have been considered the possessions of their parents.[26] Parents who severely punished their children, even beat them, were not behaving deviantly; they were merely making sure that their children obeyed. This tradition prevailed in America until the Industrial Revolution brought an abundance of new social problems. Among these social problems were the conditions of urban cities, which were often overcrowded and unsanitary and where hunger and disease were not uncommon. During this period it was thought that children from poor homes might be better raised in institutions where they could learn proper societal values. Poverty and a poor living environment were thought to be faults which children would learn from parents. Institutions such as the New York House of Refuge were established for neglected, abandoned, and delinquent youth. But the emphasis was not on protecting children from parents who harmed or neglected them. It was thought that placing children in institutions would help reverse the trend of poverty.

In the early twentieth century, the prevailing philosophy toward child care remained the "house of refuge." Even the establishment of juvenile courts in the early twentieth century did little to change this. Emphasis was on removing children from their homes, not on rehabilitating or treating parents. As the century progressed, though, more concern was expressed for children. They were removed from adult institutions, and new mothers'-aid programs provided financial security to children in their natural homes. But abusive parents were not themselves the targets of social policies or social programs; in fact, the public continued to condone parents' use of physical force on their children.

It was not the social reformers, nor the judicial personnel of the juvenile courts, nor the public at large who discovered child abuse. It was *pediatric radiologists,* who identified child abuse as a problem, or "syndrome," gave it legitimacy, and aroused public concern. John Caffey was the first to search for a cause of many of the bone fractures in children; beginning in 1946, his work led to the identification of parents as the cause of these fractures. However, Caffey and other pediatric radiologists were not the first to "see" child abuse. Emergency-room and family physicians were the first to come into contact with these children, but at least four factors prevented them from recognizing the problem. First, child abuse was not a traditional diagnosis. Second, doctors may not have believed that parents would abuse their children. Third, if the family, rather than just the child, was the doctor's patient, reporting abuse may have constituted a violation of patient confidentiality. Fourth, physicians may have been unwilling to report criminal behavior because of the time-consuming nature of criminal cases and their roles as witnesses in those proceedings.

Pediatric radiologists, rather than other physicians, exposed child abuse because they did *not* deal directly with the child and the family. Issues regarding confidentiality, who the patient was, and court proceedings were not their primary concerns. Making public the problem of child abuse also served to elevate the status of pediatric radiologists. Radiologists were not highly regarded among members of the medical profession because they did not provide direct care to patients. "Discovering" child abuse allowed pediatric radiologists to develop closer collegial relationships with physicians with whom they consulted.

It was important to the medical profession that dealing with child abuse be kept under its control. Child abuse had to be labeled a medical rather than a social or legal problem, or else physicians would be relegated to a subordinate role in its diagnosis and treatment. Child abuse was labeled "the battered-child syndrome" in 1962. Labeling child abuse as a medical syndrome legitimatized its recognition by physicians. Magazines, newspapers, and television programs, such as "Ben Casey" and "Dr. Kildare," publicized the problem.

Between 1962 and 1965 every state passed legislation on child abuse. Today child-abuse legislation is aimed more at rehabilitating parents than punishing them. Most cases are reported to welfare rather than law-

ASPCA

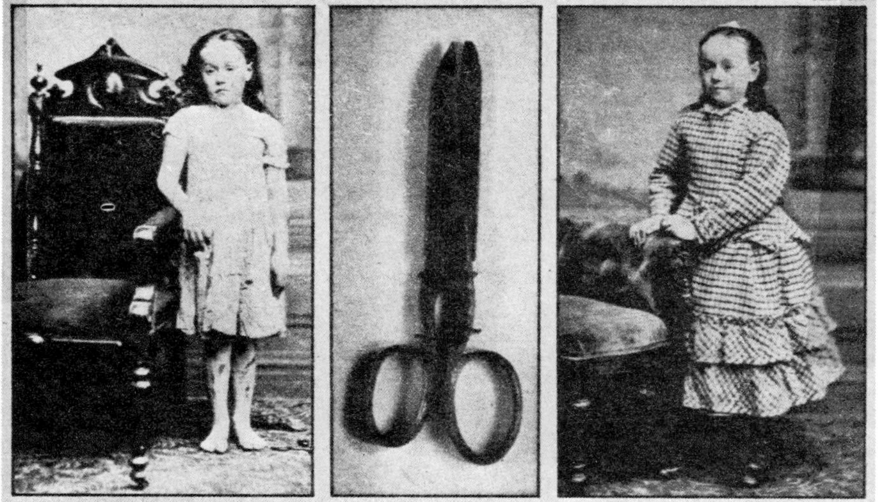

SPCA's before-and-after photos of Mary Ellen, with scissors used to punish her

Little Mary Ellen

Before 1875, U.S. authorities had no legal means to interfere in cases of battered children. The laws were changed with the help of the Society for the Prevention of Cruelty to Animals (SPCA).

A 9-year-old named Mary Ellen became the exemplar of the battered children's plight. Indentured to Francis and Mary Connolly (and rumored to be the daughter of Mary's ex-husband), the girl was whipped daily, stabbed with scissors and tied to a bed. Neighbors reported the situation to Etta Wheeler, a church worker, in 1874. When Wheeler found that there was no lawful way to rescue the child from her brutal guardians, she went to Henry Bergh of the SPCA for help.

Under the premise that the child was a member of the animal kingdom, the SPCA obtained a writ of habeas corpus to remove Mary Ellen from her home. On April 9, 1874, she was carried into the New York Supreme Court, where her case was tried. She was pitifully thin, with a scissor wound on her cheek. Mrs. Connolly was sentenced to a year in prison. Mary Ellen was given a new home. The following April, the New York Society for the Prevention of Cruelty to Children (NYSPCC) was incorporated.

Before-and-after photos of Mary Ellen (as a pathetic waif upon her rescue and as a healthy child a year later) still hang at the New York SPCA, framed with Mrs. Connolly's scissors.

(Reprinted with permission from Irving Wallace, David Wallachinsky, and Amy Wallace, "Significa," *Parade* magazine. Photos courtesy of ASPCA Archives.)

enforcement agencies. Few persons are prosecuted, and fewer are convicted. The social services that neglectful or abusive parents are most likely to receive are individual and group treatment. Self-help groups, such as Parents Anonymous, are also valuable sources of support. Social services for abusive and neglectful parents are directed at keeping the family unit intact. Most children in these families (80 percent) continue to remain at home.[27]

National Child-Abuse Legislation

In January 1974 Congress passed the Child Abuse Prevention and Treatment Act and established the National Center for Child Abuse and Neglect. The purposes of the act are to assist the states in developing programs for abused and neglected children and to conduct abuse and neglect research.

To qualify for federal funds under this act, states' child-abuse and neglect laws must (1) cover all children under eighteen years of age, (2) provide assistance in cases of mental, physical, and sexual abuse, (3) cover both neglect and abuse cases, (4) insure confidentiality of client records, and (5) see that a guardian *ad litem* (a guardian appointed for a specific purpose) is provided for children in cases which come before the court.

Since child abuse and neglect statutes are the prerogative of the states, there remains no single definition of child abuse or neglect. There is also no single piece of legislation that uniformly addresses abuse and neglect throughout the United States. Although available model legislation often serves as the basis for state statutes, it is still difficult to achieve consensus on definitions of child abuse and neglect. Even if simple definitions could be achieved, the problem of applying these definitions in specific cases would remain a problem. Child-rearing and discipline practices also vary among communities and among those from different cultures, further compounding the problems of applying uniform definitions.[28]

Reagan and Child Welfare

In fiscal year 1984 the federal government earmarked $600 million for child welfare services. Funds have been used primarily for maltreated and dependent children. Two social welfare analysts state that under the Reagan administration, "child welfare services have taken a peculiar twist."[29] Under President Carter legislation was designed to promote preventive services and to encourage keeping families together, but under the Reagan administration, less funding has been requested for preventive services with more available for foster care. Although President Reagan has not taken a stance favoring foster care over keeping children in their own homes, the result "has been to slow down or reverse the trends in the states toward more preventive and ameliorative efforts, and to increase the likelihood that children will spend more time in foster care."[30]

SERVICES FOR OLDER AMERICANS

In many cultures, the senior members are respected and revered for their wisdom and knowledge. Since they are considered important members of society, their decisions are most influential in shaping the direction of that culture. But such is not the case in America, where youth is cherished and where people spend money, time, and effort to prolong their youth. A society that worships youth and dreads old age tends to isolate older persons. The elderly are a vulnerable group. They require greater amounts of health care; they are often excluded from pursuing gainful employment; they are prime targets for crimes like theft; their mobility is limited.

The proportion of elderly persons in America is growing. Advances in medicine and technology have prolonged the lives of Americans. As the elderly population grows, older Americans become more visible and their needs and demands upon society increase.

In Chapter 4 we discussed the Social Security program and Medicare. These are important programs for the aged. In the 1960s, national policy began to recognize more social service needs of the elderly—especially in the Older Americans Act of 1965.

The Older Americans Act

The primary objectives of the Older Americans Act (OAA) are

An adequate income in retirement in accordance with the American standard of living

The best possible physical and mental health that science can make available without regard to economic status

Suitable housing that is independently selected, designed, and located, with reference to special needs and available at costs older citizens can afford

Full restorative services for those who require institutional care

Opportunity for employment with no discriminatory personnel practices because of age

Retirement in health, honor, and dignity—after years of contribution to the economy

Pursuit of meaningful activity within the widest range of civic, cultural, and recreational opportunities

Efficient community services including access to low-cost transportation, which provide a choice in supported living arrangements and social assistance in a coordinated manner and which are readily available when needed

Immediate benefit from proven research knowledge which can sustain and improve health and happiness

Freedom, independence, and the free exercise of individual initiative in planning and managing one's own life

In order to qualify for services under the OAA a person must be at least sixty years old. Income is generally not used to determine eligibility, but the poor elderly are of special concern.

The OAA created an "aging network" to express the concerns of older Americans.[31] The network operates at the federal, regional, state, and local levels. At the federal level is the Administration on Aging (AoA), which is part of the Department of Health and Human Services. In addition to its advocacy function for older Americans, the AoA coordinates all federally operated programs for the aged. The AoA also provides technical assistance to state and local governments to help them develop and implement services for elderly persons, conducts evaluations of programs, conducts research on aging, and acts as a national clearinghouse on information about the elderly. To assist in its efforts, the AoA has ten regional offices across the United States.

At the state level, the aging network is generally found within the state's human services or welfare department, subordinate to an aging-program office. The state offices assist in implementing federal policies and act as advocates for elderly citizens. They make the needs and problems of the aged known to the AoA and also to their own state legislatures, which have a great deal of influence on funding and administering state aging programs.

Most social services for the elderly are provided at the local level. At this level there are about six hundred Area Agencies on Aging (AAAs). Each AAA is guided by an advisory council primarily composed of elderly persons. The AAAs perform their advocacy function by assessing the needs of the elderly in their communities. AAAs also distribute funds to community agencies that deliver services directly to the aged. Among the social services they provide are

Nutrition programs
Senior centers
Information and referral
Transportation
Homemaker and chore services
Legal counseling
Escort services
Home repair and renovation
Home health aid
Shopping assistance
Friendly visitation
Telephone assurance (phone calls to the elderly for reassurance and to check on their needs)

The OAA and the aging network are important adjuncts to the major cash-assistance and health programs (Social Security, SSI, and Medicare) for America's elderly. These social service programs provide important links for the elderly with the community. The OAA, for instance, attempts to reintegrate elderly persons into the mainstream of American life. Social

Security checks and Medicare services are helpful in relieving some of the financial burdens faced by America's elderly, but by themselves they are inadequate to alleviate many of the social problems faced by elderly citizens. The OAA helps round out financial assistance by responding to many of the needs of senior citizens, but the aging network is only as good as its reputation. Advocacy groups for older Americans are concerned that services be well publicized to insure they are utilized.

Older Americans and the Legislature

From time to time, White House conferences on aging have been conducted, with elderly delegates from across the United States participating. The 1981 conference focused on the following issues concerning the elderly:

Improvement of their economic well-being
Availability of quality health care
Establishment of a more comprehensive social-service delivery system
Expansion of housing and long-term care facilities
Development of a national retirement policy
Offering of greater job opportunities
Overcoming of aging stereotypes
Stimulation of medical research on aging

The House of Representatives and the Senate each have special committees to address legislation concerning the elderly. Both the House and Senate committees were created in 1959. In the Senate, the committee is called the Special Committee on Aging, and in the House it is called the Permanent Select Committee on Aging. State legislatures also have committees whose functions include consideration of the financial and social needs of the elderly. In addition to these policy advisory groups, elderly people throughout the country have organized in an effort to make their needs known. Among the best-known groups are the American Association of Retired Persons (AARP) and the Gray Panthers. In the illustration on page 158, an article from the *Gray Panther Network* discusses the issue of *ageism*—discrimination against older persons—and some legislation designed to address the problem.

President Reagan, a senior citizen himself, has exerted little influence on the Older Americans Act. Attempts to place funding for social services to the elderly under a block grant have been unsuccessful. The Older Americans Act has been amended over the years, but its purpose and intent have remained the same. Provisions added in 1984 included greater emphasis on providing for the needs of minorities, assisting the elderly who have been victimized as the result of violence or abuse, and helping those with Alzheimer's disease.[32]

ILLUSTRATION: AGEISM STILL AT WORK

Nine of 10 Americans agreed, in a 1981 Harris Poll, that "nobody should be forced to retire because of age if he wants to continue working and is still able to do a good job."

One would think, then, that it would be easy to stamp out age discrimination that stemmed from mandatory retirement policies. That is not the case. The battle against discriminatory mandatory retirement policies is being fought on three major fronts: Congress, the courts, and state legislatures. And the outcome is still in doubt.

The Age Discrimination in Employment Act (ADEA) of 1967, with amendments, protects most workers ages 40 to 69 from discrimination in job retention, hiring, and promotion. But when an employee reaches 70, the protection stops. (Federal employees continue to be protected past 70, although there are some exceptions, most notably in the law enforcement and fire fighting fields, where a mandatory retirement age of 55 has been set.)

Legislation to remove the "70 cap" on age discrimination protection stalled in Congress last session as bills introduced by Sen. John Heinz, R-Penn., and Rep. Claude Pepper, D-Fla., didn't get out of committee, let alone to a floor vote.

The legislation is expected to be taken up again this session, but its prospects for passage remain unclear. The Democratically-controlled House is seen as friendlier to anti-cap legislation than the Republican-controlled Senate. Proponents of the legislation view Republicans as more attentive to the concerns of businessmen, who, in general, prefer a freer hand in their employment practices.

The anti-cap legislation would stand a much better chance of passage if the Reagan administration would get fully behind it, according to David Certner, legislative representative of the American Association of Retired Persons (AARP), an organization which has lobbied for legislation to eliminate the cap.

In April of 1982, President Reagan, who turns 74 this February, said: "When it comes to retirement, the criterion should be fitness for work, not year of birth. . . . We know that many individuals have valuable contributions to make well beyond 70 years of age and they should have the opportunity to do so if they desire."

But when it came time to testify on anti-cap legislation before the House Select Committee on Aging, administration officials were in favor of protecting persons over 70 from forced retirement, but not protecting them in hiring and promotions.

This led Pepper to ask: ". . . Why do we have to limit the protection we extend only to one phase of activity of the elderly people?"

The administration, with a nod to the business community, took the position that passage of protection limited to retirement was politically feasible, while full protection was not. Supporters of the anti-cap legislation were concerned that by accepting only a half-way measure, momentum for full protection of the rights of the elderly against age discrimination would be lost.

Now, many proponents of anti-cap bills say that the best chance for enactment lies with attaching them to other legislation.

Meanwhile, a movement is afoot in Congress to exempt state and local governments from the ADEA in setting policies for the retirement of public safety officials. Bills introduced late last session by Sen. Bill Bradley, D-N.J., and Rep. William Hughes, D-N.J., would have enabled state and local governments to set their own retirement ages for law enforcement and firefighters. Similar legislation is expected to be considered this session.

The Bradley-Hughes initiative parallels an effort in the New Jersey State Legislature to establish a mandatory retirement age of 55 for state troopers.

"The danger is, where will this stop?" asks Jo Turner, a member of the Gray Panther's Steering Committee and a New Jersey resident who has been supporting a group of older state troopers in their battle to stop the New Jersey legislators from enacting a 55-age limit for state policemen.

The battle pits older troopers against younger troopers, who are eager for promotion. The younger troopers dominate the State Trooper Fraternal Association, which backs the 55-age limit. The president of the association, Trooper Thomas Iskrzycki, has been quoted as saying "We need young, aggressive blood, not toothless troopers."

Turner says that the situation in New Jersey and some other states shows that "ageism is creeping back into society." And she adds, "This proves that education and consciousness raising on ageism need to be an ongoing process."

Pension rights are intimately bound up with mandatory retirement. Theoretically, if the government is going to force you to retire, it has an obligation to make it economically feasible to retire. Turner argues that older troopers can help keep a pension fund solvent because they continue to put money into it, rather than withdrawing from it. Turner also points out that studies have shown that older workers have better attendance and safety records, while producing at the same levels.

Turner notes that for many persons retirement can be a "life-shattering" experience, particularly so for law enforcement officials because of the "macho" nature of the job. Troopers who are able to continue working safely and efficiently should be allowed to do so, if they desire, she says.

Many states, including New Jersey, in the past have had mandatory retirement policies for public safety workers of less than 70 years. But these policies were cast in doubt by a 1983 Supreme Court ruling in the case of *Wyoming v. the Economic Employment Opportunity Commission,* which upheld the constitutionality of a 1974 amendment to the ADEA binding state and local authorities to the 40 to 69 rule.

Therefore, unless the ADEA is amended again, even proponents of mandatory retirement say that it is unlikely that legislation, such as that proposed in New Jersey to set a 55-age limit on state troopers, will survive court challenges.

As it is, state and local governments must show that age is a "bona fide occupational qualification" (BFOQ) in mandatorily retiring persons, ages 40 to 69. A showing of this qualification provides an employer exemption from the ADEA. Other exemptions involve business executives, aged 65 or more, who would retire to annual pensions of at least $44,000, and university and college professors who have turned 70.

In recent years, courts have generally adhered to the rule that to establish age as a BFOQ, an employer must show that "all or substantially all" persons of a given age cannot pass an appropriate test designed to prove whether a person can do his or her job with safety and efficiency, or that no such test can be designed.

However, proponents of mandatory retirement established a beachhead in the court system this past January when a federal Appeals Court allowed the city of Baltimore to force its firefighters to retire at age 55 without proving that such a policy was necessary for safety and efficiency. Six Baltimore firefighters, backed by the EEOC, had challenged the 55-age limit. The Appeals Court ruled that an age-55 limit was valid because Congress has settled on retirement at age 55 for law enforcement officers and firefighters in the federal Civil Service. But the U.S. Supreme Court has agreed to take up the case, and a decision, expected by June, should shed more light on what criteria may be used in establishing a BFOQ.

Some opponents of mandatory retirement argue that the federal government is guilty of age discrimination in forcing some employees to retire at age 55, and that such a policy sets a bad example that should be changed.

An EEOC official familiar with mandatory retirement litigation says the Appeals Court ruling on the Baltimore firefighters is probably a bad decision that stands a good chance of being overturned by the Supreme Court. If the Supreme Court agrees with the EEOC, early retirement dates will not necessarily become invalid. Rather, cities and states will have to justify them with specific health and safety data.

And it is on the basis of specific data that opponents of mandatory retirement ages with respect to police and firefighters expect to win court cases.

A report issued by the House Select Committee on Aging, "The Myths and Realities of Age Limits for Law Enforcement and Firefighting Personnel," tears apart many arguments for mandatory retirement among public safety workers, and by logical inference, all lines of work.

The report shows that chronological age is a poor indicator of ability to perform on the job. The study backs up arguments made by the Gray Panthers before the New Jersey Legislature that older workers can perform as well, and, in some cases, noticeably better than their younger counterparts.

The report cites research on the Los Angeles Fire Department that shows that an individual firefighter can be tested for his or her fitness to perform the job, that fitness testing and training can reduce injuries, that such programs can be cost efficient, and that many firefighters in their 50's and 60's have passed their fitness tests.

The report is being circulated on Capitol Hill, and may help some legislators see the light on lifting the 70 age cap, while not lifting protection of state and public safety employees.

While opponents of the age discrimination permitted against workers over 70 have been stymied thus far in Congress, they have been making headway at the state level. At least 20 states, including most recently New York and Florida, have eliminated the 70 cap.

Gray Panthers across the country have been instrumental in educating legislators about the issue and lobbying to end mandatory retirement in their own states. Last April, Boston Gray Panthers organized a statewide coalition to help pass such legislation and held an intergenerational rally on the steps of the Massachusetts State House. They attribute their success—the age cap was lifted in Massachusetts shortly after these actions—to their intergenerational focus which had a unifying, rather than divisive, effect. Gray Panthers are pressing for similar measures in other states, including New Jersey.

This issue, like so many others, proves there may be more than one way to achieve a goal.

Mark Graven, "Ageism Still at Work," *Gray Panther Network,* Winter 1985, 12–13.

Philanthropy, Voluntarism, and the Private Sector

Many social services—from child day care to nursing-home care and from preventive to remedial services—are provided by private agencies. Many of these agencies are the not-for-profit type and others are for-profit (proprietary) organizations. Estimates are that 375,000 not-for-profit agencies exist in the United States, employing 1.4 million workers and with expenditures of $114 billion in 1980.[33] When President Reagan took office, his philosophy was clearly one of involving the private sector in solving many of the country's social problems. He wanted to see the service capacity of private organizations expanded. Private agencies have long provided social services in this country, and the role of some of these agencies has recently grown. For example, in the area of developmental disabilities, services provided by private agencies in smaller, residential settings are expanding as states shut down their large institutions. Deinstitutionalization and normalization are forcing states to look for alternatives to serving even the most severely disabled clients, and many states are choosing to purchase these services rather than provide them directly.

Along with the encouragement of the private sector to serve the disadvantaged came the encouragement of citizens to donate more, to be more philanthropic, thereby enabling private not-for-profit agencies to provide more social services.[34] But social policies do not always complement each other, and many times they work at cross-purposes. At the same time that the administration was encouraging Americans to give more, it also cut their personal income tax rates. As a result, Americans gained less by making philanthropic contributions. Some social scientists estimate that decreased taxes resulted in a loss of $10 billion in donations between 1981 and 1984! Reductions in federal spending along with reduced incentives to give have hurt many not-for-profit agencies. Among the hardest hit were agencies providing housing, employment, training, legal, and social services, while health-related services have fared better. In addition, other federal government actions, including elimination of the Community Services Administration, appointment of an "ardent conservative" to head ACTION (the federal volunteer agency), and attempts to increase postal costs and change accounting procedures for agencies engaged in political advocacy activities, have served to alienate the not-for-profit sector.

Finally, the president's desire to encourage voluntarism, although well intentioned, cannot make up for many of the cuts in social welfare spending. It is true that citizen involvement is an important aspect of the quality of human services. Volunteers can do many things to assist their communities by promoting better and increased social services, but they are only a part of providing the professional services needed by many clients.

DO SOCIAL SERVICES REALLY WORK?

Do social services really help people? Evaluating any social welfare program or policy is difficult because social-service programs are often without well-defined goals. There is a "confusion between policy ends and policy means. . . . While federal and state governments are committed to 'doing something' about certain vulnerable populations, the end product of their efforts has not been specified."[35]

Even if we knew the specific goals of various social services, evaluating these services is not easy. There are two types of major obstacles to evaluation: political and methodological. Political obstacles operate at all levels of the social service delivery system. Evaluation is threatening to federal, state, and local government, to social service administrators, to social service workers, and last but not least, to the recipients themselves. Evaluation is threatening to governments because it might imply that they have developed poor policies, passed inadequate laws in response to those policies, or funded ineffective programs. Evaluation is threatening to social service administrators because it might imply that they have done a poor job of implementing and managing the programs, laws, and policies developed by legislators. Evaluation is threatening to social service workers because it might imply that they are not adequately skilled in delivering and providing social services to clients. Finally, evaluation may be threatening to recipients because the process may invade their privacy, place pressure on them in times of personal crisis, and make them even more embarrassed about receiving social services.

A second major source of difficulty in conducting evaluations of social services is methodological. Methodological problems are problems found in the design of the evaluation. For example, there are difficulties in obtaining truly random samples and difficulties in generalizing from special samples to the whole population. In addition, there is a "halo effect": Groups that are selected to receive services are more likely to improve because they are given attention, regardless of the quality of the service. Experimentation in the social services is also difficult since governments often cannot deny services to people. Many studies that are called *evaluations* are actually little more than a tabulation of the number of people seen, or the amount of services provided, rather than an evaluation of the actual effects or impacts of programs or services on these people.

But in spite of these political and methodological obstacles to evaluation, more efforts are being made to determine the effectiveness of social service programs. For example, one writer concluded that while there is very little empirical evidence of the overall effects of social service programs for the elderly, two demonstrable effects are "(1) an increase in the ability of the aged to maintain homes apart from younger relatives, and (2) an increase in proprietary nursing home beds for the sick aged."[36]

In the 1970s a number of studies were conducted to evaluate the success of community mental-health centers.[37] A study conducted by the United States government's General Accounting Office spoke of the positive effects of CMHC programs. One effect cited was an increase in the availability of community care. In another report the Senate Committee on Labor and Public Welfare also discussed the positive results that have been achieved by CMHCs through provision of community-based care in lieu of institutional care. But other reports have not been as complimentary. A 1974 Nader Report states that community mental-health centers have not reduced the number of persons admitted to state mental-health institutions. The Nader Report accused psychiatrists of benefiting unfairly from the programs and of neglecting service to the poor.

A study of reports on child welfare services tells us that the effects of counseling services on families and children have not been clearly identified. Evaluation of services provided by family-service and child-guidance agencies has suggested that "the service is helpful, but available research does not establish this helpfulness at statistically significant levels."[38] Generally, half of those clients served by family service agencies show some improvement.[39] But the results of studies of child welfare services must be interpreted carefully.[40] Evaluative studies of child and family welfare programs suffer from the same methodological problems as other social service programs.

We see that it is difficult to determine the effects of social-service programs. Studies that have attempted to evaluate the effectiveness of these programs often show mixed results. While there is no doubt that the *number* of social services available to those in need has increased, the demonstrable *effects* of these services are often limited or ambiguous.

Should we conclude from this evaluation that social services are not very effective? This may be an unfair and premature assumption to make. Each of us can think of individuals who benefit greatly from social services: an elderly person who receives adequate meals through a nutrition program such as Meals on Wheels, a friend whose depression has been relieved through services provided by a mental-health center, a child whose adoption prevented transfer from foster home to foster home. In the aggregate, however, effects of social service programs cannot always be demonstrated easily, yet there is more pressure on human service professionals to justify that their work is useful.

Evaluation studies seem to be most useful when they contain recommendations for future service delivery. A major 1985 study of the effectiveness of mental-health services conducted by the National Association of Social Workers concluded with the following suggestions for providing better services:

1. Clients should be involved in defining the problems to be solved.
2. The treatment should be clearly specified.
3. Treatment expectations should be made clear to the client.
4. Paraprofessionals can play an important role in assisting mental-health clients.
5. Short-term treatment tends to produce better outcomes than long-term treatment.
6. Outpatients and hospitalized and posthospitalized patients benefit from different types of services.[41]

As attempts are made to improve client services, researchers and program evaluators are also striving to develop strategies and techniques which take into account the political and methodological obstacles faced in evaluating social service policies and programs.

SUMMARY

Social services include many types of programs, including day care, mental health care, juvenile-delinquency-prevention programs, child welfare programs, and nursing-home care. Not all social services are directed toward the poor. People from all walks of life may require social services. Social services are provided by both public and private agencies. The federal government chose to reimburse the states at a generous rate for providing social services, especially those to public assistance recipients. Spending increased rapidly, and the federal government exercised its option to control social service spending through Title XX of the Social Security Act and more recently through the Social Services Block Grant.

Mental-health services are one example of social services that may be needed by an individual regardless of economic and social status. Mental-health services were first provided in large institutions where patients were often poorly treated. Better treatment methods—for instance, "moral treatment"—were regarded as too costly to provide. Dorothea Dix and other reformers helped improve institutional treatment, but it was not until the 1960s that greater emphasis was placed on community care. Two factors that paved the way for improved mental-health legislation were (1) the identification of many young men with mental-health problems during World War II and (2) the improvement of drugs that help the mentally ill function in society. The Community Mental Health Act of 1963 was the landmark legislation that encouraged the building and staffing of community mental-health centers (CMHCs). CMHC services are available in most communities today and are financed in large part through the Alcohol, Drug Abuse and Mental Health Block Grant.

One of the biggest obstacles faced by CMHCs is the fear that community residents have of mental-health clients. Residents may oppose locating a mental-health facility within their community because they believe that clients may harm their children, that the neighborhood will deteriorate, and that they will be forced to sell their property for less than it is worth. While these claims have not been substantiated, residents may resort to adopting zoning ordinances that prohibit the location of mental-health facilities within their communities.

The United States has no official social policy for families and children, largely because of the belief that families should be relatively free from governmental intervention. In the United States a variety of policies govern family relations; some of these laws are used to intervene in cases of child abuse and neglect. Child abuse was not "discovered" in the United States until the 1960s when pediatric radiologists began looking for the cause of bone fractures and other unexplained traumas suffered by children. Prior to that time, punishment of children was considered a parental right. Children whose parents were incapable of caring for them were often sent to institutions to learn appropriate societal values, but parents were not the focus of treatment. Today public social service agencies are largely responsible for intervening in cases of neglect and abuse and for providing services to abusive parents.

The most important legislation that recognizes the social service needs of the elderly is the Older Americans Act of 1965. The act emphasizes a variety of services for the elderly, including nutrition programs and services that increase the capacity of the elderly to remain in the community. The Administration on Aging is the federal agency that is primarily responsible for administering this act by determining the needs of America's elderly and insuring that services are provided to address these needs. Some elderly persons may not be aware that a network of services is available to them within their communities.

Some attempts to evaluate the effectiveness of social services have produced positive results while others have been unclear about the benefits of social services. Social-service providers and program evaluators can work together to develop better methods of assessing the effectiveness of social services.

NOTES

1. Alfred J. Kahn, *Social Policy and Social Services* (New York: Random House, 1979), pp. 12–13.
2. Robert Morris, *Social Policy of the American Welfare State: An Introduction to Policy Analysis* (New York: Harper & Row, 1979), p. 120.
3. Department of Health, Education and Welfare, *First Annual Report to Congress on Title XX of the Social Security Act*, 1977, p. 1.
4. John L. Palmer and Isabel V. Sawhill, eds., *The Reagan Record* (Cambridge, Mass.: Ballinger, 1984), p. 375.
5. Ibid., p. 376.
6. David Mechanic, *Mental Health and Social Policy, 2nd ed.* (Englewood Cliffs, N.J.: Prentice-Hall, 1980), pp. 15–16.
7. Department of Health and Human Services, Public Health Service, Alcohol, Drug Abuse, and Mental Health Administration, *Report of the Administrator, Alcohol, Drug Abuse, and Mental Health Administration*, 1979, p. 1.
8. Department of Health and Human Services, National Institute on Drug Abuse, *Highlights from Student Drug Use in America 1975–1981*, cited in Oakley Ray, *Drugs, Society and Human Behavior* (St. Louis: C. V. Mosby Co., 1983), p. 15.
9. Thomas R. Vischi, Kenneth R. Jones, Ella L. Shank, and Lowell H. Lima, Department of Health, Education and Welfare, Public Health Service, *The Alcohol, Drug Abuse, and Mental Health National Data Book: A Reference Book of National Data on Incidence and Prevalence, Facilities, Services Utilization, Practitioners, Costs, and Financing*, January 1980, p. 6.
10. Ibid.
11. Mechanic, *Mental Health and Social Policy*, pp. 51–52.
12. Ibid., p. 52.
13. Ibid., p. 53.
14. G. Grob, *The State and the Mentally Ill* (Chapel Hill: University of North Carolina Press, 1966), cited in ibid., p. 54.
15. Ibid.
16. Ibid., p. 61.
17. See ibid., pp. 55–56, for a discussion of these psychiatric screenings.
18. Ibid., pp. 61–62.
19. Clara Claiborne Park with Leon N. Shapiro, *You are Not Alone: Understanding and Dealing*

with Mental Illness—A Guide for Patients, Doctors, and Other Professionals (Boston: Little, Brown, 1976), pp. 93–94.

20. For a description of these programs see Department of Health, Education and Welfare, *Report on Federal Government Programs That Relate to Children,* 1979, prepared by the representatives of the Federal Interagency Committee on the International Year of the Child, no. (OHDS) 79-30180.
21. Data reported in this section are taken from Department of Health, Education and Welfare, Office of Human Development Services, National Center for Child Advocacy, U.S. Children's Bureau, Administration for Children, Youth and Families, *National Study of Social Services to Children and Their Families: Overview,* prepared by Ann W. Shyne and Anita G. Schroeder, (Washington: Government Printing Office, 1978), pp. 1, 3, 5, 6, 9, 12, 13, 17, 21, and 22.
22. *Highlights of Official Child Neglect and Abuse Reporting 1982* (Denver: American Humane Association, Child Protection Division, 1984), p. 2.
23. Ibid., p. 5.
24. Perspectives on Child Maltreatment in the Mid '80s, Department of Health and Human Services, DHHS publication no. (OHDS) 84-30338, p. 15.
25. *Highlights of Official Child Neglect and Abuse Reporting 1982,* p. 9.
26. This section relies on Stephen J. Pfohl, "The Discovery of Child Abuse," *Social Problems* 24, no. 3 (February 1977), pp. 310–23.
27. Alfred Kadushin, *Child Welfare Services,* 3rd ed. (New York: Macmillan, 1980), p. 199.
28. Ibid., pp. 214–20.
29. Palmer and Sawhill, *Reagan Record,* p. 376.
30. Ibid.
31. This section relies on Linda Hubbard Getze, "Need Help? What the Aging Network Can Do for You," *Modern Maturity* (March 1981), pp. 33–36.
32. Janet Hook, "Congress Clears $4 Billion Bill for Elderly Services, Nutrition," *Congressional Quarterly,* September 29, 1984, p. 2408.
33. Lester M. Salamon, "Nonprofit Organizations, The Lost Opportunity,'" in Palmer and Sawhill, *Reagan Record,* p. 273.
34. For a more extensive discussion of the nonprofit sector and the Reagan administration see ibid, pp. 261–85, on which this paragraph relies.
35. Morris, *Social Policy of the American Welfare State,* p. 133.
36. Ibid., p. 150.
37. See Lucy D. Ozarin, "Community Mental Health: Does It Work? Review of the Evaluation Literature," in Walter E. Barton and Charlotte J. Sanborn, eds., *An Assessment of the Community Mental Health Movement* (Lexington, Mass.: D.C. Heath, 1977), pp. 122–23.
38. Kadushin, *Child Welfare Services,* pp. 107–8.
39. Ibid., p. 99.
40. Ibid.
41. Lynn Videka-Sherman, "Harriett M. Bartlett Practice Effectiveness Project, Report to NASW Board of Directors," Silver Springs, Md.: National Association of Social Workers, July 10, 1985.

chapter 8

Fighting hunger: federal nutrition programs

IS AMERICA HUNGRY?

The pictures of Ethiopians, their bodies reduced to flesh over bones, have recently made clear to us the dire consequences of starvation. It is frightening to know that such conditions exist in the world. Americans shocked by television and newspaper accounts of the famine have responded with an outpouring of aid. Fortunately, Americans do not face this crisis, but unfortunately, some Americans do face serious problems of undernutrition, such as anemia.[1] Technically, "malnutrition is an impairment or risk of impairment to mental or physical health resulting from failure to meet the total nutrient requirements of an individual."[2] But it has been suggested that in the United States, "a person should be considered malnourished if for economic or other reasons beyond his control he experiences repetitive periods of prolonged hunger even though his total intake of nutrients is sufficient to protect him from symptoms of deficiency disease."[3]

Most Americans consume about the same amount of calories daily, regardless of whether they are poor, and most get enough of the essential nutrients, except for iron. (Only whites above the poverty level take in 100 percent of the standard for iron.) But for other nutrients such as calcium and vitamins A and C, nearly everyone, rich or poor, averages more than 100 percent of the standard.[4] However, in the United States, *patterns* of eating are more important than counting grams of protein or other numbers on the backs of food packages.[5] For example, in the United States poor people may eat adequately at the beginning of the month, but when food stamps, AFDC checks, or SSI checks run out near the end of the month, eating habits may change. Or the poor may have to decide between buying more food and paying other bills. Other patterns are also important. Children may attend school without breakfast and without money to buy lunch; a snack and supper may be their main sources of nutrition. The poor elderly are sometimes unable to get to the store or have no teeth with which to chew food. An increasing number of people are turning to food kitchens, which have sprung up across the country to obtain meals (see pages 179–180). When low-income families in southeast Washington, D.C., were asked what they would purchase if they had an additional $50 per month, eight out of twelve said, "Food!" Starvation may be rare or nonexistent in the United States, but patterns of inadequate nutrition do exist.

EARLY POLICIES: COMMODITY FOOD DISTRIBUTION

Prior to the 1930s, states and communities used their own methods to feed their "deserving" poor. But with the advent of the Great Depression, more and more people were unable to obtain enough food to eat. Today mention of the Great Depression conjures up pictures of men and women standing in bread lines and waiting in soup kitchens to obtain their only means of survival. Bread lines and soup kitchens were some of the first widespread attempts to deal with poverty and hunger in the United States. But these methods of feeding needy persons were inadequate to meet the country's needs. In 1933 Congress established the Federal Surplus Relief Corporation to provide surplus commodity foods as well as coal, mattresses, and blankets to the poor.[6] Overproduction of food and encouragement by farmers to purchase surplus goods helped prompt the federal government to feed the poor. The Federal Surplus Relief Corporation provided as much relief to the agricultural industry as it did to the hungry.[7] The early commodity-distribution program was characterized by recipients waiting in long lines to receive food, an experience which some public officials believed was degrading for beneficiaries.[8]

There were other problems with the commodity food distribution program as well. Perishables were difficult to preserve, and alternatives to helping the hungry were needed. As a solution, the nation embarked on its first Food Stamp program in 1939. The program used two types of stamps, blue and orange. Orange stamps could be used to purchase any type of food; blue stamps could be redeemed only for surplus commodities. For every dollar spent on orange stamps, the beneficiary received fifty cents worth of blue stamps free.[9] Four years later, in 1943, the program ended. The American Enterprise Institute for Public Policy Research believes the program was terminated for three reasons: (1) families who were poor but not receiving other public assistance payments were not eligible to receive assistance; (2) widespread participation was discouraged by purchase requirements, which were believed to be too high; and (3) products other than surplus foods were sometimes purchased with the stamps.[10] These factors contributed to the early demise of the program.

With the termination of the original Food Stamp program came a return to the commodity-food-distribution method. Commodity distribution was a popular method for feeding poor persons for at least two reasons. First, it insured that surplus foods would be utilized. Second, the poor were given foods which were supposed to meet minimum nutritional requirements. But the new commodity-food-distribution program left unsolved many problems of the original commodity program. Food preservation remained a problem; large containers of food were inconvenient for use by small families; and some foods were unappealing.

Alternatives to commodity distribution were continually considered. In 1961 President John F. Kennedy was able to begin a new Food Stamp program on a pilot basis. There was some early evidence that recipients purchased more and better goods under the program. This provided encouragement for passage of the Food Stamp Act of 1964.[11] The illustration on pages 169–170 further describes America's concerns about nutrition.

THE FOOD STAMP PROGRAM

Today's Food Stamp program is the responsibility of the United States Department of Agriculture (USDA), but state and local welfare agencies certify eligible recipients and provide them with the stamps. Recipients are given an allotment of stamps based on their income and family size. The stamps or food coupons, like money, come in various denominations and may be exchanged for food products in regular retail stores that choose to accept the coupons. Eligibility requirements and coupon allotments are established at the federal level.

The Food Stamp program was originally designed to be broader than the commodity distribution program. The states were to give food stamps to any persons whose incomes prevented them from acquiring an adequate diet. This meant that persons who were not welfare recipients but whose incomes were low (the near-poor) could also qualify.[12]

ILLUSTRATION: POLITICS DISCOVERS AND REDISCOVERS HUNGER

"Hunger in America was conceived as a national issue in April 1967 by two northern senators in an alien rural South. On a mission guided by politics, they came to study poverty programs, but in the small Delta town of Cleveland, Mississippi, they found more than they had bargained for.

The United States Senator from New York felt his way through a dark windowless shack, fighting nausea at the strong smell of aging mildew, sickness, and urine. In the early afternoon shadows, he saw a child sitting on the floor of a tiny back room. Barely two years old, wearing only a filthy undershirt, she sat rubbing several grains of rice round and round on the floor. The senator knelt beside her.

"Hello . . . Hi . . . Hi, baby . . . ," he murmured, touching her cheeks and her hair as he would his own child's. As he sat on the dirty floor, he placed his hand gently on the child's swollen stomach. But the little girl sat as if in a trance, her sad eyes turned downward, and rubbed the gritty rice.

For five minutes he tried: talking, caressing, tickling, poking—demanding that the child respond. The baby never looked up.

The senator made his way to the front yard where Annie White, the mother of the listless girl and five other children, stood washing her family's clothes in a zinc tub. She had no money, she was saying to the senator, couldn't afford to buy food stamps; she was feeding her family only some rice and biscuits made from leftover surplus commodities.

For a few moments Robert F. Kennedy stood alone, controlling his feelings, which were exposed to the press entourage waiting outside the house. Then he whispered to a companion, "I've seen bad things in West Virginia, but I've never seen anything like this anywhere in the United States."

Senators Kennedy of New York and Joseph Clark of Pennsylvania discovered hunger that day, raw hunger imbedded in the worst poverty the black South had known since the Depression of the 1930s. Driving along muddy, forgotten roads, the two senators and their aides stopped at shack after shack to see with their own eyes hungry, diseased children; to hear with their own ears the poor describe their struggle for survival."[1]

At the same time that political figures such as Robert F. Kennedy were discovering hunger, others were also investigating the problem. The Field Foundation, supported by the Field family of Chicago's Marshall Field department store, also documented the problems of eating, or not eating, in America.[2] Ten years later, in 1977, the Field Foundation conducted a follow-up study. The findings showed that there were fewer cases of malnutrition. And the doctors who conducted the study, four of whom had conducted the original 1967 study, suggested that federal food programs were responsible for much of the difference.[3]

But social problems reappear, and the 1980s brought with them new charges of hunger in America. Increased unemployment and social-program cuts were blamed. Concerned that reports of hunger were exaggerated,[4] the President's Task Force on Food Assistance was appointed and its findings published in 1984. It concluded that undernutrition was *not* problem. Social-action groups lambasted the report. The president of the National Association of Social Workers called it a "political document that has not treated the problem of deprivation in this country in the objective manner that it deserves."[5] And nutrition experts said, "Despite their almost total lack of qualifications, the task force members did manage to find that hunger has reappeared in America. But because of their ineptitude, they were unable to qualify its extent, or to discern the presence of chronic malnutrition."[6]

Meanwhile, the Food Research Action Center publicized results of its work indicating increased infant-mortality rates in some areas of the country, and the Citizens' Commission on Hunger in New England also concluded that malnutrition and hunger again confronted America. While the President's Task Force recommended block grants to the state to fund nutrition programs and penalizing states that failed to lower error rates in the Food Stamp program, the Citizens' Commission proposed quarterly reporting to Congress on efforts to reduce hunger and a bipartisan commission to develop legislation that would put hunger to rest.

The Physicians Task Force on Hunger in America recently identified 150 "hunger counties" in the U.S.—counties in which substantial numbers of poor people are not receiving food stamps. In order to reduce hunger, the physicians recommend: giving cash or credit cards to recipients to reduce the embarassment of using coupons; improving outreach efforts to nonparticipants; simplifying the entire process of obtaining food benefits.[7]

Politics has played its part in attempts to achieve the goal of reducing hunger. The goals of rational planning suggest that no American should go hungry; the politics of hunger in America suggest that nutrition programs remain part of the political struggle over welfare.

1. Nick Kotz, *Let Them Eat Promises: The Politics of Hunger in America* (Englewood Cliffs, N.J.: Prentice-Hall, 1969), pp. 1-2.

2. Ibid, pp. 7–9.

3. Nick Kotz, *Hunger in America: The Federal Response* (New York: Field Foundation, 1979), p. 9.

4. "Hunger Reports Prompt Food Aid Expansion," *Congressional Quarterly Almanac 1983*, p. 412.

5. "Report on Hunger Overlooks Role of Cuts," *NASW News*, February 1984, p. 19.

6. Jean Mayer and Jeanne Goldberg, "New Report Documents Hunger in America," *Tallahassee Democrat*, March 29, 1984, p. 16E.

7. James Pinkerton, "Overhaul of Food Stamp Program Advised to Bypass Bureaucracy," *Austin American-Statesman*, May 21, 1986, p. A9

But food stamps have not always been provided at no charge. At first, the program worked like this: Those who qualified for benefits paid a specific price for their stamps; the amount depended on income and family size. The amount paid was supposed to be the amount the family would have spent on food. Recipients received stamps, which had a greater value than the amount they paid. The difference between the amount paid and the value of the stamps was called the bonus.

"In theory," says one observer, "the food stamp plan 'sounded' simple and workable, and should have been an enormous improvement over commodity distribution." But, he says, what really happened was "extortion."[13]

> It was no accident that the stamp payment formula produced the outcries "We can't afford the stamps" and "The stamps run out after two weeks." Following their congressional leaders' twin desires of helping the farmers but not providing welfare to the poor, Agricultural Department bureaucrats had designed a Food Stamp program so conservative that reformers called the plan "Scrooge stamps."[14]

A number of changes were made in the Food Stamp program in the 1970s. Benefits were increased, and eligibility and application procedures were standardized so that applicants are now treated similarly regardless of where they live or where they apply for stamps. Unemployed adult recipients who are capable of working are required to register for work and accept it if a suitable job can be found.

A troublesome requirement had been that recipients were required to buy either all the stamps to which they were entitled or none at all. This requirement was modified so that a portion, rather than all of the stamps, could be purchased. The price of stamps could not exceed 30 percent of the household's income, and in the poorest cases, families could receive the stamps at no charge. Efforts were made to increase participation rates through advertising campaigns and outreach to nonparticipating eligible persons. In addition, communities were not immediately forced to choose between food stamps and commodity distribution. They could operate both programs until 1973, when food stamps had to be the program available in all communities.

THE ELIMINATION OF PURCHASE REQUIREMENT

The most significant change in the Food Stamp program since its inception has been the elimination of the purchase requirements in 1977. Critics had held that the Food Stamp program did not necessarily make eating better or easier for the poor. For many families, the amount they had to spend for food stamps was more than they could actually afford—except by taking from the rent or other necessities. Other reasons for low participation have been the stigma attached to "being on welfare," lack of knowledge of the program, and inability to get to the Food Stamp office to apply. The elimination of the purchase requirement helped to increase participation rates. In the Southeast, participation rose by over 32 percent; in the Mountain Plains, by almost 32 percent; and in the Southwest by almost 31 percent. These areas include many rural states. In New England, participation increased by 7 percent.[15] Although estimates indicate that fifteen million eligible persons are not participating,[16] the Food Stamp program has come closer to being available to all needy Americans than any other welfare program.

FOOD STAMPS: PARTICIPANTS AND COSTS

Nearly twenty-two million persons, or approximately 9.5 percent of all Americans, receive food stamps. Of all food-stamp households, about 58 percent are white, 33 percent are black and 9 percent are of Spanish origin.[17] Unlike the AFDC program, single persons and married persons without children are also eligible for food stamps. About 34 percent of households are headed by a married couple; 41 percent are headed by women only, and many of the remaining 25 percent are composed of single individuals. Most households (63) percent are in metropolitan areas. Much of America's poverty is found in the South, a fact that is borne out by the statistics of the Food Stamp program. Forty-one percent of recipients reside in the South, 23 percent in the North Central part of the United States, 20 percent in the Northeast, and the remaining sixteen percent in the West. Many recipients (43 percent) have annual incomes under $5,000 while 31 percent earn between $5,000 and $10,000. Another 14 percent earn between $10,000 and $15,000, and 12 percent make $15,000 or more. Sixty-seven percent have incomes below the poverty line. Forty-one percent of all families in the United States below the poverty line and 3.2 percent of families above the line receive food stamps. Many public assistance recipients, such as AFDC families, are automatically eligible for food stamps. Eligibility is determined by gross income, which cannot exceed 130 percent of the poverty line, and net income cannot exceed 100 percent of the poverty line. In determining payments, certain deductions are made from income. Eighteen percent of earned income is deducted along with a flat amount (about $90). Child-care expenses are allotted while a parent is working or seeking employment. Some housing allowances are also made. Medical expenses for aged and disabled persons are also deducted. Assets generally cannot exceed $1,500.

Some special categories of people receive stamps. Victims of natural disasters may qualify. Alcoholics and drug addicts, blind and disabled persons, women and children and aged persons who reside in nonprofit facilities such as halfway houses, shelters, or group homes may also be eligible. However, the eligibility of students has been tightened owing to work requirements of the program.

Because food stamps have been available to so many Americans, the cost of the program has been considerable, even after controlling for inflation (see figure 8-1). In 1965 the program cost a modest $32 million. By 1970 costs had risen to $473 million, but by 1980 costs had escalated to more than $9 billion. In 1983 they were about $12 billion.

FIGURE 8-1 Annual bonus value of food stamps, 1965–83. (Sources: *Social Security Bulletin, Annual Statistical Supplement,* 1983, p. 250, and *Statistical Abstract of the United States, 1982/1983*, p. 129.)

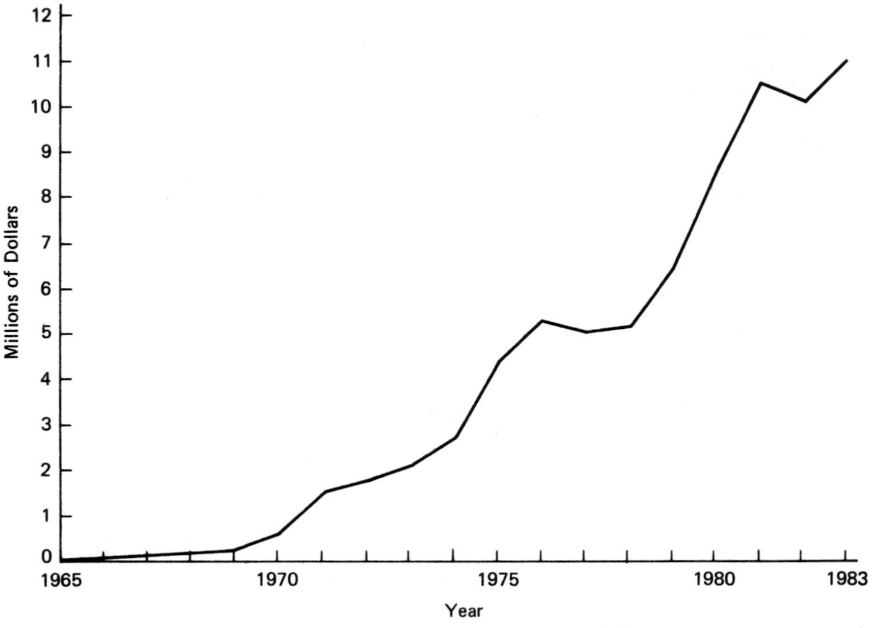

PURCHASING HABITS OF FOOD-STAMP RECIPIENTS

Do food-stamp recipients shop differently from other people? An exploratory study conducted in Cookeville, Tennessee in 1978 compared food-stamp with non-food-stamp recipients and found the differences shown in table 8-1. According to this study, there are a number of differences between food-stamp shoppers and those who do not receive stamps. Food-stamp shoppers are less likely to prepare for trips to the grocery store by making shopping lists. They shop in small, nearby stores, unlike other shoppers, who generally buy in supermarkets. In addition, food-stamp recipients shop in stores that are located close to home, rather than in stores that charge lower prices. Food-stamp shoppers are more satisfied with their local stores and appear to be less concerned about price, although they do buy in larger quantities than non-food-stamp shoppers. But we cannot necessarily blame the poor for their shopping habits. They may have less access to information about sales and other shopping values. The poor are less likely to own automobiles and are thus prevented from taking advantage of sales at faraway supermarkets. Neighborhood stores tend to offer less selection at higher prices than large chain grocery stores, but without transportation the poor may be forced to shop in these nearby establishments.

In contrast to the study represented in table 8-1, other studies suggest that food-stamp shoppers spend their money and stamps in the same fashion as middle-class shoppers. For example, one study reports that the poor and the middle-class spend about the same percentage of their shopping dollar on meat and dairy products but that the poor buy less expensive

TABLE 8-1 Comparison of Food-Shopping Behavior of Food-Stamp Recipients and Nonsubsidized Food Purchasers

FOOD-STAMP RECIPIENTS	NONSUBSIDIZED SHOPPERS
1. Engage in less prepurchase preparation	1. Engage in extensive prepurchase preparation
2. Have less shopping experience	2. Have wide shopping experience
3. Shop in small, nearby stores	3. Shop in supermarkets, traveling as necessary
4. Choose a store on basis of location	4. Choose a store on basis of price
5. Are relatively unconcerned with selection	5. Are highly concerned with selection
6. Are not inclined to believe that supermarkets offer price, quality, or selection advantages	6. Believe that supermarkets offer price, quality, and selection advantages
7. Are well satisfied with their regular store	7. Express frustration and suggest store improvements
8. Do not perceive private brands favorably	8. Believe private brands offer acceptable quality at lower prices
9. Buy larger unit sizes	9. Buy smaller unit sizes
10. Are not very price-conscious	10. Are highly price-conscious

Source: Gerald Underwood Skelly, "*A Study of the Differential Food Purchasing Behavior of Federal Stamp Recipients and Non-Subsidized Food Purchasers,*" dissertation, Florida State University, 1978, p. 231.

foods within these categories.[18] The illustration on pages 175–176 tells us about the type of diet that can be purchased with food stamps. Stamp allotments allow recipients to purchase only the most economical foods under the "basic thrifty food plan" established by the United States Department of Agriculture.

ILLUSTRATION: GROCERY SHOPPING WITH FOOD STAMPS

Food-stamp allotments are calculated according to the "thrifty food plan."[1] Although it is the least costly of the USDA's four food plans, the thrifty food plan is still supposed to provide an adequate diet. But the thrifty food plan has been criticized by some nutrition experts as less than adequate, with fewer than 10 percent of participants at this level receiving the recommended daily allowance (RDA) of nutrients and fewer than half getting two-thirds of the RDAs. The Food Stamp program bases stamp allotments on family size but does not take into consideration whether recipients are small children, teenagers, or older or younger adults, who may require varying amounts of food. According to the USDA, a family spends approximately 30 percent of its net income for food. A family with no countable income receives $253 a month in food stamps or about $58 a week. As countable income rises, 30 percent of it is deducted from the base of $253. For example, a family whose countable income is $100 a month receives $223 in food stamps.

What can a family of four eat with $58 per week allotted for food? One USDA official set out to answer the question.[2] The test site was Atlanta, Georgia. She shopped at one grocery store in the city and one grocery store in a suburban neighborhood and spent $58.61 and $56.90 respectively. Here is what she bought in the first store and what she paid for it.

ITEM	AMOUNT PURCHASED	COST
Produce		
Cabbage	1/2 small head	.29
Carrots	2-lb. bag	.79
Celery	1 medium bunch	.59
Lettuce	1 small head	.79
Onions	3 lbs.	.69
Potatoes	5-lb. bag	.99
Apples	5 medium	.58
Bananas	4 medium	.24
Oranges	12 small	1.00
Pears	2 medium	.63
Canned and Dried		
Tomatoes	3 1-lb. cans	1.37
Tomato puree	2 10-1/2 oz. cans	.53
Peaches, juice-packed	1-lb. can	.59
Raisins	1 box (15 oz.)	1.79
Tuna fish, chunk-style	1 can (6-1/2 oz.)	.85
Flour, Mixes and Shortening		
Flour, enriched	10-pound bag	1.54
Gingerbread mix	1 14-oz. box	1.09
Cornmeal, whole ground	2-lb. bag	.79
Fruit-flavored gelatin, dry mix	3-oz. package	.35

Shortening	3-lb. can	1.19
Salt	26-oz. container	.23
Baking powder	4-oz. can	1.25
Rice, Macaroni and Beans		
Noodles, enriched	16-oz. package	.59
Macaroni, enriched	16-oz. package	.59
Rice, regular enriched	1-lb. package	.38
Navy beans, dry	1-lb. package	.29
Cereals		
Shredded wheat	10-oz. package	1.09
Cornflakes	24-oz. package	1.49
Cookies and Crackers		
Oatmeal cookies	11-1/2 oz. package	.89
Saltines	1-lb. package	.49
Bread		
White, enriched	3 22-oz. loaves	1.19
Whole wheat	1-lb. loaf	1.00
Dressings, Jelly and Peanut Butter		
Vinegar	1 pint	.44
Jelly	18-oz. jar	.99
Peanut butter	18-oz. jar	.99
Dry and Canned Milk		
Nonfat dry milk	Box to make 20 quarts	5.49
Frozen		
Mixed vegetables	1 package (2 for $1.09)	.55
Green beans	1 package (2 for 99¢)	.50
Peas	1 package (2 for $1.09)	.54
Orange juice, concentrate	1 12-fl. oz. can	.79
Lemonade, concentrate	1 6-fl. oz. can (6 for $2.09)	.35
Meat		
Ground beef	2 lbs.	2.23
Liver, beef or pork	1 lb.	1.13
Beef, bottom round	3.31 lbs (@ $1.89 lb.)	6.37
Chicken, mixed parts	4.18 (@ 38¢ lb.)	1.59
Dairy and Deli		
Milk, lowfat	1 gal. and 1/2 gal.	1.79
American process cheese	16-oz. package, sliced	1.29
Cottage cheese, lowfat	12-oz. carton	.69
Bacon, sliced	1-lb. package	1.69
Bologna	16-oz package	1.59
Eggs, large	1 dozen (extra large)	.79
Margarine	2 sticks	.39
	Tax:	$2.26
	Total Costs:	$58.61

The USDA defends its meal plans, stating that it "can develop much lower-cost food plans, but they would be very monotonous and less like families' food consumption practices and preferences." But probably no one disagrees that it takes a very careful shopper to feed a family of four for $58 a week.

[1]Much of this paragraph relies on Harrison Donnelly, "Congress to Decide Fate of Food Stamps," *Congressional Quarterly,* February 7, 1981, p. 278.

[2]See Brenda Schuler, "Making Food Dollars Count," *Food and Nutrition* 13, no. 3 (July 1981): 16–19.

NUTRITION PROGRAMS FOR SCHOOL CHILDREN

The National School Lunch Act became law in 1946. Under this program, school-age children obtain hot lunches at reduced prices or free if their parents are unable to pay. The program operates in the following way: The federal government, through the Food and Nutrition Service of the Department of Agriculture, provides cash assistance and food commodities to state departments of education. The departments of education then distribute the cash and food to public and private nonprofit schools that have agreed to participate in the program. Federal expenditures for the program were $3 billion in 1983, and 3.7 billion lunches were served to 22.9 million children (4 million fewer than in previous years). Free lunches are given to children whose family income is at or below 130 percent of the poverty level. Schools receive $1.26 from the federal government for each lunch served to these children. Reduced-price lunches are given to children whose family income is between 130 and 185 percent of the poverty level. Eighty-six cents per meal is given to schools for each of these meals, and children cannot be charged more than 40 cents per meal. The lunches of all children are actually subsidized since schools receive 22 cents for all other lunches served, and the approximate cost of these lunches to children is about 85 cents per meal.[19]

Figures on the number of children served through the lunch program over the years sound impressive, but they might be more impressive if we could be certain that the bulk of the program's benefits went to poor children. Historically, there has been concern that many of the benefits went to nonpoor children.[20] And there were reasons why. Schools had to have kitchen facilities to participate, and schools in poor neighborhoods often did not. Meals to these schools could have been catered, but school-lunch administrators had been known to lobby against earmarking federal funds for free meals to poor children, for fear that private caterers would take over their jobs.[21] The administrators contended that they could take care of poor children out of general federal school-lunch aid; yet critics argued that they provided free lunches to less than half of the poor children in school.[22]

The School Breakfast program is much smaller than the School Lunch program, but it is operated in a similar fashion. Eligibility requirements for students are the same. The federal government provides 60¢ for each free breakfast, 30¢ for reduced-price breakfasts, and 8¢ for all other breakfasts. A reduced-price breakfast cannot exceed a cost of 20¢ to a child. In 1983, 553 million breakfasts were served to 3.4 million children at a cost of $327 million.[23] But because resources allocated for the program are not enough for all school districts, a priority system has been established. Schools in the poorest areas and schools to which children must travel long distances are given preference. While this may be considered a rational approach to allocating scarce resources, the School Breakfast program, like the School Lunch program, has sometimes not operated in a rational fashion. As with some other programs, school districts must choose to participate. Why would schools choose *not* to participate in a program that would benefit hungry children? First, the program means more administrative responsibilities for school personnel. Second, adoption of the program may mean that teachers and other school personnel must monitor the breakfasts and come to school earlier when the breakfasts are served before class. These factors may make the program unpopular among school personnel who already feel taxed by heavy workloads and who do not wish to see the school day lengthened.

There are other programs designed to provide nutritional benefits to school- and preschool-age children. The Summer Food program offers lunches to children in poor areas during the school-year recess, and the Child Care Food program offers funds for breakfasts, snacks, lunches and dinners to children in day-care centers. The School Milk program began in 1954 at a time when the market was full of surplus dairy products. In 1983, $20 million was spent on the program, and 210 million half-pints of milk were distributed each day.[24] Unfortunately, the program is now restricted to schools and child-care facilities which are not participating in other federal food programs.

The Reagan administration has not been kind to child-nutrition programs. Funds for meals to needy children were cut; a number of schools lost the milk program, and the summer program was restricted to especially impoverished areas, but, block grant proposals to fund these nutrition programs have been rejected by Congress.

WIC

The Special Supplemental Nutrition Program for Women, Infants, and Children, called WIC, was ten years old in 1984. WIC's purpose is to upgrade the nutrition of low-income women, infants, and young children. The Food and Nutrition Service of the Department of Agriculture operates the program in conjunction with fifteen hundred local agencies, mostly health clinics and departments. Pregnant women and those who are breastfeeding and children to age four with nutritional problems are given foods (iron-fortified formula and cereal, eggs, juice, cheese, and milk) high in important nutrients. Participants are given WIC food coupons valued at about $28 monthly to obtain these food products in grocery stores. About $1.2 billion was spent in 1983, and 2.5 million women and children were reached by the program.[25] A similar but much smaller program, the Commodity Supplemental Food program, provides food products in lieu of coupons. The WIC program has withstood the president's budget axe; in fact, Congress has increased funding for this more popular of the social welfare programs. However, a 1985 suit by the National Anti-Hunger Coalition and others charged the federal government with failure to spend all appropriated WIC funds. If all funds are not spent, thousands of potential beneficiaries may not receive services.

MEALS FOR THE ELDERLY

In addition to the Food Stamp program, there are two important nutrition programs targeted for the elderly. One is the Meals on Wheels program. Meals on Wheels began in 1972 as part of a federal effort to improve the nutrition of the elderly. States receive funding and coordinate the program through local agencies. The agencies are responsible for seeing that the meals are prepared and delivered to elderly persons at their homes. Elderly individuals who receive food stamps can pay for these meals with stamps, and a donation amount is suggested for others who can afford to pay in cash. The second type of service is the congregate meal program in which meals are provided at sites such as senior citizens' centers. In addition to improved nutrition, there is a positive spillover effect from these meal programs for the elderly. They provide an opportunity for older Americans, who may be isolated, to maintain contact with others in their community. A visit by the Meals on Wheels volunteer provides a check, in case the elderly individual has become ill or needs other assistance. A visit to the congregate meal site offers the elderly a chance for socialization. Staff and volunteers may also identify other social service needs of the participants and assist them in obtaining services.

ILLUSTRATION: HOW PEOPLE SURVIVE ON LEFTOVERS

At 3 A.M. on a wet, bone-chilling night, Carol Fennelly is grubbing around in a garbage dumpster at the Maryland Wholesale Produce Market, south of Baltimore. Bundled against the cold, she quickly fills four large cardboard boxes with green peppers, then moves to the loading dock. A few words with a merchant yield three cases of blemished tomatoes and some bananas too ripe to make it to a supermarket shelf.

By 4 A.M., Fennelly and two co-workers have enough to fill their van—15 cases each of broccoli and pears, 12 of tomatoes, four each of peppers and bananas and a couple of boxes of grapes.

By 10 that morning, the produce has been cleaned and sorted by Fennelly and fellow members of a religious activist group called the Community for Creative Non-Violence. Some 150 needy people are lined up outside its free food pantry in Washington, D.C., soon to receive the recovered produce, along with donated day-old bread, packets of chicken giblets and U.S. government cornmeal. Later, street people may drop in for a cup of coffee and doughnuts to tide them over. Still more produce—salvaged from small truck farms, market loading docks and supermarket dumpsters—will supply an evening meal. Nearly 1000 men and women are fed here each day.

In the war against hunger, members of small groups such as this one are shock troops on the front lines of a growing national movement to reclaim food for the poor that otherwise would be thrown away.

About a fifth of the food produced in the U.S. is wasted, a federal study revealed. Much is lost or spoiled during storage, transportation and processing, still more during meal preparation and as plate waste. Little is recoverable.

More than $6 billion worth of food at the wholesale and retail level is wasted—or used to be. Recently, the food banks have begun recovering some of this: surplus items, mislabeled goods, food whose shelflife has expired, and marred but edible items. Situated in population centers and equipped with warehouses, freezers and coolers, the food banks ask large food companies for donations, which they then distribute to soup kitchens, emergency feeding programs and food pantries, as well as to various social welfare agencies.

By asking the agencies to contribute from 5 cents to 12 cents a pound for such goods, the food banks are largely self-supporting. The agencies, which often purchase food at wholesale or retail prices, in turn have a cheap, reliable supply of consumables. And the companies making the food donations are eligible for a tax write-off on the items.

"It's a tremendous idea, and everyone benefits," says Bill Ewing, director of marketing for Second Harvest, a network of 74 food banks. Begun as a small operation in Phoenix in 1967, Second Harvest has expanded nationwide since 1977. Last year, the organization distributed 85 million pounds of food across the U.S.

While food banks are geared to function efficiently by gathering, storing and distributing in large quantities, small neighborhood-based programs also are a vital link in the food chain. It takes little more than desire and hard work to have a significant impact.

In November 1982, Celeste McKinley of Las Vegas went to a garbage dumpster behind a supermarket, seeking waste produce to feed her pet cockatoo. "I couldn't believe what they were throwing away," she recalls. "Most of the food was still attractive and edible but no longer shelf-perfect. It was a terrible waste."

McKinley began soliciting surplus from supermarkets in the city. Today, she operates Gleaners, Inc., a free food pantry furnishing groceries to more than 15,000 needy families a month.

In New York, an organization called City Harvest operates a different type of salvage program, providing the physical link between food supplies and the agencies that need them. Six people, one office, a telephone and two vans net 2 million pounds of surplus food a year from a network of restaurants, bakeries, food suppliers and other sources.

"We have no warehouse—don't need one," says Helen Palit, the founder of City Harvest. "The whole thing is done by telephone. Food suppliers have always wanted to give away their surplus, but they never knew where to send it or who would pick it up."

Manhattan is an especially rich resource. On any day, Palit may get donations of 100 pounds of pâté and 20 wheels of Brie cheese from a gourmet supplier, or thousands of pounds of lamb from a wholesaler who overbought, or surplus meals from expensive restaurants where the tab for one might run $100 or more. Food banks in other cities have similar luck.

Unfortunately, the salvage operations still claim only a fraction of the food being thrown away. Many possible donors remain untapped, while others are reluctant to contribute their surplus. Fast-food chains, for example, routinely toss out any items that sit much longer than 10 minutes under a heat lamp. The chains have resisted suggestions to freeze these foods and donate them to the hungry.

Though it is seen as a holding action to help just a few of the 35.3 million Americans living below the poverty level, the food-bank movement is growing. As Celeste McKinley says, "We help feed people, and it doesn't cost the taxpayers one cent."

Source: Michael Satchell, "How People Survive on Leftovers," *Parade* magazine, February 10, 1985, p. 9.

CASHING OUT FOOD STAMPS

The older of the major welfare programs—for example, AFDC and SSI (formerly Old Age Assistance, Aid to the Blind, and Aid to the Permanently and Totally Disabled)—are *cash* assistance programs. The newer welfare programs—for example, Food Stamps and Medicaid—are *in-kind* programs. Why are the benefits of newer welfare programs administered differently from older welfare programs?

It might be argued that *cashing-out*—administering all welfare programs on a cash basis would be more efficient. AFDC and SSI recipients who qualify for food stamps would simply have their checks increased as a more efficient means of providing nutritional benefits. While the use of food stamps does allow recipients greater choice of food products than commodity distribution, the use of stamps is still stigmatizing to recipients as they stand in grocery store checkout lines. A cash allowance equal to the value of the stamps would reduce or eliminate this stigma and still allow the beneficiary a choice of food products. Other savings and benefits might also result from cashing out. The costs of printing the stamps, transferring and destroying them—about $41.5 million annually—would be eliminated.[26] Underground markets for selling and trading stamps would also be eliminated.

But the choice of a cash allowance has been rejected. Part of the explanation is found in the nature of in-kind programs. Politicians who allot funds to the poor may believe that the use of stamps will insure a more adequate diet for the poor, since the stamps may be legally used only to purchase food. Proponents of the use of stamps believe that this plan reduces the chances that food allowances will be used for other purposes. Most stamps are used for basic food needs. We do hear reports of recipients who use stamps to buy "gourmet" food items or sell the stamps for cash, but there is little evidence to suggest that a cash allowance would not be used to purchase food, and neither cash nor stamps can insure that recipients will purchase the most nutritious foods. In fact, many Americans, rich and poor, need guidance in obtaining a healthy diet.[27]

HOW MUCH FRAUD AND ERROR IN WELFARE?

Do a large number of welfare clients cheat? Would recipients rather collect benefits than work? Are merchants who accept food stamps profiting unfairly from the Food Stamp program by overcharging food-stamp recipients? Do the doctors who accept Medicare and Medicaid payments order more diagnostic tests and treatments than patients need? In addition to fraud, are welfare-program administrators concerned about reducing errors in processing welfare applications? Are payments workers careful in their calculations of eligibility and payments to recipients? When we talk about fraud and error in welfare, we cannot limit our concerns to welfare clients alone. Those who provide services to welfare clients and those who administer welfare programs must also be considered.

Figures on the number of clients who "cheat" vary. Several years ago the Department of Health, Education and Welfare reported that less than 1 percent of welfare recipients were reported for possibly committing fraud and that even fewer were prosecuted for fraud.[28] Admittedly, methods of detecting welfare fraud are limited, although they have improved, and those who believe that there are larger numbers of welfare cheats could argue that fraud often goes undetected or ignored. Estimates indicate that 7 percent of those receiving AFDC are ineligible or receiving overpayments; the error rate for the Food Stamp program is 10 percent.[29] In 1982 about $950 million was issued in food stamps overpayments and $242 million in underpayments.[30] While it is unlikely that those receiving overpayments would be considered well off, media accounts of welfare fraud dramatize the most extreme cases and incite the public about abuses. For example, the widely read *Reader's Digest* published an article entitled "Time to Crack Down on Food-Stamp Fraud," which began with the sentence, "In Kentucky undercover policemen discover that federal food stamps are being traded for automobiles, drugs and automatic weapons."[31] And a newspaper account declared, "Food Stamps are Fast Becoming Second U.S. Currency, Official Says."[32]

Error rates may be attributed in part to welfare administrators and payment workers—the people who process welfare applications and determine eligibility, amounts of payments, and the conditions under which welfare clients must apply if they wish to receive benefits. Some reports suggest that about half of administrative errors are made by caseworkers.[33] Administrative errors such as overpayment and underpayment can be attributed to miscalculations by workers, failure by workers to understand the complicated rules which govern eligibility, the large number of cases to be processed, the volume of paperwork, and other unintentional or careless mistakes.

"Quality control" is a term and a method borrowed from business and industry.[34] In industry it refers to a process whereby samples of products—for example, cars—are checked or tested to insure that they perform adequately. In welfare the term *quality control* refers to the process of taking a sample of cases to insure that welfare recipients are actually eligible and that they are being paid neither too much nor too little. Sampling is based on scientific techniques to assure that the cross section of cases reviewed truly represents the range of recipients.

The federal government sets the standards and procedures for quality control, and the state welfare agencies actually review and investigate the cases by interviewing clients and verifying records such as rent receipts and paycheck stubs. In any system which serves large numbers of people, some error is bound to occur. The federal government, however, believes that only a certain amount of error is tolerable. Error-tolerance levels are 3 percent for ineligible persons receiving AFDC and 5 percent in cases where persons are eligible but are receiving overpayments. In 1985 the tolerance level in the Food Stamp program was reduced to 5 percent. When a state determines that its error rate is too high, it is required to take steps to reduce error.

Some successful measures to reduce error rates in welfare programs were instituted prior to President Reagan's election, and additional management controls under the Reagan administration also resulted in savings. But according to some welfare experts, further attempts may not be as successful.[35] For example, the Social Security Disability program was especially troublesome, however, the president may have been too zealous in his efforts to control abuse there.[36] Many of those who were eliminated from the program as a result of stricter screening procedures have been restored to the rolls by judges who felt that they had been unfairly excluded. Other aggressive attempts are being made by the federal government to curb error and abuse in the Food Stamp program. The USDA euphemistically calls its effort "Operation Awareness" and is encouraging states to experiment with new alternatives to counter abuse. The government is generously reimbursing states at a rate of up to 75 percent for installing computer systems and for investigating, conducting hearings, and prosecuting cases of fraud in the Food Stamp program.

Other accounts of welfare fraud have focused on the "vendors" of welfare services. Vendors include doctors and others who provide care to Medicare and Medicaid patients, food-store retailers who exchange food stamps for groceries, and landlords who receive rent payments for those who qualify for subsidized housing. Television programs and newspaper reports have exposed doctors and operators of health clinics for overcharging for Medicare and Medicaid services and for charging for services that patients never received. Some individuals question whether grocers might overcharge those food-stamp recipients who are forced to shop at neighborhood stores. Also, landlords may collect the rent in subsidized housing units but fail to provide adequate heating or needed repairs.

There is no single formula for determining whether the rates of fraud and error are extraordinarily high. Certainly, we would all like to see fairly administered welfare programs that cover those in need, result in few errors and no fraud, and actually help people! We often produce welfare policies that sound rational but result in unfair treatment of people, thus raising public concern that programs are poorly administered and that benefits sometimes go to persons who do not qualify. And we know that other government programs, such as defense, are also subject to abuse. Perhaps the focus on fraud would be better directed at government programs in general.

NUTRITIONAL POLITICS

The early commodity-distribution programs were closely tied to federal agricultural policy. The U.S. government purchased agricultural products to guarantee a minimum income for farmers; the distribution of these products from federal stockpiles to the poor was viewed as a means of disposing of food surpluses. The federal government's commodity-distribution programs had the support of the powerful farm lobby, the American Farm Bureau Federation, and the nation's farmers.

The current Food Stamp program, initiated in 1964, was also tied to agricultural policy—at least in its early years. The Food Stamp program began as a modest part of the activities of the U. S. Department of Agriculture. Initially the program had the support of farmers and of organizations who viewed the program as a means of increasing the demand for farm goods. But by the mid-1970s the Food Stamp program had outgrown all other farm programs and was on its way to becoming a multibillion-dollar enterprise. The Food Stamp program eventually grew much larger than all other programs of the U.S. Department of Agriculture. Agriculture interests came to believe that the Food Stamp program was not directly linked to farm prices, farmers' incomes, and farm surpluses; the stamps were used for a wide variety of packaged foods sold at retail stores. At the same time, U.S. farmers began to acquire major markets for surplus foods in foreign trade. Indeed, by 1980 nearly half of U.S. farm production was sold in international markets. Farmers became less dependent on federal purchases of surpluses. Thus, the Food Stamp program lost an important political base—farmers and farm organizations.

Politically, it may be easier to win support for an in-kind program, which distributes food to the poor, than a cash program, which distributes money to the poor. "Feeding the poor" appeals to nearly everyone. But cash payments do not carry the same urgency. Money can be spent for many purposes; not all of these purposes are viewed as "worthy" by the taxpayers whose money is being spent. It is true that it might be more "natural" to provide the poor with cash to purchase whatever they need most. But food stamps focus the aid on a recognized need—eating. No one really wants to see hunger or malnutrition in America.

Although measures have been taken to curb the growth of the Food Stamp program, there is little chance that the basic structure of the program will be altered. The Reagan administration has, however, attempted to "reform" the Food Stamp program "to re-focus the program on its original purpose–to insure adequate nutrition for America's needy families." The administration believes that the program grew too large during the 1970s by allowing many families with higher than poverty-level incomes to participate. The result was "to divert the Food Stamp program away from its original purpose toward a generalized income transfer program, regardless of nutritional need."[37]

The Reagan reforms have included (1) tightening income deductions and income limitations so that only families near or below the poverty line can participate, (2) calculating family income partly on past income rather than current income, (3) monitoring programs to reduce fraud and error, (4) cutting benefits by 1 percent, and (5) delaying adjustments for inflation. Some of these measures have resulted in eliminating from the rolls persons who would have formerly qualified.

In what might be considered one irony of federal food programs, Congress in 1983 directed the Secretary of Agriculture to give surplus foods to emergency food kitchens and similar programs in addition to schools and institutions. The surplus commodities were acquired from price-support programs and farmers who had defaulted on loans. But when surplus cheese was offered, some community-based programs had difficulty taking advantage of it because they lacked administrative funds to transport and store the products.[38] In spite of the size and scope and the Food Stamp program, we have again resorted to the use of surplus commodities to supply nutritional benefits to some people. Another irony is that as farmers have come upon bad times, some may need the social welfare services that they once supported through their labor.

SUMMARY

Food is the most basic necessity of life. The United States has more than enough food for all of its people, and starvation is rare in America. Programs such as commodity distribution and Food Stamps have helped to improve the nutrition of poor Americans, but not all Americans eat adequately every day. Some do not eat well because they select foods that are not nutritious. Others do not eat well because they cannot afford enough food. The high costs of food may make food-stamp allotments insufficient for recipients to afford enough food at the end of the month. Most poor people say that if they were provided with additional income, they would spend it on food.

The first food programs provided surplus commodity foods to the poor. The programs were as much welfare programs for farmers, who were unable to sell their surplus foods, as they were for the poor. Commodity food programs were replaced by the Food Stamp program because perishables were difficult to keep and because the poor had been restricted in selecting foods. Stamps are a cumbersome method of providing food to the poor, but the idea of a cash allotment has been rejected by those who want to insure that the money goes to buy food. There is little evidence, however, to suggest that the poor would use a cash allotment for other purposes.

The major revision of the Food Stamp Act of 1964 came in 1977 with the elimination of the requirement that recipients pay for the stamps. Recipients' inability to afford the stamps had been blamed for low participation. Eliminating this requirement has increased the number of recipients.

The Food Stamp program is still criticized by those who insist it is riddled with fraud. Research shows that there is a 7 to 10 percent error rate in welfare programs.

The Food Stamp program has come closer to covering all poor persons than any other welfare program. Recent restrictions, however, have limited the number of formerly eligible persons. Soup kitchens, food banks, and other emergency nutrition programs at the community level run by churches and other charitable organizations have responded to people in need across the country.

NOTES

1. Barbara Bode, Stanley Gershoff, and Michael Latham, "Defining Hunger Among the Poor," in Catherine Lerza and Michael Jacobson, eds., *Food For People, Not for Profit* (New York: Ballantine, 1975), pp. 299–300.
2. See Nick Kotz, *Let Them Eat Promises: The Politics of Hunger in America* (Englewood Cliffs, N.J.: Prentice-Hall, 1969), p. 35.
3. Bode et al., *Hunger among the Poor,* p. 301.
4. Bureau of the Census, *Statistical Abstract of the United States, 1979* (Washington, 1979), p. 128.
5. The rest of this paragraph relies on Bode et al., *Hunger among the Poor,* pp. 300–302.
6. Lucy Komisar, *Down and Out in the USA* (New York: New Viewpoints, 1977), p. 51.
7. Ibid., p. 51; and Kotz, *Let Them Eat Promises,* p. 45.
8. Komisar, *Down and Out,* p. 51.
9. Paul A. Brinker, *Economic Insecurity and Social Security* (Englewood Cliffs, N.J.: Prentice-Hall, 1968), pp. 390–91.
10. American Enterprise Institute for Public Policy Research, *Food Stamp Reform,* Washington, D.C., 1977, p. 3.
11. American Enterprise Institute, *Food Stamp Reform,* p. 4
12. Laurence E. Lynn, Jr., "A Decade of Policy Developments in the Income-Maintenance System," in Robert H. Haveman, ed., *A Decade of Federal Antipoverty Programs: Achievements, Failures, and Lessons* (New York: Academic Press, 1977), pp. 55–117.
13. These statements from Kotz, *Let Them Eat Promises,* pp. 52—53.
14. Ibid., p. 53.
15. Department of Agriculture, "Food Stamp Changes Help the Rural Poor," *Food and Nutrition* 10 (February 1980), 2.
16. Ronald Alsop, "These Ads Sell Food Stamps and Sobriety—and with Style," *Wall Street Journal,* January 31, 1985, p. 27.
17. Data on recipients rely on *Statistical Abstract, 1984,* p. 373.
18. Donald A. West, "Food Expenditures by Food Stamp Participants and Non-Participants," *National Food Review,* U.S. Department of Agriculture, June 1978; cited in Kotz, *Hunger in America: The Federal Response* (New York: Field Foundation, 1979), p. 16.
19. "Hunger Reports Prompt Food Aid Expansion," *1983 Congressional Quarterly Almanac,* p. 414.
20. Dorothy James, *Poverty, Politics and Change* (Englewood Cliffs, N.J.: Prentice-Hall, 1972), pp. 58–59.
21. Kotz, *Let Them Eat Promises,* p. 59.
22. Ibid.
23. "Hunger Reports Prompt Food Aid Expansion," p. 414.
24. Ibid., p. 415.
25. Ibid.
26. Randy Fitzgerald, "Time to Crack Down on Food-Stamp Fraud," *Readers' Digest,* February 1983, p. 141.
27. Kotz, *Hunger in America,* p. 16.
28. Department of Health, Education and Welfare, "Welfare Myths vs. Facts," pamphlet SRS-72-02009; cited in Ronald C. Federico, *The Social Welfare Institution: An Introduction,* 3rd ed. (Lexington, Mass.: Heath, 1980), p. 83.
29. Raymond J. Struyk, "Administering Social Welfare: The Reagan Record," paper on changing domestic priorities (Washington: Urban Institute, April 1984), p. 35; cited in D. Lee Bawden and John L. Palmer, "Social Policy: Challenging the Welfare State," in John L. Palmer and Isabel V. Sawhill, eds., *The Reagan Record* (Cambridge, Mass.: Ballinger, 1984) pp. 212–13.

30. Jane Mattern Vachon, "Building a Better Food Stamp Program," *Food and Nutrition* 14 (October 1984).
31. Fitzgerald, "Time to Crack Down," p. 138.
32. "Food Stamps are Fast Becoming Second U.S. Currency, Official Says," *Tallahassee Democrat,* March 13, 1983.
33. National Food Stamp Information Committee, *The Facts about Food Stamps* (November/December 1975), p. 9.
34. Department of Health, Education and Welfare, *Quality Control in Aid to Families with Dependent Children,* no. (SRS) 74-04009, rev. 1973.
35. Bawden and Palmer, "Social Policy," p. 212.
36. Ibid., p. 213.
37. *America's New Beginning: A Program for Economic Recovery,* Washington, D. C., February 18, 1981, p. 1.
38. "Hunger Reports Prompt Food Aid Expansion," p. 413.

chapter 9

Warring on poverty: victories, defeats, and stalemates

THE CURATIVE STRATEGY—THE "WAR ON POVERTY"

American confidence in the ability of government to solve problems was once so boundless that President Lyndon Johnson was moved to declare in 1964: "This administration today, here and now, declares unconditional war on poverty in America." And later when signing the Economic Opportunity Act of 1964, he added: "Today for the first time in the history of the human race, a great nation is able to make and is willing to make a commitment to eradicate poverty among its people."[1] Ten years later, after the expenditure of nearly $25 billion, Congress abolished the Office of Economic Opportunity. There were still twenty-five million poor people in the country; this was approximately the same number of poor as when the "war on poverty" began. The government had passed a law—the Economic Opportunity Act of 1964; it had created a new bureaucracy—the Office of Economic Opportunity; and it had thrown many billions of dollars in the general direction of the problem. But according to many critics, nothing much had happened.

An especially stinging critique of the social welfare policies of the 1960s and 1970s is that they spawned more poverty. Rather than reduce poverty, this argument goes, the United States created additional misery through antipoverty programs that actually encouraged welfare dependency.[2] But others disagree. They believe that many programs of the Great Society were successful and that the programs that remain in place, such as Food Stamps (see chapter 8), Medicaid, and Medicare (see chapter 10), have continued to prevent or mitigate human suffering. But the fact remains that large numbers of Americans continue to fall below the poverty level. The failures as well as the successes of the war on poverty are important lessons in policy analysis.

The Curative Strategy

The war on poverty was an attempt to apply a *curative strategy* to the problems of the poor. In contrast to the *alleviative strategy* of public assistance, which attempts only to ease the hardships of poverty, and in contrast to the *preventive strategy* of social insurance, which attempts to compel people to save money against the future possibility of old age, death, disability, sickness, and unemployment, the curative strategy stresses efforts to help the poor become self-supporting by bringing about changes in these individuals and in their environment. The curative strategy of the war on poverty was supposed to break the cycle of poverty and to allow the poor to move into America's working classes and eventually its middle classes. The strategy was "rehabilitation and not relief." The Economic Opportunity Act of 1964, the centerpiece of the war on poverty, was said to "strike at the causes, not just the consequences, of poverty."

Area Poverty and Case Poverty

The first curative antipoverty policies originated in the administration of President John F. Kennedy. Kennedy was said to have read socialist Michael Harrington's *The Other America*—a sensitive description of the continuing existence of a great deal of poverty that had gone unnoticed by the majority of middle-class Americans. But Kennedy, the Harvard-educated son of a multimillionaire business investor, was visibly shocked when he first saw the wooden shacks of West Virginia's barren mountains during his 1960 presidential primary campaign. And Kennedy's economic advisor, John Kenneth Galbraith, had in 1957 written an influential book, *The Affluent Society*, which called attention to the continued existence of poverty in the midst of a generally affluent society. Galbraith distinguished between *case poverty* and *area poverty*. Case poverty was largely a product of some personal characteristics of the poor—old age, illiteracy, inadequate education, lack of job skills, poor health, race—which prevented them from participating in the nation's prosperity. Area poverty was a product of economic deficiency relating to a particular sector of the nation, such as West Virginia and much of the rest of Appalachia. "Pockets of poverty" or "depressed areas" occurred because of technological change or a lack of industrialization—for instance, decline in the coal industry, the exhaustion of iron ore mines, the squeezing out of small farmers from the agricultural market.

Kennedy Initiatives

The initial forays in the war on poverty were begun in the Kennedy administration. The fight against area poverty began with the Area Redevelopment Act of 1961, which authorized federal grants and loans to governments and businesses in designated "depressed areas." This program was later revised in the Economic Development Act (EDA) of 1965. The EDA has not been without its critics. Some have labeled it a trickle-down approach to alleviating poverty, with most benefits going to business and not the poor. Republicans have called it a pork-barrel program to aid Democrats in getting elected. Since coming into office, the Reagan Administration has tried to abolish the Economic Development Administration. Congress has had other ideas, however, and has continued to support the EDA with a current annual appropriation of about $267.5 million.

The fight against case poverty began with the Manpower Development and Training Act (MDTA) of 1962—the first large-scale, federally funded job-training program. Eventually, MDTA was absorbed into the Comprehensive Employment and Training Act (CETA) of 1973. Dissatisfaction with CETA led the Reagan administration to replace it with the Job Training Partnership Act of 1982.

Enter LBJ

When Lyndon B. Johnson assumed the presidency in 1963, he saw an opportunity to distinguish his administration and to carry forward the traditions of Franklin D. Roosevelt. Johnson believed that government work and training efforts, particularly those directed at youth, could break the cycle of poverty by giving young people the basic skills to improve their employability and making them self-sufficient adults.

Johnson's war on poverty included:

The Elementary and Secondary Education Act of 1965: The first major, general federal aid-to-education program, which included federal funds to "poverty-impacted" school districts and which remains today as the largest source of federal aid to education.

The Food Stamp Program: The development of a major in-kind benefit program, which continues today to provide major relief to the poor.

Medicare: Amendments to the Social Security Act to provide health-care insurance for the aged.

Medicaid: The first major federal health-care program for the poor.

Job Training: An expansion of the Manpower Development and Training Act and the initiation of a series of new job-training programs, including the Job Corps and the Neighborhood Youth Corps for young adults and the Work-Study program to encourage college attendance among the poor.

The Economic Development Act of 1965 and *The Appalachia Regional Development Act of 1965*: Efforts to encourage economic development in distressed areas.

THE ECONOMIC OPPORTUNITY ACT— "COMMUNITY ACTION"

The Economic Opportunity Act created a multitude of programs that were to be coordinated in Washington by a new, independent federal bureaucracy—the Office of Economic Opportunity (OEO). OEO was given money and authority to support varied and highly experimental techniques for combating poverty at the community level. As evidence of the priority given OEO, its first director was Sargent Shriver, brother-in-law of the slain President John F. Kennedy and later Democratic vice-presidential candidate with George McGovern in 1972. OEO was encouraged to bypass local and state governments and establish new "community action" organizations throughout the nation—semiprivate organizations, with the poor participating in their own governance. OEO was *not* given authority to make direct grants to the poor as relief or public assistance. All of the OEO programs were aimed, whether accurately or inaccurately, at curing the causes of poverty rather than at alleviating its symptoms.

Youth Programs

A number of OEO programs were oriented toward youth—breaking the cycle of poverty at an early age. The Job Corps was designed to provide education, vocational training, and work experience in rural conservation camps for unemployable youth between the ages of sixteen and twenty-two. Job Corps trainees were supposed to be "hard core" unemployables who could benefit from training away from their home environment—breaking habits and associations that were obstacles to employment while learning reading, arithmetic, and self-health care as well as auto mechanics, clerical work, and the use of tools. Another youth program was the Neighborhood Youth Corps, designed to provide work, counseling, and on-the-job training for young people in or out of school who were living at home. The Neighborhood Youth Corps was intended for young people who were more employable than those who were expected in the Job Corps. A Work-Study program helped students from low-income families remain in high school or college by providing them with federally paid, part-time employment in conjunction with cooperating public or private agencies. The Volunteers in Service to America (VISTA) program was modeled after the popular Peace Corps idea, but volunteers were to work in domestic poverty-impacted areas rather than in foreign countries.

Community Action

The core of the Economic Opportunity Act was a grassroots "community action" program to be carried on at the local level by public or private nonprofit agencies, with federal financial assistance. Communities were urged to form a "community action agency" composed of representatives of government, private organizations, and, most important, the poor themselves. It was originally intended that OEO would support antipoverty programs devised by the local community action agency. Projects might include (but were not limited to) literacy training, health services, homemaker services, legal aid for the poor, neighborhood service centers, vocational training, and childhood development activities. The act also envisioned that a community action agency would help organize the poor so that they could become participating members of the community and could avail themselves of the many public programs designed to serve them.

Finally, the act attempted to coordinate federal and state programs for the poor in each community.

Community action was to be "developed, conducted, and administered with the maximum feasible participation of the residents of the areas and members of the groups served." This was one of the more controversial phrases in the act. Militants within the OEO administration frequently cited this phrase as authority to "mobilize" the poor "to have immediate and irreversible impact on their communities." This language implied that the poor were to be organized as a political force by federal antipoverty warriors using federal funds. Needless to say, neither Congress nor the Democratic administration of President Lyndon Johnson really intended to create rival political organizations that would compete for power with local governments in those communities.

The typical community action agency was governed by a board consisting of public officials (perhaps the mayor, a county commissioner, a school board member, or a public health officer), prominent public citizens (from business, labor, civil rights, religious, and civic affairs organizations), and representatives of the poor (in some cases elected in agency-sponsored elections, but more often hand-picked by ministers, social workers, civil rights leaders, and so on). A staff was to be hired, including a full-time director, and paid from an OEO grant for administrative expenses. A target area would be defined—generally it was the low-income area of the county or the ghetto of a city. Neighborhood centers were established in the target area, perhaps with counselors, employment assistance, a recreation hall, a child-care center, and some sort of health clinic. These centers assisted the poor in contacting the school system, the welfare department, employment agencies, the public-housing authority, and so on. Frequently, the centers and the antipoverty workers who staffed them acted as advocates for the poor and as intermediaries between the poor and public agencies. This activity was called *outreach*.

Head Start

Community action agencies also devised specific antipoverty projects for submission to the Washington offices of OEO for funding. The most popular of these projects was Operation Head Start—usually a cooperative program between the community action agency and the local school district. Preschool children from poor families were given six to eight weeks of special summer preparation before entering kindergarten or first grade. The idea was to give these disadvantaged children a "head start" on formal schooling. Congress (as well as the general public) was favorably disposed toward this program and favored it in later budget appropriations to OEO.

Legal Services

Another type of antipoverty project was the legal services program. Many community action agencies established free legal services to the poor to assist them in rent disputes, contracts, welfare rules, minor police actions, housing regulations, and so on. The idea behind the project was that the poor seldom have access to legal counsel and are frequently taken advantage of because they do not know their rights. Congress amended the act in 1967 to insure that no OEO funds would be used to defend any person in a criminal case. But antipoverty lawyers using federal funds have been active in bringing suits against city welfare departments, housing authorities, public health agencies, and other government bodies.

More OEO Projects

Other kinds of antipoverty projects funded by OEO include family-planning programs—the provision of advice and devices to facilitate family planning by the poor; homemaker services—advice and services to poor families on how to stretch low family budgets; job training—special outreach efforts to bring the hard-core unemployed into more established work-force programs; Follow Through—to continue Head Start efforts with special educational experiences for poor children after they enter school; Upward Bound—educational counseling for poor children; as well as other programs.

POLITICS AND THE WAR ON POVERTY

The war on poverty, specifically OEO, became an unpopular stepchild of the Johnson administration even before LBJ left office. The demise of the OEO programs cannot be attributed to political partisanship—that is, to the election of a Republican administration under Richard Nixon. Nor can the demise of the poverty program be attributed to the Vietnam War—since both "wars" were escalated and later deescalated at the same time. The Nixon administration "reorganized" OEO in 1973, transferring the Job Corps, the Neighborhood Youth Corps, and all job-training programs under a reorganized CETA to the Department of Labor. The administration also transferred the Work-Study Program, Head Start, and Upward Bound to the then Department of Health, Education and Welfare. VISTA became part of a larger federal volunteer program called ACTION. The Ford administration abolished OEO in 1974. It turned over a greatly reduced community action program to an independent (and now defunct) Community Services Administration; and it turned over legal services to an independent Legal Services Corporation.

The reasons for the failure of the war on poverty are complex; the Office of Economic Opportunity was always the scene of great confusion. Personnel were young, middle-class, and inexperienced, and there was always a high turnover among administrators. Community action agencies throughout the country appeared directionless. Aside from Head Start, there were no clear-cut program directions for most community action agencies. Many of the poor believed that the poverty program was going to provide them with *money*; they never really understood that community action agencies could provide only organization, outreach, counseling, training, and similar assistance. Many community action agencies duplicated, and even competed with, existing welfare and social-service agencies. Some community action agencies organized the poor to challenge local government agencies. As a result, more than a few local governments called upon the Johnson administration and Congress to curb community action agencies that were using federal funds to "undermine" existing programs and organizations. There were frequent charges of mismanagement and corruption, particularly at the local level. Finally, some community action agencies became entangled in the politics of race; some big-city agencies were charged with excluding whites; and in some rural areas, whites believed that poverty agencies were "for blacks only."

Perhaps the failures of the war on poverty can be explained by our lack of knowledge about how to *cure* poverty. In retrospect, it seems naive to believe that passing a law, creating a new bureaucracy, and passing out money to local agencies to find their own cures could have succeeded in eliminating or even reducing poverty.

Can poverty be cured? The evidence is frequently conflicting. For example, some social commentators have pointed to evaluation studies of the Job Corps program which indicate that after completing the program, enrollees have had increases in their annual incomes ranging from less than $200 a year to no more than about $500 a year, and they conclude that "the programs were seldom disasters; they simply failed to help many people get and hold jobs that they would not have gotten and held anyway."[3] On the other hand, government officials who reviewed the same evidence stated: "While there are always uncertainties, the size of this increment provides reasonable certainty that the Job Corps investment in human resources is profitable."[4] And some social scientists also consider the Jobs Corps among the "well-regarded programs."[5]

In some cases, initial evidence conflicts with later results. Early evidence on Head Start revealed that the program was very popular among parents. But after two or three years in school, differences in educational achievement or aspiration levels of poor children who attended Head Start and poor children who did not attend seemed to vanish. More recent longitudinal evidence confirms that IQs of former Head Start children declined after they were in school, which may not be surprising considering the quality of some public schools.[6] But research also indicates that Head Start produced long-term gains that could not have been measured in earlier studies. For example, enrollees are less likely as they grow older to be dependent on welfare and less likely to be involved in crime; they are more likely to have remained in school and are more likely to hold jobs.

The war on poverty has not been won, and we may be forced to conclude that social science simply does not know enough about social behavior to end poverty. It might be argued that the war on poverty was never funded at a level that would make a substantial impact. OEO funds were spread over hundreds of communities. Such relatively small amounts could never offset the numerous, deep-seated causes of deprivation. The poverty program raised the expectations of the poor, but it never tried to cope with poverty on a scale comparable to the size of the problem. Often the outcome was only to increase frustration.

In an obvious reference to public policies affecting the poor and the black in America, Aaron Wildavsky wrote:

> A recipe for violence: Promise a lot; deliver a little. Lead people to believe they will be much better off, but let there be no dramatic improvement. Try a variety of small programs, each interesting but marginal in impact and severely underfinanced. Avoid any attempted solution remotely comparable in size to the dimensions of the problem you are trying to solve. Have middle-class civil servants hire upper-class student radicals to use lower-class Negroes as a battering ram against the existing local political systems; then complain that people are going around disrupting things and chastise local politicians for not cooperating with those out to do them in. Get some poor people involved in local decision-making, only to discover that there is not enough at stake to be worth bothering about. Feel guilty about what has happened to black people; tell them you are surprised they have not revolted before; express shock and dismay when they follow your advice. Go in for a little force, just enough to anger, not enough to discourage. Feel guilty again; say you are surprised that worse has not happened. Alternate with a little suppression. Mix well, apply a match, and run. . . .[7]

It would be difficult to find a better summary of the unintended consequences of public programs for the poor and the black.

It is possible to view the war on poverty as failing because it promised too much, raised people's hopes, and delivered too little. Daniel P. Moynihan observed:

> Over and again the attempts by official and quasi-official agencies . . . to organize poor communities led first to the radicalization of the middle-class persons who began the effort; next to a certain amount of stirring among the poor, but accompanied by heightened radical antagonism *on the part of the poor* if they happened to be black; next to the retaliation from the larger white community; where upon it would emerge that the community action agency, which had talked so much, been so much in the way of change in the fundamentals of things, was powerless. A creature of a Washington bureaucracy, subject to discontinuation without notice. Finally, much bitterness all around.[8]

CAN WE "CURE" POVERTY?: NEW EVIDENCE ABOUT HEAD START

Can we "cure" poverty? Is the curative strategy effective? Recent evidence indicates that at least some strategies are more effective than we once thought. As an example, let us consider at greater length attempts to evaluate the effectiveness of one of the most popular antipoverty programs, Head Start.

When the Economic Opportunity Act of 1964 first authorized the creation of local community action agencies throughout the nation to fight the war on poverty, the responsibility for devising community antipoverty projects was placed in the hands of local participants. But within one year, the Office of Economic Opportunity in Washington and its director, Sargent

Shriver, decided that Head Start programs were the most desirable antipoverty projects. OEO earmarked a substantial portion of funds for local community action agencies for Head Start programs. The typical local Head Start project was a cooperative program between the community action agency and the local school district. Preschool children from poor families were given six to eight weeks of special summer preparation before entering kindergarten or first grade. The idea of helping to prepare disadvantaged children for school is more appealing to the middle class than programs which provide free legal aid for the poor, help them get on welfare rolls, or organize them to fight city hall. Indeed, Head Start turned out to be the most popular program in the war on poverty. Nearly all of the nation's community action agencies operated a Head Start project, and over one-half million children were enrolled throughout the country at the height of the program in the late 1960s. Some communities expanded into full-year Head Start programs and also provided children with health services and improved daily diets. Head Start became OEO's showcase program.

Evaluating Head Start

Head Start officials within OEO were discomforted by the thought of a formal evaluation of their program. They argued that educational success was not the only goal of the program; that child health and nutrition, and even parental involvement in a community program, were equally important goals. After much internal debate, Director Shriver ordered an evaluative study, and in 1968 a contract was given to Westinghouse Learning Corporation and Ohio University to perform the research.

When Richard Nixon assumed the presidency in January 1969, hints of negative findings had already filtered up to the White House. In his first comments on the poverty program, Nixon alluded to studies showing the long-term effect of Head Start as "extremely weak." This teaser prompted the press and Congress to call for the release of the Westinghouse Report. OEO claimed that the results were still "too preliminary" to be revealed. However, after a congressional committee investigation and considerable political pressure, OEO finally released the report in June 1969.[9]

The report stated that the researchers had randomly selected 104 Head Start projects across the country. Seventy percent were summer projects; and 30 percent were full-year projects. Children who had gone on from these programs to the first, second, and third grades in local schools (the experimental group) were matched in socioeconomic background with children in the same grades who had not attended Head Start (the control group). All children were given a series of tests covering various aspects of cognitive and affective development (the Metropolitan Readiness Test, the Illinois Test of Psycholinguistic Abilities, the Stanford Achievement Test, the Children's Self-Concept Test, and others). The parents of both groups of children were matched on achievement and motivation.

The unhappy results can be summarized as follows:

1. Summer programs were ineffective in producing any gains in cognitive and affective development that persist into the early elementary grades;
2. Full-year programs produced only marginally effective gains for certain subgroups, mainly black children in central cities.

However, parents of Head Start enrollees voiced strong approval of the program.

Political Reaction

Head Start officials reacted predictably in condemning the report. Liberals attacked the report because they believed that President Nixon would use it to justify major cutbacks in OEO. *The New York Times* reported the findings under the headline "Head Start Report Held 'Full of Holes.' " This newspaper warned liberals that "Congress or the Administration will seize the report's generally negative conclusions as an excuse to downgrade or discard the Head Start Program"[10] (not an unreasonable action in the light of the findings but politically unacceptable to the liberal community). Academicians moved to the defense of the war on poverty by attacking various methodological aspects of the study. In short, scientific assessment of the impact of Head Start was drowned in a sea of political controversy.

Ten Years Later

It is difficult for educators to believe that education, especially intensive preschool education, does *not* have a lasting effect on the lives of children. The prestigious Carnegie Foundation decided to fund research in Ypsilanti, Michigan—research which would keep tabs on disadvantaged youngsters from preschool to young adulthood. In 1980 a report was released on an eighteen-year study of the progress of 123 low-IQ children, fifty-eight of whom (the experimental group) were given special Head Start-type education at ages three and four and continued to have weekly visits throughout later schooling.[11] The others (the control group) received no such special educational help. Both groups came from low socioeconomic backgrounds; half of their families were headed by a single parent, and half received welfare. Because the sample was small and local, researchers were able to track the children's progress to age nineteen.

The initial results were disappointing: Most of the gains made by the children with preschool educations disappeared by the time the children had completed second grade. As children in the experimental group progressed through grade school, junior high school, and high school, their grades were not better than the children in the control group.

However, throughout the school years, children with preschool educations scored slightly higher (8 percent) on reading, mathematics, and language-achievement tests than the control group. More important, only 19 percent of the preschoolers ended up in special classes for slow learners, compared to 39 percent for the control group. The preschoolers also showed fewer delinquent tendencies and held more after-school jobs. The key to this success appeared to be a better attitude toward school and learning among children with preschool educations. Finally, more former preschoolers were likely to finish high school and find jobs than those in the control groups, and the preschoolers were less likely to end up on welfare.

Positive results of this study continue to be touted, and Head Start is a good example of the need for longitudinal research. Researchers estimate that current benefits have exceeded per pupil costs at least seven times over.[12] Their conclusion is that a Head Start–type experience is a bargain to society in the long run because it reduces the later need for social-support systems such as welfare.

JOB PROGRAMS: MAKE-WORK VERSUS THE REAL THING

The Comprehensive Employment and Training Act of 1973 (CETA) was originally proposed by the Nixon administration as a means of reforming and reorganizing the large array of job-training programs that had emerged from the Great Society programs of the 1960s. CETA was designed to accomplish two general goals: (1) *consolidation* of job programs from the Manpower Development and Training Act of 1962; the Economic Opportunity Act of 1962, including community action programs featuring job training, the Job Corps, and the Neighborhood Youth Corps; and a separate Job Opportunities in the Business Sector (JOBS) program; and (2) *decentralization* of these progams, giving control and implementation to local governments. The U.S. Department of Labor was given overall responsibility for consolidating various job-training programs and distributing funds to city, county, and state governments, which serve as "prime sponsors" for the programs.

Initially, CETA was directed at "structural" unemployment—the long-term, "hard-core" unemployed with few job skills, little experience, and other barriers to productive employment. But later, particularly in response to the economic recession of 1974–75, Congress extended the target population to include individuals affected by "cyclical" unemployment—temporary unemployment caused by depressed economic conditions. Indeed, Congress forced the Nixon and Ford administrations to accept more "public-service jobs" through CETA than either administration requested.

CETA provided job training for over three and one-half million persons per year. Programs included classroom training, on-the-job experience, and public-service employment. "Prime sponsor" local governments contracted with private community-based organizations (CBOs) to help recruit poor and minority trainees, to provide initial classroom training, and to place individuals in public-service jobs. Indeed, it is sometimes argued that CBOs do a better job of "getting down to the people" than local governments do.

As it turned out, a major share of CETA funds were used by cities to pay individuals to work in regular municipal jobs. CETA offered local governments the possibility of substantially lowering their labor costs by "substituting" federally paid CETA workers for regular municipal employees. In addition, CETA enabled many local governments to shift regular municipal employees (police, firefighters, refuse collectors, and others) to the CETA budget and off the city's payroll. Instead of creating new jobs, a substantial portion of CETA money simply funded a continuation of existing jobs. Obvious substitution occurred when a government laid off employees and then rehired them in their old jobs with CETA funds.

Although CETA regulations officially prohibited such substitution, most observers agreed that the practice was widespread. Indeed, it has been estimated that about half of all CETA jobs were jobs formerly paid for by local governments.

Defenders of CETA argued that substitution was not necessarily wasteful if municipal employees were going to lose their jobs without assistance from CETA. Substitution allowed cities facing financial stress to cut back on their own spending and yet not force large numbers of their employees to go jobless.

On the other hand, it was clear that CETA funds were not all "targeted" to those who needed the assistance most—the economically disadvantaged and long-term, hard-core unemployed. One estimate was that only one-third of CETA workers came from welfare families. Prime sponsors tended to focus on the "cream" of the labor market—skimming off the most skilled of the unemployed. Nonetheless, according to federal figures, about 40 percent of the participants were minorities, about 45 percent had less than high school educations, 39 percent were age twenty-one or less, and 73 percent were classified as "low income."[13]

The Humphrey-Hawkins Act of 1978 "guarantees" jobs to every "able and willing" adult American. The ambitious language of the act reflects the leadership of its sponsor, the late Senator Hubert H. Humphrey (D.-Minn.). The act views the federal government as "the employer of last resort" and pledges to create public-service jobs and put the unemployed to work on public projects. Lowering the unemployment rate to 3 percent is to be a "national goal." But the Humphrey-Hawkins Act is more symbolic of liberal concerns than it is a real national commitment. Doubtless, pressures on Congress and the president to expand funding for public-service jobs will increase during periods of recession. But it is unlikely that the national unemployment rate will ever be reduced to 3 percent. Increasingly, Congress and the president have become concerned with the creation of "real," permanent, private-sector jobs rather than government-funded public-service jobs.

Job Training Partnership Act

In order to focus on private-sector employment, the Reagan administration allowed CETA legislation to expire and replaced it with the Job Training Partnership Act (JTPA) of 1982. The goals of the JTPA are to provide the unemployed and underemployed with skill training and to meet the employment needs of local communities. Under the JTPA about six hundred Private Industry Councils have been established. These councils are composed of volunteers from the business sector who are supposed to be knowledgeable about the job skills most needed in their communities. The councils pass their advice on to job-training centers established by state and local governments with federal funds.

Under the Reagan administration, the amount of funds for job-training programs has decreased after taking inflation into account, but more important than funding levels is whether the JTPA will put more economically disadvantaged people to work than CETA did. Early projections are mixed. An enthusiastic editorial in the *Wall Street Journal* reported that 70 percent of 115,000 participants graduating during a six-month period had found jobs. The editorial praised the Reagan administration for replacing CETA's costly make-work jobs in the public sector with "real" jobs in the private sector.[14]

Others are less enthusiastic about the JTPA's potential for success, contending that private employers are still likely to "cream" while the hard-core unemployed remain jobless.[15] Since 85 percent of JTPA funds must be used for training, little is available for support services like living allowances and child care, which might make the difference in getting some of the disadvantaged into the job market. An early indictment of the program is that "the most disadvantaged portion of the JTPA-eligible population will receive less priority because these people will often be unable to participate in training without some income or social service support. Adults not on welfare and troubled youths in need of counseling will be hardest hit."[16]

THE U.S. EMPLOYMENT SERVICE: FINDING JOBS

The labor market does not always coordinate jobs with workers. This is particularly true at the levels of unskilled and semi-skilled jobs. In 1933 the United States Unemployment Service (USES) was established under the Wagner-Peyser Act to help the millions of depression-era unemployed find jobs.[17] Today the USES consists of twenty-four hundred offices throughout the nation. The USES reports that it places about five million workers in jobs each year. The poor make up about one-quarter of these placements. The USES is funded from federal unemployment insurance taxes paid by employers on their employees' wages. Although federally funded, USES offices are staffed and administered separately in each state. As a result, services may vary from state to state. The current administration is working with the states to develop legislation that would transfer responsibility for financing and administering employment services to state governments.[18]

The USES is supposed to serve both employers and unemployed workers. It accepts job listings from private and public employers, and it accepts job applications from individuals seeking employment. For both employers and job-seekers USES is a "free" job service. But USES sometimes has difficulty in getting employers to list jobs with the service, especially highly skilled or professional jobs. Most of the USES job applicants possess limited skills.

One reason for the difficulty confronting the USES in placing people may be that some individuals list themselves as job seekers in order to fulfill requirements of public assistance, or unemployment insurance programs. Most state unemployment insurance programs require recipients to register with USES, to check with the service every week to see if there is a job opening in their field, and to state that they did not decline a job in their regular occupation as conditions of receiving their unemployment benefits. In some cases, food stamps and other welfare benefits are being distributed to adults, whether or not there is a real likelihood that they will be employed, on the condition that they register with the USES.

THE MINIMUM WAGE: HELPING OR HURTING?

Laws establishing minimum wages for working people have been an accepted strategy in fighting poverty since the federal Fair Labor Standards Act of 1938. The purpose of this law was to guarantee a minimum wage level that would sustain health and well-being and a decent standard of living for all workers. The minimum wage began in 1938 at 25¢ per hour; by 1981 it had been increased to its current rate of $3.35 per hour. A basic work week of forty hours was established; employees can work longer, but overtime work requires additional pay. Today over 90 percent of nonsupervisory personnel in the American work force are covered by the law, with certain exceptions in retail trade, services, and agriculture.

It is sometimes argued that the minimum wage is the most direct and comprehensive measure to increase the earnings of the working poor. Indeed, it might be argued that the minimum wage ought to be higher than it is. A minimum wage worker earning $3.35 per hour on a forty-hour work week would earn $134 weekly, or $6,968 for a fifty-two-week year. The poverty guideline for a family of four for 1985 was $10,650. If there was only one worker in this family, and the worker was paid only the minimum wage, the family would live well below the poverty line.

Certainly a high minimum wage helps the person who has a job, particularly an unskilled or semiskilled job, which is likely to be affected by minimum wage levels. There are some persons, though, who believe that workers may not be hired by employers because government-imposed wage levels are too high to justify adding these people to the payroll. In other words, does a high minimum wage create unemployment by discouraging employers from taking on additional workers—especially workers who have few skills and whose labor is not "worth" the minimum wage?

The persons most likely to be excluded from jobs because of a high minimum wage are teenagers. It has been argued that they have not yet acquired the job skills to make their labor worth the minimum wage; with a high minimum wage, fast-food chains, movie theaters, retail stores, and the like tend to cut back on their teenage help to save costs. At a lower minimum wage, more teenagers could be expected to find work. The teenage unemployment rate is approximately three times higher than the unemployment rate for adults. Some economists claim that this youth-employment problem is partly a result of the minimum wage. But there is no real consensus about whether the reduction or elimination of the minimum wage for teenagers would substantially reduce youth unemployment.

One alternative that has been proposed to alleviate teenage unemployment and still maintain wage standards for adults is the "dual minimum" or "subminimum" wage. The president's most recent idea along these lines is to reduce the minimum wage for those under twenty years old for the summer months only. Other proposals have called for amending the Fair Labor Standards Act to permit all youths under eighteen years old and youths between the ages of eighteen and twenty in the first six months of employment to receive a lower minimum wage than the minimum wage fixed for persons over eighteen or with more than six months on the job. Criticisms of these proposals include the concern that employers would replace older workers with younger workers at the subminimum wage.

ILLUSTRATION: LEGAL SERVICES UNDER FIRE

The federal government's Legal Services Corporation grew out of the early legal services provided as part of the OEO "community action" programs in the 1960s. Today the Legal Services Corporation is a separate nonprofit corporation, financed by Congress from tax dollars to provide legal services to the poor. The corporation is headed by an eleven-member board appointed by the president. More than three hundred regional legal service groups around the nation are staffed by about five thousand attorneys.

According to the corporation, most of its work consists of advising the poor of their legal rights in everyday cases—rental contracts, loans, credit accounts, welfare rules, housing regulations, and other day-to-day civil law. The corporation is prevented by law from representing the poor in criminal cases. (The states are required by the U.S. Constitution to provide legal counsel to persons accused of felonies.) The corporation reports that only 15 percent of its cases ever reach the courtroom. Others are resolved by the parties before litigation begins.

Defenders of the Legal Services Corporation argue that the poor require legal protection as much as or more than the affluent. Most case work, they claim, revolves around survival issues of food, shelter, or clothing. "We represent the most powerless people in America." Government-paid poverty lawyers are prohibited from taking fees, such as a percentage of damages in accident-injury suits. Moreover, legal-service money cannot be used for political activity, public demonstrations, or strikes.

But opponents of the Legal Services Corporation say that it is irrational to establish a government agency to sue other government agencies. The Legal Services Corporation has been involved in several well-publicized "class-action" suits. In these suits, lawyers from the corporation claim to represent a whole "class" of poor people, not just one individual or family, and they usually bring these suits against another government agency. For example, the Bay Area Legal Services in Tampa, Florida, using federal funds, sued the state of Florida to stop the state from requiring its high school graduates to pass a functional literacy test. Corporation lawyers argued that the test was discriminatory because larger proportions of black students failed it than white students. Should the Legal Services Corporation take on such class action cases? Even when the cause is just, it might be argued that taxpayers should not have to foot the bill for these class-action suits. Or according to one critic of the corporation: "Why should the taxpayers have to cough up $300 million a year for an elite corps of radical lawyers who want to move this country to the left?"[1]

Alternatives to the Legal Services Corporation have been proposed by those who agree that the poor need lawyers but complain that the government should not pay for class-action suits:

A voucher system, similar to food stamps. Poor people would qualify for a certain number of vouchers to be redeemed at private law firms.

Judicare, which, like Medicare, would be a national insurance program. Everyone would contribute a small amount and everyone would be insured against legal expenses.

A prohibition against class-action suits by lawyers paid through the Legal Services Corporation.

Pro bono (no fee) services to the poor donated by private-practice attorneys and law-school clinics.

Since 1981 President Reagan has tried to abolish the Legal Services Corporation (LSC), but Congress—composed largely of lawyers—has continued to support it. The president's failed attempts have led him to make nineteen appointments to the Legal Services board while the Senate has been in recess, thereby avoiding the nomination and approval process. The president has submitted twenty-five nominations to Congress, but none have been approved because Congress has viewed these nominees as unsympathetic to the LSC. The Senate has also retaliated by limiting the board's power to cut funds to LSC-funded programs until such time as the president's nominees are confirmed by the Senate. Meanwhile, the new appointees have left the LSC with less than a clear mandate for the future.[2] Changes in the LSC board, funding cutbacks, loss of positions, and the numbers of people unable to obtain legal assistance have contributed to the demoralization of LSC attorneys.

Some states have responded to the funding cuts by establishing Interest on Lawyer Trust Accounts (IOLTA). Sometimes private attorneys hold small amounts of money for clients. The amount involved is so small and the money is held for such a short period that opening a separate interest-bearing account for the client is not feasible. In thirty-five states these small amounts of money are pooled into a single account, and interest earned goes to subsidize legal services for the poor. While questions have been raised as to propriety of this practice, Henry G. Miller, president of the New York State Bar Association, believes that "nothing could be further from the truth."[3] He explains that no one has ever successfully challenged IOLTA programs in the U.S. or in other countries that have them, such as Canada and Australia. No harm is done to clients whose money is held because their funds would not have earned them interest anyway. Mr. Miller questions the motivations of those who see IOLTAs as unethical, suggesting that their opposition may not be to "IOLTA itself but to provisions for civil legal services to the poor."[4]

1. *Congressional Quarterly Weekly Report,* April 18, 1981, p. 660.

2. "Reagan's Recess Appointments Rankle Hill," *Congressional Quarterly Weekly Report,* July 14, 1984, p. 1699.

3. Letter to the editor, *Wall Street Journal,* February 25, 1985, p. 31.

4. Ibid.

SUMMARY

The curative strategy of the war on poverty was an attempt to eradicate many of America's social problems. But this attempt to combat poverty by creating a variety of new social welfare programs failed to reduce poverty. Twenty-five million people remained poor in the United States. The groundwork for the war on poverty was laid during the administration of President John F. Kennedy with the passage of the Area Redevelopment Act, but it was President Lyndon B. Johnson who succeeded in establishing the Office of Economic Opportunity (OEO). The purpose of OEO was to assist the poor in establishing community action agencies to get at the causes of poverty rather than providing direct cash grants to the poor. Job programs, literacy programs, legal-aid programs, and child-development programs were among the many services offered. Community action agencies were to be operated with the "maximum feasible participation of the poor."

The war on poverty sounded like a rational approach to remedying poverty, but the war was plagued by a number of problems that led to its demise. Many OEO staff members were inexperienced at administering social programs. The goals of the many programs were not clear and services were often unnecessarily duplicated. Others contended that the war raised the expectations of poor Americans but provided so little funding for *each* community that it was doomed to failure. Accusations of racism toward whites and corruption and mismanagement within the programs all contributed to pressures against OEO. The agency was abolished in 1974, with its remaining programs transferred to other federal departments.

Case studies of Head Start programs, the Comprehensive Employment and Training Act (CETA), and the Legal Services Corporation help to illustrate how politics interferes with rational approaches to policy making. Conservatives attacked Head Start programs for having few long-term effects on participants. Liberals attacked conservatives for looking for a way to eliminate the Head Start programs. Conservatives believed that CETA funded jobs that local governments would have paid for anyway. Liberals believed that paying for these jobs was better than allowing financially troubled city governments to lay off workers. Opponents of the Legal Services Corporation reject the idea of lawyers being paid by the federal government to sue government agencies. Proponents believe that all citizens should be entitled to legal services, regardless of their financial status. Head Start and the Legal Services Corporation have survived, but CETA has been replaced with the Job Training Partnership Act.

NOTES

1. Quoted in Daniel Patrick Moynihan, *Maximum Feasible Misunderstanding* (New York: Free Press, 1969), pp. 3–4.
2. For an extensive elaboration of this argument, see Charles Murray, *Losing Ground, American Social Policy, 1950–1980* (New York: Basic Books, 1984).
3. Ibid., p. 37.

4. This is a quote from Robert Taggart, Office of Youth Programs, U.S. Department of Labor, in the introduction to Charles Mallar et al., *Youth Knowledge Development Report 3.4, The Lasting Impacts of Job Corps Participation,* U.S. Department of Labor, May 1980, p. ii.
5. D. Lee Bawden and John L. Palmer, "Social Policy: Challenging the Welfare State," in John L. Palmer and Isabel V. Sawhill, eds., *The Reagan Record* (Cambridge, Mass.: Ballinger, 1984), p. 201.
6. Ann Crittenden, "A Head Start Pays Off in the End," *Wall Street Journal,* November 29, 1984, p. 32.
7. Aaron Wildavsky, "The Empty Headed Blues: Black Rebellion and White Reactions," *Public Interest* no. 11, (Spring 1968), 3–4.
8. Moynihan, *Maximum Feasible Misunderstanding,* pp. 134–35.
9. Westinghouse Learning Corporation, Ohio University, *The Impact of Head Start* (Washington Office of Economic Opportunity, 1969).
10. James E. Anderson, *Public Policy-Making* (New York: Holt, Rinehart & Winston, 1975), p. 150.
11. *Newsweek,* December 22, 1980, p. 54.
12. Crittenden, "A Head Start Pays Off."
13. *Budget of the United States Government, Fiscal Year 1982.*
14. "A Real Jobs Program," *Wall Street Journal,* September 24, 1984, p. 32.
15. Palmer and Sawhill, *Reagan Record,* pp. 211–12.
16. Ibid., p. 367.
17. Henry P. Guzda, "The U.S. Employment Service at 50: It Too Had to Wait Its Turn," *Monthly Labor Review,* June 1983, pp. 12–19.
18. *Budget of the United States Government, Fiscal Year 1986,* p. 4–10.

chapter 10

Improving health care: treating the nation's ills

National health policy in America presents many examples of the problems of rational policy making. Political issues intervene at every stage of the rational decision-making process—in defining the goals of health policy, in identifying alternative courses of action, in assessing their potential costs, and in selecting policy alternatives that maximize the quality and accessibility of health care while minimizing its cost.

Health care is a basic human need. Most of us would argue that no one should suffer or die for lack of financial resources to obtain adequate medical attention. But how much health care is "enough"? How much are people willing and able to pay for health care? If all of us cannot have all of the health care we want (that is, if health care is a "scarce resource"), then how do we decide who will get what care and how? As we shall see, these are largely *political* questions that do not lend themselves easily to rational planning.

Health care is an issue that affects all of us directly. For years Congress debated the issue of subsidizing health care for the poor and the elderly and made only modest gains in covering these vulnerable populations. Then in 1965, as part of the war on poverty, major health-care programs were established for both groups. These programs were important for several reasons: (1) The poor and the aged, on the average, require more medical attention than the general population. Indeed, health problems are a contributing cause of unemployment, inadequate income, and poverty. (2) Preventive health care for the poor is infrequent. In addition to health risks facing the poor, even minor costs can delay treatment of health problems until they develop into major crises. (3) Health-care facilities and personnel (the "delivery system" for health care) are particularly disorganized and inadequate in poor areas, both in inner cities and in poor rural communities.

We might think that providing more health-care coverage for the elderly and poor has reduced our concerns about medical services in this country, but on the contrary, health care in the United States continues to be a pressing social welfare issue. The costs of health care for all citizens, rich and poor, are so astronomical that policy makers can no longer be concerned about how to provide health care for the poor and elderly alone. As we shall see, politicians, health care providers and citizens in general are concerned about the cost of health care for the entire population.

GOOD HEALTH OR MEDICAL ATTENTION?

The first obstacle to a rational approach to health policy is deciding upon our goal. Is health policy a question of *good health*—that is, whether we live at all, how well we live, and how long we live? Or are we striving for good *medical care*—that is, frequent and inexpensive visits to doctors, well-equipped and accessible hospitals, and equal access to medical attention by the rich and poor?

Good medical care does not necessarily mean good health. Good health is related to many factors over which doctors and hospitals have no control: heredity, lifestyle (smoking, eating, drinking, exercise, worry), and the physical environment (sewage disposal, water quality, conditions of work, and so on). Of course, doctors can set broken bones, stop infections with drugs, and remove swollen appendixes. Anyone suffering from any of these or similar problems certainly wants the careful attention of a skilled physician and the best of hospital facilities. But in the long run, infant mortality, sickness and disease, and life span are affected very little by the quality of medical care.[1]

If you want to live a long, healthy life, choose parents who have lived long, healthy lives, and then do all the things your mother always told you to do: don't smoke, don't drink, get lots of exercise and rest, don't overeat, relax, and don't worry.

Historically, most of the reductions in infant morality (deaths during the first year of life) and adult death rates, in the United States and throughout the world, have resulted from improved public health and sanitation—including immunization against smallpox, clean public water supply, sanitary sewage disposal, improved diets and nutrition, and increased standards of living. Many of today's leading causes of death (see table 10-1), including cancer, heart disease, stroke, cirrhosis of the liver, emphysema, accidents, and suicides are closely linked to heredity and personal habits.

The overall death rate in the United States (the number of deaths per one hundred thousand people) has continued its general decline (see figure 10-1). Considerable progress has been made in reducing both infant and adult death rates for many of the major killers—infant diseases, heart disease, stroke, pneumonia and influenza, accidents, and atherosclerosis

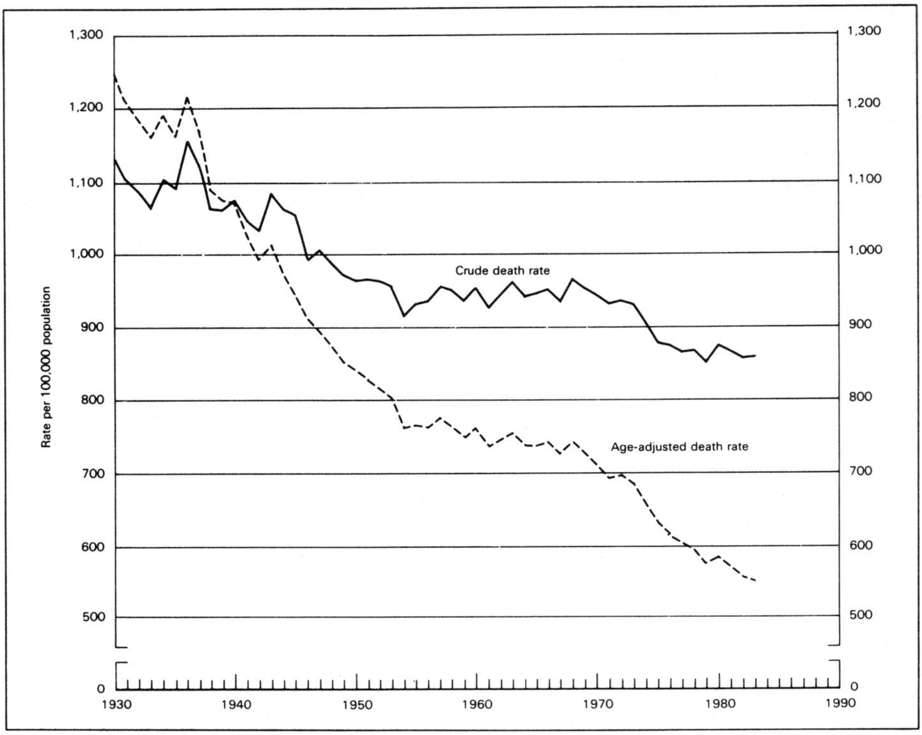

FIGURE 10-1 Crude and age-adjusted death rates, United States, 1930–83. (National Center for Health Statistics, "Annual Summary of Births, Deaths, Marriages, and Divorces: United States, 1983," *Monthly Vital Statistics Report* 32, no. 13 [September 21, 1984], 4.)

TABLE 10-1 Leading Causes of Death (per 100,000 population per year)

	1960	1970	1979	1983
All causes	954.7	945.3	852.2	858.9
Heart disease	369.0	362.0	326.5	327.6
Cancer	149.2	162.8	179.6	188.3
Cerebrovascular disease (stroke)	108.0	101.9	75.5	66.8
Accidents	52.3	56.4	46.9	39.0
Pulmonary diseases[a]	9.9	15.2	22.2	28.4
Pneumonia and influenza	37.3	30.9	20.1	22.9
Diabetes	16.7	18.9	14.8	15.2
Suicide	10.6	11.6	12.1	12.4
Liver disease (including cirrhosis)	11.3	15.5	13.2	11.9
Atherosclerosis	20.0	15.6	12.8	11.1
Homicide	4.7	8.3	10.0	8.2
Infant diseases	37.4	21.3	10.4	8.1

[a]Figures for 1960 and 1970 include bronchitis, emphysema, and asthma.

Sources: U.S. Bureau of the Census, *Statistical Abstract of the United States, 1984*, p. 78; *Monthly Vital Statistics Reports* 32, no. 13 (September 21, 1984), 5.

(see table 10-1). However, the cancer death rate continues to rise despite increased medical spending. Suicide rates have increased, and less progress has been achieved in the areas of alcoholism (cirrhosis), homicide, and diabetes. Moreover, death rates for the poor and for blacks, although declining over time, remain much higher than the death rates for the nonpoor and for nonblacks.

MEDICAID: HEALTH CARE FOR THE POOR

The poor and the black in America have greater health problems than the affluent and the white. A case in point is the infant mortality rate, which is considered to be especially sensitive to the adequacy of health care and is therefore frequently used as a general indicator of well-being. Infant deaths have declined rapidly over the last thirty years for both whites and blacks. But black infant death rates, which have been consistently higher than those for whites, remain almost twice as high as white infant death rates (see figure 10-2). These and other health statistics clearly suggest that black Americans and the poor do not enjoy the same good health as more affluent white Americans.

Prior to 1965 medical care for the poor was primarily a responsibility of state and local governments and private charity. But interest in national health care for the poor dates back to the turn of the century, when reform groups during the Progressive Era first proposed a national health insurance plan. In 1935 potential opposition from the American Medical Association (AMA) forced President Franklin D. Roosevelt to drop the idea of including health insurance in the original Social Security Act; he feared its inclusion would endanger passage of the entire act. Every year from 1935 to 1965, health insurance bills were introduced into Congress. But all of them failed, in part because of the opposition of the AMA. National health insurance became a major issue in the Truman administration in the late 1940s, but the AMA succeeded in branding national health insurance as "socialized medicine." (Proposals for national health insurance generally tried to "socialize" health *insurance* but did not call for government ownership of hospitals and employment of physicians as in Great Britain.) Fear of government interference in medical practice, along with opposition of the medical community, succeeded in defeating national health plans for thirty years. Nonetheless, in 1950 the federal government did authorize states to use federal-state public assistance funds (under the Old Age Assistance, Aid to the Blind, Aid to the Permanently and Totally Disabled, and Aid to Families with Dependent Children programs) for medical services. In 1957 the Kerr-Mills Act began a separate federal and state matching program for hospital care for the elderly and the poor, but not all of the states chose to participate in the program.

Medicaid is the federal government's largest single welfare program for the poor. The costs of Medicaid now exceed the costs of all traditional welfare programs—including SSI, AFDC, and the Food Stamp programs. A combined federal and state program, Medicaid was initiated in 1965 under Title XIX of the Social Security Act. It replaced earlier medical assist-

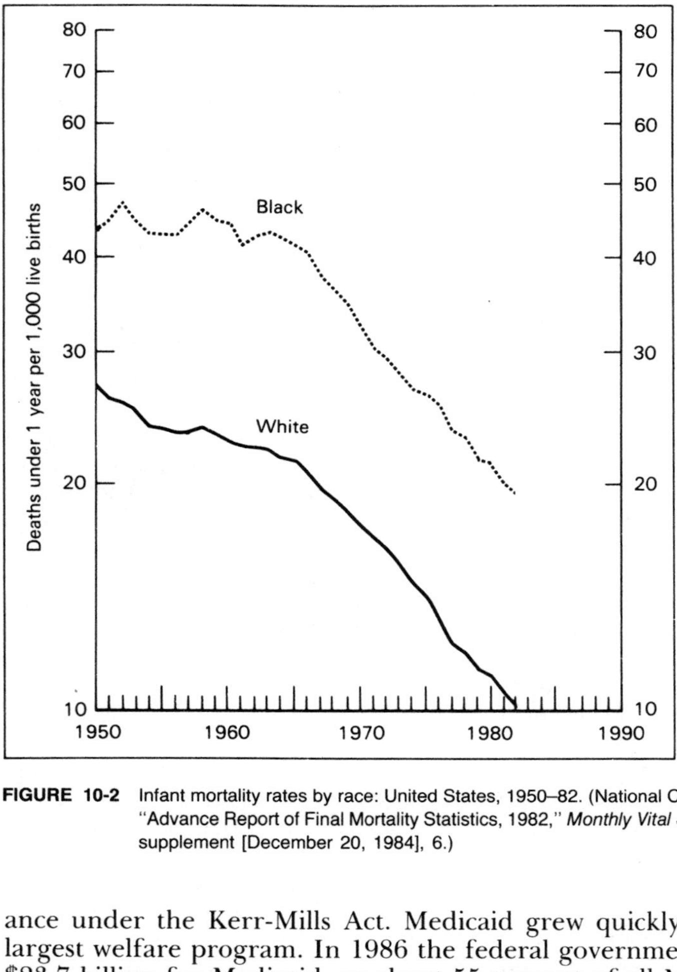

FIGURE 10-2 Infant mortality rates by race: United States, 1950–82. (National Center for Health Statistics, "Advance Report of Final Mortality Statistics, 1982," *Monthly Vital Statistics Report* 33, no. 9, supplement [December 20, 1984], 6.)

ance under the Kerr-Mills Act. Medicaid grew quickly into the nation's largest welfare program. In 1986 the federal government allocated about $23.7 billion for Medicaid, or about 55 percent of all Medicaid costs (see figure 10-3).[2] States receive 50 to 78 percent of their Medicaid expenditures from the federal government depending on their per capita incomes. The states carry the rest of the financial burden and also exercise broad administrative powers.

Medicaid is an in-kind public assistance program designed for needy persons. Medicaid patients receive services from physicians and other health-care providers, and these providers are directly reimbursed by the government. No prior contributions are required by the beneficiaries; monies come from general tax revenues. Although states differ in their eligibility requirements for Medicaid, they must cover all AFDC families. (Remember, however, that the states determine who receives AFDC.) As a result of recent legislation, states must also cover poor, first-time pregnant women if they would qualify for AFDC upon the birth of the child. They

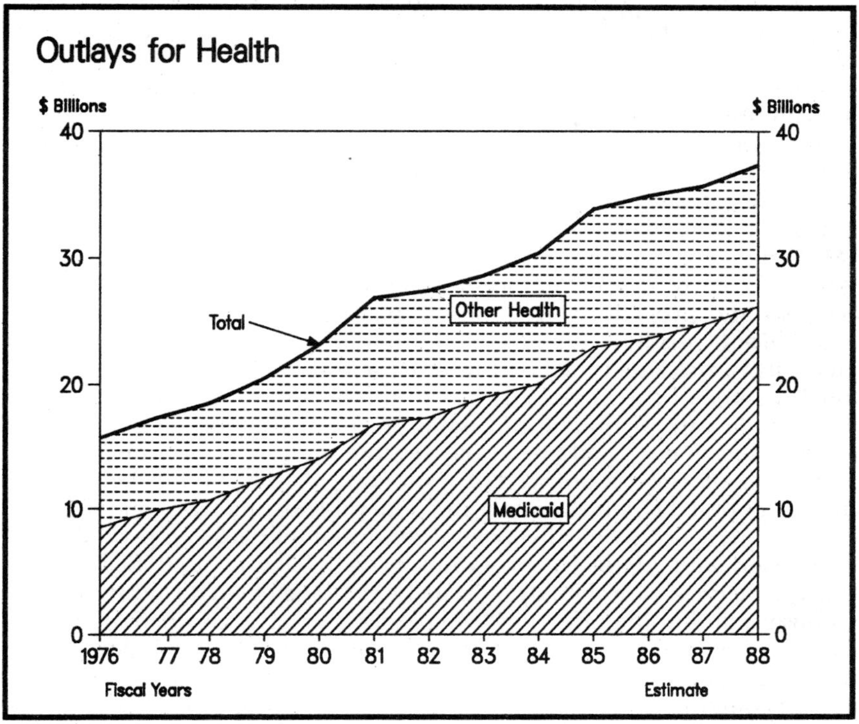

FIGURE 10-3 Federal outlays for Medicaid and other health expenditures (excluding Medicare). (*The United States Budget in Brief, Fiscal Year 1986,* p. 45).

must also cover pregnant women in two-parent families in which the primary breadwinner is unemployed. Poor children to age five in two-parent families are also eligible. Although there are some exclusions, most SSI recipients are eligible for Medicaid. In addition, thirty-one states extend coverage to other "medically needy" individuals who do not qualify for public assistance but whose incomes are low enough to prevent them from obtaining medical care.[3] About half the states extend Medicaid to families headed by an individual receiving unemployment compensation.

States also help set benefits under Medicaid. All states are required by the federal government to provide inpatient and outpatient hospital care; physicians' services; laboratory and x-ray services; skilled-nursing-home services for adults; home health care; family planning; rural health clinics; nurse-midwife services; and early, periodic screening, diagnosis, and treatment (EPSDT) services for children. States may offer other benefits if they wish such as prescription drugs and dental care.

Approximately twenty-two million people per year receive Medicaid payments.[4] This figure is considerably less than the thirty-four million persons whose incomes fall below the poverty level. AFDC families comprise two-thirds of Medicaid beneficiaries, but their medical bills account for only one-fourth of Medicaid expenditures.[5] Much of the funding for Medicaid (rather than Medicare) actually goes to pay for the long-term nursing-home care of elderly and disabled recipients.

Under the Medicaid program, the states have a great deal of latitude in determining the extent of benefits offered, such as the number of allowable physician visits, and they determine reimbursement rates for services with some restrictions on the amount they can reimburse hospitals for services. When states set their reimbursement rates low, hospitals and physicians may be discouraged from providing good care or any care at all under Medicaid. To compensate for low payments, health-care providers may schedule too many patients in too short a span of time or prescribe unnecessary tests and procedures designed to make treatment more expensive.

Medicaid costs have far exceeded original estimates. The rapid rise in AFDC rolls in the late 1960s and in SSI for the disabled in the 1970s accounts for some of the increased costs of the program. Another factor has been the high rate of inflation in medical-care prices. Hospital costs and physicians' fees have raced ahead of even the high inflation rate affecting all segments of the economy. For example, in 1982 alone health-care inflation stood at 11 percent while the general consumer price index rose by only 3.9 percent.[6] Ironically, part of this inflation has been produced by the Medicaid and Medicare programs, which have created heavier demands for medical care. Finally, a large percentage of Medicaid funding is spent on nursing-home care. These expenditures have spawned many new nursing homes and have resulted in many more aged and disabled people being placed in nursing facilities. Thus, Medicaid costs have escalated because of (1) increases in welfare rolls, (2) inflation in medical costs, (3) increased use of nursing homes, and (4) greater accessibility of health-care services.

Can anything be done to curb the costs of Medicaid and still provide adequate medical care for the poor and the near poor who are not covered by other medical insurance?[7] There have been few good solutions. Currently, there are no limits on the amount of federal matching funds available to the states under Medicaid. President Reagan would like to see such a cap instituted, but Congress has been unsympathetic to this approach. Some states have been making plans to add new beneficiaries to their Medicaid programs, but these plans will probably be scrapped if Medicaid funding is capped or otherwise reduced. The Reagan administration sees it this way: caps on federal spending would force states to develop reimbursement plans for doctors and hospitals that would result in greater cost savings. But others see it differently. They believe that budget cuts in Medicaid will result in fewer and less adequate services for Medicaid recipients as well as elimination of potential recipients from the program. Those in the poorest states—for example, in South Carolina where allowable countable income under the Medicaid program for a family of four generally cannot exceed $2,748—would probably be hurt the worst.

In the past, hospitals have often made up for the costs of providing services to those who could not pay their bills by shifting costs to third-party payers (government programs and private health insurers) and to patients who could afford the bills. But today it is becoming increasingly difficult for hospitals to do this because of cost-containment strategies in Medicare and because private insurance companies are also interested in holding down the costs of medical care. Consumers, and employers who purchase medical benefits for their employees, are also complaining about medical costs. Hospitals, public and private, are businesses. When they cannot recoup their costs, one solution they see is to provide fewer services to those who cannot pay. However, public hospitals cannot refuse to treat the indigent, and they feel that they are unfairly burdened for treating nonpaying patients when cuts in hospital benefits are made.

The old saying that "an ounce of prevention is worth a pound of cure" also applies here. When the poor are denied access to health care, they may be forced to wait until their health has severely deteriorated before they seek or are able to obtain health care. This strategy does nothing to save health-care dollars but instead adds to the costs of health care. What is needed is a health-care program that will cover all medically needy persons and reimburse health-care providers at reasonable rates, but the formula for achieving this balance has eluded policy makers.

LONG-TERM CARE: THE ELDERLY AND THE DISABLED

The nation would certainly feel better about Medicaid if it could develop a more rational plan for providing for the long-term-care needs of elderly and disabled persons. Nursing-home residents are only 7 percent of Medicaid beneficiaries but they account for 40 percent of the program's costs. "The Health Care Financing Administration estimates that the nursing home population will increase four times faster than the U.S. population as a whole in the next 50 years." Much of the increase will be due to the baby-boom generation reaching retirement age. "In Florida the population age 85 or older is expected to increase by 73 percent from 1980 to 1990."[8] Although many elderly people enter nursing homes with some funds, the high costs of care can quickly deplete their savings and force them onto Medicaid. What can be done? Some alternatives include controlling the amounts that nursing homes can be reimbursed for Medicaid patients, restricting the number of nursing-home facilities, and making greater use of home-health-care and independent-living services (which can be less expensive than nursing-home care). Newer ideas are to encourage private insurance companies to offer policies that would cover people in the event they need long-term nursing-home care and to give tax breaks to families who care for relatives who would otherwise seek nursing-home placements.

MEDICARE: HEALTH CARE FOR THE AGED

The provision of adequate health care for the nation's aged is an issue of critical concern. The proportion of America's population that is over sixty-five is steadily increasing (see table 10-2). More important, the process

TABLE 10-2 Population over Age 65

	1950	1960	1970	1980	1983
Millions	12.4	16.7	20.1	25.7	27.4
% of population	8.1	9.2	9.8	11.3	11.7

Source: Bureau of the Census, *Statistical Abstract of the United States, 1981,* p. 27, and *1985,* p. 26.

of aging is associated with an increased incidence of chronic conditions and disabilities. The aged have about two and one-half times as many restricted activity days as the general population and more than twice as many days in bed and in hospitals.[9] Older Americans now enjoy higher incomes than ever before and fewer live in poverty,[10] but without some form of health insurance, a serious or long-term illness would result in financial ruin for most of them.

Medicare, like Medicaid, was enacted in 1965 as an amendment to the nation's basic Social Security Act. Medicare provides prepaid hospital insurance for the aged under Social Security and low-cost voluntary medical insurance for the aged, directly under federal administration. Medicare includes (1) Hospital Insurance (HI), a compulsory basic health insurance plan covering hospital costs for the aged financed out of payroll taxes (1.35 percent in 1985) that are collected under the Social Security system; and (2) Supplemental Medical Insurance (SMI), a voluntary, supplemental medical insurance program that will pay doctors' bills and additional medical expenses and is financed in part by contributions from the aged and in part by general tax revenues.

The largest group of Medicare beneficiaries are persons aged sixty-five or older who are eligible for Social Security retirement benefits or who would be eligible if they retired. Eligibility is not dependent on income. Long-term disabled workers and those with end-stage renal disease may also qualify as well as some aged persons who do not have enough earning credits to qualify for Social Security. As part of the Social Security system, Medicare compels employers and employees to pay into the program during working years in order to enjoy the benefits, including health insurance, after retirement. Benefits under HI include a broad range of hospital services as well as some skilled-nursing-home care and home health care following a hospital stay. After the beneficiary pays a deductible ($400 in 1985), Medicare pays for the remainder of the first sixty days in the hospital and a portion of additional days. Although there is some disagreement on this point, projections are that the HI fund may be depleted by 1994.[11]

Benefits under SMI include physicians' services, outpatient hospital care, and other medical services. The cost of SMI, $15.50 per month, is so low that participation by the elderly is almost universal. SMI payments can be deducted automatically from Social Security payments. Beneficiaries of SMI must pay for the first $75 of services themselves, after which Medicare pays 80 percent of most services and the patient pays the remaining 20 percent. Home health services do not require any deductibles or coinsurance payments. Medicare now includes benefits for hospice services.

Note that both the HI and SMI provisions of Medicare require patients to pay an *initial* charge. The purposes are to discourage unnecessary medical care and to recover some of the costs of the program. HI generally pays the full hospital charge, but many doctors charge higher rates than allowable under SMI. Indeed, it is estimated that only about half of the doctors in the nation accept SMI allowable rates as payment in full. Many doctors bill Medicare patients for charges above the allowable SMI payments. Medicare does *not* pay for custodial nursing-home care, most dental care (including dentures), private-duty nursing, eyeglasses and eye examinations, most prescription drugs, routine physician examinations, and hearing tests and hearing devices.

DIAGNOSIS-RELATED GROUPS: CUTTING MEDICARE COSTS

Medicare serves thirty million people, and costs were projected to be $77.2 billion in 1986, a huge increase from the $3.4 billion Medicare cost in its first year.[12] In 1983 Congress enacted a system of payment by "diagnosis-related groups" (DRGs) in order to curb the costs of the program. Under Medicare there were some restrictions on the fees hospitals could charge, but Medicare generally reimbursed hospitals for the total amount billed for each patient. This was a "retrospective" (after the fact) method of paying for hospital care. Now a "prospective" method of payment is being utilized in which the federal government specifies *in advance* what it will pay for the treatment of 468 different illnesses or diagnosis-related groups. (At this time the plan pertains only to hospital costs, not physician fees, and only to the Medicare and not the Medicaid program.) DRGs are interesting because hospitals that spend more to treat Medicare patients must absorb excess costs, but if the hospital spends less than the amount allotted to treat a patient, it gets to keep the difference. Hospitals may not charge Medicare patients more than the DRG allotment. Obviously, the idea behind DRGs is to encourage hospitals to be more efficient in their treatment of Medicare patients. It appears DRGs have had an effect because in 1984 the average hospital stay was 7.5 days, down from 9.5 in 1983.[13] But critics are already charging that DRGs may be doing more harm than good. According to a study done by the General Accounting Office, "Patients are being discharged 'quicker and sicker,' sometimes more 'prematurely,' and are 'being sent out into a no-care zone, without access to the health care they so urgently need.' "[14] DRG rates do take into consideration regional cost differences. Some exceptions to the DRG rates can be made (for example, in the case of very long hospital stays), and some types of hospital facilities are exempt, such as psychiatric and rehabilitation units, hospitals that are the only facilities in a community, and those which serve large numbers of poor patients.

The DRGs apply to part A of Medicare (HI) but not to part B (SMI). Steps to control costs under the SMI portion have included freezes on the amount that "participating" physicians can charge to Medicare patients. Participating physicians agree to accept Medicare reimbursement as payment in full for their services while "nonparticipating physicians" may charge clients in addition to fees reimbursed by Medicare. There are some incentives for participating physicians, such as prompter reimbursement by Medicare, and these physicians have been promised they will receive future fee increases from the government that will be denied to nonparticipating physicians. The Reagan administration has suggested continuation of freezes on physicians' fees, but there is sentiment that participating physicians should not be affected. The Reagan administration is also proposing increasing out-of-pocket costs to Medicare beneficiaries, but Congress seems more amenable to freezing provider (physicians, therapists and other health-care professionals) fees than raising beneficiary costs again.[15]

ILLUSTRATION: THE DEBATE OVER HEALTH CARE

MEDICARE'S HEALTHY; LET'S KEEP IT THAT WAY

Twenty years ago this week, it was hard to find a happy doctor in the USA.

Congress had just enacted a health insurance plan for the elderly: Medicare. Doctors called it socialized medicine.

They angrily predicted that Medicare and Medicaid, its sister program for the poor, would kill private medicine. They warned that patients would not be able to pick their physicans. They flatly refused to help government plan the new programs.

But the programs worked. And doctors benefited. Virtually every hospital and 90 percent of the physicians in the USA now get income from the programs. A third of all doctors' salaries come from Medicare and Medicaid.

And the programs' major beneficiaries are the elderly and indigent patients who have been treated by some of the best physicians in some of the best hospitals in the world.

New medical technology has meant many older citizens have been able to afford heart by-pass surgery, artificial joints, and man-made lenses to cure cataracts.

So on Medicare's 20th birthday, the USA could celebrate: The elderly were getting quality care, with dignity, from good doctors who were amply paid for their services.

But there are symptoms of illness in the system.

Health care costs have soared. They skyrocketed from $1 billion in 1965 to $70 billion last year. Over a decade, Medicaid costs accelerated by about 25 percent a year.

Periodic scandals persist. There are documented cases of doctors who robbed the system through overcharges. A recent congressional committee disclosed a $2 billion fraud in kickbacks to doctors treating patients for cataracts. Such abuses further drive up costs.

Our elderly now pay about $1,500 out of their own pockets for health care. That could be $2,500 by the year 2000.

A step toward cost control was taken last year when the Reagan administration imposed a policy of paying the bills on a flat, per case fee. That innovation has helped.

Still, by the year 2030, there will be more than 60 million people over 65—double the present number. That will put intense financial strains on the system.

The government will have to further control costs. Many patients who can continue to work after 65 will have to do so. The medical establishment will have to police its own ranks, end unnecessary, expensive treatments; eliminate overcharges and cut out fraud. The insurance industry will have to help serve a larger, older constituency.

As the system continues to suffer, there will be new prognoses that we can't afford Medicare, that it will bankrupt the country, that it will bring on socialized medicine.

Twenty years after they refused to help plan Medicare, doctors must join government and other players in the health care industry to write a new prescription to make sure Medicare stays healthy.

MEDICARE IS SO SICK IT OUGHT TO BE JUNKED
by John C. Goodman, President, National Center for Policy Analysis

Medicare has been a bonanza for the elderly—a bonanza which they did not pay for and which many of them do not need.

According to the federal government's own projections, on the average, a 65-year-old male can expect to receive about $28,255 in Medicare benefits before he dies.

Yet he has paid only $2,640 in Medicare taxes.

If the man has a dependent spouse, the couple together can expect to receive almost $60,000 more in benefits than they paid in taxes.

When Medicare was signed into law, it was widely viewed as a poverty program.

Yet the most recent statistics show that the elderly have more after-tax income and more assets than people under 65.

Far from being poor, many Medicare beneficiaries are quite wealthy. There are about 254,000 millionaires in the USA today who are eligible for Medicare coverage.

Unfortunately, the workers who pay taxes to support the program will never get the same great deal.

It is almost certain that young workers entering the labor market today will pay considerably more in Medicare taxes than they will receive in benefits.

They may have trouble getting any benefits at all.

According to the Social Security Administration, by the year 2035, the payroll tax may have to be almost *40 percent* of workers' income in order to fund Social Security and Medicare.

Yet, future workers may be unwilling to fork over that much of their paychecks.

There is a better way.

The National Center for Policy Analysis has proposed an alternative:

Allow workers to make tax-free deposits to medical individual retirement accounts (they might be called "MIRAs," like "IRAs") during their working years.

Upon retirement, the funds in these accounts would allow people to buy private health insurance and to pay for their own medical bills, rather than rely on the federal government.

This proposal would avert Medicare's financial crisis and would allow future generations of workers to pay their own way.

Source: *USA Today*, August 5, 1985, p. 8A. Copyright, 1985 *USA Today*.Reprinted with permission.

HEALTH SERVICES BLOCK GRANTS

In addition to Medicaid and Medicare, other health services are provided under block grants. These services include community health centers, which provide medical care to the poor and near-poor persons in areas with few doctors or medical facilities; treatment for those with specific health problems, such as hypertension; health programs for migrant workers; rodent-control programs; and others. Fewer federal funds have been available for health services since the block grants replaced numerous categorical grants.

HOW MUCH MEDICAL CARE IS ENOUGH?

No health-care program can provide as much as people will use. Each individual, believing that his or her health and life is at stake, will want the best trained medical specialists, the most thorough diagnostic treatment, the most constant care, and the best and most sophisticated facilities available. And doctors have no strong incentive to try to save on costs; they want the best and most advanced diagnostic and treatment facilities for their patients. Doctors can always think of one more thing that might be done for any patient—one more consultation with another specialist, one more diagnostic test, one more therapeutic approach. Any tendency doctors might have to limit testing or treatment is countered by the threat of malpractice suits; it is always easier to order one more test or procedure than to risk even the remote chance that failure to do so will someday be used as cause for a court suit. So both patients and doctors are encouraged to push up the cost of health care, particularly when public or private insurance pays the cost.

Although there is some disagreement about actual figures, it appears that *85 percent* of the population is covered by some sort of health insurance—most by private insurers that offer group insurance for workers and their families through employers, and the rest by Medicaid or Medicare. But this method of "third-party financing" of health care has vastly increased the nation's medical bill. Until recently there have been few incentives for doctors or patients to keep the bill low, when it seemed that "someone else" was paying. The result has been skyrocketing health costs.

Total national health-care expenditures have risen from nearly $30 billion in 1960 to more than $400 billion today (see figure 10-4)! Instead of spending 5 percent of the nation's gross national product (the total of all goods and services produced) for health care, we are now spending nearly 11 percent. Future projections are higher, and we have still failed to provide health insurance for all the poor.

Over the years several diverse causes of "medical inflation" have been identified:

1. Certainly, "third-party financing" has contributed to these rapidly increasing health costs. This includes the expansion of private insurance plans as well as the rapid expansion of the federal government's Medicaid and Medicare programs.

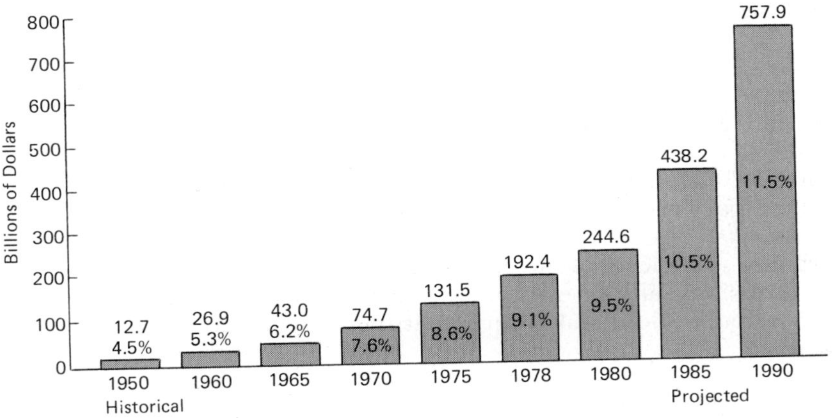

FIGURE 10-4 Total national health expenditures, selected years 1965 to 1990, in billions of dollars and percentage of gross national product. (*Congressional Quarterly, Health Policy* [Washington, D.C.: Congressional Quarterly. 1980], p. 3.)

2. The growing number of the nation's elderly population (persons over sixty-five) has contributed to rising expenditures in all areas of health care. The elderly spend more time in hospitals, visit doctors more often, purchase more drugs, and need more nursing services than the rest of the population.
3. Advances in medical technology have added to health-care expenses. These advances have helped to diagnose and treat illnesses—including cancer and heart disease—that were considered surely fatal a decade ago. Yet the installation of such equipment as CAT scanners (which by means of a computer, can take a detailed x ray of a person's entire body) and intensive cardiac-care units as well as organ transplants and other extraordinary life-sustaining procedures have dramatically increased hospital costs.
4. The nation has also seen a vast expansion of hospital facilities—an expansion which has created an excess of expensive-to-maintain hospital beds. It was the federal government, through the Hill-Burton Act, that encouraged new and modernized hospital facilities from the 1950s through the early 1970s. Now the complaint is that the nation is "overbedded." (Although some rural areas may not have a hospital or even a doctor.)

While medical "cost containment" remains on the national policy agenda, a growing number of economists and physicians have defended the increased costs of medical care. If people place a high value on medical care, they should be free to make this choice. Perhaps the nation *should* spend 10 or 15 percent of the gross national product on medical care. "Neither the level nor the rate of increase in medical care spending in the United States is unique compared with other industrialized countries."[16] After all, so the argument goes, the combined revenues of the alcohol and tobacco industries amount to almost as much as medical care. Medicaid and Medicare have enabled the poor and the aged to enter the marketplace for medical care; it is understandable that this increased demand will raise prices. And who does not *want* a sophisticated cardiac-intensive-care unit close by when a heart attack strikes?

WHAT AILS MEDICINE?

What has national health policy accomplished for the poor in America? There is no doubt that *access to medical care* for the poor has improved with Medicaid and Medicare. Contrary to popular stereotypes, the poor in America see doctors more often than the nonpoor. Indeed, the poor see doctors about 20 percent more often than the nonpoor.[17] We must assume, then, that the poor are receiving more, if not better, medical care than the nonpoor.

Certainly some level of government spending is necessary to insure adequate access to health care for all Americans, and there is evidence that for *some* conditions additional government spending is particularly useful. For example:

> Evidence that poor people with hypertension can benefit from free medical care comes from a "natural experiment" in which some adults were terminated from the California medicaid program in 1982. Blood pressure levels among terminated people with hypertension increased significantly during the 6-month study period, compared with a control group.[18]

However, the general health of the poor remains worse than that of the nonpoor, despite increases in medical care for the poor. That is to say, infant mortality rates, death rates due to specific causes, and average life spans of the poor remain below those of the nonpoor. It is true that these measures of health are improving over time for both groups, but there is no indication that Medicaid and Medicare have been mainly responsible for these improvements. Indeed, improvements in health statistics were just as great prior to the enactment of Medicaid and Medicare as they have been since the enactment of these programs.

So we are faced with a paradox in rational health-care policy: We can increase access to medical care, but we cannot always improve health. As Aaron Wildavsky observes:

> If the question is, "Does health increase with government expenditure or medicine?" the answer is likely to be "No." Just alter the question: "Has access to medicine been improved by government programs?" and the answer is most certainly with a little qualification, "Yes."[19]

"MEDIGAPS"

Another problem with the current health-care system in America is the inadequate coverage provided by health insurance programs—both private and public. Private health insurance plans often leave gaps in medical coverage. These "medigaps" include: limitation to the first thirty or sixty days of hospital care; overall dollar limits on payments made to hospitals and physicians for particular services; exclusion of various diagnostic tests, outpatient care, or office visits; and so on. Moreover, private insurance often will not cover individuals initially found to be in poor health who need this insurance most. And perhaps the most serious concern about private insurance is that it frequently fails to cover "catastrophic" medical costs—costs that may run to tens or hundreds of thousands of dollars for serious, long-term illnesses. Many middle-class families would lose their life savings and become "medically indigent" if faced with a serious illness.

Medigaps also exist in Medicare. We have already mentioned a number of services, such as prescription drugs and eyeglasses, that Medicare does not cover but that older Americans are likely to need. In addition, the amount of deductibles and other out-of-pocket costs for Medicare recipients have risen since 1965. As a result, many older Americans supplement their Medicare coverage with additional insurance to cover these medigaps. Many insurance companies provide these policies. To curtail potential abuse (selling needless coverage to the elderly), Congress has set legislation to regulate Medicare supplemental insurance. Although a number of policies are good supplements to the services provided by Medicare, some do not provide much help with items already excluded under the Medicare program.

HEALTH SYSTEMS AGENCIES

As the nation solved one problem—health care for the poor and aged—it helped to create a new problem: spiraling health-care costs, which in turn require new policies. It is still not clear, however, that the federal government is really capable of holding down medical inflation, and it is less clear that the government can hold down costs without hurting the quality of health care and limiting the availability of sophisticated diagnostic and treatment facilities. One previously tried approach to cost containment is found in the National Health Planning and Resources Development Act of 1974. The act created two hundred *health systems agencies* (HSAs) across the nation with authority to grant or withhold "certificates of need" for new medical facilities. These HSAs were designed to prevent duplication of facilities, overbuilding and unnecessary costs, but more than ten years later it is clear that HSAs have not made significant contributions to reducing medical inflation or controlling the growth of medical facilities. The Reagan administration wanted to abolish HSAs as a deregulation measure, but even conservatives worried that some cost-control measures were needed; liberals, however, contended that the HSAs were too weak to exert control over medical facilities.[20] Although it has not abandoned the HSAs, Congress has severely reduced funding for these agencies.

HEALTH MAINTENANCE ORGANIZATIONS

The federal government has also experimented with health costs and health care delivery by supporting *health maintenance organizations* (HMOs). HMOs are membership organizations. Some hire doctors and other health professionals at fixed salaries to serve dues-paying members in a clinic-type setting. Others contract with private physicians who treat patients in their own offices. HMOs typically provide comprehensive health care for enrolled members. The members pay a regular fee, and they are usually entitled to hospital care and physicians' services at no extra cost. Advocates of HMOs say that the organizations are less costly than fee-for-service medical care because doctors have no incentive to overtreat patients. Moreover, HMOs emphasize preventive medicine and therefore attempt to treat medical problems before they become serious illnesses. In 1973 Congress endorsed the HMO concept by passing a Health Maintenance Organization Act offering federal assistance for the development of HMOs. Complaints about HMOs are similar to complaints about service in other bureaucratic settings: Patients may see different doctors on different days; doctors in HMOs do not work as hard as private physicians; care is depersonalized; there is less choice in seeking the services of specialty physicians. On the average, private insurance premiums are about the same as fees charged by HMOs. There are 343 HMOs in the country with about fifteen million enrollees, and these numbers are expected to grow.[21] The federal government is expanding the availability of HMOs to older Americans who can now use their Medicare benefits to join a HMO.

ILLUSTRATION: HOW TO REFORM HEALTH-CARE POLICY

Many social welfare advocacy groups develop and support specific legislative agendas. Below is an agenda for health-care-policy reform that is supported by two of these groups.

A 15-POINT PROGRAM TO STRENGTHEN MEDICARE, MEDICAID AND HEALTH CARE FOR ALL

The purpose of Medicare and Medicaid was to ease the financial burdens of illness which fall with particular harshness on the elderly, the severely disabled, the blind and the poor. Yet runaway health care costs, coupled with reductions in Federal outlays for these programs, mean that these are still an unmet goal.

To make this worthy goal a reality, we *support* the following:

1. **Legislation to control health's escalating costs** as incorporated in bills introduced by Senator Edward Kennedy, Representative Richard Gephardt, and others to put a brake on cost escalation and halt further reductions in benefits or decreases in the number eligible for health care.

2. **Prospective budgeting for *all* payors and providers,** public and private; assuring access to the health care system without reducing the quality of health care. Reimbursement by Diagnostic Related Groups, a prospective payment schedule incorporated in the Social Security Amendments of 1983, is a *partial* approach to hospital cost-containment. We have serious reservations about it because it is limited to Medicare and because its effects are uncertain.

3. **Mandatory assignment under Medicare for all physician payments.** This means all physicians would have to accept the reimbursable amounts set by Medicare as *payment in full* for every Medicare patient and for every episode of illness.

4. **Combining Part A (hospitalization) and Part B (physician's services)** under Medicare and paying part of this combined cost from Federal general revenues.

5. **Improved access to a full range of health care services for the chronically ill**, including home help, hospice and out-patient care.

6. **Improved coverage for preventive care needs,** with particular emphasis on health education, to help focus our priorities on keeping people healthy, instead of waiting to care for them until they become sick or disabled.

7. **Catastrophic insurance coverage** built on top of a basic comprehensive benefit program and made available, as a matter of right, for people with long-term medical problems.

8. **Improvements in Medicare benefits,** including reimbursement for prescription drugs, immediate coverage for the disabled, and improved long-term care provisions.

9. **Federal financing of Medicaid,** with the entire cost paid from Federal general revenues, accompanied by uniform benefit levels throughout the nation; and liberalization of the income and assets test. *This must be accomplished without reducing existing entitlements and/or services.*

10. **Extension of Medicaid benefits** to all pregnant women and to children under 6 living in families with incomes below the poverty level.

11. **Uniform levels of reimbursement** for all public and private payors, so that costs would be consistent throughout the health care system and cost-shifting from Medicare and Medicaid to private insurance would end.

12. Prompt enactment of, and adequate funding for, **health insurance for the unemployed** on a continuing basis so that workers and their families will not lose health care coverage when they lose their jobs.

13. **Federal financial and technical aid for non-profit Health Maintenance Organizations** which serve as models of efficient and cost-effective health delivery systems.

14. Creation of mechanisms in all health care programs to **protect the quality of care.**

15. **Consumer participation** in the decision-making process in all public health care programs to make these programs more responsive to the needs of the American people.

Source: Health Security Action Council and Coalition to Protect Social Security, "Health Care in the United States in the Mid-1980's, An Action Agenda," publication no. HSAC 8105.

POLITICS AND THE HEALTH-CARE INDUSTRY

As mentioned, the health-care industry dwarfs all other sectors of the American economy. The largest portion of these health-care expenditures (41 percent in 1983) go to hospitals (see table 10-3). Physicians' services comprise the second largest portion of all health-care expenditures (19 percent). Nursing-home care is now the third largest category of health-care expenditures (8 percent), followed by drugs (7 percent). Public health accounts for only 3 percent of all health-care expenditures and research for only 2 percent. The proportion of total health care expenditures paid for by the government has risen consistently from 25 percent in 1965 to 37 percent in 1970 and now stands at about 42 percent. Thus, the government's role in keeping America healthy has expanded rapidly.

TABLE 10-3 National Health Expenditures

	1970	%	1983	%
Total	$74.7 billion		$355.4 billion	
Spent by				
Consumers	43.1	58	195.7	55
Government	27.8	37	148.8	42
Philanthropy & industry	3.8	5	10.9	3
Spent for				
Personal health care				
Hospital care	27.8	37	147.2	41
Physicians' services	14.3	19	69.0	19
Nursing home care	4.7	6	28.8	8
Drugs	8.0	11	23.7	7
Dentists' services	4.7	6	21.8	6
Other	3.7	5	16.5	5
Eyeglasses & appliances	1.9	3	6.2	2
Administration	2.7	4	15.6	4
Public health	1.4	2	11.2	3
Construction	3.4	4	9.1	3
Research	2.0	3	6.2	2

Sources: Bureau of the Census, *Statistical Abstract of the United States, 1984,* p. 103; "Health Status and Medical Care," *Economic Report of the President,* House document no. 99-19, 99th Cong. 1st Sess., February 1985, p. 133.

The health-care industry consists of many groups—hospitals, physicians, dentists, nurses and other professionals, drug companies, nursing-home operators, private medical insurance companies, and others—all with a vested interest in the delivery and financing of health care. These interests make up the health-care lobby. The most powerful group in the lobby is the American Medical Association (AMA), which has operated since 1847. Opposed for years to government intervention in medicine, physicians have benefited tremendously from Medicaid and Medicare. Certainly, doctors are among the most highly paid and highly respected professionals in the country. Nevertheless, the AMA has been accused of being "far more concerned with preserving the economic health of doctors than promoting the physical health of the rest of the country."[22] We would expect at least some physician opposition to government intervention that seeks to regulate physicians' practices or cap their earnings, but the AMA defends itself by pointing to the many other types of health issues, such as the quality of care, it also addresses.[23] Insurance companies, which have a strong interest in holding down health-care costs, also reject what they consider to be too much government regulation. They have led the opposition to proposals for national health insurance. Groups that lobby for the large hospital industry are the Federation of American Hospitals and the American Hospital Association. One group on the health-care scene of a liberal persuasion is the American Public Health Association (APHA), but it lacks some of the clout of other organizations with larger financial bases.[24] APHA members represent professionals from many health fields. Although nurses, many of whom belong to the American Nursing Association, comprise a large portion of all health-care providers, they have been poorly organized in the past but may be the "sleeping giants among the health lobbying community."[25] There are many smaller groups of professionals representing the concerns of other health specialists such as nurse-midwives, physical therapists, and social workers. And it is difficult to overlook groups representing the elderly, who consider health care one of their primary issues. For example, the American Association of Retired Persons, with its eighteen million members, can hardly be ignored—if not for its concerns, for the number of votes it represents.[26] There are times when the groups of the health-care lobby come together and others when the groups are at opposition to each other. For example, the groups have united to stave off cuts in Medicare, but should the president or Congress choose to select certain groups to sustain cuts or absorb more cost burdens, the political glue now holding these groups together is sure to weaken.[27]

THE POLITICS OF NATIONAL HEALTH INSURANCE

When the original Social Security Act of 1935 was passed, efforts were made in Congress to include "a comprehensive national health insurance system with universal and mandatory coverage." But, as mentioned earlier, President Franklin D. Roosevelt was forced to back off from this program when he became fearful that its inclusion in the original Social Security bill would bring about defeat of the entire bill. Representatives of the AMA contended that the plan would not work without the political support of the nation's physicians. President Harry S. Truman pushed hard for a national health insurance program tied to Social Security, but again opponents in the medical community succeeding in branding it socialized medicine and defeated the proposal. President Lyndon B. Johnson chose to pursue a somewhat narrower goal—compulsory health insurance for the aged, Medicare, and a related program for the poor, Medicaid. Johnson was successful in amending the Social Security Act to achieve these goals in 1965. In more than fifty years of attempts to implement a plan of national health insurance for all citizens, none have succeeded. Today much of the emphasis in health policy is on cost containment and the role of the private sector in current government programs. It is unlikely that we will see the government expand its role in the near future by providing health care for all Americans, yet a discussion of health care cannot ignore the concept of national health insurance.

NHI—Protecting the Nation's Health

The United States remains one of the few industrial nations in the world where medical-care expenses can cause poverty. Even though most people are covered by some kind of private or public medical insurance program, there are major gaps in this coverage. Some American families whose incomes are too high to qualify for Medicaid either do not purchase insurance at all or they purchase inadequate coverage—perhaps $25 or $50 per day against $100 to $150 per day hospital room charges. Or sometimes private insurance runs out after the first thirty or sixty days of hospital care, and eventually the seriously ill are impoverished by medical bills.

Until the 1940s most people did not have health insurance. One careful 1980 study of the nation's health insurance produced the following information: (1) About 85 percent of the population was "covered by private insurance or public medical programs for basic hospital room and board costs . . . but only 29.4 percent had coverage protecting them adequately against catastrophic or major medical expenses;" (2) only 40 percent of the population was covered for outpatient doctor costs and only 44 percent for nursing-home care, and (3) fewer than 20 percent of the population had insurance protection for prescription drugs.[28] Health care should be a right. Whatever other goals we may pursue, most Americans agree that lack of money should not be a barrier to adequate medical care. Access to doctors, hospitals, and drugs is necessary for a decent life.

A variety of national health insurance (NHI) plans have been introduced in Congress over the years; the proposal submitted by Senator Edward M. "Ted" Kennedy is one of the more comprehensive plans. The Kennedy plan includes the following provisions:

1. A National Health Board would be appointed by the president to set policy guidelines, oversee the program, and calculate the federal health budget each year.
2. A national insurance corporation would be formed to collect tax premiums from workers and allocate them to private insurance companies. These companies would process all claims. (Some supporters of NHI do not believe that private companies should play any role at all in national health insurance and that insurance claims should be paid directly by the federal government.)
3. Every American would be required to have health insurance coverage. (The Kennedy bill was officially named the Health Care for All Americans Act.) Workers and their families would be covered by plans developed through their employers. All others would be insured through a special federal insurance fund.
4. NHI would be funded in part by a new tax on employers (who would pay 65 percent of the costs of this insurance) and employees (who would pay 35 percent). Additional federal and state appropriations might be required to meet the expected costs.
5. Benefits would include full coverage of inpatient and outpatient hospital care, physicians' services, including office visits, laboratory and x-ray services, nursing-home care, and prescription drugs.
6. In order to contain costs, physicians' fees and hospital charges would be determined by the government for each year. The annual budget for NHI would have to be approved by Congress.

Comprehensive, universal health insurance, including the Kennedy NHI plan, would eliminate the need for separate Medicare and Medicaid programs for the aged and the poor. *All* Americans would be covered by national health insurance.

NHI would not be "socialized medicine" because hospitals would not be government owned and doctors would not be public employees. The analogous program is Canada's, not Great Britain's. The Canadians established universal hospital insurance in 1958 and universal physician insurance in 1968. Their rate of "medical inflation" over the last twenty years has been roughly the same as ours. This suggests that NHI need not be especially inflationary.

NHI—A Giant Step Sideways

Some people believe that national health insurance would be "a giant step sideways" in health care, if not an actual health hazard.[29] It would encourage the United States to continue to put scarce resources into even more sophisticated, elaborate, and costly medical care, whether or not this care had much impact on the nation's health.

We know that 85 percent of the population is covered by some form of private or public health insurance. Medicaid currently serves the poor; the poor now see doctors more often and stay in hospitals longer than the nonpoor. Medicare serves the aged; they also enjoy greater access to medical care than the rest of the population. The national "need" is *not* for more medical care. Indeed, Americans may be receiving too much medicine. The "need" is for a rational means of distributing a scarce resource—medical care—in an efficient fashion that would actually improve the nation's health.

Medical care is a "scarce resource" in that there will never be enough of it available to satisfy the unlimited demands of each individual and each physician. If all costs were eliminated, each patient and doctor could order the most elaborate diagnostic procedures (extensive lab work, CAT scans, consultations with specialists), extraordinary treatments (renal dialysis, organ transplants), long hospital stays, extensive nursing care, frequent office visits, and so on. With potential unlimited demand, medical care must be "rationed" in *some* fashion. It is difficult to assert that "health care is a right," when we know that some method of controlling aggregate demand for medical services will continue to be imposed on Americans. In Great Britain, under socialized medicine, health care is "rationed," in part by *time* rather than money: patients are required to wait many hours to see a doctor and months to undergo most types of surgery. It is persons who are willing and able to *wait,* rather than pay, who are served. And, of course, the press of patients may result in a poorer quality of care, although conclusive evidence on this point is not available.

It is really impossible to estimate what the total cost of medical care would be if NHI were adopted. If nearly 11 percent of our GNP is devoted to health now, what can we expect when *all* Americans are covered by a government program? What happens when virtually all incentives to control costs are removed? The total cost of health care could rise to 15 or 20 percent of the GNP, and *government* expenditures for health could rise to

40 percent of the entire federal budget. Yet there is no evidence that spending such a large share of the nation's resources on medical services, through the federal government or otherwise, would significantly improve the nation's health.

Americans would be required to sacrifice *something* for such an increase in medical services—whether it would be other social services, including Social Security, or education or defense or private spending. There is no "free" medical care.

Yet, once again, health studies generally suggest that medical care does not always imply good health. Often one encounters the comparisons of Utah and Nevada, two state populations with similar incomes, education, urbanization, climate, and numbers of physicians and hospital beds. Utah enjoys one of the highest levels of health in the nation—lower death rates, fewer days lost to sickness, longer life spans. Nevada, on the other hand, is at the opposite end of the ranking of the states by these measures of health.

> The answer almost surely lies in the different life styles of . . . the two states. Utah is inhabited primarily by Mormons . . . who do not use tobacco or alcohol and in general lead stable, quiet lives. Nevada . . . has high rates of cigarette and alcohol consumption and very high indexes of marital and geographic instability.[30]

Channeling more funds to help Americans adopt healthier life styles may prove to be a better use of health-care dollars.

The adoption of a limited alternative program of "catastrophic" health insurance could protect most Americans from becoming impoverished by large medical bills. "Catastrophic" health insurance, as opposed to "comprehensive" health insurance, would pay medical bills *over* some limit—for example, any bills over five thousand dollars per year. Individuals would be responsible for their care up to this limit; the government would relieve individuals of additional medical costs. The results would be to relieve Americans of the fear of major medical costs, while at the same time relying on the private market to help contain unnecessary medical treatment and cost. President Reagan has directed the Department of Health and Human Services to work with private enterprise to develop plans that would help provide Americans with catastrophic health insurance.

In addition to catastrophic health insurance for all Americans, health specialists have proposed that the nation adopt a "Kiddie Care" program for children under age seven and their mothers.[31] According to Theodore Marmor, Kiddie Care is necessary because (1) poor children are disadvantaged, even more than poor adults, in receiving medical care,[32] and (2) "the care that children need most is readily producible, relatively cheap, and reasonably likely to improve the health of preschoolers."[33] Kiddie Care focuses on routine services needed by children, such as immunizations, which will likely reduce the need for more expensive care later in life. Since the target of the program is children, Kiddie Care may be likely to gain popular support.

MEDICAID, MEDICARE, AND THE REAGAN ADMINISTRATION

The Reagan administration came into office promising that Medicare would be untouched by its budget-cutting efforts. Medicare was included among the Reagan safety-net programs, programs which would be protected from budget reductions. However, serious cost-cutting measures such as "diagnosis realted groups" have been introduced in the Medicare program. Medicaid was *not* included in the safety net. According to the Reagan officials, "High federal matching, excessive benefit provisions, and overly-generous eligibility have made the Medicaid program a very poorly managed social program that fails to provide cost-effective services to those most in need."[34] The administration pointed out that Medicaid costs have escalated at an alarming rate and that combined federal and state expenditures under Medicaid exceeded thirteen hundred dollars per year for each eligible beneficiary. The administration blamed excessive costs on the "insulation" of patients, doctors, and hospitals from the cost consequences of their decisions.

In its second term in office, the Reagan adminstration has continued to work to reform the Medicare and Medicaid programs. In spite of the cost control measures that have already been initiated, payroll taxes for the Health Insurance portion of Medicare will continue to lag far behind spending rates.[35] Although Congress defeated a cap on federal funding for Medicaid, stricter eligibility requirements have prevented many unemployed from gaining access to the program, and restrictions on AFDC eligibility have also contributed to what would have been higher utilization rates.[36] The president has been successful in consolidating and reducing public health expenditures through block grants. The use of means tests to determine veterans' eligibility for many health-care services provided by the Veterans' Administration has also been proposed. Veterans' advocacy groups, part of the health-care lobby, have attacked any such suggestions.

SUMMARY

Health care for aged and poor Americans has been on the social policy agenda since the early twentieth century. Health-care proposals have received strong public backing, but political opposition from the powerful American Medical Association helped to delay large-scale federal government involvement in medical assistance for fifty years!

The largest medical-care programs are in-kind programs called Medicare and Medicaid. Medicaid is the single *most* expensive public assistance program. It is operated jointly by the federal and state governments. All AFDC recipients and many SSI recipients are automatically eligible for Medicaid. Other medically indigent persons may also qualify. Twenty-two million Americans are Medicaid recipients.

Medicare is a social insurance program financed by the government through payroll taxes. It serves the nation's aged population. The elderly are more susceptible to illness and disease than other segments of the population and require more health services. Nearly all those aged sixty-five and over are eligible for Medicare, regardless of their income. Attempts to curb Medicare spending include diagnosis-related groups, a plan that pays fixed fees to hospitals for treating medical problems, and freezes on the amounts physicians can charge for their services.

Health-care expenditures make up a continually increasing amount of the federal budget. Rising medical costs can be attributed to the expansion of private insurance coverage, growth of the Medicaid and Medicare programs, the growing population of elderly persons, advances in medical technology, and the expansion of hospital facilities.

The access of the poor to medical care has increased, but the health of poor Americans has not improved in direct proportion to expenditures. The poor see doctors more often than the nonpoor, but their infant mortality rates are higher and their life spans are shorter. Providing more health care does not necessarily counteract the negative effects of the disadvantaged environments in which the poor live.

The goals of a rational health-care policy are to provide adequate health care for Americans while containing health-care costs. Federally established health systems agencies (HSAs), designed to keep health costs down by helping communities avoid duplication of medical services, have had little impact on cost containment.

Health maintenace organizations (HMOs) represent another attempt at keeping medical costs under control. Members pay fixed fees that are supposed to discourage doctors from providing too much care. The popularity of HMOs is growing.

National health insurance (NHI) is a controversial plan for alleviating the nation's health-care problems. Proponents believe that all Americans should be entitled to health-care services, but others argue that most Americans are already covered by private insurance companies and that such sweeping changes in the health-care-delivery system are not needed. They believe that catastrophic health-care insurance, which would prevent Americans faced with large health-care bills from financial ruin, is a more cost-efficient alternative than national health insurance. NHI does not appear to be in the offing. In spite of attempts to slow the rate of growth of health-care spending, health-care costs are taking a bigger and bigger chunk of the GNP.

NOTES

1. Although this point may seem arguable, the research literature is extensive. See, for example, Victor R. Fuchs, *Who Shall Live?* (New York: Basic Books, 1974); Nathan Glazer, "Paradoxes of Health Care," *Public Interest,* no. 22 (Winter 1971), 62–77; and Leon R. Kass, "Regarding the End of Medicine and the Pursuit of Health," *Public Interest,* no. 40 (Summer 1975), 11–42.
2. "Reagan Again Seeks to Curb Medicare, Medicaid Growth," *Congressional Quarterly,* February 9, 1985, p. 243.
3. "Congress Shies Away from Any Cap on Medicaid Outlays," *Congressional Quarterly,* May 11, 1985, p. 894.

4. Ibid., p. 891.
5. Janet Hook, "Growing Demand for Long-Term Care Drains Medicaid Coffers Nationwide," *Congressional Quarterly,* May 11, 1985, p. 892.
6. "Major Changes Made in Medicare Program," *1983 Congressional Quarterly Almanac,* p. 391.
7. The rest of this section relies on "Congress Shies Away," pp. 891–95.
8. These figures and quotes are from Hook, "Growing Demand for Long-Term Care," p. 892.
9. National Center for Health Statistics, figures cited in John L. McCoy and David L. Brown, "Health Status among Low-Income Elderly Persons: Rural-Urban Differences," *Social Security Bulletin* 41, no. 6 (June 1978), 14.
10. Bureau of the Census, *Money Income and Poverty Status of Families and Persons in the United States: 1984,* Current Population Reports, series P-60, no. 149, August 1985, p. 26.
11. "Health Status and Medical Care," *Economic Report of the President,* House document no. 99-19, 99th Cong., 1st Sess., February 1985, p. 146.
12. "Medicare Eyed for More Cuts as Congress Seeks Savings," *Congressional Quarterly,* March 30, 1985, p. 577.
13. Ibid., p. 581.
14. "Hill Panels Find DRGs Leave Patients 'Sicker,'" *NASW News,* April 1985, p.10.
15. "Medicare Eyed for More Cuts," p. 580.
16. "Health Status and Medical Care," p. 134.
17. See Ronald W. Wilson and Elijah L. White, "Changes in Morbidity, Disability and Utilization Differentials Between the Poor and the Nonpoor; Data from the Health Interview Survey: 1964 and 1973," paper presented at the 102d Annual Meeting of the American Public Health Association, October 21, 1974, cited in Dorothy P. Rice and Douglas Wilson, "The American Medical Economy: Problems and Perspectives," *Journal of Health Politics, Policy and Law* 1 (Summer 1976), 151–72; and Theodore R. Marmor, "Rethinking National Health Insurance," *Public Interest,* no. 46 (Winter 1977), 73–95. For a critique of the argument that access to health care is greater for the poor than the nonpoor, see Catherine Kohler Riessman, "The Use of Health Services by the Poor: Are There Any Promising Models?" *Social Policy,* no. 14 (Spring 1984), 30–40.
18. "Health Status and Medical Care," p. 137.
19. Aaron Wildavsky, *Speaking Truth to Power* (Boston: Little, Brown, 1979), p. 286.
20. "Health Planning," *1983 Congressional Quarterly Almanac,* p. 420.
21. Data on HMOs are from Martha Brannigan, "Variations in Health Maintenance Groups Make Comparative Shopping Worthwhile," *Wall Street Journal,* December 17, 1984, p. 29.
22. "Physicians' Lobbying Machine Showing Some Signs of Wear," *Congressional Quarterly Weekly Report,* January 7, 1984, p. 77.
23. Ibid., p. 79.
24. "Many Health Groups Influencing Congress," *Congressional Quarterly Weekly Report,* January 7, 1984, p. 80.
25. Ibid.
26. Steven Pressman, "Unity of Lobby Groups Likely to Shatter as Congress Looks for Medicare Cuts," *Congressional Quarterly,* May 30, 1985, p. 581.
27. Ibid., p. 580.
28. See *Health Policy: The Legislative Agenda* (Washington, D. C.: Congressional Quarterly, 1980), p. 11.
29. This phrase is courtesy of Peter Steinfels, "National Health Insurance: Its Politics and Problems," *Dissent* 24 (Winter 1977), 61–71.
30. Fuchs, *Who Shall Live?,* p. 53.
31. Theodore R. Marmor, "The Politics of National Health Insurance: Analysis and Prescription," *Policy Analysis* 3, no. 1:25–48. Reprinted in John E. Tropman, Milan J. Dluhy

and Roger M. Lind, eds., *New Strategic Perspectives on Social Policy* (New York: Pergamon Press, 1981), pp. 30–50.

32. Karen Davis and Roger Reynolds, "The Impact of Medicare and Medicaid on Access to Medical Care" (Washington: Brookings Institution, n.d.), p. 3; published also in Richard Rosett, ed., *The Role of Insurance in the Health Services Sector* (New York: National Bureau of Economic Research, 1976); cited in Marmor, "Politics of National Health Insurance," p. 38.
33. Marmor, "Politics of National Health Insurance," p. 38.
34. Office of Management and Budget, *A Program for Economic Recovery,* February 18, 1981, pp. 1–15.
35. John L. Palmer and Isabel V. Sawhill, eds., *The Reagan Record* (Cambridge, Mass.: Ballinger, 1984), p. 369.
36. Ibid., p. 370.

chapter 11

Challenging social welfare: Racism and sexism

Poverty and other social problems are not random events. These problems plague some groups more than others. Prejudice and discrimination against racial, ethnic, and cultural minorities and against women, the elderly, and the handicapped all contribute to perpetuating poverty and other social problems.

Racism and sexism have long been a part of American society. Women and members of minority groups are often treated in ways that reflect myths and misconceptions. For example, blacks are expected to live in certain areas of the community but not others. Women are expected to occupy some jobs but not others. Blacks are expected to excel in sports and dancing, and women are expected to be the primary child rearers.

Prejudice and discrimination occur every day. *Prejudices* are stereotyped *attitudes* that are harbored toward a group of people. *Discrimination* consists of *actions* that have negative consequences for a group of people. Prejudice and discrimination often occur simultaneously. A landlord believes that Mexican-Americans make poor tenants and refuses to rent to them. An employer avoids hiring women based on a belief that mothers are unreliable employees because they miss time from work to care for their children. A civic leader omits blacks from the annual membership-drive because "other members" will not like the idea. In this chapter we explore disadvantages that accrue to women and minorities and look at policies that seek to alter these problems.

THE FEMINIZATION OF POVERTY

When we trace the origins of public assistance, we see that some of the earliest welfare programs were directed toward dependent children and their mothers. Women became public assistance beneficiaries because they were expected to remain at home to care for their young children when their husbands were unable to support them because of death, divorce, or desertion. Even when women went to work to support themselves and their families, they were forced into low-paying jobs. These factors contributed to a pattern of female dependency on welfare. This pattern was further exacerbated during the 1970s and has come to be called the "feminization of poverty."[1] For example, from 1969 to 1978 the number of poor families headed by women increased by nine hundred thousand while the number of poor families headed by couples or males dropped by six hundred thousand.[2]

Most of those on the welfare roles continue to be women. Even though half the states operate AFDC-UP programs, few fathers participate (see Chapter 6). Efforts to reduce the number of mothers on welfare through job training and employment have not produced very positive results. These programs have not been structured in ways that would allow AFDC mothers to cross the poverty threshold. The costs of clothing, transportation, and child care coupled with the loss of welfare benefits do not make work in low-paying jobs a viable option for many AFDC mothers. Women are also overrepresented in the SSI program. Twice as many women as men receive SSI.

The historical patterns of inequities in education, status, employment, and pay have made women and their families much more dependent on welfare than men. In 1984 the poverty rate for families headed by married couples was 7 per cent, while families headed by men only had a rate of 13 percent and those headed by women only had a rate of 35 percent. As we can see, married couples are least likely to be poor, but *woman heading families alone are nearly three times as likely as their male counterparts to live in poverty.* The discrepancy is less for single persons. The poverty rate for single males is 19 percent, and for women it is 24 percent.[3] Differences in median income also make apparent the financial difficulties of women alone. Married couples had a median income of $29,612, and males heading households earned $23,325; female heads of households earned only $12,803.[4]

THE WAGE GAP

Women have long earned less than men (see table 11-1). The familiar phrase of the equal rights movement—"fifty-nine cents"—attested to the fact that women earned fifty-nine cents for every dollar earned by men. By 1984 this figure had inched up to sixty-four cents on the dollar. Many reasons have been offered to explain the difference in earning power. Among these explanations are the following:

TABLE 11-1 Ratio of Women's to Men's Annual Earnings Based on Full-time Employment

YEAR	RATIO	YEAR	RATIO
1955	64	1970	59
1956	63	1971	60
1957	64	1972	58
1958	63	1973	57
1959	61	1974	59
1960	61	1975	59
1961	59	1976	60
1962	60	1977	59
1963	60	1978	59
1964	60	1979	60
1965	60	1980	60
1966	58	1981	60
1967	58	1982	63
1968	58	1983	64
1969	61	1984	64

Source: Nancy Rytina, "Comparing Annual and Weekly Earnings from the Current Population Survey," *Monthly Labor Review,* April 1983, p. 36. Figures for later years are from the Bureau of Labor Statistics, March Current Population Survey Supplement (unpublished).

1. Traditionally, most women were not the major wage earners in a family, nor did they earn salaries comparable to their husbands even if they did work.
2. Women's wages were considered secondary to that of their spouses.
3. Women were considered temporary employees who would leave their jobs to marry and have children; they were not really serious about careers.
4. Women's work outside the home was considered an extracurricular activity to fill free time.
5. Women had fewer opportunities to obtain education that would lead to better-paying jobs.
6. Women had limited job choices because they were forced to accept jobs that did not conflict with the routines of their husbands and children.
7. "Women's work" cleaning and child rearing at home have not been wage-earning jobs.
8. Some thought that women "preferred" lower-level employment because these jobs were more compatible with characteristics they associated with women, such as lack of aggressiveness.

Today there are elements of truth in some of these statements. Some women do terminate their employment, on a temporary or long-term basis to raise families, and others prefer to select jobs that are compatible with family routines; however, we also know that many of these statements can no longer be defended. Many women must work to support their families. Fifteen percent of U.S. families are headed by women; one-third of all women who work have a spouse whose annual earnings are less than fifteen

TABLE 11-2 Ratio of Women's to Men's Annual Earnings Based on Full-time Employment for Selected Occupations, 1981

Professional and technical workers	64.3
Managers and administrators	57.9
Salesworkers	51.4
Clerical workers	63.7
Craft workers	64.9
Operatives	61.1
Transport-equipment operatives	73.7
Nonfarm laborers	71.3
Service workers	60.5

Source: Nancy Rytina, "Comparing Annual and Weekly Earnings from the Current Population Survey," *Monthly Labor Review,* April 1983, p. 35.

thousand dollars.[5] Many women find their work satisfying and an integral component of their lives, regardless of their marital status.

Today women comprise 43 percent of the work force, and these numbers continue to grow,[6] but women continue to earn less than men, although many have earned advanced degrees and more women now hold higher-level jobs. Women who hold professional and technical jobs earn only 64 percent of their male counterparts' salaries (see table 11-2). Women managers and administrators are even worse off, earning only about 58 percent of men in the same fields. Even in the "pink-collar" clerical field where many women are employed, the ratio is less than 64 percent. Women in the blue-collar fields, operating transportation equipment and working as laborers, seem to do better, earning as much as 74 percent of their male coworkers' wages.

COMPARABLE WORTH

One approach to narrowing the wage gap has been to press for equal pay for equal work. For example, it is difficult to justify paying a male accountant more than a female accountant if their job responsibilities are the same. By law, men and women who do the *same* work are supposed to be paid equally. A more recent effort to reduce the gap in earnings between women and men is based on the argument of "comparable worth." According to this argument, workers should be paid equally when they do *different* types of work that require the same level of responsibility, effort, knowledge, and skill. Many jobs done by men are valued or weighted more heavily in terms of monetary compensation because the idea of the "dual labor market" creates a situation in which "women's professions"—secretarial, teaching, nursing, social work—tend to be valued less than professions dominated by men. To phrase the argument this way, are the jobs in question of equal value in society?

One White House official recently called compensation based on comparable worth a "truly crazy proposal."[7] However, others argue that comparable worth is a truly rational proposal. Twenty states have passed laws or resolutions which make comparable worth a requirement or a goal of state employment.[8] The rub occurs when officials attempt to actually implement such a proposal.[9] In theory most people can agree on the principle of equal pay for work of equal value, but how do we determine what constitutes work of equal value? How can we determine if the work of a secretary is comparable to the work of an automobile mechanic? Some contend that even if the value of jobs could be calculated in a way agreeable to everyone, the cost of implementing far-reaching comparable-worth plans would be so tremendous as to be unfeasible; while others say it is about time that women are paid equitable salaries.

The U.S. Commission on Civil Rights has failed to support comparable worth saying it would reek havoc on the market place. Thus far the courts have responded to the issue of comparable worth by supporting salary differentials that appear to arise from labor-force competition.[10] In a case against Brown University, a male faculty member accused the university of paying an equally qualified female faculty member a higher salary. The First Circuit Court ruled in favor of the university, which argued that the female professor was paid more because she had planned to take a position at another school, which had offered her a higher salary. Brown wanted to retain her. The university contended that she had greater market value than the male professor, and the court agreed. In another case in higher education, nursing faculty at the University of Washington filed suit stating that they were paid less than male faculty in other university departments. The Ninth Circuit Court ruled that under Title VII of the Civil Rights Act, suits cannot be brought before the court if salary inequities are due to labor-market conditions. Whether we agree with the courts or not, the issue of comparable worth is gaining increasing attention, and ways to implement it will continue to be sought.

EQUAL RIGHTS FOR WOMEN

Women have been striving for equality through political participation since the suffragette movement. This movement culminated in 1920 in the Nineteenth Amendment to the United States Constitution, which gave women the right to vote.

But despite the right to vote, the percentage of women who hold political office is small, though growing. In the early 1980s women held 12 percent of the seats in state legislatures, 7 percent of those on county commissions, 9 percent of mayoralties, and 4 percent of township and local council seats.[11] From 1960 to 1985 the percentage of women in state legislatures grew from 4 to 14.3 percent.[12] In 1985 only two of the 100 U.S. senators, and 21 of the 435 U.S. representatives were female.[13]

Since the 1960s the federal government has attempted to address the inequities women face in employment, education, and the marketplace.

ILLUSTRATION: TITLE IX: SEX DISCRIMINATION IN EDUCATION

Two events in 1970 helped a few Washington women to organize an information network that would first make sex discrimination issues visible and would then foster the passage of women's rights legislation in education.

In January 1970, Bernice Sandler, under the auspices of the Women's Equity Action League (WEAL), requested the Office of Federal Contract Compliance (OFCC) in the Department of Labor to enforce Executive Order 11246, as amended. She then began to file class-action complaints of sex discrimination against 250 colleges and universities.

Sandler had discovered the executive order quite by accident, while reading a report on civil rights enforcement. A part-time instructor at the University of Maryland and a recent Ph.D recipient, she had experienced sex discrimination in her search for academic positions, including being told that she "came on too strong for a woman." Encouraged by an OFCC official to file a class-action complaint through a national organization, she turned to WEAL. At the time, WEAL's advisory board included several congresswomen: Edith Green (chair of the House Special Subcommittee on Education), Shirley Chisholm, Patsy Mink, and Martha Griffiths. Griffiths supported WEAL's involvement in the complaint, and Green used the charges as a basis for committee hearings on discrimination against women. Several years later, Chisholm and Mink were to figure prominently as supporters of sex-equity legislation in education.

In June and July of 1970, Representative Green held seven days of hearings on sex discrimination. The hearings focused on a bill that Green had just introduced and that was designed to eliminate the loopholes in coverage under the Equal Pay Act and Title VII of the 1964 Civil Rights Act, authorize the U.S. Commission on Civil Rights to study discrimination against women, and most important, to prohibit sex discrimination in federally assisted programs and in the field of education. Testifying at the hearings were women employed in higher education institutions across the country, as well as representatives from women's organizations and from the President's Task Force on Women's Rights and Responsibilities. Several professional associations in higher education were invited to participate but they declined. Representing the Department of Health, Education, and Welfare (HEW), which would administer the law, was the associate commissioner for higher education for the U.S. Office of Education, who supported the principle of equal rights but questioned whether "the provisions are the proper vehicle for expanding existing law"—the standard language used to oppose a bill. In fact, the Nixon Administration consistently opposed sex-equity legislation. No immediate action was taken on Green's bill, but the 1300 pages of testimony comprised the first comprehensive compilation of statistics on the status of women in education and were widely distributed.

Green's bill later became Title IX of the Education Amendments of 1972, which Green saw through to passage before she retired. Initially, Green sought to amend Title VI of the 1964 Civil Rights Act to include sex, but she later proposed a separate title at the urging of black civil rights leaders and others who feared that opening Title VI for amendment would weaken its coverage and enforcement.

In its final form, Title IX had wording identical to Title VI, except that it was restricted to educational activities:

> No person in the United States shall, on the basis of sex, be excluded from participation in, be denied the benefits of, or be subjected to discrimination under any education program or activity receiving federal financial assistance.

The parallel wording with Title VI was to become very important in the enforcement of the new measure. Its sponsor in the Senate, Birch Bayh, deliberately defined its program coverage as identical to that of Title VI, so that no federal funds were to go to any institutions practicing discrimination on the basis of sex. Hence, the Title IX regulation was written to cover an entire institution, not just the federal projects housed within it. As with Title VI, presidential approval of the regulation was also required.

Title IX was more inclusive than Title VI, in that it covered employment, but it would take a decade of litigation and a 1982 Supreme Court decision (North Haven Board of Education v. Bell) to affirm it. There were also exceptions to the Title IX coverage. Some educational institutions were allowed to maintain admission restrictions, and military schools were exempt. Also, some religious schools were exempt under certain circumstances.

There was no organized lobbying for Title IX; indeed, Green actively discouraged lobbying. As Sandler recalls:

> Mrs. Green's advice was: "Don't lobby for this bill." She was absolutely right. She said: "If you lobby, people are going to oppose it. Leave it. The opposition is not there right now so don't call attention to it." We knew it was going to cover athletics; it was no surprise. We just didn't tell many people.

Title IX passed on June 23, 1972, and was signed into law by President Richard Nixon on July 1.

It was a banner year for women's rights in Congress. Margot Polivy, then an administrative aide to Representative Bella Abzug, remembers that session of Congress well:

> 1972 was a watershed year. We put sex discrimination provisions into everything. There was no opposition. Who'd be against equal rights for women? So we just kept passing women's rights legislation.

The Equal Rights Amendment passed both houses and was sent to the states. Title IX also passed, and the loopholes in the Equal Pay Act and in Title VII of the 1964 Civil Rights Act were closed. Finally, Title IV of the Civil Rights Act, which provides federal funds to schools in race desegregation efforts, was amended to provide assistance to school districts in combating sex discrimination.

Source: Mary Ann Millsap, "Sex Equity in Education," pp. 92-94 in *Women in Washington, Advocates for Public Policy*, edited by Irene Tinker.

1. The Equal Pay Act of 1963 requires employers to conpensate male and female workers equally for performing the same jobs under similar conditions. The law does not cover all groups, but amendments to the act have added to the types of jobs and employers who must comply.
2. Title VII of the Civil Rights Act of 1964 prohibits sexual discrimination in employment practices and provides the right to court redress. The Equal Employment Opportunity Commission is the agency charged with interpreting and enforcing Title VII.
3. Executive Order 11246, as amended by Executive Order 11375, prohibits employers who practice sexual discrimination from receiving federal contracts. Employers are also required to develop plans for "affirmative action" (positive steps taken to recruit and promote women to remedy inequities). The order also established the Office of Federal Contract Compliance Programs under the Department of Labor as an enforcement agency.
4. Title IX of the Education Amendments of 1972 prohibits sexual discrimination by elementary, secondary, vocational, professional, and higher education institutions that receive federal funds.
5. The Equal Credit Act of 1975 prohibits discrimination by lending institutions based on sex or marital status.

The equal rights amendment (ERA) attempted to guarantee women equal rights through the U.S. Constitution. The equal rights amendment simply stated:

> Section 1. Equality of rights under the law shall not be denied or abridged by the United States or by any state on account of sex.
> Section 2. Congress shall have the power to enforce by appropriate legislation the provisions of this Article.
> Section 3. This amendment shall take effect two years after the date of ratification.

Proponents of the ERA argued that this guarantee of sexual equality under law should be part of the Constitution—"the supreme law of the land." It is true that a number of existing federal and state laws prohibit sexual discrimination, but there were concerns that these laws were inadequate to address the problem. ERA proponents contend that like many other social policy issues, sexual discrimination is best addressed by a national policy rather than by a multitude of federal, state, and local laws that are each subject to change, modification, and repeal. Proponents continue to contend that women have long been disadvantaged and that the ERA can only contribute to more equitable treatment for women.

However, opponents of the ERA were successful in halting this constitutional amendment just three states short of the thirty-eight states (three-quarters) needed for ratification. In 1972 the United States Congress passed the ERA and set a 1979 deadline for state ratification. But by 1978 the amendment had not been ratified. Congress granted an extension of the deadline until June 30, 1982. Despite the endorsement of 450 organizations with 50 million members—unions, churches, civil rights groups, legal associations, educational groups, medical organizations[14]—the ERA failed.

The "stop ERA" movement" was based on fears about what *might* happen if the ERA passed. It was argued that the ERA would lead to an extension of military registration and perhaps even a military draft and combat duty for women. The ERA did not specifically address the role of women in the armed services. Other issues—marriage, divorce, child custody, inheritance—were also not specifically mentioned in the ERA. It was thus difficult to predict the long-range consequences of the ERA. Some feared that passage of the amendment would cause laws governing relationships between men and women to change in ways that might disadvantage women. Others claimed that the ERA would not have much of an impact at all. "Stop ERA" Chairperson Phyllis Schafly announced to women:

> ERA won't do anything for you. It won't make your husband do half the dirty diapers and dishes. It won't make your ex-husband pay support. I think the defeat of ERA is a tremendous victory for women's rights.[15]

Do Americans want the ERA? Some national polls report that majorities of Americans—both men and women—support equal rights. (Support for ERA was reported at 71 percent by the NBC-Associated Press poll in 1980; 64 percent by Gallup, 1980; 61 percent by *Time* magazine, 1981; 61 percent by the *Washington Post*-ABC Poll, 1981).[16] Although it was not ratified, supporters have not given up efforts to see the ERA returned to the national agenda.

Equal rights and affirmative-action proponents are now concerned about new threats to existing policies. In February 1984 the Supreme Court, in the case of *Grove City* v. *Bell,* delivered a ruling affecting the interpretation of Title IX of the Civil Rights Act which prohibits sex discrimination in federally funded education programs. The Court declared in a 6-3 vote that Title IX applies only to those individual programs receiving federal aid and not to all programs of an institution. This interpretation is in sharp contrast to the spirit with which Title IX has been applied since its enactment. The fear of those opposed to the Court's decision is that it will also affect application of Title VI of the Civil Rights Act barring discrimination based on race, color, or national origin in federally sponsored programs, as well as the Rehabilitation Act of 1973 barring discrimination against the handicapped and the Age Discrimination Act of 1975. Another fear is that the Court's action lends support to what critics believe is the president's deemphasis of affirmative action.

THE SUPREME COURT: REAFFIRMING ABORTION RIGHTS

Before the 1960s abortions were rarely permitted in any states, except in cases where the mother's life was in danger. Then about a quarter of the states made some modifications in their abortion laws, extending them to cases of rape, incest, or when the physical or mental health of the mother was in jeopardy. Obtaining an abortion was still difficult because each case had to be reviewed individually by physicians and by the hospital where the abortion was to be performed.

In 1970 abortion policy began to change.[17] Four states (New York, Alaska, Hawaii, and Washington) liberalized their abortion laws, permitting women to obtain an abortion upon the woman's request with her physician's agreement. In 1973 the Supreme Court made decisions which fundamentally changed abortion policy. In the cases of *Roe* v. *Wade* and *Doe* v. *Bolton,* the Supreme Court ruled that the Fifth and Fourteenth Amendments to the Constitution, which guarantee all persons "life, liberty and property," did not include the life of the unborn fetus. In addition, the First and Fourteenth Amendments guaranteeing personal liberties were said to extend to child-bearing decisions. The Supreme Court did stipulate some conditions under which abortions could and could not be restricted by the states: (1) during the first three months of pregnancy the states cannot restrict the mother's decision for an abortion; (2) from the fourth to six months of pregnancy the states cannot restrict abortions, but they can protect the health of the mother by setting standards for how and when abortions can be performed; (3) during the last three months of pregnancy the states can prohibit all abortions except those to protect the mother's life and health.

Under the Medicaid program, poor pregnant women used to be able to obtain federally funded abortions. But in 1976 antiabortion groups were able to tack an amendment on to the appropriations bill for the former Department of Health, Education and Welfare. Known as the Hyde Amendment, it prohibited the federal government from paying for abortions except in cases that endanger the mother's life. The amendment does not restrict women from obtaining a privately funded abortion but limits their ability to do so if they are unable to arrange to cover the costs. The National Abortion Rights League lost a Supreme Court battle to change Congress's decision. The Supreme Court upheld the Hyde Amendment, declaring that the poor do not have the right to abortions financed by the federal government, except in cases endangering the mother. In 1977 the federal funding ban was lifted in promptly reported cases of rape and incest and in cases where "severe and long-lasting" harm would be caused to the woman.

In 1983 the Supreme Court reaffirmed its 1973 decisions concerning abortion and also extended some provisions.[18] Abortions early in the second trimester do not have to be performed in hospitals since medical advances now make it possible to conduct these procedures safely on an outpatient basis. The court also struck down regulations adopted in Akron, Ohio, which required physicians (1) to obtain parental consent prior to performing any abortions on minors under age 15; (2) to recite to women lengthy information about abortion complications; and (3) to inform women of risks while preventing others (such as nurses and counselors) from doing so. The Court also struck down regulations which designated a twenty-four hour waiting period between the time the woman signed an informed consent form and the time the abortion was actually performed. A 1986 Supreme Court decision also reaffirmed a woman's right to abortion when it struck down a Pennsylvania law aimed at discouraging women from obtaining abortions.

Opponents of abortion, usually referred to as "right-to-life" groups, have been distressed by the Court's recent actions. They oppose the freedom to obtain an abortion and generally base their arguments on religious, moral, and biological grounds, contending that the viability of the fetus (its ability to survive outside the womb) is evidence that a human life is at stake.

Abortion, they argue, is tantamount to taking a human life. Prolifers demonstrate annually in Washington on the anniversary of the *Roe* v. *Wade* decision. A controversial film entitled "The Silent Scream" is said to depict the horrors of abortion for the fetus and has been shown around the country to increase opposition to abortion rights.

Proponents of abortion, who often call themselves the "prochoice" movement, believe that a woman has the right to make decisions about her own body, including the decision to terminate an unwanted pregnancy. Without recourse to legal abortions they fear that women may turn to illegal abortions that can result in health risks or even death for the mother. Proponents believe that misery and suffering may be avoided when a parent or parents can make a decision about unwanted children. In 1985 prochoice groups including the National Abortion Rights Action League, Planned Parenthood (a family-planning organization), and Catholics for a Free Choice joined together to again counter the arguments of prolife activists through letter campaigns to the president and "speakouts" across the country.[19]

Since Roe v. Wade, the number of abortions performed annually has increased from 750,000 in 1973 to about one and one-half million in 1980[20] and has remained at that level. Although the Court's decisions have reaffirmed Roe v. Wade, there is concern from prochoice groups about the future of abortion policy. The 1973 decison was supported 7-2, the 1983 decision 6-3, and the 1986 decision 5-4. Since it is the older rather than younger members of the Court who have been most supportive of the decisions, deaths or resignations could cause a shift in the Court's opinion. Sandra Day O'Connor, a Reagan appointee and the only woman on the bench, has voted with the opposition. With the resignation of Chief Justice Warren Burger, the president has another opportunity to make a nomination to the Supreme Court. Any other changes on the bench during the president's second term may have a drastic effect on Roe v. Wade.

Unfortunately, the controversy over abortion has not been limited to rhetoric, verbal debate, and court decisions. The anniversary date of *Roe* v. *Wade* has become a tense time for employees of abortion clinics owing to a number of bombings of these facilities. Some recent bombings have not been confined to the anniversary date and have also included Planned Parenthood offices. Leaders of the right-to-life movement deny involvement, asserting that the bombings are another form of the violence they abhor. But more bombings have occurred and most of the responsible parties have not been identified.

SPOUSE ABUSE

Like many other issues related to the family, domestic violence has remained largely outside the public policy arena until the last decade. Domestic violence may occur among any family members. Generally we think of this as violence against children, spouses, and elderly parents. In this section our primary concern is spouse abuse. Although physical abuse of husbands and wives does occur, most victims are women. In the late 1970s some states officially recognized that battered women were not receiving adequate legal protection.[21] In effect, this amounted to a form of sexual discrimination toward women who were victimized by their partners.[22] All states have now enacted some type of legislation to protect battered women, although provisions are not consistent among states. Battered spouses have two types of legal recourse: civil and criminal. Civil laws are used to "settle disputes between individuals and to compensate for injuries," while criminal laws are used to "punish acts which are disruptive of social order and to deter other similar acts."[23] In 1979 the federal government established the Office on Domestic Violence under the Department of Health and Human Services. The office was responsible for administrative activities including planning, policy development, and technical assistance, and demonstration activities. It was abolished in 1981, and its functions were turned over to the National Center on Child Abuse and Neglect. Although federal legislation to assist victims of domestic violence has been introduced, there is no federal law which substantially addresses the problem. Instead, states and communities have responded with their own laws and services. Most prominent among the services are shelters for battered women. Many are operated through local agencies with limited resources and are able to assist only a portion of those in need of services. Domestic violence is another issue in the broad area we call family policy.

WOMEN, MEN, AND SOCIAL SECURITY

When the Social Security system was first adopted, the roles of men and women were different than they are today. Women were less likely to work outside the home, and divorce was less common. The Social Security system reflected the social conditions of the 1930s when most women received Social Security benefits because they were "dependents" of their working husbands. Since women are poorer than men they rely more heavily on transfer payments such as Social Security, but their benefits are often smaller than men's. Social Security is the sole source of income for 60 percent of elderly women.[24] In 1984, 15 percent of women aged sixty-five and over were in poverty compared with 9 percent of men.[25] Older women are less likely than men to have additional sources of income like pensions.

The Social Security system has not kept pace with the changing roles of men and women.[26] Women have been inadequately treated by the Social Security system for a number of reasons:

1. Women's wages remain lower than men's wages, resulting in lower benefits paid to women when they retire.
2. Women are still likely to spend less time in the work force than men because they also carry the major responsibilities for home and children. This also results in lower benefits paid to women.
3. Divorced women are entitled to only one-half of their former husbands' benefits. If this is the woman's only income it is generally not adequate.

4. Widows generally do not qualify for benefits unless they are sixty years old or unless there are children under age eighteen in the home.
5. Homemakers are not covered on their own unless they have held jobs in the labor force.
6. Social Security benefits are often based on the earnings of the primary worker, generally the husband. The wages of a second earner may not raise the couples' combined Social Security benefits very much.
7. Couples in which one worker earned most of the wages may receiver higher benefits than those in which the husband and wife earned equal wages.
8. Married workers benefit from Social Security more than single workers. An individual who has never worked can benefit from Social Security payments based on the work of a spouse. Single workers do not receive additional benefits, even though they have made Social Security payments at the same rate as married workers.

Two major options have been suggested for remedying inequities in the Social Security system.[27] The "earnings-sharing" option would divide a couple's earnings equally between the husband and wife for each year they are married. This option would allow benefits to be calculated separately for the husband and the wife and would eliminate the ideas of the "primary wage earner" and the "dependent spouse." This option would also recognize that the spouse who takes care of the home is an equal partner in the marriage. A second option is the "double-decker plan." Under this option everyone would be eligible for a basic benefit, whether or not he or she has worked. Individuals who have also contributed to the paid labor force would receive a payment in addition to the basic benefit.

As a result of the Social Security Amendments of 1983, some disqualifications for benefits based on sex were eliminated, but most brought only a limited number of new recipients to the rolls. One provision allows divorced spouses to qualify for benefits at age sixty-two based on a former spouse's earnings even if the ex-spouse has not claimed benefits. Another measure allows divorced husbands to claim benefits based on the earnings records of their former wives.

In 1984 the Social Security Administration conducted a survey of new beneficiaries who had retired in the early 1980s.[28] The survey compared the average monthly benefits of men and women. As we would expect, couples received the highest benefits (see figure 11-1). Their average monthly benefit was $815, while widowed men received $520 and widowed women received $432. Divorcees received less than widowed beneficiaries. Divorced women received less than divorced men. But it is interesting to note that single (never married) women averaged $50 per month more than their male counterparts. For all groups, average benefits exceeded the poverty level, an improvement over ten years ago when benefits for unmarried men and women were about two-thirds of the poverty level.

The number of women who qualify for benefits based on their own work records has increased considerably from 2.9 million in 1960 to 10.3 million in 1983. However, many women still receive higher payments based on their husband's earnings rather than on their own, but this is expected to change in the future.

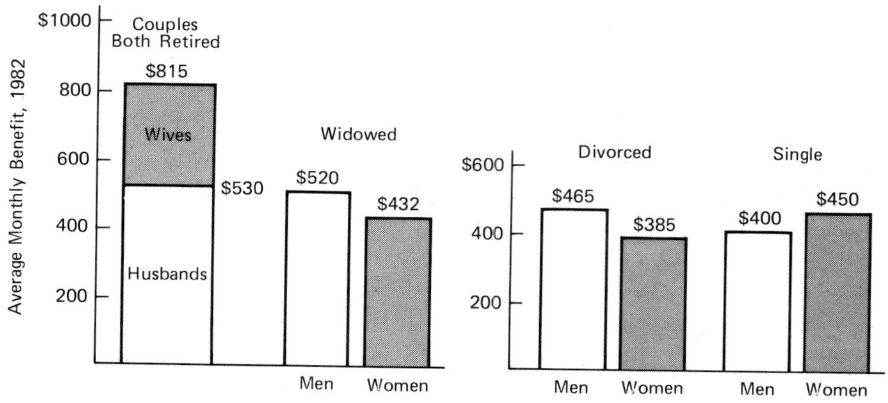

FIGURE 11-1 Monthly benefits of new Social Security Recipients, 1982. ("Women and Social Security," *Social Security Bulletin* 48, no. 2 [February 1985], p. 18.)

BLACKS, HISPANICS, AND WELFARE

The living conditions of white, black and Hispanic* Americans continue to differ. On the average, blacks do not live as long as whites; they are in poorer health; they earn less, and they are overrepresented in public assistance programs. The effects of poverty also contribute to a less adequate lifestyle for many Hispanic-Americans. Table 11-3 compares the incomes of those three groups. Twenty-five percent of black families earn less than $7,500 annually, compared with 18 percent of Hispanic and 8 percent of white families. Whites are twice as likely as blacks to earn $35,000–50,000 annually. Hispanic families have somewhat better earning records than black Americans. In 1984 the median income of black families was $15,432, compared with a Hispanic median income of $18,833 and a white median income of $27,686.

Since black Americans earn less than white Americans and those of Hispanic origin, they are also more likely to be poor. Table 11-4 compares poverty rates for these three groups from 1966 to 1984. For each year blacks were at least three times as likely to be poor as whites; those of Hispanic origin were less likely to be poor than blacks. Although poverty rates generally decreased for all Americans in the 1960s and 1970s, they began rising in the 1980s. Twelve percent of whites, 34 percent of blacks, and 28 percent of Hispanics are now poor.

Even after controlling for education, blacks are more likely to be poor than whites and those of Hispanic origin. While educational attainment is closely related to income, the income of blacks in America is less likely than whites to increase with education (see table 11-5). For example, 14 percent of whites with an eighth-grade education have incomes below the poverty level, compared with 36 percent of blacks and 29 percent of those of His-

*Hispanics may be of any race.

TABLE 11-3 Income Levels for White, Black, and Hispanic Families, 1984

INCOME	% OF TOTAL WHITE	% OF TOTAL BLACK	% OF TOTAL HISPANIC ORIGIN[a]
Under $2,500	1.6	4.7	3.4
$2,500 to $4,999	2.2	10.1	6.3
$5,000 to $7,499	3.7	10.2	8.1
$7,500 to $9,999	4.4	9.0	7.6
$10,000 to $12,499	5.3	8.3	8.0
$12,500 to $14,999	5.0	6.6	7.0
$15,000 to $19,999	10.7	12.3	11.7
$20,000 to $24,999	11.0	9.4	12.1
$25,000 to $34,999	19.8	13.1	16.7
$35,000 to $49,999	19.4	10.5	12.3
$50,000 and over	16.9	5.8	6.7
Median Income	$27,686	$15,432	$18,833

[a]Persons of Hispanic origin may be of any race.

Source: Bureau of the Census, *Money Income and Poverty Status of Families and Persons in the United States: 1984,* Current Population Reports, series P-60, no. 149, August 1985, p. 9.

panic origin. These differences persist at the high school and college levels. There are more than three times as many poor black as poor white high school graduates. College attendance does not eliminate this difference in earning patterns.

Considering the depressed incomes of black Americans, their overrepresentation in public assistance programs should come as no sur-

TABLE 11-4 Poverty Rates for White, Black, and Hispanic Persons for Selected Years, 1959–84.

	% OF TOTAL	% OF WHITE	% OF BLACK	% OF HISPANIC ORIGIN[a]
1984	14.4	11.5	33.8	28.4
1983	15.3	12.2	35.7	28.1
1981	14.0	11.1	34.2	26.5
1979	11.7	9.0	31.0	21.8
1977	11.6	8.9	31.3	22.4
1975	12.3	9.7	31.3	26.9
1973	11.1	8.4	31.4	21.9
1971	12.5	9.9	32.5	[b]
1969	12.1	9.5	32.2	[b]
1966	14.7	11.3	41.8	[b]
1965	17.3	13.3	[b]	[b]
1960	22.2	17.8	[b]	[b]
1959	22.4	18.1	55.1	[b]

[a]May be of any race.
[b]Not available.

Source: Bureau of the Census, *Money Income and Poverty Status of Families and Persons in the United States: 1984,* Current Population Reports, series P-60, no. 149, August 1985, p. 21.

TABLE 11-5 White, Black, and Hispanic Families Below Poverty by Educational Level, 1982 (in thousands)

	WHITE		BLACK		HISPANIC ORIGIN[a]	
EDUCATION	NUMBER	%	NUMBER	%	NUMBER	%
Elementary:						
Less than 8 years	917	24.7	388	39.4	400	41.0
8 years	490	13.7	145	36.4	77	28.8
High School:						
1–3 years	970	15.6	525	40.7	164	35.3
4 years	1,433	8.0	576	28.4	133	16.1
College:						
1 year or more	747	3.9	208	15.8	37	6.4

[a]May be of any race.

Source: Bureau of the Census, Current Population Reports, series P-60, no. 140, cited in Bureau of the Census, *Statistical Abstract of the United States, 1984,* p. 476.

prise. Although blacks comprise about 12 percent of the total U.S. population, they comprise 44 percent of all AFDC recipients, 27 percent of SSI recipients, and 35 percent of all Food Stamp recipients (see table 11-6). The proportion of blacks in public assistance programs serves to reinforce stereotypes that blacks are less motivated to work than white Americans, despite recognition of the effects of racial discrimination. In fact, patterns of racial discrimination are so firmly entrenched in American society that the term *institutional racism* has been used to refer to these practices.

However, we should not obscure the progress that blacks have made in recent years. While their income in relation to whites remains substantially lower, the proportion of blacks below the poverty level has decreased from 55 percent in 1959 to 34 percent today. The quality of housing

TABLE 11-6 Participation in Social Welfare Programs for Whites and Blacks (in thousands)

	WHITES		BLACKS	
	NUMBER	% OF ALL RECIPIENTS	NUMBER	% OF ALL RECIPIENTS
Aid to Families with Dependent Children (families)	1772	51.7	1505	43.9
Food Stamps (families)	4424	62.2	2522	35.4
Supplemental Security Income (individuals)	2335	60.5	1043	27.0

Source: Bureau of the Census, *Statistical Abstract of the United States, 1984* (Washington, 1984), pp. 373, 393, 396.

occupied by blacks has improved, and blacks are also more likely to hold professional jobs and to graduate from college.

HOUSING AND RACIAL DISCRIMINATION

One of the largest items in the average household budget is housing. Whether payments come in the form of the monthly rent or the mortgage payment, housing costs are consuming an increasing portion of the personal budget. As far back as the Housing Act of 1949, Congress acknowledged the need for a "decent home and a suitable living environment for every American family." Yet the poor often have little choice except to rent apartments and homes that the more affluent have left behind.

Housing policy in the United States—public and private, formal and informal—is perhaps the most pervasive tool of racial discrimination. Despite laws which prohibit discrimination in the sale and rental of property, neighborhood segregation remains a fact of life in most communities. Integration, required by law in schools and work places, has not been realized in the area of housing. The integration of neighborhoods could eliminate the need for busing or other aids to school integration.

Segregation and discrimination have been evident in government housing programs. Section 235 of the 1968 Housing Act became "the largest single subsidized housing program and the most controversial."[29] According to the U.S. Civil Rights Commission, the Federal Housing Administration (FHA) contributed to the sale of inferior homes to minorities under section 235 by delegating too much authority to private industry, which had failed to comply with the spirit of the 1968 Fair Housing Act and other civil rights legislation.[30]

Redlining has also contributed to inferior living arrangements for blacks and other minorities. Redlining occurs when a bank, mortgage company, home insurance company, or other enterprise refuses to finance or insure property in certain areas. Redlined areas are generally those occupied by poor and minority groups. Inability to obtain financing and insurance further depresses the community. It is not only private enterprise that has been accused of redlining. During the 1960s the National Commission on Urban Problems charged the FHA with neglecting loans to poor and black persons and with condoning policies that "aided, abetted, and encouraged" neighborhood deterioration.[31] Congress took measures to stop such practices.

Over time, housing patterns have shifted. As the middle classes left the inner cities to move to the bedroom communities of the suburbs, the poor were left to live in the deteriorating apartment buildings of America's cities. Now, in some areas, a countertrend has developed in which affluent whites are returning to the cities, buying and renovating homes, and displacing poor inner-city residents. According to a University of Wisconsin sociologist, the greater visibility of blacks in suburban areas may make it appear that housing segregation has diminished, but while some blacks have moved into white communities, the reverse is rarely true.[32]

Fifteen years ago Henry Aaron, an authority on housing, wrote:

> Over the years public housing has acquired a vile image—highrise concrete monoliths in great impersonal cities, cut off from surrounding neighborhoods by grass or cement deserts best avoided after dark, inhabited by large, mostly black, families, exhibiting the full range of social and economic difficulties.[1]

Today, Cabrini-Green, a Chicago housing project, still seems to fit this description.

Cabrini-Green became the focus of national press coverage when then Chicago mayor, Jane Byrne, decided to move in.[2] The project is a ghetto of its own composed of 78 towerlike buildings—some 19 stories high. There are 13,500 residents at Cabrini-Green who are black, poor, mostly children, and mostly welfare recipients. More than half the residents do not even have telephones. Cabrini-Green is one example of the condition of many large public housing projects.

One advantage of living at Cabrini-Green is that the rent is low. Some two bedroom apartments rent for as little as $50 a month. But Cabrini-Green's residents do not look at their home as a blessing. In fact, one is hard pressed to hear residents say anything positive about Cabrini-Green. Some call the place a prison. Crime is rampant at Cabrini-Green. Murders, shootings, rapes, robberies, and gang wars are nothing new to the neighbors at Cabrini-Green. Some residents go to work, come home, lock their doors, and do not venture out. Crime is a major problem, but there are others. Cockroaches and rodents are not uncommon. City exterminators come by, but some residents are not convinced that this helps. One little girl said she was afraid of mice so she liked to play on the front porch where she "can get away from them quick." Cabrini-Green's towers are equipped with elevators but complaints are that the elevators are on the fritz—a major problem if you live on the ninth floor. One elderly resident broke an elevator door down to get a child out because, he says, the repairman never came. Drugs are used by some of the young at Cabrini-Green, and drinking liquor at neighborhood taverns provides some escape for the adult population.

Cabrini-Green is very close to a wealthy Near North Side neighborhood. In fact, Mayor Byrne lived just a mile away from the project. Byrne agreed that Cabrini-Green needed cleaning up; so she and her husband moved into one of Cabrini-Green's apartments, and some conditions at the project changed. Cabrini-Green became cleaner, there were more police around and crime decreased. Byrne's stay at the project lasted less than one month, although she kept the apartment for occasional visits during her term in office. Mayor Byrne was not the only one to move out of Cabrini-Green. The city began evicting residents who failed to pay their rents. Bruce Conn, who had lived twenty of his thirty-one years at Cabrini-Green, and his family were evicted, but Conn looked at the positive side of the situation. "This may be the best thing. I've been wanting to get out of the place for a while now, but once you're in it's almost impossible to get out."

[1]Henry J. Aaron, *Shelter and Subsidies, Who Benefits from Federal Housing Policies?* (Washington: Brookings Institution, 1972), p. 108.

[2]Information and quotations about Cabrini-Green rely on David J. Blum, "Cabrini-Green Project, Big Ghetto in Chicago, Fights a Losing Battle," *Wall Street Journal*, May 5, 1981, p. 1 & 18.

SEPARATE BUT NOT EQUAL

The Fourteenth Amendment guarantees all citizens equal protection under the law, but this amendment is also an example of how ideas that sound rationale can be used to maintain and perpetuate racial discrimination. Until 1954 the Fourteenth Amendment served as legal grounds for equal but separate protection under the law. Segregation of blacks and whites in public schools, on public buses, and in other public (and private) places was condoned. Public facilities for blacks were supposed to be equal to facilities for whites (see *Plessy* v. *Ferguson*), but this was generally not the case. Yet it was not until the middle of the twentieth century that the Supreme Court exercised its power in overturning the separate but equal doctrine set forth in the case of *Plessy* v. *Ferguson.*

In 1954 a growing black dissatisfaction with the separate but equal doctrine resulted in a Supreme Court ruling that marked the official recognition of racial inequality in America. Schools in Topeka, Kansas, were segregated but essentially equal in terms of physical conditions and quality of education. However, in the case of *Brown* v. *Board of Education of Topeka, Kansas,* the Supreme Court ruled that separate was not equal. In its decision the Court took the position that "the policy of separating the races is usually interpreted as denoting the inferiority of the Negro Group." The Court also stated that "segregation with the sanction of law, therefore, has a tendency to retard the education and mental development of Negro children." The *Brown* decision remains a landmark case in the history of equal rights.

However, de facto segregation of schools due to neighborhood segregation continues to exist. When children from inner-city black neighborhoods attend their neighborhood schools, the schools are almost totally composed of black students. One solution to de facto school segregation is busing. In 1971 in the case of *Swann* v. *Charlotte-Mecklenburg Board of Education,* the Supreme Court approved court-ordered busing of children to achieve integration in school districts that had a history of discrimination. However, in 1974 in *Milliken* v. *Bradley,* the Supreme Court ruled that mandatory busing across city-suburban boundaries to achieve integration is not required unless segregation has resulted from an official action. This decision means that de facto segregation will remain in areas where schools in largely black central cities are surrounded by predominantly white suburbs.

Busing remains an American controversy. Parents often reject the idea of sending a child to a school several miles away when a neighborhood school is nearby. Parents—generally white parents—who purposely purchased homes in certain school districts, are often angered when their child must be bused to a school that they feel is inferior. Critics point to the irony of forced busing. They believe busing has contributed to "white flight"—white families moving to avoid busing. Furthermore, they point to the trend toward private-school enrollments, which also thwarts efforts to integrate public schools. However, concern remains that without school integration poor children will continue to receive their education in disadvantaged situations.

Educational inequality also results from the way public education is financed. The major source of school funding is the local property tax. Schools in middle- and upper-class areas have larger financial bases than schools in poor areas. These financial inequities have led to a call for equal educational expenditures for all school children, regardless of their families' economic status. Unequal educational opportunities continue to prevent minority persons from obtaining jobs that would increase their earning capacity and reduce their dependence on welfare programs. And as one social researcher has noted, less progress has been made in integrating institutions of higher education than in integrating elementary and secondary schools. Colleges and universities which traditionally served white students and those which traditionally served black students continue to do so. They have failed to become highly integrated.[33]

CIVIL RIGHTS ACT

Since the 1954 *Brown* decision, the single most important reform with regard to racial equality has been the Civil Rights Act of 1964. The act states:

1. It is unlawful to apply unequal standards in voter registration procedures, or to deny registration for irrelevant errors or omissions on records or applications.
2. It is unlawful to discriminate or segregate persons on the grounds of race, color, religion, or national origin in any public accommodation, including hotels, motels, restaurants, movies, theaters, sports arenas, entertainment houses, and other places that offer to serve the public. This prohibition extends to all establishments whose operations affect interstate commerce or whose discriminatory practices are supported by state action.
3. The attorney general shall undertake civil action on behalf of any person denied equal access to a public accommodation to obtain a federal district court order to secure compliance with the act. If the owner or manager of a public accommodation should continue to discriminate, he would be in contempt of court and subject to peremptory fines and imprisonment without trial by jury.
4. The attorney general shall undertake civil actions on behalf of persons attempting orderly desegregation of public schools.
5. The Commission on Civil Rights, first established in the Civil Rights Act of 1957, shall be empowered to investigate deprivations of the right to vote, study, and collect information regarding the discrimination in America, and make reports to the President and Congress.
6. Each federal department and agency shall take action to end discrimination in all programs or activities receiving federal financial assistance in any form. This action shall include termination of financial assistance.
7. It shall be unlawful for any employer or labor union with 25 or more persons after 1965 to discriminate against any individual in any fashion in employment, because of his race, color, religion, sex, or national origin, and an Equal Employment Opportunity Commission shall be established to enforce this provision by investigation, conference, conciliation, persuasion, and if need be, civil action in federal court.

Amendments to the act in 1968 prohibited housing discrimination. It has been more than twenty years since passage of the first Civil Rights Act, yet the balance of racial power has not shifted as dramatically as many blacks would like. As we shall see, recent actions of the Reagan administration and the Supreme Court have made civil rights activists wary of the future.

MINORITIES AND POLITICS

There are many aspects of equal rights that continue to engender political concern. Affirmative action, for example, refers to policies to achieve equality in admissions and employment among racial groups. The success of affirmative-action programs is based on the notion that minority groups should be admitted, hired, and promoted in proportion to their representation in the population. But to what extent should affirmative-action policies be pursued? Why is it not enough to pursue policies which do not discriminate against persons because of racial background? Should policies go much further in order to reduce inequities in employment? Originally the federal government pursued an approach of nondiscrimination. Examples of nondiscrimination are found in President Truman's decision to desegregate the military in 1946 and in Titles VI and VII of the 1964 Civil Rights Act. Nondiscrimination simply means that preferential treatment will not be given to selected racial groups.[34]

The quest for civil rights among blacks brought dissatisfaction with this method of achieving racial equality. There was concern that a more aggressive approach should be taken to promote equality in college admissions and in employment. One aspect of this concern spurred a debate as to whether quotas rather than goals should be used to achieve racial equality. Quotas are defined as "imposing a fixed, mandatory number or percentage of persons to be hired or promoted, regardless of the number of potential applicants who meet the qualifications,"[35] while a goal is a

> numerical objective, fixed realistically in terms of number of vacancies expected, and the number of qualified applicants available. . . . If . . . the employer . . . has demonstrated every good faith effort to include persons from the group which was the object of discrimination . . . but has been unable to do so in sufficient numbers to meet his goal, he is not subject to sanction.[36]

In addition, the employer is not obligated to hire an unqualified or less qualified person in preference to a prospective employee with better qualifications.[37]

The Philadelphia Plan of 1967 issued by the U.S. Office of Federal Contract Compliance was one of the first examples of an affirmative-action plan. The plan required that those bidding on federal contracts submit plans to employ specific percentages of minority groups.[38] Another quota-type plan was adopted in 1971 by the Federal Aviation Administration. This plan essentially placed a freeze on hiring any additional employees if every fifth vacant position was not filled by a minority.[39]

Opponents of quota setting generally believe that giving preferential treatment to minorities constitutes a violation of equal protection of the laws provided in the Fourteenth Amendment to the U.S. Constitution. In 1974 a federal court upheld this belief in its decision that the University of Washington Law School should admit Marco DeFunis, Jr. DeFunis had protested the university's decision to reject his application while admitting blacks with lower grades and test scores. Other cases charging "reverse discrimination" have also been heard by the courts. The Supreme Court ruled on the issue of admitting less qualified minority applicants over white applicants in the case of Alan Bakke. The Court determined that Bakke had been unfairly denied admission to the University of California Davis Medical School because his qualifications were stronger than those of some minority candidates admitted to the school. Proponents of the decision hoped the Bakke case would help change what they perceived to be a trend of reverse discrimination against whites. Opponents feared that the *Bakke* decision threatened the future of affirmative action.

Concerns about threats to affirmative action have mounted under the Reagan administration. Those critical of the administration accuse the president of attempting to reverse a pattern of improvement in civil rights that began in the 1960s and has been supported under both Democratic and Republican administrations. The president's recommendations for appointments to the U.S. Civil Rights Commission and his attempts to get rid of some members raised the ire of most civil rights groups. The Justice Department has also become a place of controversial appointments. During the Carter presidency the Justice Department had taken a strong role as a proponent of civil rights. It had, for example, helped to implement a court decree requiring the police and fire departments of Indianapolis to establish quotas for hiring and promoting women and blacks. But in 1984 the Supreme Court ruled in the case of *Firefighters Local Union No. 1784* v. *Stotts* that the jobs of blacks with less seniority cannot be protected at the expense of jobs of whites with more seniority. The Justice Department, under its new chief, William Bradford Reynolds, has used this Supreme Court decision in an effort to get Indianapolis and forty-nine other jurisdictions to abandon the use of quotas. The National Association for the Advancement of Colored People (NAACP) and others have contended that the Justice Department action is illegal. Lower federal courts have also supported quota systems established under affirmative-action plans.

Another aspect of affirmative action challenged by the Reagan administration is the use of class action suits to benefit groups of people rather than individuals. The Equal Opportunity Employment Commission, for example, has expressed its desire to tackle cases of discrimination against particular individuals rather than assisting classes of people in obtaining preferential treatment. Reynolds, head of the Justice Department, has declared that what is needed is a color- and sex-blind society rather than a color- and sex-conscious one. He extols the dedication of the Reagan administration to affirmative action and contends that quotas are a form of discrimination.

But the NAACP, NOW, and other groups dedicated to the protection of the rights of minorities of color and women have taken a much different view and express grave concerns about slippage in civil rights. They pointed to the reductions in the number of discrimination cases pursued by the federal government in education, employment, and housing as indications of dwindling concern.[40] The question being seriously debated was whether to continue implementing policies and programs to make up for past inequities or to concentrate on equal treatment of persons currently seeking employment or admission to colleges and universities. The Supreme Court addressed that issue and dealt a serious setback to the Reagan administration and a clear victory for affirmative action with two 1986 decisions (one involved Cleveland firefighters, the other a New York sheet metal workers union). According to these decisions, ". . . federal judges may set goals and timetables requiring employers guilty of past discrimination to hire or promote specific numbers of minorities, even if the jobs go to people who are not themselves the proven victims of bias."[41]

But some black scholars have taken the position that affirmative action is no longer helping blacks. Glenn Loury, a Harvard political economist, credits the civil rights movement and affirmative action for doing much to help some blacks, but he is concerned about solutions to the problems of other blacks who remain poor.[42] Loury believes the current problems of black communities must be attacked through mutual "self-help" among blacks whether or not government continues to help.

The 1980s have brought other concerns about minority rights, such as renewal of the Voting Rights Act. When President Lyndon B. Johnson signed the Voting Rights Act in 1965, he stated:

> The right to vote is the most basic right, without which all others are meaningless. . . . The vote is the most powerful instrument ever devised by men for breaking down injustice and destroying the terrible walls which imprison men because they are different from other men.

Since the 1940s a number of major steps have been taken to insure that minorities are provided the same opportunities to vote as whites. The Voting Rights Act was designed to further insure, protect, and encourage the right to a voice in the electoral process. The act is periodically reviewed by Congress and was renewed in 1982. At times concern has been expressed that support for the act may be waning, but there is little chance that Congress would fail to voice continuing reapproval of this legislation. Of greater concern is the question of

> how much blacks can gain through the exercise of their vote. In the North, blacks have voted freely for decades, but conditions in the urban ghettos have not been measurably improved through political action. . . . It is probably true that people can "better" protect themselves from government abuse when they possess and exercise their voting rights, but the right to vote is not a guarantee against discrimination.[43]

Few blacks have served in Congress. Black mayors have been elected in some of America's larger cities—Los Angeles, Detroit, and Cleveland, for example—but there continues to be a lack of minority leadership in important political posts. Among members of the 98th Congress there were twenty-one black U.S. representatives but no black senators.

NATIVE AMERICANS AND WELFARE

Native Americans are among the groups most seriously affected by social welfare problems. "Indians have the lowest income, worst health and the largest indice [sic] of social problems in the U.S."[44] Native Americans have faced unusual hardships. These hardships have been attributed to attempts to force them to assimilate into the majority culture, despite substantial differences between their cultures—family structure, religion, and communication patterns—and that of whites. Native Americans have also faced displacement from their own reservations and have encountered problems in adapting to urban life.

The Bureau of Indian Affairs (BIA) is responsible for assisting Native Americans in meeting their welfare needs, but the BIA has been criticized for its paternalistic or authoritarian attitude toward its clientele. According to some, "The BIA takes care of Indians' money, land, children, water, roads, etc. with authority complete as that of a prison."[45] One of the worst degradations has been the removal of Native American children from their families to be raised by others. This practice was rationalized by welfare professionals who viewed Native American child-rearing practices as overly harsh.[46] The Indian Child Welfare Act of 1978 was designed to remedy problems concerning the placement of Native American children by restoring greater control over child-placement disposition to Indian tribes. Priority for placement of Native American children is now given to members of the child's own tribe, rather than to non-Indian families.

In recognition of the abuses experienced by Native Americans, the Indian Self-Determination and Education Assistance Act of 1975 emphasizes tribal self-government and the establishment of independent health, education, and welfare services. The extent to which this act can address the needs of the Native American population is questionable. The act cannot serve as retribution for those whose survival and culture have been threatened over the years.

IMMIGRATION POLICY

Immigration and naturalization policy are also issues to consider in our discussion of discriminatory practices. The United States population is composed of people from virtually every country, every culture, every religion, and every race. In 1906 the Bureau of Immigration and Naturalization was established to assist persons entering the country. From time to time, however, immigration policies have prohibited certain groups from entering the United States. Laws such as the Chinese Exclusion Act of 1833 and the Oriental Exclusion Law of 1924 severely restricted the entrance of these groups of people. The Quota System Law of 1921 and the Immigration Act of 1924 also limited the number of Asians entering the United States. Immigration policies have been much more favorable to certain other groups, such as northern Europeans.

The treatment of Japanese-Americans after the Japanese attack on Pearl Harbor in 1941 serves as an example of the discriminatory treatment given to American citizens of foreign backgrounds. Following Pearl Harbor, Japanese-Americans were interned in ten relocation camps by President Franklin D. Roosevelt for fear that they might threaten U.S. security. Another reason given for the relocation was to protect Japanese-Americans from potential attacks by Americans angered by the Japanese attack.[47] However, interned Japanese-Americans did not believe this action was either necessary or benevolent. They were forced to give up their jobs and their possessions. To prove that they were indeed Americans, many Japanese-Americans volunteered to serve in the armed services. Internment ended in 1943 with the recognition that citizenship and loyalty to one's country, not racial characteristics, make one an American. But it was not until 1983 that the U.S. government actually acknowledged wrongdoing. The statement came as a result of the work of the Commission on Wartime Relocation and Internment of Civilians. The commission, which was appointed by Congress, recommended that certain reparations be made to Japanese and Japanese-Americans interned during World War II. The fact that American citizens were deprived of their freedom because of the military actions of a foreign government remains an important lesson in American history.

In 1965 stringent national-origin quotas limiting the number of entrants from various countries were abolished. But new issues are at the forefront of American immigration policy. The Vietnam War displaced and impoverished many Vietnamese people who later sought refuge in the United States and in other countries. Of special concern is the number of "Amerasian" children, children born to American servicemen and Vietnamese women. An estimated six to eight thousand of these children still live in poverty in Vietnam since they were not brought to the United States by their fathers or charitable organizations.[48] Considered "half-breeds" in their place of birth, these children have found themselves ostracized. Establishing their fathers' identities is difficult; thus many have been unable to come to the United States. Squalid life conditions in Vietnam had left these children with little hope for a brighter future, but the Reagan administration is attempting to bring more of these Amerasian children as well as some Vietnamese political prisoners to the United States.

CAN WE AGREE ON IMMIGRATION REFORM?

The issue of immigration to the United States, especially that of Hispanics from Mexico and Central American countries, has become an increasingly pressing issue. Concerns are due to the large volume of people who attempt to enter the United States. In 1984 the Border Patrol of the U.S.

Immigration and Naturalization Service (INS) made more than one million arrests of illegal aliens at the expansive Mexican-American border, and the number of those who successfully avoid arrest is probably as many, if not more.[49] Is this type of immigration helpful or harmful to the United States? Illegal aliens are considered useful by farmers who hire them as cheap labor at critical times when others may not be willing to do the work. But some believe that in other sectors of the economy illegal aliens take jobs away from legal aliens and Americans who also need work.[50] While some point to the high costs of providing social services and education for the children of illegal immigrants, others believe that these costs are probably offset by income and Social Security taxes that are paid on their wages but from which the illegal aliens never collect benefits. Since we really do not know how many illegal aliens reside in the United States (estimates range from two to six million[51]), it is difficult to weigh these costs and benefits.

In addition to those fleeing from Mexico, other groups such as Cuban, Haitian, and Central American refugees have also aroused the attention of Americans. Like the entrance of illegal aliens from Mexico, the arrival of many Cubans and Haitians was not planned for by the United States. Since Cuba and Haiti are so close to the tip of Florida, people have virtually arrived en masse in boats, some losing their lives in the process. Cubans originally began immigration to the United States in the 1960s in order to seek political asylum from the communistic Castro regime. Then in 1980 and 1981 a new influx of Cuban refugees prompted President Carter to institute an airlift program and to open three refugee-processing centers at Eglin Air Force Base in Florida, Fort Chaffee in Arkansas, and Fort Indiantown Gap in Pennsylvania. Some refugees came to join their families in the United States, but some were convicted criminals in Cuba, and others were also considered "undesirables." This resulted in concern that Castro had used the United States as a dumping ground for those he wished to deport. In 1986 Cuba and the United States reopened talks that may reinstitute immigration from Cuba to the U.S.

Haitians have also made attempts to come to the United States. The poverty on the small island of Haiti is overwhelming (and the now overthrown Duvalier government was also considered repressive). Under the Refugee Act of 1980, the definition of *refugee* does not include those leaving their country for economic reasons. Those wanting to leave for economic reasons are considered to be requesting "asylum." The issue is critical because refugees are entitled to the same social welfare benefits (AFDC, food stamps, Medicaid) as U.S. citizens. If they are considered to be asking for asylum, however, provision of welfare benefits is subject to question.[52] During his first term, the president called for an immigration policy which would "integrate refugees into our society without nurturing their dependence on welfare."[53] While the Reagan administration also views Central American aliens as coming for economic reasons, others believe that they should be given the status of political refugees. Some blame the U.S. for contributing to the political strife of Central Americans through its foreign policies. They believe political strife has increased the desire of Central Americans to come to the U.S.

The "sanctuary movement" is another aspect of the immigration issue. Americans involved in the movement have provided food, clothing, shelter and jobs to immigrants. Most of those helped through the movement have been Salvadorans and other Central Americans. Sanctuary workers feel their actions are justified even if they are housing people who entered the country without permission. They believe many Central Americans face grave political oppression and persecution in their homeland. But the INS and other officials disagree. They believe certain actions, such as transporting illegal aliens into the country, are a violation of the law. As a consequence, several religious and lay persons active in the movement have been brought to trial or are awaiting trial.

In an attempt to stem the heavy tide of both legal and illegal immigration to this country—more immigrants came to the U.S. in 1983 than in any previous year during this century[54]—Senator Alan K. Simpson (R-Wyo.) and Representative Romano L. Mazolli (D-Ky.) offered a bill which would have (1) imposed sanctions on those employers who hired aliens who did not have permission to work in this country; (2) offered amnesty or legalization to immigrants who showed they were assimilated into the United States (the definition of assimilation was not agreed on); (3) increased enforcement of immigration laws; (4) limited the number of immigrants; (5) provided more restrictive methods for legally admitting aliens; and (6) provided for a "guest worker" program which would have allowed some aliens to enter the country to work for limited periods of time. Like other social policy measures, the bill offered too much for some people's tastes and too little for others. Conservatives found it to be too permissive—perhaps as many as one million illegal immigrants would have been eligible for amnesty.[55] They also thought the policy unfair to those aliens who had abided by the law. Liberals thought the amnesty provision was too restrictive.[56] In conjunction with Hispanic civil rights groups, liberals also sharply criticized the provision for punishing employers, for fear that employers would be reluctant to hire anyone with Hispanic features or accents, whether or not they had proof of citizenship.

Can policies like those included in this bill solve the problem? Certainly, no one thinks they can do the whole job. While the bill's sponsors did think it would be effective in reducing immigration, others think that it had the wrong answers. One professor of international economics at Columbia University believes that the legislators chose a set of "internal solutions" when they should have chosen "external solutions."[57] External solutions are those which focus on better enforcement at the border and fewer internal controls of the kind suggested in the bill. According to this perspective, internal solutions could ultimately increase the number of illegal aliens because INS resources would have to be used to police employers rather than to stop more illegal aliens from crossing the border. With fewer border patrols it is easier for illegal aliens to cross into the United States. Furthermore, the bill would increase, not reduce, the underclass status of aliens by making it more undesirable for employers to hire them. Experience in other countries suggests that employer sanctions have not been very effective in reducing alien employment. It is also more effective to keep people out in the first place because once they enter, the United States hesitates to deport them. Amnesty might also contribute to the numbers who attempt to enter the U.S.

Except for Native Americans, all other Americans are the descendants of immigrants or were themselves immigrants. Certainly, America continues to be enriched by people of many different nationalities who have made this country their home. It is perhaps ironic that in 1986 as our country celebrated the 100th birthday of the Statue of Liberty—a symbol of freedom for many immigrants—we were still debating immigration reform.

GAY RIGHTS

The legal rights of many groups—women, blacks, Hispanics, the elderly, and the handicapped—have become common topics of public debate. Traditionally, the rights of homosexuals rarely appeared on the public policy agenda. But today questions about *gay rights*—the legal rights of homosexual men and women—are being discussed more openly. For many people gay rights is much more than a legal or political issue. Debate is frequently colored by religious interpretations, moral judgments, and emotionalism. Some cities have taken up the issue of gay rights. For example, voters in Houston recently rejected two gay rights proposals. One would have forbidden discrimination based on sexual preference in city employment practices, and the other would have prevented the city from maintaining employment records on sexual orientation. For almost twenty years the Supreme Court refused to hear cases of gay rights. It had not involved itself in issues such as the right of homosexuals to child custody. But the Supreme Court broke its silence in 1985 by hearing the case of *Oklahoma City Board of Education* v. *National Gay Task Force.* In its evenly divided 4-4 decision (Justice Powell was ill), the Supreme Court upheld a lower-court ruling that public-school teachers cannot be forbidden to advocate homosexuality but that homosexuals can be prohibited from engaging in homosexual activity in public. The Oklahoma law had permitted school boards to bar from employment teachers who advocated homosexuality in ways that might become known to students or school employees. The Gay Rights Task Force had criticized the law as a First Amendment violation of free speech while the Board of Education contended that the law was only concerned with those who publicly endorse certain sexual acts between homosexuals. In what was considered a serious setback to the rights of homosexuals, the Supreme Court in 1986 refused to strike down laws in Georgia and Texas forbidding individuals from engaging in similar types of sexual activity.

SUMMARY

Sexism and racism manifest themselves in many areas of American life—education, employment, income, and political participation. The disadvantages that women and blacks and other groups have endured place them in a position of being poorer than the rest of the population. Poverty, in turn, results in greater dependence on social welfare programs for these groups.

Ever since women won the right to vote there have been movements to enact an equal rights bill for women. Opposition to equal rights centers on concerns that women may be forced into combat or may lose other privileges. Other arguments suggest that there are already a number of laws which prohibit discrimination in hiring and payment of wages to women workers. However, since women continue to encounter discrimination, supporters of an equal rights amendment believe that a guarantee of equality should be a part of the U.S. Constitution. They have vowed to continue to press the issue.

The Social Security program treats women inequitably in several ways. For example, homemakers are not entitled to Social Security payments unless they are the dependent or survivor of a worker; as a result, many divorced women are not entitled to benefits earned by their former husbands. The "double-decker plan" and the "earnings-sharing plan" have been proposed to remedy some of these problems.

Women earn sixty-four cents for every dollar earned by men. Because women are poorer, they receive welfare payments more often then men. As a result, they are also more likely to be hurt by welfare cutbacks. Efforts to promote comparable worth are aimed at increasing women's earnings, but they have met with opposition.

Another welfare issue that concerns women—and also men—is abortion. The Supreme Court has upheld the right of women to abortions, with the states reserving the right to place more stringent restrictions on abortions done late in the pregnancy. Right-to-life groups have continued to oppose abortions on moral, religious and biological grounds while prochoice groups have defended a woman's right to abortion on demand. Another issue is that of federally funded abortions. While abortions are a legal means of birth control, the government no longer insures the right to a federally funded abortion for poor women, except in cases where the mother's life is in danger or in cases of rape or incest.

Black Americans have faced a number of struggles in their fight for civil rights. A Supreme Court decision struck down the "separate but equal" doctrine, stating that separate public facilities are not equal facilities. One result of this decision has been the integration of public schools, although integration has not been achieved in many communities, because neighborhood segregation continues to contribute to segregation in public schools. The Civil Rights Act of 1964 addressed a number of black Americans' concerns, including equal treatment in employment. However, discrimination remains an issue. Even after controlling for education, black Americans earn less than whites. Blacks continue to be disproportionately represented on the welfare rolls. The use of quotas and time tables designed to promote the hiring of more minorities and women is not enjoying the same support under the Reagan administration that it did during the 1960s and 1970s, although recent Supreme Court decisions have supported the use of affirmative action to remedy past discrimination.

Other minority groups also face discrimination. Native Americans are among the most severely affected. The Bureau of Indian Affairs has been criticized for its treatment of Native Americans, even though this government agency was established to assist them. The Indian Self-Determination and Education Assistance Act of 1975 was an attempt to restore to Native Americans planning power over their social welfare programs.

The current refugee situation also poses problems. Vietnamese immigrated to the United States as a result of the Vietnam War, and Cubans sought political asylum from the communistic Castro regime. Haitians tried to escape dire poverty under the Duvalier government, and Mexicans continue to leave their country to seek jobs and escape poverty. Central Americans are looking for an escape from poverty and many argue that they are also victimized by political violence. The United States has been a haven for many seeking freedom from oppression, but the unprecedented numbers of people entering this country illegally have caused the introduction of legislation designed to restrict illegal immigration. The debate on immigration policy continues.

NOTES

1. Diana Pearce and Harriette McAdoo, *Women and Children: Alone and in Poverty* (Washington, D.C.: National Advisory Council on Economic Opportunity, 1981).
2. Ibid., p. 2.
3. Bureau of the Census, *Money Income and Poverty Status of Families and Persons in the United States, 1984,* Current Population Reports, series P-60, no. 149, p. 3.
4. Ibid., p. 2.
5. Nina Totenberg, "Why Women Earn Less," *Parade* magazine, June 10, 1984, p. 5.
6. "Notes and Brief Reports," *Social Security Bulletin* 48, no. 2 (February 1985), 27.
7. Jill Johnson Keeney, "Not a Crazy Proposal," *Louisville Times,* 1984, reprinted in *The Office Professional* 5, no. 2 (February 15, 1985), 7.
8. Ibid.
9. Ibid.
10. "Job Discrimination Limits," *Wall Street Journal,* January 7, 1985, p. 18.
11. Bureau of the Census, *Statistical Abstract of the United States 1984* (Washington, 1983), p. 262.
12. Joann S. Lublin, "Women Gain Statehouse Roles," *Wall Street Journal,* December 31, 1984, p. 28.
13. Bureau of the Census, *Statistical Abstract of the United States 1985* (Washington, 1985), p. 247.
14. "ERA Ratification Status Summary," *ERA Countdown Campaign* (Washington: National Organization for Women, 1981), p. A.

15. Quoted in David Klein, "The ERA Is Wanted Dead or Alive in Florida," *Tallahassee Democrat,* January 21, 1982.
16. These polls are summarized in "Strong Public Support for ERA," in *ERA Countdown Campaign* (Washington: National Organization for Women, 1981), p. C.
17. Much of this section relies on Thomas R. Dye, *Understanding Public Policy,* 4th ed. (Englewood Cliffs, N.J.: Prentice-Hall, 1978), pp. 78–79.
18. "Court, Senate Rebuff Anti-Abortion Efforts," *1983 Congressional Quarterly Almanac,* p. 306.
19. Jacob V. Lamar, "Silent No More," *Time,* May 27, 1985, p. 32.
20. Bureau of the Census, *Statistical Abstract of the United States 1984,* p. 71.
21. United States Commission on Civil Rights, *The Federal Response to Domestic Violence* (Washington: Government Printing Office, January 1982), pp. iv–v.
22. Ibid.
23. Lisa G. Lerman, "Legal Help for Battered Women," in Joseph J. Costa, ed., *Abuse of Women: Legislation, Reporting, and Prevention* (Lexington, Mass: Lexington Books, 1983), p. 29.
24. "ERA and Social Security," in *ERA Countdown Campaign* (Washington: National Organization for Women, 1981), p. 4.
25. *Money Income and Poverty Status of Families and Persons in the United States 1984,* p. 26.
26. This section relies on Department of Health, Education and Welfare, *Social Security and the Changing Roles of Men and Women* (Washington: Government Printing Office, February 1979), chaps. 1 and 2.
27. Ibid.
28. "Women and Social Security," *Social Security Bulletin* 48, no. 2 (February 1985), pp. 17–26.
29. Chester W. Hartman, *Housing and Social Policy* (Englewood Cliffs, N.J.: Prentice-Hall, 1975), p. 136.
30. Ibid., p. 139.
31. Ibid.
32. "Housing Integration Moves Slowly Study Finds," *Tallahassee Democrat,* May 13, 1983, p. 3A.
33. "Racial Progress Assessed," *Tallahassee Democrat,* April 9, 1984, p. 3A.
34. Dye, *Understanding Public Policy,* pp. 67–69.
35. *Federal Policies on Remedies Concerning Equal Employment Opportunity in State and Local Government Personnel Systems,* March 23, 1973, cited in Felix A. Nigro and Lloyd G. Nigro, *The New Public Personnel Administration* (Itasca, Ill.: F. E. Peacock, 1976), p. 21.
36. Ibid.
37. Ibid.
38. Dye, *Understanding Public Policy,* p. 69.
39. Nigro and Nigro, *New Public Personnel Administration,* p. 21.
40. For a summary of reductions in litigation see D. Lee Bawden and John L Palmer, "Social Policy, Challenging the Welfare State," in John L. Palmer and Isabel V. Sawhill, eds., *The Reagan Record* (Cambridge, Mass.: Ballinger, 1984), pp. 204–6.
41. Frank Trippett, "A Solid Yes to Affirmative Action," *Time,* July 14, 1986, p. 22.
42. Glenn C. Loury, "The Moral Quandry of the Black Community," *Public Interest* no. 79 (Spring 1985): 9–22.
43. This section relies on Thomas R. Dye and L. Harmon Ziegler, *The Irony of Democracy,* 5th ed. (Monterey, Calif: Duxbury Press, 1981), p. 212.
44. Thomas H. Walz and Gary Askerooth, *The Upside Down Welfare State* (Minneapolis: Elwood Printing, 1973), p. 25.

45. Ibid.
46. Joseph J. Westeroreyer, "Indian Powerlessness in Minnesota," *Society*, no. 10 (March/April 1973), 50, cited in ibid, p. 31.
47. Donald Brieland, Lela B. Costin, and Charles R. Atherton, *Contemporary Social Work: An Introduction to Social Work and Social Welfare*, 2nd ed. (New York: McGraw-Hill, 1980), p. 404.
48. Walter W. Miller, "Vietnamese Society Rife with U.S. 'Footprints,' " *Austin American-Statesman*, April 2, 1985, p. A16.
49. Cheryl Arvidson, "Phantom Barrier," *Austin American-Statesman*, November 11, 1984, p. A8.
50. Ibid.
51. R. A. Zaldivar, "Independent Study Casts Doubt on U.S. Illegal Alien Estimate," *Austin American-Statesman*, June 25, 1985, p. A4.
52. Nadine Cohadas, "Cuban Refugee Crisis May Prompt Introduction of Special Legislation," *Congressional Quarterly Weekly Report*, May 31, 1980, p. 1496.
53. Statement issued by President Reagan on July 30, 1980, in *Congressional Quarterly Weekly Report*, August 22, 1981, p. 1577.
54. Leonel Castillo, "Immigration: Compassion vs. Resources," *NASW News*, September 1984, p. 7.
55. Ibid.
56. Arvidson, "Phantom Barrier," p. A8.
57. This argument is based on Jagdish N. Bhagwati, "Control Immigration at the Border," *Wall Street Journal*, February 1, 1985, p. 22.

chapter 12

Implementing and evaluating social welfare policy: what happens after a law is passed

Americans once believed that social problems could be solved by passing laws, creating bureaucracies, and spending money. Americans generally believed that if Congress adopted a policy and appropriated money for it, and the executive branch organized a program, hired people, spent money, and carried out the activities designed to implement the policy, then the effects of the policy felt by society would be those intended by the Congress. But today there is a growing uneasiness among both policy makers and the general public about the effectiveness and cost of many government programs. Americans have lost their innocence about government and public policy.

IMPLEMENTING PUBLIC POLICY

Many problems in social welfare policy arise *after a law is passed*—in the implementation process. Policy implementation includes all of the activities designed to carry out the intention of the law: (1) creating, organizing, and staffing agencies to carry out the new policy, or assigning new responsibilities to existing agencies and personnel; (2) issuing and entering directives, rules, regulations, and guidelines to translate policies into specific courses of action; and (3) directing and coordinating both personnel and expenditures toward the achievement of policy objectives.

There is always a gap—sometimes small, sometimes very large—between a policy decision and its implementation. Some scholars of implementation take an almost cynical view of the process:

> Our normal expectation should be that new programs will fail to get off the ground and that, at best, they will take considerable time to get started. The cards in this world are stacked against things happening, as so much effort is required to make them move. The remarkable thing is that new programs work at all.[1]

THE POLITICS OF IMPLEMENTATION

What are the obstacles to implementation? Why isn't implementation a *rational* activity? Why can't policies be directly implemented in decisions about organization, staffing, spending, regulation, direction, and coordination?

The obstacles to successful implementation are many, but we might categorize them in terms of (1) communications, (2) resources, (3) attitudes, and (4) bureaucratic structure.[2]

Communications

The first requirement for effective policy implementation is that the people who are running the program must know what they are supposed to do. Directives must not only be received but must also be clear. Vague, inconsistent, and contradictory directives confuse administrators. Directives give meanings to policies—meanings which may not be consistent with the original intention of the law. Moreover, poor directives enable people who disagree with the policy to read their own biases into programs. The Department of Health and Human Services, the largest department of the federal government, is divided into many offices that are responsible for administering numerous programs. These programs affect every community in the United States. The DHHS must constantly struggle with the problem of maintaining accurate communications (see figure 12-1).

Generally the more decentralized the administration of a program, the more layers of administration through which directives must flow, and the less likely that policies will be transmitted accurately and consistently. Whatever the advantages of decentralization, prompt, consistent and uniform policy implementation is *not* usually found in a decentralized structure.

Frequently Congress (and state legislatures) is deliberately vague about public policy. Congress and the president may pass vague and ambiguous laws largely for *symbolic* reasons—to reassure people that "something" is being done to help with a problem. Yet in these cases Congress and the president do not really know exactly what to do about the problem. They therefore delegate wide discretion to administrators, who act under the "authority" of broad laws, to determine what, if anything, actually will be done. Often Congress and the president want to claim credit for the high-sounding principles enacted into law but do not want to accept responsibility for the unpopular actions that administrators must take to implement these principles. It is much easier for political leaders to blame the "bureaucrats" and pretend that government regulations are a product of an "ungovernable" Washington bureaucracy.

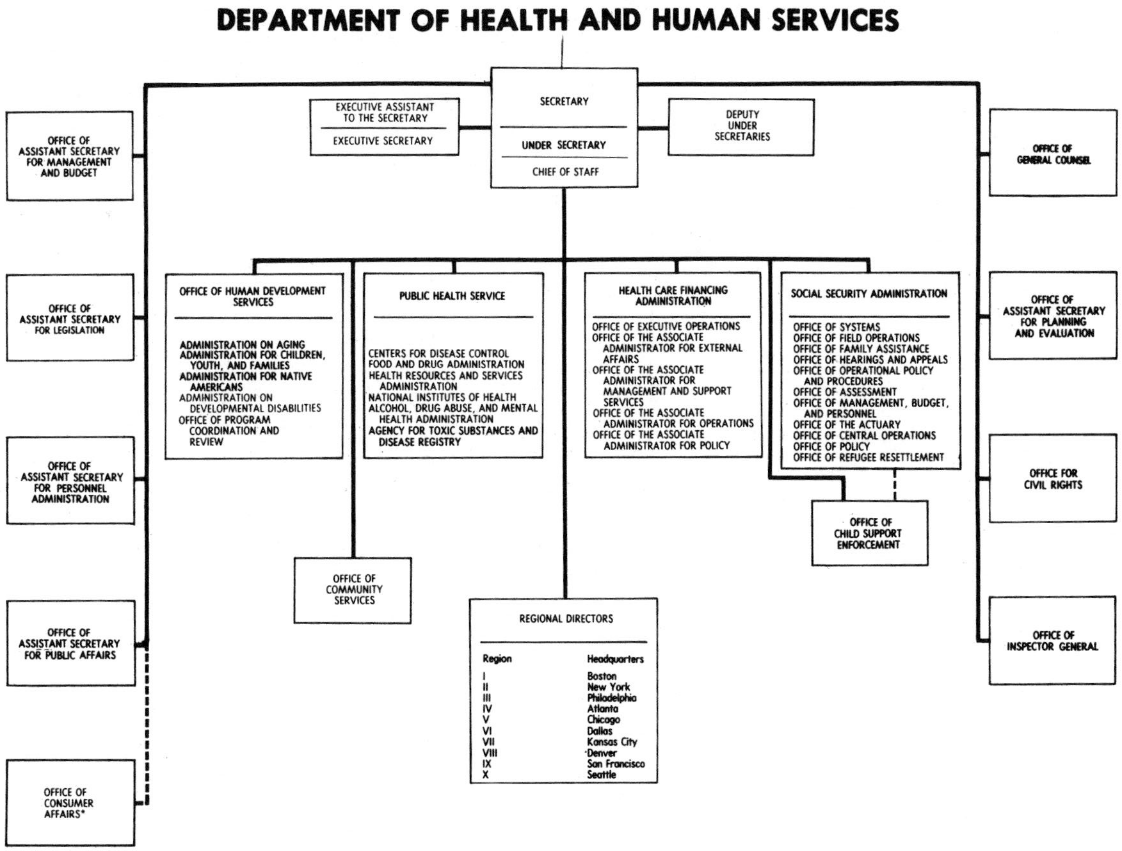

*Located administratively in HHS, but reports to the President.

FIGURE 12-1 (*The United States Government Manual, 1984/85,* p. 831).

For example, in the Economic Opportunity Act of 1964, Congress and President Johnson wrote into the law a provision calling for "maximum feasible participation of the poor" in community action agencies and programs supported by the Office of Economic Opportunity. But no one knew exactly what that phrase meant. How were the poor to help plan and run the programs? Did this phrase authorize poverty workers to organize the poor politically? Did this phrase mean that social activists paid by the government should help organize the poor to pressure welfare and housing agencies for better services? The policy was not clear, and its implementation was confusing and frustrating. Eventually, of course, the Office of Economic Opportunity was abolished, in part because of its problems in administering an unclear mandate from Congress.

Resources

Policy directives may be clear, accurate, and consistent, but if administrators lack the resources to carry out these policies, implementation fails. Resources include *staffs* with the proper *skills* to carry out their assignments, and with the *authority* and *facilities* necessary to translate a paper proposal into a functioning public service.

It is common for government agencies to claim that problems of implementation arise from undersized staffs. And many of the claims are true. Indeed, one tactic of opponents of a particular policy, even after they lose the fight over the actual policy in Congress, is to try to reduce the size of the budget and staff that is to implement the policy. The political battle does not end with the passing of a law. It continues each year in fights over resources to implement the law.

It is not enough that there be adequate funds to hire personnel to carry out a policy. In addition, the personnel must have the skills necessary for the job. Staffing is especially difficult in new programs. There are no ready-made reserves of people who are trained for the program and who know what to do. Yet there is always pressure to "show results" as quickly as possible to insure the continuation of the program the next year.

Sometimes agencies lack the authority, even on paper, to implement policy. Agencies may not be authorized to issue checks to citizens; or to purchase goods or services; or to provide funds to other government agencies; or to withdraw funds in the case of noncompliance; or to go to court to force compliance. Some agencies may have the necessary authority (for example, to withdraw federal funds from a local government agency or a nonprofit corporation), but they may be reluctant to exercise this authority because of the adverse political repercussions that might ensue. Agencies that do not have the necessary authority to carry out policy (or agencies that fear that exercising that authority may be politically risky) must rely on *persuasion and cooperation.* Rather than order local agencies, private corporations, or individual citizens to do something, higher level officials may consult with them, ask for their cooperation, or appeal to their sense of public service. Successful implementation generally requires goodwill on the part of everyone involved. Agencies or administrators who must continually resort to sanctions will probably be unsuccessful in the long run.

Physical facilities may also be critical resources in implementation. Programs generally need offices, equipment, and supplies. It is difficult to run an agency without telephones. Yet many government agencies (especially new agencies) find it difficult to acquire the necessary facilities to carry out their programs. Again, most government administrators must rely on persuasion and cooperation to get other government agencies to provide them with offices, desks, telephones, travel approvals, and so on.

Attitudes

If administrators and program personnel sympathize with a particular policy, it is likely to be carried out as the original policy makers intended. But when the attitudes of agency administrators and staff personnel differ from those of the policy makers, the implementation process becomes very complex. Because administrators always have some discretion (and occasionally a great deal) in implementation, their attitudes toward policies have much to do with how a program is implemented. When people are told to do things with which they do not agree, inevitable slippage will occur between a policy and its implementation.

Generally, social service personnel enter the field because they want to "help people"—especially the aged, poor, handicapped, and less fortunate in society. There is seldom any attitudinal problem in social agencies in implementing policies to *expand* social services. But highly committed social service personnel may find it very difficult to implement policies to *cut back* or eliminate social services.

Conservative policy makers are aware of the social service orientation of the "welfare bureaucracy." They do not believe, for example, that welfare administrators really try to enforce work provisions of the welfare law.[3] They believe that the welfare bureaucracy has been partially responsible for the growth in numbers of recipients over the years; eligibility requirements, these conservatives say, have been given liberal interpretation by sympathetic administrators. They believe that welfare administrators are a major obstacle to policies designed to tighten eligibility, reduce overlapping benefits, and encourage work.

In government agencies it is generally impossible to remove people simply because they disagree with a policy. Direct pressures are generally unavailable: pay increases are primarily across-the-board; promotions are infrequent and often based on seniority. Again, "selling" a policy—winning support through persuasion—is more effective in overcoming opposition than threatening sanctions is. If those who implement policy cannot be convinced that the policy is good for their clients or themselves, perhaps they can be convinced that it is less offensive than other alternatives which might be imposed by policy makers.

Bureaucratic Structure

Previously established organizations and procedures in bureaucracies may hinder implementation of new policies and programs. Bureaucratic "inertia" slows changes in policy. Administrators become accustomed to ways of doing things (standard operating procedures, or SOPs), and administrative structures have a tendency to remain in place long after their original functions have changed or even disappeared.

Standard operating procedures are routines that enable officials to perform numerous tasks every day; SOPs save time. If every worker had to invent a new way of doing things in every new case, there would not be enough time to help very many people. SOPs bring consistency to the handling of cases; rules are applied more uniformly.

However, SOPs can also obstruct policy implementation. "Once requirements and practices are instituted, they tend to remain in force long after the conditions that spawned them have disappeared."[4] Routines are not regularly reexamined; they tend to persist even when policy changes. If SOPs are not revised to reflect policy changes, these changes are not implemented. Moreover, many people prefer the stability and familiarity of existing routines, and they are reluctant to revise their patterns. Organizations have spent time, effort, and money in developing these routines. These "sunk costs" commit organizations to limit change as much as possible.

SOPs can make it difficult to handle nonconforming cases in an individual fashion. Even though particular cases may not conform to prewritten SOPs, many administrators try to force these cases into one or another of the established classifications.* Frustrations also arise for social workers when they attempt to obtain services for those in need who do not meet specific eligibility criteria. Over a period of time these frustrations may lead to staff "burnout."

The organization of bureaucracies also affects implementation, especially when responsibility for a policy is dispersed among many governmental units. There are 80,000 governments in the United States: a national government, 50 state governments, 3,000 county governments, over 18,000 city governments, 17,000 township governments, 16,000 school districts, and 24,000 special districts. Even within the national government, various departments have responsibility for major social welfare programs: The Department of Health and Human Services has responsibility for AFDC; the Department of Agriculture administers the Food Stamp program; the Department of Labor administers job-training programs and employment services.

The more governments and agencies involved with a particular policy, and the more independent their decisions, the greater the problems of implementation. Separate agencies become concerned with their own "turf"—areas they believe should be their exclusive responsibility. Agencies may fight each other to hold onto their traditional areas of responsibility. Proponents of particular programs may insist in Congress that their programs be administered by separate agencies that are largely independent of traditional executive departments. They fear that consolidating program responsibilities will downgrade the emphasis that the larger department may give to their particular program.

*Consider, for example, the conversations reported in the accompanying illustration. How often have you experienced a similar conversation yourself? How much more frustrating these conversations must be for poor or elderly people or people with less formal education.

ILLUSTRATION: BUREAUCRACY AND IMPLEMENTATION

SWITCHBOARD:	City Hall, may I help you?
CALLER:	My daughter is handicapped and needs special transportation to her therapist. Who can I speak to in the city about this?
SWITCHBOARD:	I think the Office of Aging handles things like that.
(after a pause):	Let me connect you.
OFFICE OF AGING:	Good morning. Office of Aging, can you hold please? (Several minutes later.) Sorry to keep you waiting; can I help you?
CALLER:	My daughter is handicapped and needs special transportation to her therapist. Usually someone in the family helps out but it's not always. . .
OFFICE OF AGING:	How old is your daughter?
CALLER:	She's only a teenager, but the switchboard. . .
OFFICE OF AGING:	I'm sorry but your daughter isn't eligible. Our program is only for senior citizens. Ask the switchboard to connect you to the Youth Bureau. I'll connect you back. (There are several clicks and the connection is lost. The caller dials the main city hall number again.)
SWITCHBOARD:	City Hall, may I help you?
CALLER:	The Youth Bureau please.
SWITCHBOARD:	Do you want the Delinquency Program or the Recreation Program?
CALLER:	I think it must be the Recreation Program. It's my daughter. I called earlier and was cut off, but I don't think I talked to you. I just want to. . .
YOUTH BUREAU:	Youth Bureau, Recreation, can I help you?
CALLER:	I hope so. My daughter is handicapped and needs special transportation to her therapist. I was wondering if you. . .
YOUTH BUREAU:	I'm sorry; we don't have information on that kind of program. You might try the Office of Aging. . .
CALLER:	But I. . .
YOUTH BUREAU:	. . . or the School Board. Their number is. . .

Source: Reprinted by permission of the publisher from Wayne Anderson, Bernard J. Frieden, and Michael J. Murphy, eds., *Managing Human Services* (Washington: International City Management Association, 1977), p. 193; also cited in Bruce L. Gates, *Social Program Administration* (Englewood Cliffs, N.J.: Prentice-Hall, 1980), p. 163.

Some fragmentation may be desirable. The argument for federalism—the division of governmental responsibilities between the national government and the fifty state governments—is that it allows each state to deal more directly with conditions confronting that state. Government "closer to home" is sometimes thought to be more flexible and manageable than a distant bureaucracy in Washington.

However, when programs and services are fragmented, coordination of policy is difficult. This is true whether we are talking about the fragmentation of responsibilities among different agencies of the national government or the division of responsibilities between the national government and the fifty states. Uniformity is lost. Consider, for example, the nation's fifty separate AFDC programs. These are *state*-administered programs with federal financial assistance. The federal government pays over half of the costs of AFDC. Yet actual average benefits given to AFDC families range from less than $140 per month in six (southern) states to over $300 per month in several other (northern and western) states.[5]

EVALUATING SOCIAL POLICY

In recent years there has been a growing interest in *policy evaluation*—in learning about the consequences of public policy. Government agencies regularly report how much money they spend, how many persons ("clients") are given various services, and how much these services cost. Congressional committees regularly receive testimony from influential individuals and groups about how popular or unpopular various programs and services are. But *even* if programs and policies are well-organized, financially possible, efficiently operated, widely utilized, and politically popular, the questions still arise: "So what?" "Do they work?" "Do these programs have any beneficial effects on society?" "What about people *not* receiving the benefits or services?" "What is the relationship between the costs of the program and the benefits to society?" "Could we be doing something else of more benefit to society with the money and human resources devoted to these programs?"

Can the federal government answer these questions? Can it say, for example, that AFDC, SSI, Food Stamps, and Medicaid are accomplishing their objectives; that their benefits to society exceed their costs; that they are not overly burdensome on taxpayers; that there are no better or less costly means of achieving the same ends? One surprisingly candid report by the liberal-oriented think tank, the Urban Institute, argues convincingly that the federal government *does not know* whether most of the things it does are worth doing:

> The most impressive finding about the evaluation of social programs in the federal government is that substantial work in this field has been almost nonexistent.
>
> Few significant studies have been undertaken. Most of those carried out have been poorly conceived. Many small studies around the country have been carried out with such lack of uniformity of design and objective that the results rarely are comparable or responsive to the questions facing policy makers. . . .
>
> The impact of activities that cost the public millions, sometimes billions, of dollars has not been measured. One cannot point with confidence to the difference, if any, that most social programs cause in the lives of Americans.[6]

POLICY EVALUATION AS A RATIONAL ACTIVITY

From a rational perspective, policy evaluation involves more than just learning about the consequences of public policy. Consider the following definitions by leading scholars in the field:

> Policy evaluation is the assessment of the overall effectiveness of a national program in meeting its objectives, or the assessment of the relative effectiveness of two or more programs in meeting common objectives.[7]
>
> Policy evaluation is the objective, systematic, empirical examination of the effects ongoing policies and programs have on their target in terms of the goals they are meant to achieve.[8]
>
> Evaluation research is viewed by its partisans as a way to increase the rationality of policy making. With objective information on the outcomes of programs, wise decisions can be made on budget allocations and program planning. Programs that yield good results will be expanded; those that make poor showings will be abandoned or drastically modified.[9]

These definitions of policy evaluation assume that the goals and objectives of programs and policies are clear, that we know how to measure progress toward these goals, that we know how to measure costs, and that we can impartially weigh benefits against costs in evaluating a public program. In short, these definitions view policy evaluation as a *rational* activity.

Ideally, the evaluation of a program would include all of its effects on real world conditions. Evaluators would want to (1) identify and rank all of the goals of a program; (2) devise measures to describe progress toward these goals; (3) identify the "target" situation or group for which the program was designed; (4) identify nontarget groups who might be affected indirectly by the program ("spillover" effects) and nontarget groups who are similar to the target groups but did not participate in the program or receive its direct benefits ("control group"); (5) measure program effects on target and nontarget groups over as long a period of time as possible; (6) identify and measure the costs of the program in terms of all the resources allocated to it; and (7) identify and measure the indirect costs of the program, including the loss of opportunities to pursue other activities.

Identifying target groups in social welfare programs means defining the part of the population for whom the program is intended—the poor, the sick, the ill-housed, and so on. Then, the desired effect of the program on the target population must be determined. Is it to change their physical or economic conditions in life—their health, their nutrition, their income? Or is it to change their behavior—put them to work in the private or public sector or increase their physical activity? Is it to change their knowledge, attitudes, awareness, or interest—to organize poor neighborhoods, to pressure slum landlords into improving housing conditions, to increase voter turnout among the poor and the black, to discourage unrest, riots, and violence? If multiple effects are intended, what are the priorities (rankings) among different effects? What are the possible *un*intended effects (side effects) on target groups—for example, does public housing achieve better physical environments for the urban poor at the cost of increasing their segregation and isolation from the mainstream of the community?

In making these identifications and measurements, the evaluators must not confuse *policy outputs* (what governments do) with *policy impacts* (what consequences these government actions have). It is important *not* to measure benefits in terms of government activity. For example the number of dollars spent per member of a target group (per pupil educational expenditures; per capita welfare expenditures; per capita health expenditures) are not really measurements of the *impact* of government activity. We cannot be content with counting how many times a bird flaps its wings; we must learn how far the bird has flown. In assessing the *impact* of public policy we cannot simply count the number of dollars spent or clients served, but rather we must identify the changes in individuals, groups, and society brought about by public policies.

ILLUSTRATION: A RATIONAL MODEL OF PROGRAM EVALUATION

Several ideal, rational models of program evaluation have been proposed. One noted evaluation team, headed by the sociologist Peter H. Rossi, has suggested that evaluation research includes four important types of questions.

1. Program Planning Questions:
   What is the extent and distribution of the target population?
   Is the program designed in conformity with its intended goals, and are chances of successful implementation maximized?
2. Program Monitoring Questions:
   Is the program reaching the persons, households, or other target units to which it is addressed?
   Is the program providing the resources, services, or other benefits that were intended in the project design?
3. Impact Assessment Questions:
   Is the program effective in achieving its intended goals?
   Can the results of the program be explained by some alternative process that does not include the program?
   Is the program having some effects that were not intended?
4. Economic Efficiency Questions:
   What are the costs to deliver services and benefits to program participants?
   Is the program an efficient use of resources compared with alternative uses of the resources?

It is also possible to identify a "Theoretical Model of Program Development" to assist in understanding exactly what stage of the policy process is being evaluated. One such model is shown here:

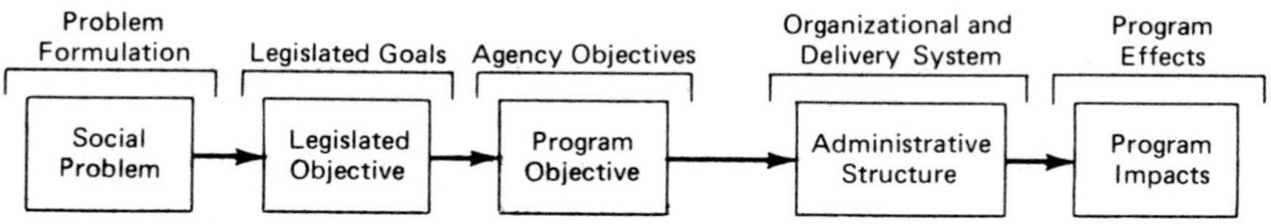

Evaluative research might be directed at any of the linkages suggested here. For example, one might want to inquire whether congressional legislation is related to the social problem, or whether the agency's objectives are consistent with the goals of Congress, or whether the program's activities have any impact on society.

See Peter H. Rossi, Howard E. Freeman, and Sonia R. Wright, *Evaluation: A Systematic Approach* (Beverly Hills, Calif.: Sage Publications, 1979).

Identifying the effects of a program on *nontarget* groups is equally important. For example, what effects will proposed welfare reforms have on social workers, social welfare bureaucracies, working families who are not on welfare, taxpayers, and others? Nontarget effects may turn out to be either benefits or costs.

Evaluators must also determine whether the program's goals are long-range or immediate. When will the benefits and costs be felt? Is the program designed for a short-term, emergency situation or is it a long-term, developmental effort? Many impact studies show that new or innovative programs have short-term positive effects—for example, Head Start and other educational programs. The newness of the program, or the realization by the target group that is being given special treatment and being watched closely, may create measurable changes (the *Hawthorne effect*). But these positive effects may disappear as the novelty and enthusiasm of the new program wear off. Another problem is that longitudinal studies that assess the far-reaching impacts of social welfare programs are rarely conducted owing to constraints of time and money. This leaves us with little information with which to assess the positive and negative consequences of most social welfare programs.

Perhaps the most difficult problem confronting evaluators is the weighing of costs against benefits. Benefits may be measured in terms of bettering human conditions—improved education, improved medical care for the poor, better nutrition, steady employment, and so on. Costs are usually measured in dollars. But how can we measure many of the values of education, health, or self-esteem in dollars?

THE MANY FACES OF PROGRAM EVALUATION

Most government agencies make some attempt to assess the utility of their programs. These efforts usually take one or more of the following forms.

Public Hearings

This is the most common type of program review. Frequently legislative committees ask agency heads to give formal or informal testimony regarding the accomplishments of their programs. This usually occurs near budget time. In addition, written "program reports" or "annual reports" may be provided to legislators and interested citizens by agencies as a "public information" activity. However, testimonials and reports of program administrators are not very objective means of program evaluation. They frequently magnify the benefits and minimize the costs of programs.

Site Visits

Occasionally teams of legislators, high-ranking federal or state officials, or expert consultants (or some combination of all of these people) will descend upon agencies to conduct investigations "in the field." These teams can interview workers and clients and directly observe the operation of the agency. These teams can accumulate impressions about how programs are being run, whether they have competent staffs, and perhaps even whether or not the "clients" (target groups) are pleased with the services.

Program Measures

The data developed by the agencies themselves generally describe program or *output* measures—for example, the number of recipients of various welfare programs; the number of persons in work-training programs; the number of hospital beds available; the number of persons treated. But these output measures rarely indicate the *impact* these numbers have on society—for example, the conditions of life confronting a poor family; the success of work trainees in later finding and holding useful employment in the nation's work force; the actual health of the nation's poor in terms of sickness, life spans, death rates, and so on.

Comparison with Professional Standards

In some areas of social welfare activity, professional associations have developed their own "standards" of benefits and services. These standards may be expressed in terms of the maximum number of cases that a welfare case worker can handle effectively; or in the minimum number of hospital beds required by a population of one hundred thousand people; or in other ways. Actual governmental outputs can be compared with these "ideal" outputs. While this kind of study can be helpful, it still focuses on the *outputs* and not on the *impacts* that government activities have on the conditions of target and nontarget groups. Moreover, the standards are usually developed by professionals who may have questions about what the ideal levels of benefits and services should be. There is really very little hard evidence that ideal levels of government outputs have any significant impact on societv

Formal Designs: Experimental Research

The "classic" research design for evaluating policies and programs employs two comparable groups—an *experimental group* and a *control group*—that are equivalent in every way *except* that the policy has been applied only to the experimental group. After the application of the policy for a given length of time, its impact is measured by comparing changes in the experimental group with changes, if any, in the control group. Initially, control and experimental groups must be identical in every possible way, and the program must be applied only to the experimental group. Postprogram differences between the two groups must be carefully measured. Also every effort must be made to make certain that any observed postprogram differences between the two groups can be attributed to the program and not to some other intervening cause that affected one of the groups as the program was administered. This classic research design is

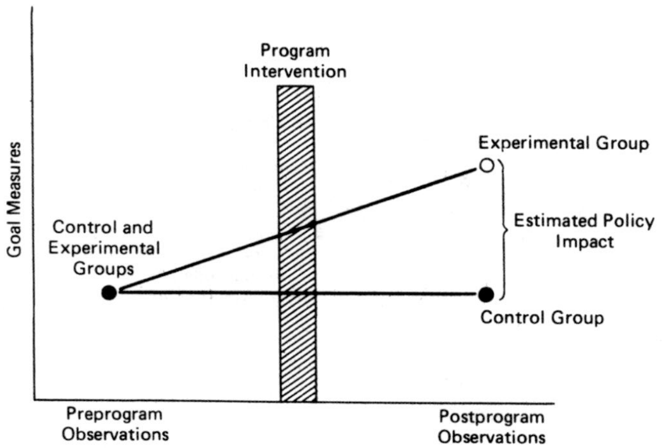

FIGURE 12-2 "Classic" research design.

preferred by social scientists because it provides the best opportunity for estimating changes that can be directly attributed to policies and programs (see figure 12-2 for a model of the classic research design).

Formal Designs: Quasi-Experiments

It is frequently impossible to conduct controlled experiments in public policy, because sometimes the human beings involved cannot be placed arbitrarily in experimental or control groups just for the sake of program evaluation. (Indeed, if experimental and control groups are really identical, the application of *public* policy to one group of citizens and not the other may violate the "equal protection of the laws" clause of the Fourteenth Amendment of the U.S. Constitution.) Frequently, it is only possible to compare individuals and groups that have participated in programs with those that have not, or to compare cities, states, and nations that have programs with those that do not. Comparisons are made of the extent to which the groups that have participated in the program have achieved the desired goals in relation to those groups that have not participated in the program. The problem is to try to eliminate the possibility that any difference between the two groups in goal achievement may really be caused by some factor *other than* experience with the program. For example, we may compare the job records of people who have participated in JTPA programs with those who have not. The former JTPA participants may or may not have better job records than other groups. If they do not, it may be because the JTPA trainees were less skilled to begin with; if they do, it may be because the JTPA officials "creamed off" the local unemployed and trained only those who already possessed good skills and job experience. Thus, quasi-experimental research designs, like most social science research, still leave room for discussion and disagreement. (See figure 12-3 for a model of the quasi-experimental research design.)

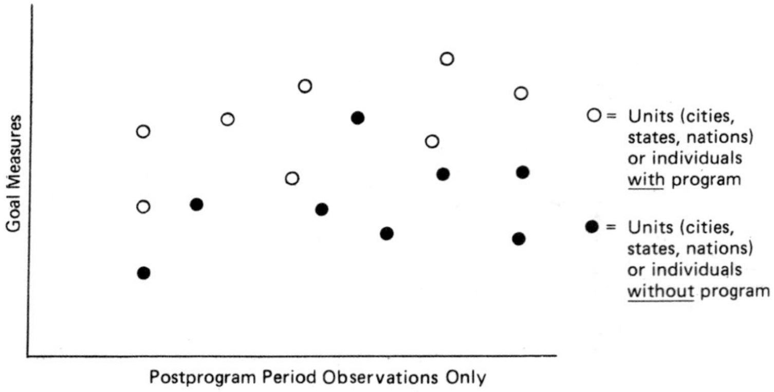

FIGURE 12-3 Quasi-experimental research design.

Formal Designs: Time Series

Another research design is the before-and-after study—a comparison of conditions before and after a policy or program has been adopted. Usually only the target group is examined. This design is essential in jurisdictions where no control groups can be identified. When several observations are made of conditions *before* the program is adopted, and then several observations are made *after* the program is adopted, this is generally referred to as a *time series*. These observations are designed to show program impacts; *but* it is very difficult to know whether the changes, if any, have come about as a result of the program itself or as a result of other changes which were occurring in society at the same time. (See figure 12-4 for a model of the time-series research design.)

FIGURE 12-4 Time-series research design.

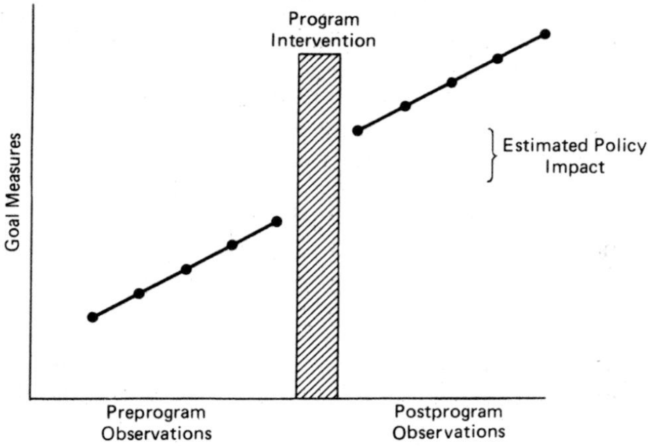

POLICY EVALUATION AS A POLITICAL ACTIVITY

Program evaluation may resemble scientific and rational inquiry, but it can never really be separated from politics. Let us consider just a few of the political problems that make rational policy evaluation difficult, if not impossible.

Unclear, Ambiguous Program Goals

Evaluators are often told to evaluate a program and yet are not informed of its goals or purposes. Reading the language of the original legislation that established the program may not be very helpful; legislative language frequently uses fuzzy words—"improve the conditions of life of the poor," "improve the health of society," "enhance the quality of life," for example. Even interviews with the original legislative sponsors (Congress members who sponsored a federal bill or state legislators who did so at the state level) may produce ambiguous, or even contradictory, goals. Often the evaluators, at the risk of offending someone, must define the goals or purposes themselves. In this way, evaluation itself becomes a political activity.

Symbolic Goals

Many programs and policies have primarily symbolic value. They do not actually change the conditions of target groups but rather make these groups feel that their government "cares." Of course, a government agency does not welcome a study that reveals that its efforts have no tangible effects. Indeed, such a finding, if widely publicized, might reduce the symbolic impact of the program by telling target groups of its uselessness.

Unhappy Findings

Agencies and administrators usually have a heavy investment—organizational, financial, psychological—in current programs and policies. They are predisposed against findings that these programs do not work, involve excessive costs, or have unexpected negative consequences. If a negative report is issued, the agency may adopt a variety of strategies to offset its recommendations.

Program Interference

Most serious studies of public programs involve some burdens on ongoing program activities. Accomplishing the day-to-day business of an agency is generally a higher priority in the mind of an administrator than making special arrangements for evaluation. Program evaluation also requires funds, facilities, time, and personnel, all of which administrators may not like to sacrifice from regular programs.

Usefulness of Evaluations

Program administrators are clearly dissatisfied with evaluative studies that conclude that "The program is not achieving the desired results." Not only is such a finding a threat to the agency, but standing alone, it fails to tell administrators *why* the program is failing. Evaluative studies are better received at the agency level when they include some action recommendations that might conceivably rescue the program. But even when evaluative studies show programs to be failures, the usual reaction is to patch things up and try again.

Evaluation by Whom?

One of the central political questions in evaluation is the determination of who will do the evaluation. From the perspective of the agency and its clients, the evaluation should be done by the agency or by an organizational representative of its clients. This type of "in-house" evaluation is most likely to produce favorable results. The next best thing, from the agency's perspective, is to allow the agency to contract with a private firm for an "outside" evaluation. A private firm that wants to win future contracts from the agency, or from any other agency, is very hesitant about producing totally negative evaluations. The worst evaluation arrangement, from the agency's perspective, is to have an outside evaluation conducted by an independent office (the Congressional Budget Office, the General Accounting Office, or a state comptroller's office, for example). Agency staff fear that outsiders do not understand clearly the nature of their work or the problems faced by the clients they serve.

THE GUARANTEED ANNUAL INCOME EXPERIMENTS

Many policy evaluators argue that "policy experimentation" offers the best opportunity to determine the impact of public policies. Such experimentation includes selection of matching experimental and control groups, the application of the policy to the experimental group only, and careful comparisons of differences between the experimental and the control groups after the application of the policy. The argument for experimental social research is that it can save money in the long run. The opposite approach is taken when giant public programs are created without any prior knowledge about whether they will work. One economist writes:

> The fact is that there have been few effective ways for determining the effectiveness of a social program before it is started; indeed, in most cases it is impossible even to forecast the cost of a new program until it has been in operation for a long time.
>
> Clearly this situation is not conducive to sound and effective decision making.[10]

ILLUSTRATION: WHAT TO DO IF YOUR AGENCY'S PROGRAM RECEIVES A NEGATIVE EVALUATION

Even in the face of clear evidence that your favorite program is useless, or even counter-productive, there are still a variety of administrative strategies:

1. Claim that the effects of the program are long-range and cannot be adequately measured for many years.
2. Argue that the effects of the program are general and intangible, and that these effects were not identified in the crude statistical measures used in the evaluation.
3. If an experimental research design was used, claim that withholding services or benefits from the control group was "unfair"; and claim that there were no differences between the control and experimental groups because of a knowledge of the experiment by both groups.
4. If a time series research design was used, claim that there were no differences between the "before" and "after" observations because of other coinciding variables that hid the effects of the program. That is to say, claim that the "after" group would be even worse without the program.
5. Argue that the lack of differences between the persons receiving the program services and those not receiving them only means that the program is not sufficiently intensive and indicates the need to spend *more* resources on the program.
6. Argue that the failure to identify any positive effects of the program is a result of the inadequacy of the evaluation research design and/or bias on the part of the evaluators.

Perhaps the most well-known example of an attempt by the federal government to experiment with public policy is the New Jersey Graduated Work Incentive Experiment funded by the Office of Economic Opportunity. The experiment was designed to resolve some serious questions about the effect of welfare payments on the incentives for poor people to work.[11] In order to learn more about the effects of the present welfare system on human behavior and, more important, to learn more about the possible effects of proposed programs for guaranteed family incomes, the OEO funded a three-year social experiment involving 1,350 families in New Jersey and Pennsylvania. The research was conducted by the Institute for Research on Poverty of the University of Wisconsin.

Debates over welfare reform had generated certain questions that social science could presumably answer with careful, controlled experimentation. Would a guaranteed family income reduce the incentive to work? If payments were made to poor families with employable male heads, would the men drop out of the labor force? Would the level of the income guarantee or the steepness of the reductions in payments dependent on increases in earnings make any difference in working behavior? Because current welfare programs do not provide a guaranteed minimum family income, do not generally make payments to families with employable males, and do not graduate payments substantially in relation to earnings, these questions could only be answered through *policy experimentation.* But policy experimentation raised some serious initial problems for the OEO. First of all, any experiment involving substantial payments to a fair sampling of families would be expensive. For example, if payments averaged $1,000 per year per family, and if each family had to be observed for three years, and if one thousand families were to be involved, a minimum of $3 million would be spent even *before* any consideration of the costs of administration, data collection, analysis and study, and reporting. Ideally a *national* sample should have been used, but it would have been more expensive to monitor than a local sample, and differing employment conditions in different parts of the country would have made it difficult to sort out the effects of income payments from variations in local job availability. By concentrating the sample in one region, it was hoped that local conditions would be held constant. Also ideally, *all* types of low-income families should have been tested, but that procedure would have necessitated a larger sample and greater expense. So only poor families with an able-bodied man between the ages of eighteen and fifty-eight were selected; the work behavior of these men in the face of a guaranteed income was of special interest.

To ascertain the effects of different levels of guaranteed income, four guarantee levels were established. Some families were chosen to receive 50 percent of the Social Security Administration's poverty-level income, others 75 percent, others 100 percent, and still others 125 percent. In order to ascertain the effects of graduated payments in relation to earnings, some families had their payments reduced by 30 percent of their outside earnings, others 50 percent, and still others 70 percent. Finally, a control sample was observed—low-income families who received no payments at all.

The experiment was initiated in August 1968 and continued until September 1972. But political events moved swiftly and soon engulfed the study. In 1969 President Nixon proposed to Congress the Family Assistance Plan (FAP), which guaranteed all families a minimum income of 50 percent of the poverty level and a payment reduction of 50 percent for outside earnings. The Nixon administration had not waited to learn the results of the OEO experiment before introducing the FAP. Nixon wanted welfare reform to be his priority domestic legislation, and the bill was symbolically numbered HR 1 (House of Representatives Bill 1).

After the FAP bill had been introduced, the Nixon administration pressured the OEO to produce favorable supporting evidence in behalf of the guaranteed income—specifically, evidence that a guaranteed income at the levels and graduated sublevels proposed in FAP would *not* reduce incentives to work among the poor. The OEO obliged by hastily publishing a short report, "Preliminary Results of the New Jersey Graduated Work Incentive Experiment," that purported to show that there were no differences in the outside earnings of families receiving guaranteed incomes (experimental group) and those not (control group).[12]

The director of the research, economics professor Harold Watts of the University of Wisconsin, warned that "the evidence from this preliminary and crude analysis of the results is less than ideal." But he concluded that "no evidence has been found in the urban experiment to support the belief that negative-tax type income maintenance programs will produce large disincentives and consequent reductions in earnings."[13] Moreover, the early results indicated that families in all experimental groups, with different guaranteed minimums and different graduated payment schedules, behaved in similar fashion to each other and to the control group receiving no payments at all. Predictably, later results confirmed the preliminary results, which were used to assist the FAP bill in Congress.[14]

However, when the results of the Graduated Work Incentive Experiment were later *reanalyzed* by the RAND Corporation (which was not responsible for the design of the original study), markedly different results were produced.[15] The RAND Corporation reports that the Wisconsin researchers working for OEO had originally chosen New Jersey because it had no state welfare programs for "intact" families—families headed by an able-bodied, working-age male. The guaranteed incomes were offered to these intact families to compare their work behavior with control-group families. But six months after the experiment began, New Jersey changed its state law and offered *all* families (experimental *and* control-group families) generous welfare benefits—benefits equal to those offered to participants in the experiment. This meant that for most of the period of the experiment, the control group was being given benefits equivalent to those given the experimental group—an obvious violation of the experimental research design. The OEO-funded University of Wisconsin researchers failed to consider this factor in their research. Thus, they concluded that there were no significant differences between the work behaviors of experimental and control groups, and they implied that a national guaranteed income would not be a disincentive to work. The RAND Corporation researchers, on the other hand, considered the New Jersey state welfare program in their estimates of work behavior. RAND concluded that recipients of a guaranteed annual income would work six and one-half fewer hours per week than they would work in the absence of such a program. In short, the RAND study suggests that a guaranteed annual income would produce a substantial disincentive to work.

The RAND study was published in 1978 after enthusiasm in Washington for a guaranteed annual income program—or "welfare reform"—had already cooled. The RAND study conflicted with the earlier OEO study and confirmed the intuition of many Congress members that a guaranteed annual income would reduce willingness to work. The RAND study also suggested that a *national* program might be very costly and involve some payments to nearly half the nation's families. Finally, RAND noted that its own estimates of high costs and work disincentives may "seriously understate the expected cost of an economy-wide . . . program." In spite of the conflicting evidence, one conclusion can be drawn from the analyses of the New Jersey Graduated Work Incentive Experiment. We are still unable to agree on many of the conditions that might produce a serious disincentive to work.

SUMMARY

Implementing public policy can be a difficult task for administrators of social welfare programs. Implementation involves a number of activities, including organizing and staffing agencies, translating policies into specific courses of action, and spending funds to operate programs. One major obstacle to successful implementation is to determine the intent of social policies, which is not always clearly defined in the legislation. Other problems include obtaining sufficient resources, overcoming any negative attitudes toward a program and seeing that bureaucratic structures do not prevent the program from operating smoothly.

Americans no longer believe that social problems can be eliminated by merely passing laws and spending money for new welfare programs. We are increasingly concerned with obtaining evidence about whether social programs actually work. But policy evaluation is no less political than any other part of the policy process.

A rational approach to social policy evaluation includes identifying and ranking program goals and objectives, developing units to measure these goals, identifying target and nontarget groups that might be affected, measuring tangible and intangible program effects, and measuring direct and indirect program costs. Several types of research designs lend themselves to evaluative studies of social welfare policies and programs. These are experimental designs, quasi-experimental designs, and time-series designs.

Evaluating social welfare programs is a political activity for a number of reasons. Program goals and objectives are not always clear, but evaluators must evaluate something even if everyone does not agree. Some program goals are more symbolic than tangible, and the symbolic goals are even more difficult to evaluate than the tangible. No program administrator wants to receive a negative evaluation. Negative evaluations are generally criticized, and administrators will take steps to counteract negative findings. Evaluations are disruptive to the day-to-day work of the agency and take time and resources from other activities. Also, an evaluation may not provide useful information about how to improve the program. In-house evaluations tend to be positive, and outside evaluations are more likely to be critical or ambivalent about the program. The well-publicized evaluations of the Graduated Work Incentive Experiment are examples of the politics of policy evaluation.

NOTES

1. Jeffrey Pressman and Aaron Wildavsky, *Implementation* (Berkeley: University of California Press, 1973), p. 109.
2. This discussion relies on George C. Edwards, *Implementing Public Policy* (Washington: Congressional Quarterly, 1980).
3. See Daniel P. Moynihan, *The Politics of a Guaranteed Income* (New York: Vintage Books, 1973), p. 220.
4. Herbert Kaufman, *Red Tape* (Washington: Brookings Institution, 1977), p. 13.

5. Bureau of the Census, *Statistical Abstract of the United States, 1984* (Washington, 1983), p. 395.
6. Joseph S. Wholey and associates, *Federal Evaluation Policy* (Washington: Urban Institute, 1970), p. 15.
7. Ibid.
8. David Nachmias, *Policy Evaluation* (New York: St. Martin's, 1979), p. 4.
9. Carol H. Weiss, *Evaluation Research: Methods of Assessing Program Effectiveness* (Englewood Cliffs, N.J.: Prentice-Hall, 1972), p. 2.
10. David N. Kershaw, "A Negative Income Tax Experiment," in David Nachmias, ed., *The Practice of Policy Evaluation* (New York: St. Martin's, 1980), pp. 27–28.
11. See Harold M. Watts, "Graduated Work Incentives: An Experiment in Negative Taxation," *American Economic Review* 59 (May 1969): 463–72.
12. U.S. Office of Economic Opportunity, *Preliminary Results of the New Jersey Graduated Work Incentive Experiment,* February 18, 1970. Also cited in Alice M. Rivlin, *Systematic Thinking for Social Action* (Washington: Brookings Institution, 1971).
13. Harold M. Watts, "Adjusted and Extended Preliminary Results from the Urban Graduated Work Incentive Experiment," (University of Wisconsin, Institute for Research on Poverty, rev. June 10, 1970), p. 40. Also cited in Rivlin, *Systematic Thinking,* p. 101.
14. David Kershaw and Jerelyn Fair, eds., *Final Report of the New Jersey Graduated Work Incentive Experiment* (University of Wisconsin, Institute for Research on Poverty, 1974).
15. John F. Cogan, *Negative Income Taxation and Labor Supply: New Evidence from the New Jersey-Pennsylvania Experiment* (Santa Monica, Calif: RAND Corporation, 1978).

Index

NAME INDEX

SUBJECT INDEX